Jewish
Pastoral Care

*A Practical Handbook from Traditional
and Contemporary Sources*

התלוות רוחנית

Edited by Rabbi Dayle A. Friedman

For People of All Faiths, All Backgrounds
JEWISH LIGHTS Publishing
Woodstock, Vermont

Jewish Pastoral Care:
A Practical Handbook from Traditional and Contemporary Sources

© 2001 by Dayle A. Friedman

For information regarding permission to reprint material from this book, please mail or fax your request in writing to Jewish Lights Publishing, Permissions Department, at the address / fax number listed below.

About the Hebrew: *Hitlavut Ruchanit,* or "spiritual accompanying," is a Hebrew term used to describe one who assists others in their life journeys.

Grateful acknowledgment is given to Rabbi Rami M. Shapiro for permission to reprint the poem "Unending Love," © by Rami M. Shapiro, Simply Jewish Foundation.

Helping Styles Inventory diagram republished with permission of Journal of Pastoral Care Publications, from *Journal of Pastoral Care*; permission conveyed through Copyright Clearance Center, Inc.

Library of Congress Cataloging-in-Publication Data

Jewish pastoral care : a practical handbook from traditional and contemporary sources / edited by Dayle A. Friedman.
p.   cm.
Includes bibliographical references and index.
ISBN 1-58023-078-4 (hc.)
1. Pastoral counseling (Judaism) 2. Sick—Pastoral counseling of.
3. Visiting the sick (Judaism) 4. Consolation (Judaism)
5. Bereavement—Religious aspects—Judaism.
6. Jewish mourning customs. I. Friedman, Dayle A., 1956–
BM652.5 .J48 2000
296.6'1—dc21
00-011768

10 9 8 7 6 5 4 3 2 1

Manufactured in the United States of America
Jacket/cover design: Bridgett Taylor
Text design: Sans Serif, Inc.

For People of All Faiths, All Backgrounds
Published by Jewish Lights Publishing
A Division of LongHill Partners, Inc.
Sunset Farm Offices, Route 4, P.O. Box 237
Woodstock, VT 05091
Tel: (802) 457-4000   Fax: (802) 457-4004
www.jewishlights.com

Contents

SECTION III

Jewish Pastoral Care for Specific Needs and Settings

To David, Anya, Anat, and Avram, my beloveds,
and to the memory of Anne Ritter, *z'l*, my Grammy Anne,
who taught me about presence.

Acknowledgments

Many people helped to bring this book to fruition. My most powerful teachers—the residents, families, and staff of Philadelphia Geriatric Center with whom I worked from 1985 to 1997—taught me about the blessings and challenges of pastoral care. My students at Philadelphia Geriatric Center and the Reconstructionist Rabbinical College have prompted me to articulate what I have learned from my professional practice.

The authors whose original work is collected here have generously contributed their rich clinical experience and wisdom. As partners and collaborators, they unstintingly gave of their time and talent.

This book would not have been possible without David Ferleger, my partner in all things. The gestation of this book occurred simultaneously with the gestation, birth, and first year of our precious Anat and Avram. The miracle of their birth helped me to believe in the possibility of bringing forth this book. David's incredible kindness, endless patience, astute but gentle critiques, and wise counsel are blessings for which I daily give thanks. My daughter, Anya, lights up my days and my path, and she has sweetly encouraged me in this journey.

Chaplain Sheila Segal, Reverend Priscilla Denham, Rabbi Zahara Davidowitz-Farkas, Rabbi Leonard Gordon, and Rabbi Sheldon Zimmerman all assisted with the launching of this project. Rabbi Margot Stein graciously offered her discerning eye and incisive editorial judgment. Dr. Lori Lefkowitz also loaned me her wonderful mind. Moti Rieber's careful and capable editorial assistance was enormously helpful. I am profoundly grateful to all of them.

I am indebted to Elie Wise, Director of the Reconstructionist Rabbinical College library, for generously sharing "the thrill of the hunt" in the search for sources and information. I also thank the Reconstructionist Rabbinical College for affording me "a room of my own" in which to do the writing of this book.

Stuart Matlins, publisher of Jewish Lights, had the vision to take this project on and has been unceasingly encouraging and supportive. Sandra Korinchak and Martha McKinney have been wonderfully reliable resources in helping at every turn to transform this idea into a book. Their patience, knowledge, and help are enormously appreciated. Sarah Swartz's keen editorial judgment and gentle challenges enabled the book to reach a higher *madrega* than would have otherwise been possible.

Most of all, I am grateful for the sustenance I have received from the All Merciful One in the creation of this book, to be sure, but even more important, throughout all of the moments of my life.

Introduction

Hitlavut Ruchanit:
Spiritual Accompanying

"I am with you in sorrow. I will strengthen you and honor you . . ."
—ADAPTED FROM PSALMS 91:15

It was Yom Kippur, the awesome and holiest moment of the year. All of the Jews in the community were gathered in the synagogue, anxiously opening their hearts in prayer. They had accumulated sins all year and longed for an opportunity to ask for God's forgiveness, but the rabbi, the great Shneur Zalman, the Alter Rebbe, suddenly took off his *tallit*, stepped off the *bimah*, and left the *shul*. Members of the congregation wondered in hushed whispers where the rabbi had gone. How to explain his departure at this most critical juncture?

Fifteen minutes passed, a half an hour, an hour . . . only much later did they learn what had happened. While praying in the synagogue, the Alter Rebbe had sensed that there was a woman on the edge of town who needed help. The woman had just given birth, and her family members were all praying in the synagogue. She was alone and in need. The Alter Rebbe violated the holy day's laws, ceased his prayers, and personally attended to the woman.

In this tale, the rebbe acts with great compassion and demonstrates the primacy of caring in Jewish life.[1] He recognizes the need of the woman without being told that she is in trouble. He responds with caring action; his help is simultaneously practical and deeply spiritual. At the moment when the community most needs and wants to pray, this caring action carries the force of a prayer. Although it is not explicitly stated in the tale, we might infer that the rebbe's caring intervention also mobilized the community, for his action modeled a compassionate response to the woman and encouraged his congregants to respond to others similarly.

According to the late Lubavitcher Rebbe, Menachem Schneerson, this story was long suppressed in Lubavitcher circles.[2] Such a simple act of human connection was perhaps out of character for a leader so revered for his intellectual attainments. The audacity of the Alter Rebbe's caring, which placed the needs of the new mother above concerns about modesty and above the holiness of Yom Kippur was apparently hard for his followers to accept. Yet, daring caring was called for in that moment, and in ours as well.

The Alter Rebbe's behavior is a paradigm for contemporary pastoral caregivers. Just as the rebbe sensed the need of the woman without being told, so might a contemporary rabbi perceive distress in a middle-aged woman in his congregation and, listening with compassion, learn that she is being abused by her husband. Just as the rebbe's radical caring made a difference, so does that of a chaplain visiting a man hospitalized after a heart attack as he listens deeply to this shaken man voicing his crisis of faith and comprehension. Just as the rebbe's actions pierced the isolation of the woman in labor, so does the chaplain whose presence offers solace to a depressed elderly woman.

Of course, the rebbe's actions in this story are deeply rooted in Jewish tradition and communal life. The Torah tells us that Moses prays for his sister Miriam when she is stricken with a skin ailment. The prophet Elijah reaches out to revive a boy who is thought to be dead.[3] The rabbis in the Talmud visit one another when ill, offering prayer as well as concrete help and spiritual support.[4] We are taught that Elijah will announce the coming of the Messiah when we find him among the lepers of the city.[5] Rabbinic lore is filled with accounts of rabbis reaching out to Jews in pain, both in formal counseling sessions and through informal caring action such as that exemplified by the Alter Rebbe.[6]

Clearly, acts of caring and simple presence with those in need have always been core tasks for Jewish leaders, along with their priestly, teaching, and prophetic roles. The principles undergirding the work of pastoral care are embedded in teachings about *gemilut chasadim* (deeds of loving-kindness). Certainly, responding to those in need is a *mitzvah,* a sacred religious obligation, but it is more than that. Caring and effective response to the needy is an act of *imitatio dei,* the way in which we "walk in God's ways."[7] In particular, the rich and practical laws and lore about *bikur cholim* (visiting the sick) offer guidance about how we should attend to suffering people. Although these texts address the obligations of all Jews toward their fellow human beings, they contain wisdom that is precious for the professional caregiver.

What Is Jewish Pastoral Care?

The aspects of caring embodied in the Alter Rebbe's actions form a phenomenological definition of Jewish pastoral care. How can we conceptualize such care? In Jewish pastoral care, we offer a spiritual presence to people in need, pain, or transition. Rabbi Margaret Holub suggests that the heart of the rabbinic role (and by extension, the roles of cantors and lay people engaged in pastoral care) is one of *accompanying* people.[8] We walk along with those we serve in the course of their journeys through suffering, illness, change, and joy. Like Miriam, who stood and watched as baby Moses sat in his basket on the banks of the Nile, our greatest gift is sometimes simply being alongside our people.[9] We join them, at times offering encouragement or concrete help, at other times simply witnessing their endurance, their pain, and, with God's help, their resiliency. Like the rebbe in the story, we make sure that those who suffer are not alone, and we endeavor to help them transcend their suffering.

We meet the people with whom we work, in the words of the Torah, *ba'asher hu sham* (where he or she is), in whatever they are experiencing, wherever they are.[10] We find them *ba'asher hem sham* because we try to understand their experience through careful listening and attempt to assess their needs. We offer a connection to God, Torah, and Israel; to our shared tradition; to community; and to their own spiritual resources.

Jewish pastoral care is offered in many different contexts. It occurs in a myriad of informal and formal interactions between congregants and their rabbis and cantors. From the casual mention of a problem at the Oneg Shabbat to the deliberate scheduling of a crisis counseling session in the clergy's study; from the bedside visit with a hospital patient to the pre-funeral call at the home of a newly bereaved person, pastoral encounters are demanding and rich in potential for healing and transformation. Of course, Jewish pastoral care is also the primary mission of those who serve as chaplains. Chaplains are pastoral caregivers employed by or placed by the community in hospitals, nursing homes, mental hospitals, and prisons. Wherever and by whomever Jewish pastoral care is offered, the task is to respond and be present.

What do we bring to these encounters? First and foremost, we bring ourselves. We bring the experiences we have had in life, and any wisdom we have acquired through falling down and picking ourselves up again amid life's pleasures and perils. Second, we bring our Jewish tools; we bring our knowledge of text and our facility with prayer and ritual. Lastly, we bring our technical skills. We bring our finely honed listening faculty, our ability to assess what is happening, and our capacity to connect in one-to-one relationships. We also forge links between people in need and the resources of community.

Jewish pastoral care is distinct from pastoral counseling. In the counseling relationship, an individual identifies a problem and seeks help through a structured, contractual intervention. In pastoral care, a helper meets an individual who is in a challenging situation; the person may not feel that he or she has a problem, yet help is needed to respond to the situation. The modality of the help offered in pastoral care is relationship. Pastoral care rests on the assumption that being in caring connection can transform suffering because relationship shatters isolation and provides an opportunity for reflecting on one's experience. Building relationship in a way that makes a difference is a discipline that requires training and continual, conscious use of oneself.

The term *pastoral care* is one that was developed in the Christian community. It has clear roots in the Hebrew scriptures, in which both God and human leaders such as Moses and David are depicted as pastors, or shepherds tending their flocks.[11] The concept of the pastoral nurturer is expanded in the New Testament, in which Jesus refers to himself as the "good shepherd."[12] "Pastor" does not accurately represent the Jewish pastoral care relationship we are describing. A shepherd is in charge, gives direction, and is able to sustain the flock because he or she knows better than the flock what they need. The helping role we are describing involves joining with people in trouble or transition and working to help them to use the resources within and around them to come through the experience whole. It is a relationship in which the helper meets the one in need on an egalitarian footing, not through a hierarchical power connection.

This helping relationship could better be described by the Hebrew term *hitlavut ruchanit*, spiritual accompanying. The root of this term, *lvh*, is used in biblical and rabbinic texts to refer to one who "walks with" another. Ministering angels, God's presence, friends, priests, and peers all are described as *lvh*, accompanying people as they go on their path.[13] The reflexive form of the verb connotes a person involving himself or herself in the journey with the other. A pastoral caregiver might therefore be called a *mitlaveh (mitlavah) ruchanit*.[14]

Until now, there has been little practical literature or theory to guide caregivers in the work of Jewish pastoral care. Yet, the demand for competent, inspired pastoral care is intensifying day by day. We now examine the conditions that have created this demand, and survey the existing literature.

Professionalization of Pastoral Care in the Jewish Community

Rabbis and cantors serving in congregational contexts have increasingly felt the need for clinical training. Across the spectrum of the Jewish community, the range and intensity of pastoral needs of congregants is enormous. Congregational clergy are called to respond more than ever to substance abuse, domestic violence, and all kinds of family and personal problems. Although clergy have always been needed by those facing illness and death, their desire to bring both well-honed clinical skills and spiritual resources to these crises has grown. Jews who reach out for help in times of need want help that is both Jewish and spiritual, not just concrete services or psychotherapeutic interventions. The phenomenal growth of the Jewish healing movement, including healing services and Jewish healing centers, reflects this profound hunger, which is "not . . . for bread, nor a thirst for water, but to hear the words of God" (Amos 8:11).[15] Para-rabbinic and para-chaplaincy programs, which offer training and supervision to lay volunteers serving ill and suffering people, also reflect the extent of the Jewish community's need and desire for a pastoral response.

Although the pastoral aspect of rabbis' and cantors' work has long been recognized as important, the advent of pastoral care as a distinct professional role is quite recent. The National Association of Jewish Chaplains (NAJC) was created in 1989, and has reflected and shaped this development. The organization came into being because increasing numbers of rabbis and cantors were not only serving in chaplaincy roles and providing pastoral care in healthcare facilities and institutions, but also defining their professional identity in terms of this work. Jewish chaplaincy positions in individual hospitals, nursing homes, and entire communities had earlier been filled on an ad hoc basis by interested individuals who often had had no formal clinical training. Now, newly graduated rabbis and cantors as well as those making midcareer changes have specifically sought such positions and deliberately undertaken the clinical training to qualify and to certify them.

The creation of the NAJC, which currently has over 400 members, reflects this growing professionalization. The NAJC has also shaped the professionalization of Jewish pastoral care because it provides a critical role as a credentialing body. More than eighty Jewish chaplains have been certified by the organization. There is now a shared understanding of what training and qualifications are required to serve as a professional Jewish chaplain. NAJC certification is increasingly demanded by institutions and communities employing Jewish chaplains. In addition, the NAJC's conferences and its journal, *The Jewish Chaplain*, have provided a forum for dialogue and for preliminary efforts to articulate a distinctly Jewish understanding of pastoral care.

In an attempt to fill the need and the demand for a well-trained, spiritual response to suffering, both individual Jewish clergy and the Jewish training seminaries have turned to clinical pastoral training. The major rabbinical seminaries all either require or encourage students to obtain experience in pastoral care through clinical training. Most of this training has been in Christian contexts, particularly Clinical Pastoral Education (CPE).[16] Although CPE considers itself nondenominational, it was created by Christian pastoral care educators, and is overwhelmingly led by Christian clergy. In 1988, Rabbi Jeffery Silberman was the first rabbi to be certified as a CPE supervisor. Since then, four other rabbis have been certified, and one lay Jewish chaplain is also a CPE supervisor. Given the small number of Jewish supervisors, most Jews who have completed CPE have done so with predominantly Christian colleagues and supervisors.

Rabbis, cantors, and lay Jewish chaplains who have received CPE training have received the gift of a highly developed model of training, including close clinical supervision, group interaction, and theological reflection. They have emerged with skills and perspective unavailable to most of those who have not trained in this way. They have benefited from the expertise and experience of Christian pastoral care, but they have not yet had the opportunity to articulate this enterprise in a Jewish idiom, or to search out our tradition for its wisdom and practical guidance. The Jewish Institute for Pastoral Care, created by Rabbi Israel Kestenbaum in 1998, is a promising development because it offers Jewish clergy and lay people an opportunity to receive clinical training in a Jewish setting. It creates a context that can nurture a Jewish conceptualization of the work.

The Dearth of Contemporary Literature on Jewish Pastoral Care

Although spiritual care and presence have long been part of the work of Jewish leaders, this work was not articulated as a distinctly professional role in the Jewish community until relatively recently. The twentieth-century encounter with psychiatry and psychology prompted the Jewish community to seek more sophisticated ways of understanding and of providing spiritual care. For example, Mortimer Ostow's book, *Judaism and Psychoanalysis*, explored the relationship between Jewish tradition and Freudian psychoanalysis. As a part of his analysis, Ostow compared Jewish methods of biblical exegesis with psychoanalytic principles of interpretation.[17] Offering resources to rabbis to enhance their understanding of their counseling role, Earl Grollman's 1966 *Rabbinical Counseling* collected several essays explicating the rabbi's role in counseling congregants.[18] In his essay in that work, Robert Katz, a professor of professional development at Hebrew Union College–Jewish Institute of Religion, suggested that rabbinical counseling is distinct from psychotherapy in that it addresses "moral, theological and existential [problems] in which the psychiatrist claims no competence." The aim of rabbinical counseling, according to Katz, is to explore "ultimate questions . . . [and] meaningful living."[19]

In his own 1985 book, *Pastoral Care and the Jewish Tradition: Empathic Process and Religious Counseling*, Robert Katz outlined his empathy-based theory of Jewish pastoral care. Based on the concept of *gemilut chasadim*, Katz suggested that empathy is the basis of pastoral care. Human beings can emulate God's caring by noting our similarity to other human beings, by becoming entangled in the human situation, and by participating in other humans' sorrows.[20] Drawing on classical texts, Chasidic stories, and the theology of Martin Buber, Katz stressed the uniqueness of the pastoral aspect of the rabbi's role. He noted that skills helpful in the pulpit and for teaching are not necessarily what will make the counseling relationship safe and successful. He cited Leo Baeck's powerful teaching that "the greatest gift of the rabbi is himself."[21] Certainly, this insight is fundamental to the work of pastoral care.

The earlier efforts of Ostow, Grollman, and Katz provide useful foundations for the endeavor to provide conceptual and practical guidance to Jewish pastoral caregivers, but their applicability is limited because they are focused more on counseling than on pastoral care. Their work does not reflect the clinical settings in which today's pastoral caregivers serve, nor the experience of the newly professionalized Jewish chaplains.

Joseph S. Ozarowski's 1995 book *To Walk in God's Ways* offers a wealth of insight from text and tradition. Ozarowski analyzes the paradigms of *bikur cholim* and *nichum avelim* (comforting the bereaved), and draws guidance from them for contemporary Jews engaged in the work. He provides a model for creatively drawing conceptual frameworks from rubrics within Jewish sources. Ozarowski's work is an eloquent explication of the religious obligation to visit the sick and comfort the bereaved.

The Focus of This Book

The sparse Jewish pastoral care literature that exists has not yet provided a systematic articulation of Jewish pastoral care as a professional discipline. Jewish pastoral caregivers seeking guidance have had to turn to the rich Christian literature in the field, and to the few valuable but limited Jewish works mentioned here. There has been no single source that offers insight on technique, theory, and theological implications of the work from a Jewish perspective.

This book seeks to fill that gap. *Jewish Pastoral Care* articulates what is distinctive about Jewish pastoral care and provides rabbis, cantors, and trained lay people with both conceptual and practical resources. It draws from clinical experience in outlining useful techniques and strategies; provides a Jewish spiritual perspective on pastoral care in general, and on specific applications of the work; and analyzes unique needs of Jewish people in specific circumstances and transitions. Most important, perhaps, it draws on the riches of Jewish practice, text, and communal life as resources in responding to people in need.

The contributors to this volume are pioneers in the emerging field of Jewish pastoral care. They represent all strains of contemporary Judaism, from Orthodox to Renewal, Conservative to Reform and Reconstructionist. They have drawn from the tradition to articulate the task, meaning, and methods of Jewish pastoral care. Their writing is informed not only by its grounding in rabbinic text and theology, but also by the best of clinical pastoral practice and, where applicable, by contemporary social science.

The authors use two types of sacred texts to shed light on the essence of *hitlavut ruchanit*. They present and explicate biblical and rabbinic texts. In addition, the authors draw on the texts of pastoral encounters, providing narratives that are not merely illustrations of theoretical points, but are themselves the Torah of pastoral care. Stories of actual pastoral interactions are an indispensable aid to understanding this endeavor. Only through accounts of lived encounters does the theory and practice of Jewish pastoral care make sense. In these narratives, names and details have been altered to protect the anonymity of the individuals described.

The first part of this book, "Foundational Concepts for Jewish Pastoral Care," offers a thorough examination of our tradition for precedents, frameworks, and practical guidance. Having laid conceptual and theological groundwork for *hitlavut ruchanit* in Section 1, we continue with the development of key skills. Section 2, "Basic Tools for the Jewish Pastoral Caregiver," offers both general clinical skills and specifically Jewish spiritual resources. This section is a kind of toolbox, introducing you to skills and resources you may need to be present with and help those you serve. Section 3, "Jewish Pastoral Care for Specific Needs and Settings," applies the theoretical perspectives and practical tools to specific settings and populations with whom pastoral caregivers work. Each chapter analyzes a particular context or need and offers an understanding of the Jewish pastoral role in response to it. The pastoral response is shaped by Jewish text and traditional models, as well as by the best practices of contemporary pastoral care and, where applicable, by social services.

Who Should Use This Book?

This book is for a variety of Jewish and non-Jewish professionals and laypeople. It is intended as a basic reference for rabbis, cantors, and laypeople seeking to provide pastoral care as trained volunteers or professionals. You may use this book in the process of acquiring pastoral training, as a means of building your skills once in the field, or as a reference to be drawn upon as you encounter particular pastoral issues in your work. In addition, lay readers may read this book to gain insight on struggles of people you love, Jewish perspectives, and Jewish modes of helping.

Also a resource for non-Jewish pastoral caregivers, this volume is intended to provide perspective on the spiritual needs of Jews whom you might encounter as clients or patients. It also illustrates the resources within our tradition that can be used in serving them. In addition, this text is offered to clinical pastoral educators. The theoretical and practical perspectives here may be useful in helping Jewish students understand and conceive of their work, and in helping non-Jewish students to respond to the needs of Jews whom you serve. To make the text accessible to those without facility in Hebrew or knowledge about Jewish tradition, a glossary provides translations of terms that might be unfamiliar.

Some Notes for the Reader

This book aims to reflect its inclusive orientation through the language that is used. Gender-inclusive language is included as much as possible; the alternation of "he" and "she" may at times yield prose that is less than felicitous, but accurately reflecting reality seems far more important. Traditional texts have been retranslated, where possible, so that they refer in gender-neutral fashion to both God and human beings.

In this book, we usually refer to the helper as a pastoral caregiver. In some contexts, individual authors refer to the rabbi, cantor, or both. In general, the content is directed toward anyone doing the work of Jewish pastoral care, including clinically trained lay people, trained para-chaplains, and clergy.

In reading this book, you may note that several rabbinic texts are quoted in multiple chapters. It is fascinating to see how many different aspects of wisdom can be derived from a single source. This bears out the teaching of Pirke Avot 5:25, "Turn it and turn it over again, for everything is in it." This phenomenon also reflects the paucity of collected sources available to us as we eke out the beginnings of a Jewish theology and praxis of pastoral care.

This book, for all its richness, is a preliminary charting of the territory of Jewish pastoral care. There are many able practitioners doing excellent work in areas of pastoral care not specifically addressed here. To date, practice skills in many areas outstrip theory and conceptual frameworks.

Clearly, there is much more work to do. I look forward to the time when this book is one of many items on the Jewish pastoral care bookshelf. Also, I fervently hope that the excellent practitioners in the field today will continue the work of developing distinctively Jewish pastoral care training, rooted in the concepts and tools outlined in this book.

May the Source of life, the Merciful One, accompany us as we join with those in pain and need. May we find strength and inspiration. May our presence be comforting and transformative. May we never feel alone in our caring work.

Notes

1. Variants of this story are also told about the Baal Shem Tov, the Rebbe of Nemirov, Rabbi Moshe Lieb of Sassov; and Rabbi Israel Salanter. The tale seems to have an archetypal quality.
2. Rebbe Menachem Schneerson, "The Rebbe Speaks," address on 19 Kislev 5744 (1983), videotape, Brooklyn, N.Y.: Jewish Educational Media.
3. I Kings 17:17–24.

4. See, for example, BT Berachot 5a, Berachot 34b, Nedarim 40a.

5. BT Sanhedrin 98a.

6. See Zalman Schachter-Shalomi, *Spiritual Intimacy: A Study of Counseling in Hasidism* (Northvale, N.J.: Jason Aronson, 1991), for an account of the Chasidic rebbe–disciple counseling relationship.

7. BT Sotah 14a; for a detailed analysis of this teaching, see chapter 2, of this book, "Bikur Cholim," pp. 16–18.

8. Rabbi Margaret Holub, personal communication.

9. Exodus 2:4, "And his sister stood at a distance, so that she would know what befell him."

10. Based on Genesis 21:17, in which God is described as hearing the voice of Ishmael *ba'asher hu sham*, exactly where he is, in all that he faces. The text actually does not mention that Ishmael has either spoken or cried. This offers us a model of listening and presence which meets the other wherever he or she is, a model for understanding more than is actually stated.

11. God is portrayed as the shepherd of Israel in Genesis 48:15 and Psalms 23:1. Moses is the shepherd in Isaiah 63:11 and Exodus Rabbah 24:3. David is the shepherd of Israel in I Chronicles 11:2.

12. For example, in John 10:14, "I am the good shepherd, and know my sheep."

13. For example, BT Ta'anit 11a and Shabbat 119b, among others, describe the two angels who accompany a person all the days of his or her life. Numbers Rabbah 20:19 describes God as lovingly accompanying Israel through the clouds of glory that guide Israel even after the sin of the Golden Calf. *Lvh* is the verb used to describe the *mitzvah* of accompanying the dead (burial and funeral), for example, BT Berachot 18a. It is also used to describe peers going with one another, as in BT Sotah 40a.

14. It is a recognized term, thus this book will generally use the term *pastoral care*. It is hoped that *hitlavut ruchanit* or other terms that practitioners may coin can come to serve as alternative, organically Jewish labels for this work.

15. For information about Jewish healing, contact the National Center for Jewish Healing, 850 Seventh Ave., Suite 1201, New York, N.Y. 10019, 212-399-2320.

16. In addition to courses and training programs developed at the rabbinical seminaries, training programs have emerged in clinical settings, such as Philadelphia Geriatric Center's Stern rabbinic internship program, and Ruach Ami, The Bay Area Jewish Healing Center's CPE program for Jewish lay people.

17. Mortimer Ostow, *Judaism and Psychoanalysis* (New York: KTAV, 1982), p. 10.

18. Earl Grollman, ed., *Rabbinic Counseling* (New York: Bloch Publishing, 1966).

19. Robert Katz, "Counseling, Empathy and the Rabbi," in Grollman, *Rabbinic Counseling*, pp. 9–10.

20. Robert L. Katz, *Pastoral Care and the Jewish Tradition: Empathic Process and Religious Counseling* (Philadelphia: Fortress Press, 1985), pp. 30–32.

21. Katz, *Pastoral Care*, p. 106.

Bibliography

Clinebell, Howard. *Basic Types of Pastoral Care & Counseling*. Nashville: Abingdon Press, 1992.

Gerkin, Charles V. *An Introduction to Pastoral Care*. Nashville: Abingdon Press, 1997.

Katz, Robert L. *Pastoral Care and the Jewish Tradition: Empathic Process and Religious Counseling*. Philadelphia: Fortress Press, 1985.

Patton, John. *Pastoral Care in Context: An Introduction to Pastoral Care*. Louisville, Ky.: Westminster/John Knox Press, 1993.

Schachter-Shalomi, Zalman. *Spiritual Intimacy: A Study of Counseling in Hasidism*. Northvale, N.J.: Jason Aronson, 1991.

Foundational Concepts for Jewish Pastoral Care

The Gift of Healing Relationship:
A Theology of Jewish Pastoral Care

Rabbi Israel Kestenbaum

Rabbi Israel Kestenbaum focuses on empathy as the core of *chesed* and the essence of the pastoral relationship. He builds on the Talmudic notion of the *ben gil*, the helper who is a peer of the one helped, to articulate an understanding of the nature of the empathic bond.

The concept of pastoral care does not have an exact equivalent in Jewish theology or practice; because it emerges from a wholly unfamiliar Christian paradigm, the term does not have resonance for Jews. However, if the term is without a source in Jewish tradition, the essence of pastoral care—extending oneself to another for the purpose of engendering a relief from suffering—is central to Jewish responsibility and communal life. This chapter explicates the responsibility of extending oneself to the suffering, using Jewish paradigms based on the teachings from tradition, which define this unique mode of caregiving. Moreover, this Jewish framework calls the professionals engaged in this endeavor to perform it with excellence.

Chesed *and the Healing Relationship*

Jewish tradition challenges its adherents to the *mitzvah* of *chesed*, acts of loving-kindness. Forms of *chesed* include *hachnasat orchim*, inviting guests into one's home; *hachnasat kallah*, helping to meet the needs of a bride before her wedding; and *levayat hamet*, honoring the dead by attending a funeral. More relevant to themes of pastoral care is that Judaism requires the *mitzvah* of *bikur cholim*, visiting the sick, and of *nichum avelim*, comforting the mourner. These two *mitzvot* best correspond to what Christian tradition refers to as pastoral care.

It is important to note that although *bikur cholim* and *nichum avelim* are components of the *mitzvah* of *chesed*, they are in their own ways unique. In contrast to the *chesed* of *tzedakah* (giving charity),

bikur cholim and *nichum avelim* do not involve giving one's posses-
sions but rather giving one's *self*. In contrast to *levayat hamet* (attending a funeral), *nichum avelim* and *bikur cholim* require the
establishment of a healing relationship. The Talmud identifies a source
for the *mitzvah* of *bikur cholim* in the Torah. In the biblical account of
the drama of the mutineers who joined Korach in challenging Moses'
authority in the wilderness, Moses tells the people, "If these men die
in the common death of all men and be visited after the visitation of
all men, then the Eternal has not sent me" (Numbers 16:29). The Talmud points out that the deaths of these men were unusual because
they died suddenly, with no visitors to provide *bikur cholim*. The im-
plication is that the Torah expects visitation of the sick and dying as
the norm.[1] Based on the Talmudic source for this *mitzvah* of *chesed*,
bikur cholim clearly cannot be for the purpose of cure, for it is derived
from the experience of Korach's mutineers, who were about to die.
Rather, this *chesed* aims at relieving suffering through the gift of healing relationship.

The critical link between relationship building and *bikur cholim*
can be further adduced from the Talmud's discussion in Tractate Sotah
on the source for the *mitzvah*. Here, the Talmud derives the *mitzvah*
of *chesed* in general and of *bikur cholim* in particular from the responsibility of *imitatio dei* (imitating the Divine). Just as God visits the
sick and comforts the mourner, so must all Jews. The text derives
God's visitation of the sick from God's appearance to Abraham and
the subsequent visit of Abraham by three men identified by tradition
as angels. The Talmud relates that this visit occurred on the third day
after Abraham's circumcision and that God's appearance was for the
purpose of visiting the sick.[2] One might wonder how the rabbis
gleaned from the text that God's appearance was an act of *bikur
cholim*. The rabbis noted that in the verse describing God's appearance to Abraham, there is no content or stated message attached to
the Divine Presence. In fact, the only clue to the reason for the appearance are the words "to him" which follow "And the Eternal appeared" (Genesis 18:1). Therefore, the Rabbis recognized that here,
the whole focus of God's appearance was not to reveal specific content, which is more typical, but *to be with* Abraham. This makes sense
if it is understood that God's desire to be with Abraham was in response to Abraham's recent circumcision and need to convalesce.

Through *bikur cholim,* God was not delivering a message, teaching a concept, or even curing an illness (according to the Midrash, that task is left to one of the angels). God appears simply to be with Abraham and to offer the healing gift of relationship.

Suffering as Estrangement: The Power of the Ben Gil

If the *chesed* of *bikur cholim* is centered on building a relationship for healing, what suffering is it meant to relieve? It is important to identify suffering rather than pain as the operative issue here because the distinction between the two is critical. Pain is a neurological phenomenon; it can be quantified and measured. Although each person may have a different tolerance level for pain, it is essentially an objective reality, open to scientific measurement. Suffering is a *response* to pain; it results from the emotional and spiritual meaning that the pain has in one's life.[3] Medicine treats pain; caregiving responds to suffering.

In fact, the degree to which one finds a situation unbearable usually has more to do with suffering than with pain. One can endure the pain caused by wounds that are healing, but similar levels of pain related to disease may be unbearable. Childbirth may produce pain similar to a gallbladder attack, yet it is felt entirely differently. It is the *meaning* that one attaches to the pain that differs, and so does one's level of suffering.

The suffering that is at the core of illness and loss is estrangement. When ill, one becomes estranged from the key components of life and, ultimately, even from a healthy sense of self. In Jewish tradition, the sick person is given a title, *choleh.* Similarly, one who is bereaved is not only living an experience, but has a new description, *avel.* This is not intended to brand or to label the sick and the grieving, but to acknowledge their sense of "otherness." In her classic book, *Suffering,* Dorothee Soelle describes illness as an experience of estrangement[4] that can be discerned on three levels. First, in illness the sick are estranged from their community. They are hospitalized or kept at home, separated from their jobs, their synagogues, their clubs; they lose their places as participants in the community's life. Second, illness estranges one from family. Even when the family is present, the sick feel alone; their role is compromised. For example, a frail, elderly woman suffers because she has given as a mother all her life, and finds it unbearably painful to be suddenly forced into a reversal of roles when her children take care of her. Finally, and most devastatingly, prolonged illness causes an estrangement from the self. The sick lose a relationship to the person they have been throughout their lives. The inability to function as before causes self-doubt. They do not recognize themselves in this new, compromised situation. The terms *choleh* and *avel* reflect the reality that the world of the sick and the grieving and that of the healthy may not feel the same at all.

The estrangement of the suffering, the sense of alienation from community, family, and self is at the center of the despair, sadness, and fear the caregiver encounters at the bedside. Illness and loss force the ill into an exile in a most profound way; perhaps it is this personal experience of exile encountered by the sick that explains why, in Jewish tradition, "The *Shechina* [G-d's presence] is above the bed of the ill."[5] The Rabbis have explained that there is a *galut* (exile) on high that corresponds to Israel's *galut* as a people below. The *Shechina* itself is in exile, estranged from the fullness of intimacy with the *Ein Sof* (the Infinite One), even as Israel the people are exiled from their land.[6] What abode could be more appropriate for the exiled *Shechina* than the bedside of the ill, who parallel most poignantly the heartache of estrangement? Together, they form a community of the alone.

Bikur cholim and *nichum avelim* are responses to this sense of estrangement. They represent an effort to help the *choleh* or the *avel* find community, not by pretending that he or she is a part of the world of the healthy and well, but by having members of that community enter into the world of the other, the world of the estranged. The Talmud teaches that "anyone who visits the sick takes away one-sixtieth of his or her suffering,"[7] but adds that the statement is only true if the visitor is "*ben gilo*." Some commentators interpret *ben gilo* as meaning that the visitor should be the same age as the one visited;[8] others interpret it to mean that the visitor must be of the same astrological sign.[9] In either case, we are left with the challenge of making sense of the Talmudic qualifier.

In light of the preceding explication of *bikur cholim* as a response to the estrangement of the ill, the gift of a *ben gil* is quite clear. One-sixtieth of the suffering can be alleviated if the visitor identifies and builds community with the sick. A *ben gil*, one who is either of similar age or similar temperament (as reflected in the sharing of an astrological sign) with the sick person, has a greater capacity to create an empathic bond and hence, a healing relationship. Although other visitors may provide some relief, the fullest measure (one-sixtieth) can be gained only by establishment of the deepest level of rapport, and this level is most available to a *ben gil*.

The proliferation of support groups in contemporary society reflects the wisdom embedded in this tradition. That gatherings of people facing similar life concerns, from substance abuse to child loss, have become central to recovery and healing gives witness to the unparalleled capacity of the *ben gil* to relieve suffering. Support groups are not, by definition, designed to offer solutions; rather, they create a context in which the estranged can feel a sense of belonging. For many sufferers, they offer the only sense of solace.

The laws surrounding *nichum avelim* reflect the same theme. In making a *shiva* (initial period of mourning) visit, we are mandated to sit down to be with the mourner, who remains on or near the floor. We are forbidden to initiate a conversation. We comfort the mourner by including him or her in our blessing with "all the mourners of Zion."[10] The halachic (legal) guidelines govern what can and cannot be said in the prayer service of the *tzibur* (community) that takes place in the mourner's home. As a chaplaincy intern of mine once observed about pastoral care, "We need to slow down to keep up." Indeed, it is in slowing down that it becomes possible to join with the other to build a community and relieve suffering during a time of estrangement.

"Because You Were Strangers":
Empathy as the Central Pastoral Tool

Building relationship with the suffering is the challenge of this unique form of *chesed* for all in the community on whom the *mitzvah* devolves. The expectation is that visitors are usually friends of the sick or the mourner, who share a history with them.[11] The task of chaplains, rabbis, and other professionals in this work is to develop a facility that allows them to become a *ben gil,* that is, to align at a profound level, even with those with whom they have no similarity or history. How do chaplains, rabbis, and others deeply committed to this work develop the capacity to become a *ben gil*? From where do they draw the points of identification that make possible the establishment of a rapport at the deepest level with those who may be so different from themselves?

In his classic work, *The Wounded Healer,* Henri Nouwen called upon those providing pastoral care to identify with the sick and suffering by finding a corollary woundedness within themselves to serve as a conduit to the primary woundedness experience of the other.[12] He made it clear that this vulnerability on the part of caregivers was key to the healing relationship and that, to the extent to which caregivers could access that vulnerability, they had the potential to bring healing. In Nouwen's view, it was not helpful to enter the world of the sufferer with an aura of competence and completeness because it only encouraged the sick person's feeling of isolation. Caregivers need instead to be in touch with their own inner brokenness and incompleteness to form a community and to remedy the despair.[13]

Nouwen's paradigm is compelling. He challenges caregivers to meet the suffering by taking up residence in their world. However, Nouwen's image of the wounded healer is not a Jewish one. The Christian tradition has a wounded messiah, but the God who appears to Abraham and calls his children to imitate the Divine way is not a wounded one.[14] Indeed, caregivers need to discover a point of internal identification with the suffering by entering their world. But the portal paradigm for Jews is not one of common woundedness. Jewish caregivers need an authentic and accessible paradigm that emerges out of Jewish tradition and story.

The Torah provides just such a paradigm, and it consistently reminds the Jewish people that this paradigm is at the core of their national and religious identity: "And you shall love the stranger, for you too were strangers in the land of Egypt" (Deuteronomy 10:19). Forty-five times, more frequently than any other imperative, the Torah challenges the Jew to love and to care for the stranger, and yet, one wonders how there can be a command to love. Tell us to put on *tefillin,* and we can do it; forbid us to work on the Sabbath, and we can comply; but how can we be commanded to love the stranger? Love is a feeling. How can we control what we feel? The Torah itself provides the response: "Love the stranger for *you too were strangers*" (Deuteronomy 10:19). To love another, we need to identify with the other, to find in ourselves the similarity that opens the door to empathy. Precisely because we, the Jewish people, were strangers ourselves, the experience of the stranger is emblazoned on our consciousness. Because of this, we can identify with the stranger, cultivate empathy, and experience love.[15]

Estrangement is at the root of suffering. Caregivers must find the stranger in themselves to become *benei gil* of the other and to build a community with the estranged. The other may have a different age or temperament, a different gender, socioeconomic background, or religious knowledge and observance, but Jews know and share the experience of being a stranger; it is part of our national and religious psyche. It is not the *Shechina* alone that is drawn to the bedside because of the intimacy of a mutual journey of estrangement. All the members of the community of Israel have a history that can identify with the suffering of the stranger. Moreover, all have shared a long postbiblical exile whose most compelling component has been the estrangement from our homeland, from our G-d, and, in the most profound way, from ourselves.

In his Code, Maimonides refers to *bikur cholim* and *nichum avelim* as rabbinic laws derived from the Torah injunction, "Love your neighbor as yourself" (Leviticus 19:18).[16] The work of loving the other surely is not all or nothing. The *mitzvah* requires caregivers to move to ever-deeper levels of appreciation of the other's needs to better respond to him or her. In the *chesed* of caregiving, the love that is required is that of putting oneself in the other's place, the other's current context and emotional state. At times, the sufferer may be sad, at other times angry. Underneath it all, those who are suffering are estranged. In calling on the sense of stranger within ourselves as we extend ourselves to the suffering, we create a healing alignment and offer the love G-d asks of us.

Finding the stranger within ourselves means having access to our own stories. When visiting a man suffering with AIDS (acquired immune deficiency syndrome), caregivers may need to connect to their own experiences of feeling ostracized. In engaging a parent terrified by the illness of a child, caregivers need to identify with the terror of loss and aloneness they have known in their own lives. Although caregivers will not be able to understand completely, they can build the best community possible. The richer our own stores of experiences of loss and suffering, the more we have to offer in the work of healing. Not surprisingly, the best caregivers are frequently those who have suffered greatly and who have had the "stranger" experience in both their national history and their personal odyssey.

Identification with the estranged should not be difficult for chaplains or those providing pastoral care. The medical culture has largely marginalized the place of pastoral care in the hospital milieu, and those of us in the field are frequently reminded that it is not a mandated service. Pastoral caregivers have argued for years that they provide an essential service and are thus entitled to a claim on limited institutional budgets and resources, but the chaplain's place on the treatment team remains ambiguous. Spiritual well-being has become a focus of the Joint Commission on Accreditation of Health Care Organizations (JCAHO), an accrediting body for health care institutions. Chaplains are increasingly called on to contribute to interdisciplinary treatment plans. On the other hand, chaplains' credibility at the bedside is founded on the premise that they are advocates for the patients. They earn the patients' trust precisely because they are seen as outsiders, similar to the patients themselves.

Moreover, if the patient feels estranged in a strange environment, dressed in strange clothes, and attended to by strangers, the chaplain often feels no less strange entering a patient's room unbidden, attempting to win a seat at the bedside. The awkwardness of the random initial visit is often experienced as much by the chaplain as by the patient.[17] Both are asking themselves in those first moments, "Do I belong here?" And yet, it is precisely that awkwardness that offers the possibility of community building and alignment. Indeed, the chaplain is the stranger, and well he or she should be. Our ambiguous position in the health care setting is helpful to our work precisely because it *is* uncomfortable. In our sense of being a stranger, we open the channel to connect with the estranged patient, creating an alignment and a healing response to the prevailing aloneness.

Perhaps for this reason, when the student chaplain visits a sick person for the first time, he or she may have a deeper conversation than one possible for the sick person's rabbi of twenty-five years. The student chaplain has fewer interpersonal skills and surely less wisdom, and yet, the awkwardness so evident in the student becomes a powerful place of connection with the awkwardness of the patient, allowing a sense of community that the more accomplished and sophisticated rabbi cannot engender. Visits by a chaplain from another faith may invite an even more profound intimacy than a visit by one's own clergyperson, inasmuch as both chaplain and patient struggle similarly to feel accepted.

The Price and the Challenge of Empathy

There is an interesting discussion in halachic literature about whether one can receive remuneration for performing the *mitzvah* of *bikur cholim*. The distinction has to do with the form the *mitzvah* takes, that is, whether the visitor stood or sat during the visit.[18] The Ran explains this distinction. He argues that performing the *mitzvah* while standing is its most basic form, and thus does not merit remuneration, whereas doing so while *sitting* with the sick is a higher level of performance of the *mitzvah* and thus may be compensated.[19] I suggest that professionals in the field of pastoral care may make a different argument than the Ran's about the basis on which they are entitled to payment.

One Talmudic discussion derives the responsibility to perform acts of *chesed* from a verse in the biblical portion in which Jethro advises his son-in-law Moses to establish a system of justice. Jethro tells Moses that the judges to be appointed will "enjoin upon them the laws and the teachings, and make known to them the way they are to go and the practices they are to follow" (Exodus 18:20). The Talmud analyzes the latter half of the verse: "the way" refers to acts of *chesed*, "to go" refers to *bikur cholim*,[20] and then queries: If we have already derived the charge to teach *chesed* from "the way," why do we need the extra words "to go" to teach the importance of *bikur cholim*? Is not *bikur cholim* included within the larger responsibility to do *chesed*? The Talmud answers that we need the added specificity of *bikur cholim* when the visitor is a *ben gil* because a *ben gil* takes away one-sixtieth of the illness.[21]

The passage is confusing. What does the Talmud mean in requiring the extra verse to include a *ben gil*? If a person who cannot take away one-sixtieth of suffering is charged with the *mitzvah* of visiting, surely the *ben gil*, who is more efficacious at relieving suffering, should be mandated to visit. The answer is that in removing one-sixtieth of the suffering, the *ben gil* does not simply relieve the other's suffering, but takes that one-sixtieth onto himself or herself. The *ben gil*, the visitor who identifies with the one who is ill because of similarities in temperament or age, indeed establishes a healing rapport, but at a personal cost. The *ben gil* visitor feels the other's suffering, and, in fact, might hesitate to visit precisely because of the similarity of circumstances. It is threatening and even terrifying to see oneself in the bed. Were it not for a specific charge, we might have exempted the *ben gil* from the obligation to visit, for in visiting, the *ben gil* gives more than time. The *ben gil* gives of himself or herself.

Professionals providing the *chesed* of *bikur cholim* or *nichum avelim* are charged to become the *ben gil*. They are called on to identify with those who suffer in estrangement and to facilitate an alignment for healing. The work is not without consequence. As indicated earlier, the marginalization that chaplains experience in the health care setting engenders a helpful, but nonetheless hurtful, sense of estrangement. Entering into one's own persona of the stranger during a visit will indeed help alleviate the suffering of a *choleh* or an *avel*, but at a cost. Caregivers taste the very suffering they hope to relieve. Becoming a *ben gil* is the performance of the *chesed* of *bikur cholim* in its highest form. Chaplains and others providing emotional and spiritual support give *of themselves* to do the *mitzvah* and are therefore entitled to remuneration. They have gone beyond the expected; they, too, have gone into *galut*, if only for a while, to build a community in exile with their suffering brothers and sisters.

At times, the challenge of becoming a *ben gil* is not so much the difficulty in finding an inner story that matches the experience of the sufferer, but rather, of separating the sufferer's experience from one's own. Having had experiences similar to those of the person in the bed can sometimes make visiting too difficult to be healing. A woman chaplain who has recently had a mastectomy may be unable to offer relationship to a woman of her age with breast cancer. It is not that she does not understand, but that she understands too well, and the nearness of the experience makes it too painful to reenter. To become a *ben gil*, one needs both to have had an experience similar to that of the other and to have successfully integrated that experience so that one can revisit it without becoming overwhelmed. An emotionally defenseless chaplain is as unavailable to cultivate healing relationships as an overly defended one. The ongoing challenge for chaplains is to live in a community in which they can feel safe enough to be vulnerable but secure enough to ask for help.

The challenge of taking on the persona of the stranger, if consistent with the experience of the chaplain, is quite at odds with the persona of a rabbi in a congregational context. As spiritual leaders of synagogues, rabbis are primarily identified as teachers. The Talmud makes clear that the role of teacher calls for a different paradigm: "If the teacher can be compared to an angel of the Eternal of Hosts, then seek Torah from him. If not, then do not seek Torah from him."[22] The rabbi as teacher is expected to model a level of scholarly accomplishment that the student does not yet possess. Unlike the role of the rabbi as caregiver, which calls for *vulnerability,* the role of the rabbi as teacher demands excellence, competence, and a kind of invulnerability. Becoming a good educator requires the rabbi's knowing, competent, "angel"-like qualities. However, this distances the rabbi from access to the internal "stranger," which allows him or her to empathically relate to sufferers. Undoubtedly, much of the disappointment congregants express about the pastoral abilities of their rabbi is rooted in this paradox.

The challenge for rabbis and cantors serving communities and families during the vicissitudes of life is to cultivate both aspects of themselves. To teach Torah effectively, they must indeed model the spiritual integration and excellence of angels. To do *chesed* and to demonstrate leadership in healing the suffering, they must humble themselves to enter the world of the other through sharing the experience of estrangement and vulnerability. This is no easy task. It is made more difficult by the fact that the image of "angel" and of "stranger" present striking contrasts. The rabbi or cantor is called on, not to reconcile the images, but to have the maturity to contain and to use both in facilitating growth and healing. To be successful in the caregiving role, rabbis, cantors, and pastoral caregivers have to find a caring community supportive of their vulnerability.

Conclusion

The implications of the themes presented in this chapter are clear for the provision of emotional and spiritual care in the Jewish community.

The suffering experienced in illness and loss is rooted in a sense of estrangement from community, family, and self. The responsibility of the community and its caregivers is to build a rapport with the suffering by summoning the experience of the stranger in themselves. Chaplains and those professionally committed to performing this *chesed* need to develop more than good attending skills and the desire to help. They need to develop the capacity to join the predicament of the other by temporarily surrendering the secure self that lives in the world of the healthy and whole and embracing the dimension of the self that knows what it means to be a stranger. In this way, they are able to take up residence in the world of the suffering. To bring healing and hope, they need to have the courage to suffer. Is it any wonder that the Talmud describes a host of life blessings that will be granted to the one who performs the *mitzvah* of *bikur cholim?*23 To do it well requires more than presence; it requires personal preparation, discipline, and sacrifice.

Notes

1. BT Nedarim 39b.
2. BT Sotah 14a.
3. See James G. Emerson, *Suffering: Its Meaning and Ministry* (Nashville: Abingdon Press, 1986).
4. Soelle, Dorothee, *Suffering* (Philadelphia: Fortress Press, 1975).
5. BT Nedarim 40a.
6. See BT Megillah 29a.
7. BT Nedarim 39a. Various versions of the text differ as to whether the visitor alleviates one-sixtieth of the "suffering" of the sick or of the "illness" itself.
8. "Either young like him or an elderly visitor for the elderly," Rashi, BT Nedarim 39a.
9. Rabbenu Nisim (Ran), BT Nedarim 39a.
10. The traditional words used to comfort the mourners are: "May you be comforted with the mourners of Zion and Jerusalem."
11. See Keren Orah's (BT Nedarim 40a) explanation of the Talmudic passage citing the rewards promised to those who visit the sick. Among the rewards promised is that one will have good friends because the primary way of performing the *mitzvah* is with friends and contemporaries to whom one thus demonstrates closeness.
12. Henri J.M. Nouwen, *The Wounded Healer* (Garden City, N.Y.: Image Books, 1979), pp. 82ff.
13. Nouwen, *Wounded Healer*, p. 94.

14. Nouwen does indeed use Jewish sources to support his image. He refers to the Talmudic account of Rabbi Joshua ben Levi who met the Messiah sitting at the gate among the poor covered with wounds (p. 81). However, Judaism, unlike Christianity, does not charge its adherents to imitate the Messiah.

15. Nouwen argues for a similar healing model by dint of different symbols. He identifies the woundedness of society in general and of clergy in particular as rooted in the inherent and pervasive experience of loneliness.

16. Hilchos, *Avel* 14:1.

17. See Lawrence E. Holst, "The Random Initial Visit," in *Hospital Ministry: The Role of Chaplains Today,* ed. Lawrence E. Holst (New York: Crossroads Publishing, 1985), pp. 68–81.

18. The Talmud prohibits accepting payment for the mitzvah of visiting the sick (Nedarim 39a).

19. Ran, BT Nedarim 39a. For a fuller discussion on the theme see Shita Mekubetzet, Nedarim 39a.

20. BT Bava Metzia 30b.

21. Ibid.

22. BT Chagiga 15b.

23. BT Nedarim 40a.

Bibliography

Bleich, J. David. "Visiting the Sick." In *Judaism and Healing*. New York: KTAV, 1981.

Katz, Robert L. *Empathy: Its Nature and Uses*. Glencoe, Ill.: Free Press of Glencoe, 1963.

_____. *Pastoral Care and the Jewish Tradition*. Philadelphia: Fortress Press, 1985.

Kestenbaum, Israel. "The Rabbi as Caregiver: A Clinical Model," *Tradition* 23, no. 3 (spring 1988): pp. 32–40.

_____. "A Jewish Approach to Healing," *The Journal of Pastoral Care* 51, no. 2 (summer 1997): pp. 207–11.

Schacter, Zalman M., and Edward Hoffman. *Sparks of Light: Counseling in the Hassidic Tradition*. Boulder and London: Shambhala, 1985.

Rabbi Israel Kestenbaum, M.A., M.Ed., A.C.P.E., is a Certified Supervisor of the Association for Clinical Pastoral Education. He serves as founding director of the Jewish Institute for Pastoral Care of the Healthcare Chaplaincy in New York City.

Bikur Cholim:
A Paradigm for Pastoral Caring

Rabbi Joseph S. Ozarowski

Rabbi Joseph Ozarowski examines the implications of pastoral care as an act of *imitatio dei* and offers a careful analysis of rabbinic texts on *bikur cholim*. He explicates their teachings on the meaning of pastoral care and draws from them concrete guidance on providing pastoral care.

*B*ikur *cholim,* the commandment to visit the sick, offers a paradigm for the pastoral caregiver. It embodies a theological framework, and the sacred texts surrounding it provide practical guidance for our conduct with the sick. Although it has been argued that professional pastoral caregiving is different than friendly visitation, pastoral care could be considered the specialization and professionalization of this *mitzvah.* It has also been suggested that *bikur cholim* is a *mitzvah* required of everyone, not just of specialists. We have many other examples of *mitzvot* that apply to all Jews, yet involve trained people who provide leadership in these *mitzvot,* such as *brit milah, shechita,* and *talmud torah.* Therefore, we suggest that the teachings surrounding *bikur cholim* offer invaluable guidance to trained pastoral caregivers in their work. Moreover, the Jewish tradition's teachings on *bikur cholim* constitute the primary locus of both values and practical wisdom for the developing field of Jewish pastoral care.

The Theological Framework:
Bikur Cholim *as Walking in God's Ways*

Illness is a crisis point of life, an integral and inescapable part of our existence. Jewish tradition teaches that we affirm life even while facing pain and suffering. A major way we do this is by imitating our Creator, or walking in God's paths. This idea is illustrated beautifully in rabbinic sources.

R. Hama said in the name of R. Hanina: What does it mean, "You shall walk after the Eternal your God" (Deuteronomy 13:5)? Is it possible for a person to walk and follow God's presence? Does not [the Torah] also say, "For the Eternal your God is a consuming fire" (Deuteronomy 4:24)? But it means to walk after the attributes of the Holy Blessed One. . . . The Holy Blessed One visits the ill, as it says, "And God visited him [Abraham] in Elonei Mamreh" (Genesis 18:1), so you too shall visit the ill.[1]

Jewish tradition sees *bikur cholim* as a function of *gemilut chesed*, acts of kindness performed in emulation of God's divine kindness and love.[2] One who truly wishes to walk in God's path must imitate God through loving-kindness at life's crisis points, such as illness. By visiting the ill, we follow God's paths, acting as God does. In this way, we connect to and care for one another in illness and crisis, when we are most vulnerable. At these times, we truly need to be assured of God's love and presence. Our own imitation of God's love can be most effective in helping the troubled and suffering.

The Talmudic teaching about visiting the sick is based on God's appearance to Abraham after Abraham's circumcision (Genesis 18:1–2). The Midrash provides a moving description of this visit:

When God was revealed [to Abraham], the Holy Blessed One stood and Abraham sat, as it says, " . . . and he was sitting in the doorway. . . ." It is the custom of the world that when a student is sick and the teacher goes to visit, [other] students go first and say, "[There is] a delegation of the teacher to the house of the patient," meaning that the teacher wishes to visit the student. Not so the Holy Blessed One. When Abraham was circumcised and was in pain from the circumcision, God told the messengers to go and visit. But before they arrived, God came in first, as the Torah says (verse 1), "And God appeared to him," and after that (verse 2), "And he lifted his eyes and saw three. . . . " Is there no greater Humble One than this?[3]

From this first example of *bikur cholim* in the Torah, we learn several lessons. First, the visitor must visit the sick with a sense of humility, as did God. Second, the visit is for the sake of the sick person, not the visitor. Third, there is not always a set script for a *bikur cholim* visit. In fact, there is no dialogue at all between God and Abraham recorded in the Torah's account of this encounter. Often, the presence of the visitor is far more important than the words spoken.

The Mandate for Pastoral Care

Bikur cholim is not a commandment directed at professionals. All Jews are called to care for the ill through fulfillment of this *mitzvah*. But is there any mandate or warrant for skilled pastoral caregivers in these acts of *chesed*?

As in the following example, since Talmudic times, groups of individuals within the Jewish community have been organized for the express purpose of attending to communal needs.

> Rabbi Yehuda said in the name of Rav: If there is a death in the city, all citizens are forbidden to do work [in order to tend to the needs of the deceased]. R. Hamnuna went to Daromta and heard there the sound of the funeral-*shofar*. He then saw some people who were still doing work. He said to them, "These people should be placed under the *shamta* [a limited form of excommunication]. Is there not a dead person in town?" [But] they told him, "There is a *chevra* [a committee or association] in town [that does these tasks and fills these needs]." He said, "If so, it is permitted [to do work]."[4]

A second example is the following:

> Such was the practice of the *chavurot* [associations or committees] in Jerusalem: Some went to the house of the mourners; some to the house of [marriage] feasting, some went to a circumcision, others to gather up the bones.[5]

From these texts, we see that since rabbinic times, particular individuals have represented the community in fulfilling *chesed*-based *mitzvot*. Since the twelfth century, *bikur cholim* committees have functioned in this way. If lay committees can represent the community in attending to the needs of the sick, we can deduce that a trained, pastoral caregiver may individually play the role of community *shaliach*, or representative. Halachic literature suggests that although a personal visit is ideal, sending someone else to convey good wishes also fulfills the *mitzvah*.[6] A trained professional indeed represents the entire Jewish community when serving the community's ill, and does not detract from the importance of lay volunteers who visit their ill peers, or even of congregational rabbis' visits to sick congregants. Certainly, the ill see the pastoral caregiver as a representative of the community.[7] Indeed, one of the therapeutic aspects of pastoral visits for the sick is the knowledge that they will be remembered in the living community. As the Talmud puts it, "*Shelucho shel adam kamoto*" (a representative in Jewish law) has the status of the sender.[8] In all of these aspects, the pastoral caregiver can truly be said to act as the community's *shaliach* or emissary.

The Meaning of Pastoral Care

Bikur cholim, like all of Jewish practice, has a theological foundation. If we see pastoral care as an extension of *bikur cholim*, the rich traditions of this *mitzvah* can illuminate the meaning of pastoral care as well.

The Visitor as the Representative of God

Sickness is an inevitable part of life, but like any experience, illness can be a means to help one grow spiritually. In this context, God is seen as partner, not agent of punishment. For this reason, the Talmud openly says that God's very presence (*Shechina*) rests above the sick person's bed, providing sustenance for him or her:

> Rabin said in the name of Rav: From where do we know that the Holy Blessed One sustains the sick? As it says, "The Eternal will support [the sick person] upon his bed of illness" (Psalm 41). Rabin also said in the name of Rav: From where do we know that the Divine Presence rests above the invalid's bed? From the verse, "The Eternal will support [the sick person] upon his bed of illness."[9]

This text assures the sick of God's presence and love in time of illness. By sharing their presence, visitors can truly imitate God. In the eyes of many sufferers, both clergy and lay pastoral caregivers represent the Divine Presence because they come on behalf of both Judaism and of the Jewish community.

Beyond the actual symbolism of the visit, the Talmud teaches us that the Divine Presence inhabits the place of illness and the place of the sick. If the *Shechina* is at the head of every sick person, a hospital or geriatric facility becomes a holy place. In the bottom line–oriented, contemporary health care system, Jewish tradition teaches us to reclaim the sacred as an integral part of the healing process. Real pastoral care allows both the sick person and the visitor to sense the closeness of the *Shechina*. Whether sufferers formally identify with organized Judaism or are simply Jews by birth, being aware of God's presence can help them reconnect with their spiritual self. This reconnection facilitates spiritual healing, which clearly can help effect physical healing as well.[10]

The Reward for Providing Pastoral Care

The sick are not the only ones profoundly affected by *bikur cholim;* visitors, too, may be transformed by accompanying the sick on their journey through a difficult period. As a reward for the kind act of visiting the sick, the psalmist declares in Psalm 41:

> The Eternal will deliver him in the day of evil.
> The Eternal preserve him and keep him alive, let him be called
>   happy in the land;
> And You will not deliver him unto the greed of his enemies.

The commentaries elucidate the verse as follows:

> Rashi: The Eternal will sustain him [the visitor] when he is on his own sick bed.
> Ibn Ezra: [The visitor] will live long years.
> Metzudot: [The visitor] will be praised by his peers and not given to the desires of his enemies.

Psalm 41 continues:

> The Eternal will support him upon his bed of illness
> May You turn all his lying down in his sickness.

There is a dispute among the commentaries about whether the divine support promised in the last verse refers to the visitor (as a reward, according to Rashi) or to the sufferer (God's succor of the ill person, according to the Talmud and some modern commentators). It is most interesting to note that the Targum, the Aramaic translation of the Psalms, renders the Hebrew *yis'ad,* or "support," as "visit"! Therefore, this verse would be read, "The Eternal will visit him while he is on the bed of illness." God's "visit" could mean either that God visits the sick person (as suggested regarding Abraham), or that God will visit the visitor when he or she becomes ill (as a reward for the visitor's kindness in attending to the sick).

Psalm 41 lends strong credence to the notion that true visitation of the sick involves empathy, sensitivity, and understanding. Apparently, the psalmist experienced this and assures us that the visit is a major value in Judaism, richly rewarded by God.

We may also ask a question regarding a contemporary pastoral understanding of the divine reward promised by the psalmist. How are we to understand the reward today given to either the professional pastoral caregiver or to any Jew fulfilling the commandment of *bikur cholim*? Even the Talmud itself says: "Do not be like servants who serve the master for the sake of receiving a reward, but rather be like servants who serve the master without the expectation of receiving a reward."[11]

Perhaps the key concept here is God's support, sustenance, and preservation; we are promised God's blessings in a general sense for a sensitive, compassionate visit to the ill. In a deeper way, visitors are assured that God will be with them in their time of need. Visiting the sick is thus not merely gratifying; it can also yield lasting rewards for the visitor. Recent studies have found that serving others may have a positive impact on one's life, and that people who engage in frequent volunteer activity or are part of a religious community enhance their own health.[12] I have personally experienced the mysterious and powerful benefits of visiting the sick:

> I once walked into the ICU [intensive care unit] and saw a male patient wearing a *kippah*. I had barely introduced myself before this gentlemen, through his oxygen mask, began spouting wonderful *divrei torah* comments on the weekly portion! Behind me, the patient's wife exclaimed, "I don't believe this! I don't believe this!" When I explored this further, I learned that the man had been confused and dazed for the forty-eight hours before my visit. My presence, it seems, brought this man back to reality, and I was literally able to remove a fraction of his illness! We talked further,

discovering many people and places in common. As I left, they thanked and blessed me. But there was more. As I spoke further to the patient's wife, I discovered that her parents signed the papers that brought my own grandparents to the U.S. in 1950! Her parents and my grandparents were in the jewelry business together in Lisbon during the Second World War.

We pointed out earlier that *bikur cholim* falls under the rubric of *gemilut chasadim* or *mitzvot* that are acts of kindness. *Gemilut* is related to the Hebrew word for "payback." It took two generations to pay back one act of kindness with another. This act brought healing to the son-in-law of people who had helped bring a Jewish couple to this country after the Holocaust. This "payback" benefited not only the sick person but the caregiver as well. The rewards for pastoral care can be mysterious and awe-inspiring.

Pastoral Care's Task Is Limitless

The Talmud offers valuable insights about the scope of the pastoral task in visiting the sick.

> It was taught: "*bikur cholim* has no set amount." What is meant by "*bikur cholim* has no set amount"? R. Joseph thought it means there is no set amount for its reward [the reward is unlimited]. Said Abaye to him: Does anyone have the set amount of the reward for the *mitzvot*? Do we not learn: Be as careful with an easy *mitzvah* as with a heavy one, for you do not know the reward of the *mitzvot*.[13] But Abaye said [it must mean]: Even the greater [*gadol,* goes on a visit] to the smaller [*katan*].[14] Raba said: ["No set amount" means one can visit] even a hundred times a day.

This text describes the limitlessness of *bikur cholim*—whether in terms of its reward, who must visit whom, or the quantity of visits. God's visit to Abraham is the finest example of the greater visiting the smaller. In visiting the sick, in contrast to the classic clergy roles of teacher or preacher, there is no room for hierarchy in relationship. And although multiple visits may be required, Maimonides, himself a physician, encouraged the visitor to be sensitive to the sick person's needs: "One can visit many times in the day. Whoever adds [to this] is praiseworthy, providing one does not trouble [the patient]" (Laws of Mourning 14:4).

The needs of the sick often seem limitless. But in this age of managed care, all caregivers are called on to use finite resources to treat the ill. Today's pastoral professionals may no longer be able to visit patients "many times in the day," in the praiseworthy manner of Maimonides' suggestion, but they can still offer the infinite compassion of their hearts and souls, in the hope of offering spiritual healing to the ill and in imitation of the Holy One. They can take comfort in knowing they have made a difference, even though there is always more to do.

Fostering Spiritual Healing

The process of healing may also offer a spiritual opportunity. The pastoral caregiver can have a vital role to play in the spiritual journey of the ill person. As the Talmud puts it:

> R. Alexandri said in the name of R. Hiyya b. Abba: A patient does not recover from sickness until all his sins are forgiven, as it is written, "Who forgives all your iniquities; Who heals all your diseases" (Psalms 103:3). R. Hamnuna said: He then returns to the days of his youth for it is written, "His flesh shall be fresher than a child's, he shall return to the days of his youth" (Job 33:25).[15]

This passage does not mean that people who cannot recover are unforgiven. But the illustrative quote from Psalms clarifies that healing is coupled with forgiveness and God's love. Although nearly all sick people aspire to be physiologically cured from illness, this hope is often not fulfilled. But cure can also be defined mentally, spiritually, and emotionally, as the Hebrew term *refuat hanefesh* implies. Forgiveness from sin or a sense of spiritual renewal can make one's life spiritually fresher.

The rabbinic comment on Psalm 103 also implies that good pastoral care can offer the sick a sense of reconciliation with God, as well as with other people. The presence of the familiar symbols of Judaism as well as a human, Jewish presence can help the ill make sense of life at a time when their regular routines have been disrupted.

The Means of Pastoral Care

Empathy

Human beings can imitate God through empathy. Pastoral caregivers use their minds, hearts, and imagination to share the pain of the sufferer, even though they do not necessarily feel the exact same pain. A caregiver's understanding helps alleviate the sufferer's sense of aloneness and even lessens the pain.

All Jews, not just professional pastoral caregivers, are called on to follow God's ways in acts of *chesed,* such as *bikur cholim.* However, professionals' training and skills may provide them with special gifts to share with those who are ill. This type of pastoral relationship obviously makes demands of the giver. The following Talmudic tale illustrates the heart of the pastoral task:

> R. Joshua b. Levi met Elijah [the prophet] sitting at the opening of the cave of R. Shimon bar Yohai. . . . He said to him [Elijah], "When will the Messiah come?" He answered, "Go and ask him himself." "Where is he sitting?" "At the gates of the city." "What is his sign [that I may recognize him]?" "He sits among the poor who suffer from wounds. All of them unbind and rebind [their wounds] in one act. But he unbinds and rebinds [each wound] separately, saying, 'Should I be wanted, these [wounds, all dressed at once] should not delay me.'"[16]

Rashi understands the text "and he is wounded as well" to mean that the Messiah shares in the suffering of those around him. As proof of this, Rashi quotes the passage from Isaiah 53:4, "But our illness he carried and our pain, he suffered." From this text we learn that the Messiah, descendant of King David and the very symbol of redemption in Judaism, shares the pain of those who suffer, especially of those who are sick. He is able to do this because he himself feels the wounds. In other words, he shares empathy with those who are afflicted. He is able to offer redemption and hope because he understands what suffering is.[17] Pastoral caregivers, like Elijah, are called to share the pain of suffering people, to use their own experiences of vulnerability to help and to support them.

Attending to Physical Needs

Attending to the physical needs of the sick is an integral part of *bikur cholim*. In the following Talmudic story, the great Rabbi Akiba demonstrates the importance of offering personal and practical care:

> R. Helbo took ill. R. Kahana proclaimed, "R. Helbo is sick!" but no one came to visit. He rebuked the others as follows, "Did it not happen that one of R. Akiba's students took sick and none of the sages came to visit? But R. Akiba [himself] entered to visit and because [R. Akiba] swept and sprinkled the room before him, he recovered. 'My master [said the student] you have made me live!' Following this R. Akiba went and lectured, 'Whosoever does not visit the sick is like a shedder of blood.'"[18]

We see several concepts in this story. First, the story emphasizes the greatness and importance of *bikur cholim;* second, it is an excellent example of "the greater visiting the lesser"; and third, we see that tending to the ill person's actual physical needs is part of the *mitzvah*. In fact, the Hebrew term the Talmud uses for "sweeping and sprinkling" is *kibdo v'rivtzo*. The word *kibed* also means "to honor." Even an act as mundane as sweeping the room is considered a way of honoring the sufferer. Today, making sure the ill person has adequate care is a way of fulfilling the *mitzvah*.[19] Helping the ill to arrange their personal affairs also falls into this category.

Most pastoral caregivers focus on spiritual and emotional issues during a pastoral sick call; after all, hospitals usually provide adequate medical and physical care. Nevertheless, we are obligated to inquire about physical aspects of care. From the Jewish perspective, this is a pastoral concern; other pastoral care and health care professionals may not always understand this. There is a specific pastoral value in looking after the ill person's physical needs. In fact, in another version of the Talmud's story hinted at in the Meiri commentary and quoted in the commentary of the "Netziv" (Rabbi Naftali Tzvi Berlin of Volozhin [Lithuania, nineteenth century]), Rabbi Akiba visited his student but did not do the sprinkling and sweeping himself. Rather, an attendant, noticing the presence of Rabbi Akiba, was moved to sweep and to sprinkle the room. We can learn a significant lesson for our mode of care from this version of the story. Even though we assume that the physical needs of the ill are attended to by paid staff, and that we ourselves do not have to "sweep and sprinkle," these needs are not always adequately met. However, our mere presence in visiting the patient can often prompt health care workers to do their jobs of "sweeping and sprinkling" better. By checking on the food, facilities, and even medical care of the ill, we show them our concern. We empathize with them during their time of difficulty by helping arrange their affairs when they are unable to do so. In this way, we take our lead from the Almighty Who loves us and looks after our needs in times of distress.

Timing Pastoral Visits

The Talmud teaches the following regarding visiting hours:

> R. Shisha the son of R. Idi said: A person should not visit the sick during the first three hours of the day or the last three hours of the day, for he may dismiss praying for him [the sick person]. During the first three hours his illness is easing; during the last three hours his sickness more greatly weakens him.[20]

The thrust of this *Gemara* emphasizes the importance of prayer on behalf of the ill. However, in codifying this rule, Maimonides leaves out the last part of the passage and simply states, "The patient is not visited during the first three hours and the last three hours [of the day] because they are for dealing with the needs of the patient."[21] Maimonides, a physician, saw the Talmud's idea of visiting hours as a medical necessity. One should not visit during the first or last hours of the day because this is when medical treatment is administered.

Modern sources hold that the Talmud's words here are not halachically part of the *mitzvah*, but simply good advice.[22] Visitors may come when they are able, even if the visit is during the Talmud's proscribed times; but visitors—professional or lay—should avoid times when medical treatment is given and not overtax the patient.[23] In sum, visits should be timed to maximize the potential for spiritual connection and to minimize burden.

Placing Oneself in Relation to the Ill Person

Rabbinic sources offer us the following wisdom about how to approach the patient physically:

It was also taught: One who enters to visit the sick should not sit on a bed, nor a bench, nor a chair but should enrobe himself and sit on the ground, for the Divine Presence rests above the bed of the patient, as it says, "The Eternal will support him upon his bed of illness" (Psalm 41).[24]

This Talmudic teaching underlines the reverence one should have when visiting the ill. In codifying this, the Shulchan Aruch maintains that the text applies exclusively to a case in which the ill are lying on the ground, as was usually the case in those days.[25] In such instances, the visitor should not be higher than the sick person.[26] But if the sick person is in bed, as is our universal practice today, then sitting on a chair or bench is preferable. Being on the same level as the ill indicates empathy,[27] eliminating a feeling of hierarchy that might separate visitor and sufferer and offering instead a sense of true presence and interest. By placing oneself at the same level as the sick person, pastoral visitors communicate that their true interest in the patient. Feeling the concern and closeness of pastoral caregivers through this physical gesture can help the sick. When pastoral caregivers are in this proximity to the sick person, they emulate God Who is present at the very head of the sick person and alleviates the suffering.[28]

Most contemporary halachic authorities say that the level, the position, and the posture of the visitor depend on the needs of the sick person. If the sick person requests that the visitor be in a certain spot, those wishes are to be respected.[29]

One modern source interprets "enrobe" as dressing with modesty.[30] According to this authority, visitors should dress as if going to synagogue because they will be greeting the Divine Presence as well as the sick person. Also, according to this source, visiting the sick fosters thinking about the ultimate issues of life and death associated with illness. Visitors' demeanor and dress ought to reflect the seriousness of the moment and circumstance, but one should not dress in a way that will frighten or upset the ill. Again, the tradition calls us to be aware of the impact of every aspect of our presence when visiting the sick. Every gesture, every concrete action, has the power to foster healing, or conversely, to alienate an already suffering person.

Language and Nuance

It is not always easy to find the right words to share with a patient in pain and suffering. Both Jewish tradition and human experience (at least my own experience and that of colleagues) indicate that the ill person needs companionship rather than scintillating conversation. God's visit to Abraham is a model of *bikur cholim*. There is no dialogue between God and Abraham recorded in the Torah's text. Apparently, the Divine Presence was enough to heal Abraham. God's example teaches us that the visitor's actual presence is far more important and meaningful than anything said. A smile, a touch of the hand, or some quiet time together is more healing than platitudes.

Therefore, being present with the person who is sick does not solely involve talking. Listening and feeling are perhaps even more valuable. Psalm 41 is traditionally associated with *bikur cholim* and begins, "Happy is the one who considers the poor [sick] . . ." In his commentary on this verse, Ibn Ezra says:

> Some say "considers" (Heb. *maskil*) means sees; the more correct [interpretation for *maskil*] is to understand with one's heart regarding the patient; and some say *maskil* is an active verb referring to [actual] visiting, speaking to the heart [of the sick person] and understanding him or her.

Bringing one's heart to the visit can make all the difference.

The sick sometimes have difficulty articulating their feelings. A model for responding to this can be drawn from the etiquette used for visiting a mourner during the *shiva* week after the funeral. The visitor is obligated to allow the mourners to share their concerns and to respond to whatever is on their minds. Rather than engaging in meaningless chatter of little concern to grieving people, caring visitors give mourners the chance to work through their grief in their own way.

We can draw a parallel between the ill and the bereaved, for a person in a sick bed or hospital also experiences grief or loss. Using the *shiva*-house model, the visitor lets the sick person guide the conversation, but this does not necessarily mean that one must wait for the sick person to begin the dialogue in a visit. Pastoral visitors can take the initiative by introducing themselves and starting the conversation; but from then on, they follow the lead of the sick person, and in this way, we show that he or she is their primary concern.

Praying with and for the Sick Person

Rabbinic sources also emphasize prayer as a major goal of the pastoral visit.

> When R. Dimi came, he said, "Whoever visits the sick causes [the sick person] to live, and whoever does not visit the sick causes [the sick person] to die." How does one "cause" this? Does this mean that whoever visits the sick will ask mercy [pray] that [the sick person] may live, and whoever does not visit the sick will ask mercy that [the sick person] should die? Would you think this? But [it must mean] that whoever does not visit the sick will not ask mercy, neither that [the sick person] should live nor die.[31]

This source emphasizes the importance of praying during a visit, but it does not tell us of the content of these prayers.

One of the commentaries suggests, "There are times when one must ask mercy for the ill person that he should die, such as when he suffers so much in his illness and it is impossible for him to live."[32] This perspective is derived from the Talmudic account of the death of R. Yehuda HaNasi in BT Ketubot 104a, in which the great rabbi's devoted maidservant, observing his tremendous suffering, prayed for her master's death.

At least one contemporary authority allows the suffering to pray for their own death.[33] It is clear that the content of our prayers with the sick should be tailored to their particular needs, hopes, and fears. Regardless of the content of the prayer, we learn from our tradition that engaging in prayer is an essential aspect of visiting the sick.

Attending to the Dignity of the Patient

The Talmud offers etiquette about whom to visit and proscribes visits to those with intestinal trouble, eye disease, or headaches.[34] Nachmanides applies these restrictions to anyone who has difficulty speaking.[35] In these cases, the visitor is to inquire about the sick person from someone in an outer room, to tend to the sick person's physical needs, and to "listen to [the sick person's] pain . . . and ask mercy on [his or her] behalf." These guidelines appear to be intended to protect the dignity of those whose conditions are such that they might be embarrassed by a visit. Today, halachic etiquette depends on the sick person's condition, but the principle is still to provide joy and relief for the sick without troubling them. Some contemporary authorities advise those in doubt about the appropriateness of a visit to ask family members first and to use discretion.[36] One current source writes that it is a special *mitzvah* to visit when others are not around and the sick person in this case is especially lonely, embittered of soul, and troubled. A visit may help the ill person to forget worry and pain.[37]

The Talmud offers another valuable teaching about the sick person's dignity:

> "May You turn all his lying down in his sickness" (Psalms 41:4).
> R. Joseph said: This means he [or she] forgets his [or her] learning. R. Joseph took ill and his learning was removed [forgotten]. Abaye restored it to him. Thus it is often stated, "R. Joseph said, 'I have not heard this particular lesson,' and Abaye would say, 'You yourself taught it to us and said it from this teaching.'"[38]

This story reminds us that sickness, debilitation, and hospital stays have emotional and spiritual effects on the patient. The disruption of illness, both physical and emotional, can cause forgetfulness, among other symptoms. The experience of illness can literally strip one of a sense of self. Visitors must be acutely aware of the damage that illness and hospitalization can do to one's dignity, for visitors have the opportunity of restoring dignity to the suffering through interactions that remind the sick of who they are, of their value and irreplaceable uniqueness.

Conclusion

Judaism affirms that God is with us in everyday life, but also—and perhaps especially—in sickness and in times of sorrow. Ultimately, our comfort comes from the Almighty. But at the same time, we human beings are expected to help each other when we are in need of spiritual sustenance, guidance, and shepherding. We do this in imitation of the One who is the Source of compassion because, as the Talmud teaches, "Abba Shaul says [interpreting the biblical verse, "This is my God and I will glorify God"]: Be like God, for just as God is merciful and compassionate, so you too be merciful and compassionate."[39]

Notes

1. BT Sotah 14a; also Midrash Genesis Rabba 8.
2. It is not clear whether the commandment to visit the sick is biblical, as Nachmanides opines in his commentary on this section, or rabbinic, as Maimonides suggests in his Code.
3. Midrash Tanhuma Vayera 2.
4. BT Moed Katan 27b.
5. BT Semahot Chapter 12.
6. In fact, R. Waldenberg in Tzitz Eliezer 8:5 and Ramat Rachel 8 writes this as accepted Jewish law.
7. There is a precedent for this notion in the Talmud. In BT Taanit 9a, the rabbis note that Moses, the first rabbi, was regarded by God as the representative of the community: "Because he prayed for the public, he is considered as the public."
8. BT Baba Metzia 96a, BT Brakhot 34b, BT Kiddushin 41b, and many other places in rabbinic literature.
9. BT Nedarim 40a.
10. See Herbert Benson's pioneering *Timeless Healing* (New York: Scribner, 1996) and Larry Dossey's *Healing Words* (New York: Harper, 1993), both of which offer impressive statistics about the efficacy of faith and prayer in the healing process.
11. Pirke Avot 1:3.
12. A positive attitude to life, followed with compassionate acts to others, could indeed affect a person's physical condition. Many who are quite ill are assisted in their recovery by their own attitudes. See Howard F. Andrews, "Helping and Health: The Relationship between Volunteer Activity and Health-Related Outcomes," *Advances* 4, no. 1 (1990): 25–34, and Bill Moyers, *Healing and the Mind* (New York: Doubleday, 1993), p. 157 ff. Also see the works of Benson and Dossey.
13. Pirke Avot 2:1.
14. There are differing interpretations of this particular passage. Rashi understands it to mean greater and smaller in stature. Also thus *Shita Mekuvetzet* (digest of Talmudic commentaries by R. Betzalel Ashkenazi, sixteenth century Egypt and Jerusalem): "Even the greatest personage should visit the humblest" and Soncino. See *Perisha* (commentary on Tur Shulchan Aruch by Rabbi Joshua b. Alexander ha Cohen Falk, sixteenth-century Europe) who refers in the previous way to God's visit to Abraham. However, Maimonides understands it to mean age—that an older person should visit a younger one.
15. BT Nedarim 41a.
16. BT Sanhedrin 98a and following, Rashi's interpretation.
17. *The Wounded Healer* (Garden City, N.Y.: Image Books, 1979) by Catholic theologian Henri Nouwen is predicated in large part on this Talmudic passage. Although his theological interpretations of the healing Messiah in the Talmud as

Jesus is, of course, completely unacceptable from a Jewish point of view, Nouwen's pastoral understanding of the need for the healers to feel with and understand those whom they are attempting to heal spiritually is very much compatible with Judaism.

18. BT Nedarim 40a.

19. This includes medical and other forms of therapy, as well as general care. Tending to the sick person's food and dietary needs, in my opinion, would come under this rubric.

20. Rashi and R. Nissim: When the visitor sees the sick person stronger in the morning, the visitor believes the prayers are not as necessary. When the sick person weakens in the last three hours, the visitor will not pray because he or she has given up hope for recovery.

21. Ibid. 14:5.

22. *Aruch Hashulchan* 335:8 (premodern reworking of the Code of Jewish Law by R. Yehiel Epstein, nineteenth century Lithuania); *Ramat Rachel* 12 (R. Eliezer Waldenberg, twentieth century Israel), who mentions that according to Radbaz on JT Terumot 11:5, one can even visit at night.

23. Levine, 77, note 62, cites a point from the late Rabbi Y. Ruderman of Baltimore in the name of R. Hayyim of Brisk (Lithuania, nineteenth century) that the maximum amount of time for a *bikur cholim* visit is six minutes. I also recently heard in the name of R. Hayim of Volozhin (Lithuania, eighteenth century) an interpretation of Exodus 18:20: "The way that they shall walk," explained by the Talmud as referring to *bikur cholim*, to mean that there comes a point in the visit that the visitor should walk out (e.g., know when to leave) and not tire the sick person!

24. BT Nedarim 40a.

25. Shulchan Aruch Yoreh Deah 335:3.

26. See Maimonides, Laws of Mourning 14:6, "One who visits . . . should not sit on a bed, chair, bench, or any high place, and not higher than [the sick person's] head but should enrobe and sit below his [or her] head, ask mercy for him [or her], and leave."

27. Encountering this particular selection from the Talmud has affected the way I do my hospital calls. I am much more sensitive to how I enter a hospital room and to where I place myself when I enter the room. It is not always possible to be on the same level as the sick person, but I always try to be.

28. The Bet Hillel commentary on the Shulchan Aruch confirms that the main issue in all this is the height of the visitor, not the seating position. But Rashi on BT Shabbat 12 quotes the *Zohar*, which says a person should be neither at the head because of the Divine Presence nor at the foot because of the Angel of Death.

29. N. A. Tuckaczinski, Gesher HaHaim (Jerusalem: 1960), 28.

30. R. Waldenberg, Ramat Rachel 10, based on earlier sources.

31. BT Nedarim 40a.

32. R. Nissim on Ketubot 104a.
33. R. Waldenberg in Ramat Rachel.
34. BT Nedarim 41a.
35. Torat Ha-adam.
36. Aruch Hashulchan 335.
37. Ramat Rachel 3.
38. BT Nedarim 41a.
39. BT Shabbat 133b.

Bibliography

For further study of *bikur cholim*, see the following:

Hebrew Sources

Epstein, Yehiel. Aruch HaShulchan 335. New York: Friedman, undated.

Greenwald, Y. Y. Kol Bo Al Aveilut. New York: Feldheim, 1973, pp. 16–24.

Levine, Aaron. Zikhron Meir. Toronto: Zikhron Meir, 1985, pp. 23–138.

Shulchan Aruch (Code of Jewish Law). Yoreh Deah section 335.

Tukaczinski, Y. M. Gesher HaHaim. Jerusalem: Solomon Printers, 1960, pp. 27–34.

English Sources

Benson, Herbert. *Timeless Healing.* New York: Scribner, 1996.

Dossey, Larry. *Healing Words.* New York: Harper, 1993.

Encyclopedia Judaica. 1972 ed., s.v. "Sick Care, Communal."

Katz, Robert. *Pastoral Care and the Jewish Tradition.* Philadelphia: Fortress Press, 1985.

Kestenbaum, Israel. "The Rabbi as Caregiver." *Tradition* (spring 1988): pp. 32–40.

Levine, Aaron. *How to Perform the Great Mitzvah of Bikur Cholim.* Toronto: Zikhron Meir, 1987.

Levine, Joseph. "Visiting the Sick: The Delicate *Mitzvah.*" *Moment* (December 1980): pp. 20–24.

Ozarowski, Joseph S. *To Walk in God's Ways: Jewish Pastoral Perspectives on Illness and Bereavement.* Northvale, N.J.: Jason Aronson, 1995.

_____. Curriculum on *"Gemilut chasadim"* (acts of kindness) for National Jewish Outreach Program, Orthodox Union and Yeshiva University, 1994.

_____. Curriculum on *Bikur Cholim* for Coalition for the Advancement of Jewish Education, 1999.

Schur, Tsvi G. *Illness and Crisis: Coping the Jewish Way.* New York: NCSY–Orthodox Union, 1987.

Joseph S. Ozarowski, D.Min., was ordained as an Orthodox rabbi at Chicago's Hebrew Theological College and received his doctorate from Lancaster (Pa.) Theological Seminary. He has had a distinguished career spanning over two decades as a pulpit rabbi, educator, author, and hospital chaplain. His published works include *To Walk in God's Ways: Jewish Pastoral Perspectives on Illness and Bereavement,* and he coauthored *Common Ground* (both Jason Aronson) as well as numerous articles and curricula. He is now the Executive Director of the Chicago Rabbinical Council.

Wresting Blessings:
A Pastoral Response to Suffering

Rabbi Myriam Klotz

Rabbi Myriam Klotz characterizes the pastoral response to suffering as presence and the creation of meaning. She offers theological reflections on suffering, drawing both from classic Jewish texts and from works of contemporary Jewish theology. Rabbi Klotz analyzes the *Unetaneh Tokef* prayer as a model for responding to suffering.

Walking in God's Ways: Being Present

A poignant and beautiful ritual has emerged in recent years out of tremendous, collective suffering. Every fall, in cities across the United States, thousands of people participate in AIDSWALKs. Volunteers walk to raise money for organizations that serve people living with HIV/AIDS (human immunodeficiency virus/acquired immune deficiency syndrome). However, they walk not only to raise funds: Participants in annual AIDSWALKs also do so to raise hope, to wrest the blessings of compassion and love from the painful reality of living with the AIDS virus. In a very real sense, the name of this annual ritual depicts what each of us must do every day of our lives—we must walk, one foot in front of the other, on the path of life. For those blessed with good mental, emotional, and physical health, the walk of life is perhaps a mostly joyous passage. However, most of us at some time will tread pathways of pain and suffering when either we or those we care for suffer. At these times, the life path can turn into a twisting, winding, and steeply graded thoroughfare. For some, it is not possible to walk very far, if at all. The experience of suffering can cause those buoyantly striding forward to detour from the path for a time, perhaps sitting or lying down, perhaps writhing or wrestling.

The biblical Jacob wrestled a mysterious figure in the night while he was alone in the midst of his wandering journey (Genesis 23:25 ff.). Those who suffer also often wrestle in the darkness with an opaque yet powerful force. Just as Jacob persisted in his wrestling until the break of dawn, those living with suffering are also invited to persist in their wrestling throughout their dark night. Just as Jacob did not let the figure go until he had wrested a blessing from him, sufferers have the opportunity to wrest from their situation a blessing, to find redemptive meaning and value in the experience. The biblical text is clear: Jacob does not come away unscathed; the figure badly wounds Jacob in his thigh. Even though Jacob limps for the rest of his life, wounded physically in a body that does not fully heal, his inner transformation has been so profound that it engenders a new identity. The blessing bestowed upon Jacob is represented by the new name the figure gives him: Israel, one who wrestles with God.

In my work as a Jewish chaplain for people living with HIV/AIDS, I have encountered many who have prevailed in their wrestlings.[1] The straightforward direction of their life walk has given way to a different, unpredicted journey. However, they wrested blessings from their experience and, in so doing, became a source of rich blessing for others.

> Dolores had lived a wild life of drug abuse and unstable relationships.[2] By the time we met, she was in the advanced stages of AIDS, and she also had cirrhosis of the liver. She was in great physical pain and could no longer walk easily. As I sat beside her at the hospice one gray October afternoon, Dolores talked to me in English peppered with Yiddish. She fondly recalled childhood memories and shared her desire to ask her parents for forgiveness for the life she had led. Through tears that choked her thin and weak body, Dolores told me that for the first time in her life, she believed that she was beautiful. She realized that she had not made good choices earlier in her life, but that now she could start over, believing that she was worthy of her living, and of her dying. I held Dolores's hand as she spoke, and I tried to listen deeply. I felt many emotions during the visit—sadness, rage, judgment, fear, and impotence—but I attempted to remain receptive and present to Dolores. I mirrored her verbally and nonverbally and allowed myself to open my heart to her presence and her process.
>
> Dolores's walk with physical illness had forced her to change the direction of her life. Although she grieved terribly for the loss

of her health and her future, she was grateful that this illness had enabled her to recapture her sense of integrity and her belief in herself and in God. She felt pain and fear but she also felt deep peace. For the first time, she was able to tell her sister how much she loved her, and to believe that her sister loved her a great deal, too. When Dolores died, she was at peace. Dolores was able to share the gift of renewed peace across generations as she was dying and after she died: I watched Dolores shower her sister, her young niece, and the staff with gentle, joyous love. These actions helped her family come to terms with her dying.

Dolores's words and spirit profoundly moved me; my own path changed direction because of having known Dolores. I have been blessed to receive increased awareness of how fragile our lives are, yet how strong our abilities to triumph and to love, even in the most devastating of situations.

Jewish tradition asserts that we are to emulate God's actions, to "walk in God's ways."[3] What does this mean? As pastoral caregivers, we walk with and serve as companions to those who are suffering. We become participants who aid in the walk of living, and who stop walking and wait with the other, if we must, through the night of wrestling. We must join with the ones who suffer so fully that we are pierced by the truths of their experience. We may do so at a cost, for a world that theologically and existentially makes sense to us, a world filled with the Unity of the One Merciful God, may seem for a time to be senseless, perhaps cruel. We will not be able to prevent the twisting turns or wrestlings that those we are companions to must endure in their walks toward blessing. However, through our compassionate and dedicated presence, as we adjust our stride to match that of the one with whom we walk, we help make manifest the possibility of naming and tasting the blessings to be found.

Beyond Presence: Finding Meaning

Dolores was able to find meaning and blessing in her suffering, and my pastoral caregiving role was essentially about affirming and witnessing her unfolding process. However, not everyone you encounter is as easily able to find meaning in suffering. How *can* we bear the agonizing experiences that life sometimes presents? When suffering seems utterly without rationale, how can we maintain or open to a sense of God's presence? Who or what is a God that would allow such hardship?

These difficult questions are among those with which many people wrestle, and pastoral caregivers can help as we walk beside those tasting the bitterness of suffering. By being fully present to others as we walk in God's ways, by helping them to give birth to new visions of themselves and of God, we emulate the compassionate, caring face of the Infinite, even amid the apparent eclipse of God's presence.

Jewish thought and practice offer a paradoxical tension between certainty in the revealed presence of God in and through this world, and submission to a mysteriously elusive force that is utterly beyond human comprehension and knowing. This paradox is acknowledged liturgically in the *kedushah* prayer of the Shabbat and Festival morning service. "*Kadosh, Kadosh, Kadosh, Adonai Tzvaot, m'lo col ha'aretz k'vodo*" (Holy, holy, holy is God, the whole world is filled with God's glory) is chanted just before "*Baruch k'vod Adonai mimekomo*" (Blessed is the glory of God from God's place).[4] In placing these two affirmations of God next to one another, the liturgists suggest that God is at once both known and unknowable, both in this world and utterly apart from it. The liturgy honors the paradoxical nature of God, and it invites us to participate in this mystery at the heart of creation, to honor it as a pathway toward knowing the God of many faces.[5]

The pastoral caregiver participates in this mysterious paradox, bringing to the suffering of others the perspective of God's simultaneous capacity to be known and complete, as well as mysterious and separate. In confronting God's mystery and perhaps God's eclipse, pastoral caregivers stand as human representatives of God's presence and care. They strive to remain compassionately present to the sufferer at all times, even when she or he responds to suffering with anger, mistrust, or disbelief in God. At these times of God's eclipse, pastoral caregivers can serve as human messengers of loving-kindness simply through human presence—by gentle touch, eye contact, and listening deeply to the sufferer.[6] Rabbinic tradition holds that such presence actually helps heal, taking away a portion of the suffering.[7] Simply by being compassionately present to the sufferer, caregivers help alleviate the possible psychic and physical isolation that often accompanies times of intense suffering.

Pastoral caregivers can also approach the suffering of others with rich and caring discernment. There are times when gently encouraging sufferers to articulate the meaning or context of their experiences can help them move through a painful experience with greater strength and resiliency. Pastoral caregivers walk in the ways of God by helping the sufferer craft out of the mysterious distance some sense of graspable perspective, relevance, and perhaps, redemption.[8]

Michael is a physician in his late thirties. He and his wife, Joan, have three children, the youngest of whom is five years old. I met Michael in a special cancer hospital where Joan was being treated for a deadly form of cancer. Michael and I talked while Joan was in treatment. Michael expressed his anger at God for allowing his wife to suffer. He said that he didn't even know what was meant by the term *God*. During our conversation, Michael began to articulate various dimensions of his feelings and perceptions about God, which included feeling alienated in synagogue since childhood. I did not expect Michael to solve the deep frustration and confusion unearthed by his experience. However, we began together a process of diagnosis. In our dialogue, Michael was able to put his spiritual pain and questioning into a meaningful framework and to identify his difficulties and his desires. As he reflected, he realized that he did need to be able to relate to God, to something eternal, compassionate, and strong because his wife and children were suffering, his own future seemed uncertain, and he was in great emotional pain. In articulating the spiritual context of his anguish, Michael did not eradicate the pain or find a cure for his suffering, but, through this connection and his reflections, he was able to open the door to a path of healing. Michael has begun to pray, to read books about Jewish thought and practice, and to attend synagogue services whenever he can. He is finding God's caring presence amid his pain; this process began when he was able to put language to his reality.

Joan is still suffering with cancer. Michael's children are still grieving the loss of their mother's presence in their lives, and Michael still carries the responsibility of being the primary caregiver and provider for both his wife and his children, but having given voice to his own spiritual suffering has increased Michael's resiliency in the face of his challenges.

Job's Friends: A Cautionary Tale

As it was for Michael, it can be redemptive for others who suffer to articulate an understanding of a larger context of meaning in which their suffering occurs. Theological reflection—the attempt to discern God's relationship to suffering—can be essential. The pastoral caregiver can encourage and guide this process of uncovering and articulating another's understanding of God's role in suffering. However, Jewish texts caution against our human desire to assign meaning to someone else's experience that may not be authentic for him or her at that time.

For example, one of the laws of visiting the sick *(bikur cholim)* states that visitors should be careful not to sit at the head of the bed of someone who is ill because the *Shechina,* God's presence, hovers there.[9] Rabbi Nancy Flam understands this to be a metaphorical reminder for those visiting the sick or administering pastoral care not to sit so centrally in relation to the sick person that their own concerns crowd out the experience of the one before them, thereby obstructing the perception of God's presence. Such concerns might be centered on personal anxieties or fears about the visit, distress at the suffering of the other, or personal ideas about how the sufferer should understand and respond to his or her situation.[10]

It is indeed important for pastoral caregivers to be aware of the various theological responses Judaism has offered in response to suffering, and to help inform the sufferer about these perspectives. However, greater devotion to a particular solution or concept about the experience or meaning of suffering than to the suffering person can undermine one's ability to remain open and present to the fullness of another's experience.

The dangers of imposing interpretation on a person's suffering are evident in the biblical narrative of Job, a righteous and virtuous man who suddenly undergoes tremendous trauma: He loses his wealth, his children die, and he becomes terribly ill. Job's friends are quick to try to comfort him. In their desire to help, they offer explanations that they assume will assist Job in creating meaning and finding strength. Their explanations are drawn from the prevailing biblical understanding of suffering. For example, Eliphaz tells Job that righteous people will not lose their material wealth in this world, whereas evil people will. Furthermore, Bildad assures Job that God does not try the innocent unnecessarily and that Job must have done something for which he is being punished. Lastly, Zophar contends that the wicked will suffer greatly, implying that Job must somehow deserve his fate.

Eliphaz, Bildad, and Zophar are all unable to comfort Job through asserting that his suffering must be his own fault. The text does not permit Job to be understood as guilty, but rather, as a good person whose sufferings were not deserved. What does provide comfort for Job? He begins to reach peace when he feels again the presence of God in his life. It is not that God has provided any answers to Job in his suffering. In fact, when God becomes present to Job, God explains that human beings can never fully comprehend the ways of the Infinite and Powerful One. The simple affirmation of God's presence with Job in his suffering is what comforts him.

The Job narrative reflects two possible ways to respond to those who suffer. On the one hand, like Job's friends, one might offer explanations for the suffering, perhaps even point fingers of blame at the sufferer. These answers might help them feel more security in their understanding of the workings of the universe and of God, although they did not assist Job in making personal and redemptive meaning of his own experience. The biblical narrative suggests that providing explanations for suffering only heightens the alienation of the sufferer.

On the other hand, the text suggests that developing a caring relationship with sufferers in the presence of the mystery can help to heal the suffering. It was not God's answer but God's presence that helped Job. Unlike his friends, Job is not concerned with discovering why he suffers, only with feeling God's mysterious presence before him in his journey. Furthermore, only personally knowing the presence of God can help him. Job cannot have a proxy.

It is not the role of the pastoral caregiver to diminish the awesome mystery at the heart of the experience of suffering by explaining it away, but it can be helpful to sufferers in their journey to provide them with an understanding of theological contexts in which Jews have tried to understand God's relationship to suffering. Pastoral care-givers can offer some of this understanding, and can extend validating permission for sufferers to consider these frameworks as a possible springboard of meaning. At different times in life, one perspective can be more helpful than others. This model of relationship to Jewish the-ological approaches to suffering evolves over the course of a lifetime. It reaffirms the presence of the *Shechina's* imminent mystery, hovering over those who suffer, encouraging them to respond to their suffering in a meaningful, reflective way.

Theological Reflections

For Michael, theological reflection is an essential dimension of the search for meaning in his suffering. As I did with Michael, pastoral caregivers may help a person who is reflecting on suffering to explore various classical Jewish ways of understanding suffering and God's re-lationship to it. The following is a sampling of ways that Jews have sought to find meaning and redemption in the face of their own pain, just as we attempt to do in our own lives.

As you examine the following perspectives, ask yourself: What might these Jews have been trying to resolve? How might you ap-proach such a dilemma? Do you find their answers useful? If so, how? If not, why not? Pastoral caregivers must not approach these classical Jewish responses to suffering as an academic discipline but instead in-form themselves about available tools to assist real people with their urgent need for perspectives that have depth and clarity. Thinking about how you personally respond to these reflections helps prepare you pastorally to help others articulate their own responses and to find meaning in their experience.

Suffering as Just Deserts

In early Jewish thought, many believed that suffering was simply pun-ishment for one's sins, and conversely, that good health and material blessing were the result of right behavior. In God's orderly universe, there was a clear connection between how one behaved and what one experienced in life.[11] For example, in Leviticus and Deuteronomy, God clearly states that we receive blessings for our good deeds but we will experience hardship and suffering if we do not heed God's teachings and laws:

> If you obey the commandments I enjoin upon you this day, loving
> *Adonai* your God and serving God with all your heart and soul, I
> will grant the rain for your land in season, the early rain and the
> late. . . . Take care not to be lured away to serve other gods and
> bow to them. For the anger of *Adonai* will flare up against you
> and God will shut up the skies so that there will be no rain and
> the ground will not yield its produce; and you will soon perish
> from the good land that *Adonai* is assigning to you (Deuteronomy
> 11:13–7).

> If you do not obey Me and do not observe all these commandments, if you reject My laws and spurn My rules, so that you do
> not observe all My commandments and you break My covenant, I
> in turn will do this to you: I will wreak misery upon you—
> consumption and fever, which cause the eyes to pine and the body
> to languish; you shall sow your seed to no purpose, for your enemies shall eat it. I will set My face against you: You shall be
> routed by your enemies, and your foes shall dominate you. You
> shall flee though none pursues. (Leviticus 26:14–7).

How did this belief about human suffering help biblical authors come to terms with their situations? How do you, as a pastoral caregiver, respond to this approach to suffering? Are there times in your own life when you have felt that your suffering was punishment for a misdeed or ill-conceived action? Do you believe in a God who punishes human beings for their sins? If you find yourself disagreeing with this typology of reward and punishment, is it possible to reframe this approach in a way that might be useful? If not, how might your clarity regarding this stance be helpful when working with someone who feels guilty and believes that suffering is punishment from God for his or her sins?

Suffering Is a Mystery

The narrator of the Job story rejects the view that suffering is always deserved punishment for sin. Job's experience demonstrates that there are situations in which even a person who has acted righteously might still suffer greatly. How is one to understand God's plan when it appears that neither is good rewarded with good nor evil with suffering? In the book of Job, God asserts directly to Job that this is beyond Job's ability to understand. The suffering of the righteous is a profound mystery, lessened only by the sense of God's presence. The human being's response to this mystery is to accept it with faith, remaining open to connection with God's plan. Precise answers to these ultimate questions will not be found, but the simple, utterly mysterious presence of God offers redemption and comfort.

In what ways might this response have been helpful to the author of the Book of Job? How does it mesh with the image of God as one who punishes for wrongdoings and rewards for good deeds? Has there been a time in your own life when you have been comforted by the mysterious presence of God, even though circumstances did not make sense and answers were elusive? Does this resolution satisfy you? Consider how such an approach might be helpful for someone in great pain and, as a pastoral caregiver, how you might offer this perspective as a tool.

Suffering Takes Away Sin

Neither of the previous approaches to suffering explains exactly how we are to understand the righteous person's seemingly senseless suffering. According to the first view, there *is* no senseless suffering. If we were to scratch deeply enough, we would find sin beneath the surface of even the sufferers who seem the most righteous. Conversely, the second view offers abiding faith in God's mystery as an existential resolution to suffering, yet it does not help us to solve the mystery. There may be times when one these approaches will ring true, whereas at other times a sufferer might desire to probe further.

Some biblical and later rabbinic sources do attempt to penetrate the mystery of why good people suffer.[12] One view asserts that God actually brings suffering upon those God loves and cherishes on behalf of others and to relieve them of their sins:

> My righteous servant makes the many righteous,
> It is their punishment he bears;
> Assuredly, I will give him the many as his portion,
> He shall receive the multitude as his spoil.

For he exposed himself to death
And was numbered among the sinners,
Whereas he bore the guilt of the many
And made intercession for sinners (Isaiah 53:11–12).

In this view, the one who suffers is understood to be a martyr, chosen because he or she is loved deeply by God, to serve as God's partner in taking away the sins of others.

Another view understands the suffering of a good person as a means through which the loving God enables that person to be liberated from sin, and thereby, to come into even closer relationship with God. These sufferings are seen as *yisurin shel ahavah* (loving afflictions); they enable sufferers to recognize their wrongdoings, resolve to repent for them, and thereby reestablish a purified, loving relationship with God. In this context, suffering can hold meaning because it is understood as a catalyst to help one grow and heal spiritually:

The righteous [person] may attain in himself [or herself] a large measure of brilliance and excellence. Yet on the other hand, because of the minority of evil deeds that he [or she] has done, there is in [the righteous person] an admixture of darkness and repugnance. As long as he [or she] still has this admixture, he [or she] is neither prepared nor suited to become drawn close to God.

The Highest Mercy therefore decreed that some sort of purification exist. This is the general category of suffering.

God gave suffering the power to dispel the insensitivity in the human being, allowing him [or her] to become pure and clear, prepared for the ultimate good at its appointed time.[13]

In what ways might this view that God brings suffering to righteous human beings to allow them or others to come into closer relationship with the Divine have been satisfying to the authors of these works? Have you personally ever felt that suffering was offered to you to help you grow spiritually, to come closer to God, or to help others heal through your suffering? Are there ways in which suffering has been a catalyst for growth and healing? Do you believe that God gave you suffering out of love for you? How might this view be helpful for someone attempting to find meaning in their pain?

Suffering Yields Rewards in the World to Come

Some strains of classical Jewish thought maintain that God gives suffering to people in this world so that they might experience joy and liberation in *olam habah* (the world to come).[14] The medieval Jewish mystical text, the *Zohar,* states: "God gives pain to the righteous in this world in order to make the righteous meritorious for *olam habah.*"[15] In this view, suffering can be endured because it has a long-term, redemptive, and transformative value. In what ways does this view afford comfort and meaning to people who are suffering? Have you ever felt that your immediate suffering might enable you to have greater freedom or redemption in the future?

These reflections offer several perspectives to aid in making meaning out of suffering that feels profoundly chaotic and senseless. Consider how you might use these perspectives to prompt illumination at a time of bewilderment, and to foster connection at a time of abandonment.

You may not personally find redemptive meaning or authenticity in these classical Jewish views on suffering. Not to worry; it is not the role of the pastoral caregiver to defend or to assert a particular viewpoint; in fact, doing so might hinder another's authentic search for meaning. However, if you sense that "someone's personal theology is . . . pathological, as in the case of excessive guilt, such a view might well be gently challenged."[16] The central concern is to use Jewish approaches to suffering to be fully present to sufferers. With compassionate discernment and an integrity birthed in the fires of their own honest searching, pastoral caregivers can prompt theological reflections to help them grow, even when answers or solutions are unavailable.

As you explore some of the preceding perspectives with those who are suffering, remain aware of your own reactions and avoid asserting a particular viewpoint, which might hinder their own discovery process. Encourage them to consider the different shadings of meaning and perspective in each case. Ask open-ended questions that inspire further articulation of their relationship to God in the face of suffering. Allow inconsistencies, change, and for inchoate expressions of faith or doubt to yield new understanding. Theological reflection can help people in pain wrest the blessing of meaning from their suffering.

Responding to Suffering:
The Teaching of the U'netaneh Tokef

Theological and spiritual reflection can indeed help wrest meaning's blessing from suffering. However, if you sense that the sufferer is more focused on questions of meaning than in moving toward meaningful responses, you might gently shift the focus. Regardless of *why* a person suffers, it is imperative to *respond* constructively to the suffering. It can be helpful to direct a discussion away from questions such as: "How could God have let this happen? Why me?" to "How am I going to respond to this situation of suffering?"

There are Jewish teachings that urge us to focus not on the ultimately mysterious sources of suffering, over which we have no control, but on how we choose to respond to suffering. We can often find meaning in *responding* to suffering more than in understanding why it happened. The following teaching can be useful for you to consider as a framework when working with people who are suffering. As you read this material, ask yourself: How has this perspective been helpful to others? How do I relate to it, and how might I use it in my work as a pastoral caregiver?

The *U'netaneh Tokef*, a central prayer in the High Holy Day liturgy, teaches how best to respond to the uncertain nature of our existence and to suffering. The prayer says: "On Rosh Hashanah it is written, and on Yom Kippur it is sealed. . . . Who shall live, who shall die, who shall live a full life, and who shall die before their time." The fates of human beings are considered for the coming year, and no one knows what that year will bring.

Some rabbinic views assert that evil can fall on a righteous person and good can happen to an evil person. Rabbi Shlomo Riskin points out that the discerning will notice randomness within the world. He says that it "is up to us, within the limitations of that randomness, to live as God would have us live and to make our lives as worthwhile as possible."[17] We may not be able to control the circumstances of our lives. Even righteous and good-natured people can have an accident, get cancer, or witness a partner or child suffer. In this view, there is no answer for the *why*. The existence of suffering in our world is unfathomable, no matter how hard we try to construct a plausible theology. In truth, we cannot eradicate our helplessness and powerlessness over the forces of life and death that rule our world.

What *can* we do? How can we make meaning from inexplicable misery? The *U'netaneh Tokef* addresses this question. Rabbi Alan Miller points out that the very first word of the prayer, *u'v'chen*, is used only twice in the Bible, and that in each the fate that befalls people is random. In Ecclesiastes 8:10, the verse beginning *u'v'chen* is translated as: "Surely, I saw the wicked people were given a decent burial and from a holy place they went. But those who did that which was upright were forgotten out of the city."[18] In Esther 4:16, Esther is about to approach the king unbidden. She does not know if the king will order her to be put to death or not for this act of *chutzpah*. Intent upon trying to save her people, Esther says, "If I perish, I perish." Esther understands that whether those in power will act justly or cruelly may be arbitrary. The medieval poet's deliberate choice of *u'v'chen* as the initial word of the *U'netaneh Tokef* thus clearly associates it with the randomness and unfairness of life.

U'netaneh Tokef's beginning suggests that everyone, righteous or not, may suffer, and may experience it in a random, arbitrary way. How might one respond to such powerlessness? *U'netaneh Tokef* says of the Book of Life that "the imprint of every person's hand is upon it." As Rabbi Dayle A. Friedman states, "If we can't change our fate, if we can't avoid sickness, death, or loss, what mark do we leave on our fate? . . . We cannot control the fate that will befall us, but we can leave our imprint through the way we respond."[19] One's response to suffering helps determine how painful it is. The *U'netaneh Tokef* offers an empowering message for the sufferer: Although the existence of suffering is beyond human control, how one responds is one's own choice.

It is not simple for those who suffer to craft positive responses to senseless suffering, but this is precisely what this prayer challenges us to do. The *U'netaneh Tokef* states that three acts—repentance, prayer, and deeds of righteousness—can lessen the severity of the decree. The suffering does not resolve entirely, but its harshness—the intensity of the pain experienced—can be lessened by repenting, praying, and giving of ourselves to others.

Teshuvah

Several years ago while I was in synagogue on a Saturday morning, there was a lively discussion of the week's Torah portion, and participants were reflecting on the text and relating it to their lives. A woman stood up and said with both earnestness and gentle humor, "Cancer cures neurosis—at least, it did for me!" Her remark penetrated me deeply. She explained that when she had discovered that she had cancer, her perspective on life had changed. Things that once had irritated her no longer did; she became fond of people she had previously disliked. This woman's suffering enabled her to extend compassion to herself and others. Although she had not liked having cancer and had feared what it might mean for her future, its presence in her life had catalyzed a process of *teshuvah*—a turning away from destructive patterns to more constructive ones. This woman's experience demonstrates how *teshuvah* can help bring meaning to suffering.

Suffering often challenges us to reconsider our long-held self-image and to consider carefully how we have been living. Suffering can prompt self-examination, calling us to learn from our mistakes and to move on. One can respond to suffering by doing *teshuvah*—seizing the opportunity to make a fresh start. The *U'netaneh Tokef* teaches that at every moment of life—even difficult moments—there is the opportunity to learn, to grow, to remain hopeful about one's ability to move forward. Hopefulness about life can lessen the harshness of the decree when one suffers.

Ask yourself: Has *teshuvah*—the act of repentance, of turning away from past mistakes and rededicating oneself to be and to do better—been a constructive tool in your own life? Think of a time when you have gained wisdom through painful experience, and used that wisdom to live differently. When you work with others who are suffering in circumstances beyond their control or choosing, you might encourage them to reflect on what they are learning about themselves as they go through their experience. If you notice ways in which you think they have grown, changed, or done *teshuvah* in the course of suffering, you can reflect this to them. You can validate changes as constructive and perhaps redemptive, and encourage them to respond to life with openness to growth and change. This response can help sweeten the bitterness of suffering by affording a constructive response to painful circumstances.[20]

Tefilah

The *U'netaneh Tokef* also suggests that *tefilah* (prayer) can help us avert the extreme severity of a decree of suffering. By developing an inner life through prayer, we can begin to reach deep into our souls. We can push through waves of feeling, of experience, of the defenses and the facades that our egos have built, and touch upon the mystery at the center of self. In the often quiet and textured terrain of the soul lies an expanse of unity that itself can heal and transform the painful parts of our lives.

By cultivating a life of *tefilah*, we create the opportunity to experience intimately the soul within us. *Tefilah* gives voice to our soul's longing to belong to that which hosts its existence; this process is sweet and strong. When the forces of life rip us out of a sense of meaning and purpose, of optimism and empowerment, prayer can help us open to the vast resources within us that *know*, that *can* cope, that *do* have wisdom and potency by virtue of their *essential* connection to the forces of healing and eternity that breathe through us. We learn to see through the eyes of that which prays through us, the Eternal Heart that beats as our own soul in each of our bodies. By opening to the realm of soul in our life, we transform our experience of self. We lean into the Eternal in our midst, and the harshness of a temporal experience of fragility, precariousness, and suffering is averted, softened, and transformed.

However, for each of us, the level of comfort and familiarity with a life of prayer is different and will change over time. The Jewish tradition offers a rich array of contexts in which to pray, and of ways to give voice to our prayers. From the formalized communal liturgy experiences of daily and festival prayers to the spontaneous prayers of the Psalms, we have many resources that articulate the desires, the needs, and indeed, the depth of the human soul. Pastoral caregivers can inform those who are suffering about these resources, and encourage them to spend time getting to know themselves in prayer. For many people in our contemporary culture, the art of prayerful living is one that must be developed anew. Many people need help to enter *tefilah* without embarrassment, skeptical ambivalence, and awkwardness.

Joe is a lawyer in his fifties who had attended synagogue regularly as a child and an adult. Jewish identity was an integral part of his family's life. He never doubted his affiliation or his relationship to the traditional prayers, which he said regularly and habitually. However, when he was diagnosed with a rare, painful, and incurable disease, Joe's needs changed. Suddenly, nothing was as it had been, and his most basic attachments could no longer be taken for granted. Seeking to address and to ease his suffering, Joe's first inclination was to turn to the prayers that he knew by rote. However, Joe felt awkward and unsure about praying when he was so vulnerable. Words in the prayers dealing with enemies and destruction, salvation and redemption, had not seemed relevant to him before. Now, as Joe sought healing in the face of foreign forces invading his body, these images became painfully real. For Joe, this awareness in itself was confusing and uncomfortable. To whom or to what was he really praying? It felt hard to pray from a stance of weakness and fear. At the same time, it felt more urgent than ever before to try to pray in this way.

Joe decided to attend a monthly Jewish Healing Service I lead at his synagogue; he had read about these services in the newsletter but had never felt the desire to go. After the service, Joe introduced himself to me and explained his situation. Our dialogue continued over several months. Joe focused on his feelings about his illness and God's relationship to suffering, and about the efficacy of prayer, but he could not actually bring himself to pray openly to God to help him. One day, Joe sent me an E-mail. Actually, Joe sent God an E-mail. Joe began the correspondence to me, but after a few sentences, he began to pour out his heart like water to God, in prayer. Joe asked God for help—to support him in his illness, to grant him healing and strength to deal with what lay ahead, to give him peace of mind and rest for the body. At the end of his E-mail, Joe thanked me for witnessing his prayer, which he mused might be the first E-mail to God ever written. I suspect that there have been other E-mailed *tefilot*, just as the psalmist used the technology of his day to pour out his personal prayers before

God. For Joe, this experience of *tefilah* was unprecedented, even though he had been preparing for it for months. As I read his words of prayer on my computer screen, I felt the depth and immediacy of Joe's heartfelt supplications profoundly. I cried as I experienced the poignant beauty of a soul opening itself so deeply in personal *tefilah*.

I believe that this kind of prayer is what the *U'netaneh Tokef* liturgy refers to when it asserts that *tefilah* can help avert the severity of the decree. Joe's illness has not gone away; Joe's heart, however, has opened deeply. He still has doubts and awkward moments in his prayer life, but his is now a life of prayer as he walks with his illness. For Joe, this journey has become more bearable and more meaningful because he has persisted in locating the voice of his soul in prayer.

Pastoral care helped Joe find the safety and the permission he needed to slow down and to examine the liturgy in new ways. It supported him in reflecting on its meanings and implications for him as he changed, and gingerly to gestate his own emerging spirituality. It also validated Joe's hunch that *tefilah* could be deeply personal and transformative when life was uncertain, whereas previously, *tefilah* had been relatively predictable, communal, and externally focused.

As a pastoral caregiver, ask yourself: How has prayer served to comfort, to center, to nourish, to inspire, to heal, or to challenge you during times of suffering? Have there been times in your life when you have not been comfortable praying? Have you ever not known what, or how, to pray? How can you imagine prayer working in the lives of those with whom you work? What do you anticipate might be barriers for someone who is suffering as they seek to cultivate a life of prayer? Your stance as pastoral caregiver can model an openness and a relationship to *tefilah* that can empower someone to embark on a journey of prayer. Offering prayers for healing on behalf of the one with whom you work both models this process and allows you to enter deeply into the reality of the other as you journey with them in their walk of suffering. You might explore together how spontaneous or liturgical prayers, silent or spoken, help ease the burden of suffering, creating a healing response to painful experience. A life of prayer might not take away the decree, but it can avert its severity and perhaps wrest from it profound blessing.

Tzedakah

Tzedakah is righteous action. When we suffer, we can feel absorbed and isolated in our sorrow, or we can look out and see that we are not alone, that others also suffer. We can use our personal experiences to carve within us a deeper well of compassion and empathy for the pain others endure. Having known pain, we can choose to care for those around us. As Henri Nouwen suggests, we can become "wounded healers," a stance that calls for "a constant willingness to see one's own pain and suffering as rising from the depth of the human condition."[21] Similarly, the *tzedakah* of the one who has suffered "helps to mend the world."[22]

> A breast cancer organization in a large city provides research, resources, support groups, advocacy, and training for people living with breast cancer. Selma has served for several years as program director for this foundation, devoting many hours each week speaking to groups throughout the city, providing education for women about how to do self-examinations, and what to do if they discover a lump in their breast. She also works on behalf of the foundation to lobby the federal government to increase funding for breast cancer research. Selma donates much of her time to this foundation. Why does she do this? Selma herself is a survivor of breast cancer. She recalls the terror she experienced after her diagnosis and the pain of her treatment. She is committed to helping others manage their health care effectively and proactively. Selma feels that this work has been an important continuation of her own healing process; it helps her to meaningfully integrate the experience of having cancer as she reaches out to others in similar situations.

Like Selma, many people find that compassion is an antidote to suffering. In fostering compassion and allowing it to blossom through action, we can make sense of our lives even in a context of randomness. *Tzedakah* is any compassionate giving of oneself through time, energy, or resources, that contributes to the healing of others. This act, says the prayer in *U'netaneh Tokef*, lessens the harshness of a decree of suffering in our own lives.

Sometimes, like Selma, individuals will begin to practice *tzedakah* spontaneously as they come through times of suffering, but this is not always so. Pastoral caregivers can be helpful if they sense that sufferers have become isolated or embittered as a result of their burdens. Affirming and small actions of kindness—offering someone a glass of water or giving change to a homeless person—can help remind people who suffer that they can reach beyond themselves, and that they might feel relief in that act. The pastoral caregiver can also model such acts of *tzedakah*.

Ask yourself: When in my life have I found that giving *tzedakah* has lessened my personal suffering? Has there been a time when I have benefited from others' compassionate actions? How did it affect me? How might it have served the one who gave the *tzedakah*? How might you bring this sensitivity to those with whom you work when they are suffering? What are some simple and concrete suggestions for cultivating compassionate, righteous action, and how might you convey them to those with whom you work? Allow these thoughts to inhabit your pastoral care tool kit, knowing you can pull them out when you sense that encouraging someone's practice of *tzedakah* could be a source of healing and blessing in his or her suffering.

The *U'netaneh Tokef* asserts that our world is as random as the most radical of postmodern philosophers or theorists make it out to be. Yet, the prayer also affirms that in this context of inherent randomness, we can call on the depths within us and resources around us to transform the harshness of living in a world with random suffering. As pastoral caregivers, focusing on how people respond to their suffering can be transformative, encouraging them to call on potential new strengths and sensibilities birthed by suffering. *Teshuvah, tefilah,* and *tzedakah* are three means of responding to suffering that encourage growth, change, and transformation of the individual even amid the harshness of suffering.

Pastoral caregivers can gently encourage those who are suffering to reflect on these opportunities for responding to unwanted and uncontrollable life situations. Ultimately, the pastoral caregiver's role is one of an encouraging witness, of watching as the person's own mysterious process of hatching these responses to suffering unfolds.

Responses to Suffering:
Contemporary Reflections

Although the Jewish tradition offers many resources for pastoral care-givers to use in their work, you will also encounter people for whom Jewish religious perspectives are foreign or unacceptable. Especially in the post-Holocaust age, many Jews may feel that old paradigms for understanding the nature of evil and of suffering, no longer hold. Without traditional paradigms, consideration of how to build a meaningful response to one's suffering may be impossible. Several contemporary Jewish thinkers have sought to understand the nature of suffering in light of the horrific events of the last century. As you examine the following reflections by contemporary rabbis, ask yourself: How do these contemporary theological reflections differ from classical Jewish approaches to suffering? Do they help me bridge my own life experiences and Jewish approaches to suffering? What questions might they help me address or understand in a new way? How will these thoughts help me in working with someone to construct a personally meaningful theology and response to their suffering?

Rabbi Edward Feld rejects the classical Jewish notions of a God who causes suffering, whether to punish people for their sins or lovingly to give them opportunities for growth, as unacceptable and insulting to the millions of innocent victims of the Holocaust. He suggests that contemporary Jews cannot hold with integrity overarching paradigms for meaningful understanding of the nature of evil and of suffering. What humanity has witnessed in the past century has destroyed the possibility of finding redemptive meaning in suffering, Feld argues, but we still have within us the ability to overcome even the most tremendous of suffering. Through simple acts of kindness and openness to connection, we can rescue ourselves from the torture of unredeemed suffering. Feld tells a piercingly beautiful story from Terrence des Pres about two friends who were in a concentration camp together. One friend came upon a lone raspberry and kept it close beside her for days until finally it was the right time. She knew it was her friend's birthday. On that day, she approached her friend, extended her hand, and opened it to reveal a withering but identifiable fruit. Her friend cried with gratitude.[23] Such acts of human kindness wrest blessing out of suffering, nourishing the souls of both giver and recipient.

Rabbi Harold Kushner is another contemporary theologian who deals with the notion of suffering and how best to respond to it. Kushner asserts that God is not the omnipotent cause of human suffering, but rather, that God created the world according to natural laws, including those of cause and effect. In this view, some of the tragic suffering in our world is the result of natural laws, such as when a child runs into the street after a ball and is struck by a car. God did not cause the child to be hit by the car, and likewise, God was not able to stop the ball or the child or the trajectory of the car once they were in motion. Second, God does not have the power to impose limits on human free will, thus God cannot stop us from causing suffering to ourselves or other people. Kushner's God is not omnipotent in the classical sense. However, God is present in the ways in which a human being chooses to respond to the suffering. God is found in the search for strength or courage to endure a horrendously painful situation, and God is the source of loving-kindness we may find as we reach outside ourselves in response to either our own suffering or another's. Like Feld, Kushner urges us to forgive the less-than-perfect world that God has created, to forgive God for not being perfect. If one can do this, says Kushner, "you will be able to recognize that the ability to forgive and the ability to love are the weapons that God has given us to enable us to live fully, bravely, and meaningfully in this less-than-perfect world."[24]

Rabbi Naomi Levy also seeks to find a new way of thinking about God to help heal personal suffering. She writes of her journey to healing from the enormous suffering caused by the murder of her father when she was a teenager. After a long, painful period in which she blamed God for her father's murder and subsequent abandonment of herself and her family, Levy says the following:

> I suddenly realized it was my own concept of God that had caused me to feel so abandoned by God when my father died. I had believed in a God that intervenes in our lives to protect the innocent and punish the evil [but eventually] I was no longer looking to God to *prevent* ugliness, I was looking to God to show me the way to prevent the cruelty *I* had the power to prevent. I was looking to God to show me the way to behave compassionately and honestly.[25]

Although there are meaningful differences in the particular stresses and concerns of Feld, Kushner, and Levy, they share a common understanding of a God who is found neither in explanations for suffering nor in the ability omnipotently to stop the suffering. Rather, God is found in the human being's ability to respond to suffering by seeking qualities that empower that person to grow: to give, to forgive, to learn, and to transform. In this context, God is the power that offers redemptive resiliency in the face of pain. As a pastoral caregiver, you can help suffering people think about God in this way. You can also consider how you might embody qualities of godliness such as compassion, generosity, and courage that bring God's presence into an otherwise-unredeemed situation.

Concluding Reflections: A Model for Pastoral Caregiving

There is a Talmudic story in which Rabbi Yehoshua ben Levi argues with other rabbis about how to relate to a group of people quarantined on the edge of town as they suffer from a highly contagious and incurable disease, ra'athan.[26] All of the other rabbis suggest reasons for not going near the sufferers, such as protecting their own health and that of their communities. Only Yehoshua ben Levi decides to approach the sufferers. He sits with them, learns Torah with them, and hugs each of them as well. He provides radical compassion, human contact through his very physical presence and touch, in striking contrast to his contemporaries. In addition, he offers the sufferers words of Torah, helping them connect with God through sacred teachings. Perhaps Yehoshua ben Levi taught about the nature of suffering with those who suffered. The text does not say. However, it does say how Yehoshua ben Levi was affected by his actions. In the next part of the narrative, Yehoshua ben Levi requests and is granted a vision of the world to come. This rabbi was willing to be fully present with those who suffered, even at the risk of his own health and his very life. Yehoshua ben Levi confronted death itself in the service of others, and he was rewarded with the ability to overcome the fear and mystery of death itself.

There are no simple resolutions to the nature of suffering, no guidelines for being a companion to someone who is suffering. A pastoral caregiver must first and last exude radical caring, the godly qualities of loving-kindness and empathic presence. With these, the caregiver can assist others to find those qualities within themselves and to transform the harshness of their suffering into a more blessed situation. When caregivers offer themselves in this way, those who suffer may not be the only ones who are helped. Perhaps, as Yehoshua ben Levi discovered, our own journey toward understanding the mysteries of life and death will be transformed into one of profound blessing.

Notes

1. I served as Chaplaincy Coordinator, HIV/AIDS Program of Jewish Family and Children's Service, Philadelphia, Pa. 1999.
2. The names of individual people described in this chapter are pseudonyms.
3. BT Sotah 14a.
4. Siddur Sim Shalom (New York: The Rabbinical Assembly, 1985), p. 357.
5. Pesikta d'rav Kahane, 109b–110a.
6. On the therapeutic role of touch for caregivers, see Jane Handler and Kim Hetherington, *Give Me Your Hand: Traditional and Practical Guidance on Visiting the Sick,* 2nd ed. (Berkeley, Calif.: Congregation Netivot Shalom [1841 Berkeley Way, Berkeley, CA 94703], 1997), pp. 25–26.
7. According to Jewish tradition, the *mitzvah* of *bikur cholim*, visiting the sick, takes away one-sixtieth of the person's suffering. See BT Nedarim 39b.
8. For further discussion of the helpful role that finding meaning plays in responding to suffering, see Victor Frankl, *Man's Search for Meaning*, 3rd ed. (New York: Touchstone Books, 1984), and Polly Young-Eisendrath, *The Resilient Spirit: Transforming Suffering into Insight and Renewal* (Reading, Mass.: Addison-Wesley, 1996).
9. Shulchan Aruch Yoreh Deah 335:7.
10. See Rabbi Nancy Flam, "What Do I Say?" in *The Outstretched Arm* 3, no. 1 (fall 1993). (The National Center for Jewish Healing, 850 Seventh Ave., Suite 1201, New York, N.Y. 10019, 212-399-2320.)
11. See also Rabbi Edward Feld, *The Spirit of Renewal: Finding Faith After the Holocaust* (Woodstock, Vt.: Jewish Lights Publishing, 1994), p. 33.
12. See also BT Baba Metziah 85a.
13. Moshe Chaim Luzzato, translated and annotated by Aryeh Kaplan, *Derech HaShem, The Way of God* (Jerusalem and New York: Feldheim Publishers, 1997), 2:2:5.
14. See BT Kiddushin 40b.
15. *Vayeshev 27,* as in Reuven Bulka, *Judaism on Illness and Suffering* (Northvale, N.J.: Jason Aronson, 1998), p. 191.
16. Flam, "What Do I Say?" See also Harold Kushner, *When Bad Things Happen to Good People* (New York: Avon, 1981).

17. "Community Study: Repentance and the High Holidays," 92nd Street Y, 1982.
18. Ibid.
19. Dayle A. Friedman, 1998/5758, "Sweetening the Bitterness of Suffering," unpublished Kol Nidre sermon.
20. Ibid.
21. Henri Nouwen, *The Wounded Healer* (Garden City, N.Y.: Image Books, 1979), p. 88.
22. Friedman, "Sweetening the Bitterness."
23. Feld, *Spirit of Renewal,* p. 112.
24. Kushner, *When Bad Things,* p. 148.
25. Rabbi Naomi Levy, *To Begin Again: The Journey Toward Comfort, Strength and Faith in Difficult Times* (New York: Ballantine, 1998), p. 92.
26. BT Ketubot 70b.

Bibliography

Bulka, Reuven P. *Judaism on Illness and Suffering.* Northvale, N.J.: Jason Aronson, 1998.

Feld, Edward. *The Spirit of Renewal: Finding Faith after the Holocaust.* Woodstock, Vt.: Jewish Lights Publishing, 1994.

Flam, Nancy. "Healing the Spirit: A Jewish Approach." *Cross Currents* (winter 1996–97), pp. 487–96.

Kraemer, David. *Responses to Suffering in Classical Rabbinic Literature.* New York: Oxford University Press, 1995.

Leaman, Oliver. *Evil and Suffering in Jewish Philosophy.* Cambridge: Cambridge University Press, 1995.

Levy, Naomi. *To Begin Again: The Journey Toward Comfort, Strength, and Faith in Difficult Times.* New York: Ballantine Books, 1998.

Young-Eisendrath, Polly. *The Resilient Spirit: Transforming Suffering into Insight and Renewal.* Reading, Mass.: Addison-Wesley, 1996.

Rabbi Myriam Klotz, M.A., is the Rabbinic Director of the Kimmel-Spiller Jewish Healing Center at the Jewish Family Service of Delaware. She has served as Chaplaincy Coordinator for the HIV/AIDS Services Program of Jewish Family and Children's Service of Philadelphia and as spiritual leader for the Houston Reconstructionist Havurah. She is a spiritual director at the Reconstructionist Rabbinical College.

PaRDeS: *A Model for Presence in* Hitlavut Ruchanit

Rabbi Dayle A. Friedman

In this chapter, Rabbi Dayle A. Friedman suggests that the four-tiered approach to interpreting text can be applied to the human text encountered in pastoral relationships. *PaRDeS* allows us to discern four different planes of pastoral connection: fact, emotion, meaning, and soul. She proposes that pastoral caregivers use *PaRDeS* to analyze encounters and to guide them to more profound connection.

Only connect.

—E. M. FORSTER,
HOWARD'S END

P resence and listening are the essence of *hitlavut ruchanit*, or spiritual accompanying. On the one hand, just being present to another sounds like the simplest thing in the universe. As the meditation teacher Sylvia Boorstein suggests, "Don't just do something, sit there!"[1] On the other hand, pastoral caregivers know from personal and professional experience that truly being present, reaching to enter and to understand another's reality, can be a Herculean task. In this chapter, we propose a model from Jewish tradition for examining and understanding presence and listening in our *hitlavut ruchanit*.

This analysis is rooted in an insight of the founder of Clinical Pastoral Education, Anton Boisen, who taught that the pastoral interaction is an encounter with "the human document." The individual encountered by pastoral caregivers is as complex, multilayered, rich, opaque, and in need of explication as any sacred text. The pastoral theologian Charles Gerkin suggests that:

> To understand the inner world of another is . . . a task of
> interpretation—interpretation of a world of experience that is in
> itself an interpretation of the myriad events and relationships that

make up a life. Said another way, the task of understanding another in the depth of that other's inner world is a hermeneutical task.[2]

We can bring what we know about reading texts to the task of understanding the living person we are encountering. As Rabbi Rachel Mikva has noted,[3] the Jewish idiom for the human document is the *human text*. When we conceptualize our *hitlavut ruchanit*, our pastoral care, as a textual encounter, we are empowered to draw from our tradition's wisdom about unlocking a text.

In this context, we focus on one particular set of Jewish hermeneutics, the four-tiered system of textual analysis described by Rabbi Moses deLeon in the Zohar.[4] DeLeon taught that four levels of interpretation existed in *PaRDeS* (the orchard, or paradise): *Peshat* is literal interpretation; *Remez* is the searching out of allegorical meanings and philosophical truths; *Derash* is hermeneutical, homiletical, or ethical interpretation; and *Sod* is the mystical understanding that ties words and events of the text to events in the world of the *sefirot* (emanations) of the Divine Presence. Together, the four levels constitute the *PaRDeS*, which we know from rabbinic sources can simultaneously be an exalted and forbidding place to visit.

This rabbinic system of multiple levels of interpretation and understanding can be applied to the human document, to the pastoral interaction itself. Just as a text bears multiple meanings, there are also many levels on which we experience and connect to the person we serve as pastoral caregiver. This conceptualization provides a means of analyzing our encounters and critiquing our work, as well as a vision for deepening our pastoral connections. By examining our work in light of this rabbinic interpretive scheme, we have an opportunity to meet those with whom we work in the *pardes*, the orchard/paradise, and maybe, just maybe, to have a glimpse of the Divine.

In an effort to learn from this model, I first apply *PaRDeS* to pastoral listening and presence, then examine some risks of experiencing *hitlavut ruchanit* in this manner, and finally close with some thoughts about what we ourselves as pastoral caregivers need in order to do this challenging and exhilarating work.

Applying PaRDeS *to the Pastoral Encounter*

In reading a text, the four levels of *PaRDeS* represent a hierarchy of progressively more profound understanding. Similarly, in pastoral interpretation, *PaRDeS* is a succession of ever-deeper means of comprehending and connecting to the human text, the person before us.

Peshat: Fact

The first and simplest level of listening in the *PaRDeS* model is *Peshat* (plain sense), the level of *fact*. When we are encountering another on the *Peshat* level, we're relating on the surface. We inquire after the basics, the kind of information beginning journalists are instructed to gather. We are interested in the "who, what, where, when" that is present in the person's situation. In the refrain of the television show *Dragnet, Peshat* is "just the facts, ma'am." Most of us spend most of our lives on the level of *Peshat*. It's what makes up much of everyday conversation, even among intimates. We ask our children at the end of the day, "What did you do in school today?" or our partners, "Did you pick up the *chalah*, pay the bills, feed the cats?" "What time will you be home tomorrow?"

In our pastoral encounters, we often start at *Peshat*, and sometimes *end* there, too. Chaplaincy interns whom I've supervised have often brought verbatim reports which are packed with factual inquiries. They sit down with a patient or resident, ask "How are you feeling?" and find themselves in the midst of a recital of the person's entire medical history. The intern says, "I feel like there was more to get to here, but I just didn't know how to get beyond this." Other times, in an initial pastoral encounter an intern spends a hour inquiring about the person's entire personal history: "What *shul* do you belong to?" "How many kids do you have?" "Where do you come from?" "When did you come to the hospital?" In these kinds of encounters, the interns often leave without feeling they've heard what was really on the person's mind.

Of course, the *Peshat* level of interpretation can help us acquire essential information. For example, we would respond very differently to a thirty-year-old woman on the obstetrics floor if we thought she was there following delivery of a child, than we would if we knew she had undergone a hysterectomy. Having a sense of the family or social supports of the person with HIV helps to shape our pastoral assessment and plans. But often, when we are encountering someone on the level of *Peshat,* we are not truly connecting. Staying only on the level of *Peshat* can distance us from individuals and their needs and agenda. We should remember that *Peshat* can actually emerge not just from directly focusing upon it, but in the course of interacting on the deeper levels of *PaRDeS.*

Remez: Emotion

The second level of *PaRDeS* is *Remez* (hint). While in the realm of textual studies, *Remez* refers to allegorical interpretation, in the human text of pastoral encounters, *Remez* is the level of emotion. We are connecting on the level of *Remez* when we are listening and responding to *feelings.* We can learn about *Remez* not only through verbal exploration, but also through careful attention to what pastoral counselor Charles Taylor calls body messages.[5] We discern emotion in the person we're helping by carefully observing hints offered by facial expression, posture, focus, movements, and physical reactions (breathing, blushing, crying, sighing). Taylor points out that nonverbal data help us understand a person because these "are usually more spontaneous and less contrived than verbal responses."

We can powerfully connect by reflecting feelings that are apparent from nonverbal communication. For example, when we sit down next to the elderly woman in the nursing home who is exuding sadness from every pore of her being, we can simply say, "You're looking really down today." Nonverbal cues and interpretation are especially helpful when we're confronted with a person whose verbal communication is compromised.

> Ruth was seventy-nine years old and had had a stroke. Half of her body was paralyzed, and she could utter only a few phrases. Sometimes I'd come upon Ruth using her good hand to hit the table in front of her, saying, "The bastards, the bastards, the bastards!" I didn't know, and often couldn't learn the *Peshat,* for Ruth was unable to give me the *facts.* But I could reflect and acknowledge the emotion that was present. When I got beyond my own sense of inadequacy and frustration, I would say something obvious like, "Ruth, I wish I could know all the words you are thinking but can't say; but I do sense that you are feeling

really angry!" On those occasions, Ruth's whole presence would sometimes change. Her body would relax and she would grasp my hand and look me straight in the eye. It was paltry communication, on the verbal level, but there were moments when it seemed like Ruth had felt understood.

We are often able to connect to *Remez*, the level of emotion, through what Taylor labels the "spoken messages" in the pastoral encounter. We ask: What are the emotions the person is expressing explicitly or implicitly? Taylor submits a list of six basic groups of feelings, formed by three pairs of opposites:[6]

Guilt–Acceptance

Anxiety–Hope

Anger–Love

Often the access to *Remez* information is intuitive. It's not that the person opposite us articulates his or her feelings and labels them for us, but rather, we engage in what we might call "gut listening." We open our own hearts and souls to listen to emotions that emerge within us in hearing the other. It may be that the emotion evoked in us is the very one the other is feeling, or, maybe *not*. We need to check out what we're feeling, even if only to distinguish between our counter-transference and the experience of the person we're serving. Clearly, in order to hear the person on the level of feelings, we have to be ready to experience our own feelings.

To elicit the *Remez*, it can be helpful to try out a hypothesis. Instead of asking, "How does that make you feel?" which is not only trite but off-putting, we reply, "It seems like you may be feeling . . ." We offer such a reflection with humility and respect, and invite the other to confirm or correct our impression. In risking reflecting an emotion, we signal to others that we are listening hard, and want to *know* them on the level of *Remez*.

Remez is a very real connection, and not always easy.

Quite early on in my work in the nursing home, I encountered a woman whose mother suffered from severe dementia. The mother couldn't speak or respond, and she was experiencing one devastating medical crisis after another. The daughter, Sheila, visited her mother for hours every day. She had never married, had lived with her mother before her admission, and did not work. I stopped by to see Sheila on a regular basis, especially when she was faced with a decision regarding amputating her mother's leg. I never quite knew what to say to this apparently hostile and forbidding woman, who had alienated nearly all the staff. I was stymied when Sheila turned to me one day and practically spat out, "You know, there's nothing very spiritual about this, rabbi!" I don't recall what kind of response I made as I tried to regain my composure. I probably thought it was my job to defend God, or Judaism, or both! I know I didn't think simply to acknowledge her anger, fear, and pain. I couldn't accompany Sheila because I was intimidated by her raw feelings, and failed to see that her fury was the very place she needed to be touched.

When we get there, *Remez* offers a deeper kind of entry into the world of the human text than *Peshat*, and enables us to find a richer connection.

Derash: Meaning

The third level of PaRDeS is *Derash* (seeking interpretation), the level of *meaning*. Just as midrash endeavors to dig out the meanings buried in a text, *Derash* requires listening to the person's narrative to mine the meanings he or she finds and their connection to larger sources of meaning. As we analyze the material a person shares with us, Gerkin suggests that we ask, "What does it *mean*?" He urges us to place the person's narrative in the larger theological/ethical context, a context of ultimate meaning as we listen for "the story of the self" to whom we are relating.[7]

To connect to *Derash*, we need to place individuals' stories or situations in the context of their lives. We need to investigate what meaning *they* are making of their experience.

I will never forget a visit I had with a rabbi who was ninety-five years old and whom I had watched steadily decline over several years. One morning, I found him hooked up to both an oxygen line and a feeding tube. I said, "Rabbi, I wonder what you're thinking as you lie there this morning." I felt rather sure that I knew the answer he'd give, something along the lines of *"Ad matai?"* (How long, God?) or, "Why doesn't God just take me?" What he actually said was, "I'm thinking how wonderful it is to be alive!" I could not have been more stunned or humbled. I could never have imagined the meaning the rabbi was making of a life that looked from the outside to be filled with burdensome suffering.

It is on the level of *Derash* that we can both understand the meaning the person is making of an experience and perhaps support the person in finding additional meaning. The existential psychoanalyst and Holocaust survivor, Viktor Frankl, powerfully taught us about the salvific potential of meaning to transform suffering. Frankl defined despair as "suffering without meaning," and suggested that "even a life which has been wasted, meaningless, can be flooded with infinite meaning by admission of the lack of meaning."[8]

> Once when I was visiting the nursing home, I stopped to see Sol, who had recently become a double amputee. This ninety-year-old man was extremely articulate and dignified; he had a deep spiritual and intellectual life, and even in the nursing home had taken on great challenges, such as studying *parashat ha-shavua* (the weekly Torah portion) on his own. Sol had been forced to come to the home after his first amputation. He had struggled during the years he was there with mind-altering phantom pain and nearly constant infections in his remaining leg. He had gone to great lengths to avoid a second amputation, including spending nine months in bed at one point in an effort to allow his leg to heal.
>
> As I visited with Sol and his special friend, Sylvia, it was easy to get at the *Peshat*. Both Sol and Sylvia were anxious to tell me the details of Sol's surgery and hospitalization. It was not too difficult to get to the *Remez*. Although proud and generally reserved, Sol was rather voluble in sharing his sadness and resignation. It seemed to me that the crux of Sol's experience was on the *Derash* level. The amputation was clearly a trauma, but I wondered, what else was it? Would he see it as a loss, a defeat, or another hurdle to be overcome? The most important part of our dialogue occurred in exploring the meaning he found in the amputation. "I'm not fooling myself," he said. "I know I don't have much longer. I'm just trying to get through each day. It's been pretty rough; I'm ready for whatever God has in store for me. I'm not afraid."
>
> Clearly, Sol did not feel ready to try to "beat" his latest disability. He saw his story as coming to its conclusion, and the

amputation was the signal to begin wrapping up. He was not stopping living or loving or learning, but getting ready for the moment when *malach ha-mavet* would come. He needed to be met at that place. By attending to *Derash*, I was privileged to accompany him in this final part of his journey.

Simply engaging in the exploration of *Derash* brings meaning. We can support the quest for meaning by refraining from what Frankl called "the raised finger" of judgment or condemnation, using instead "the pointed finger," directing the other toward examples of using life meaningfully. It is here that we can at times constructively offer models from the texts and narratives of our tradition, as well as from the historical experience of the Jewish people. It is here, on the level of *Derash,* that the willingness to explore the role of faith, prayer, observance, and community can be the most distinctive gift of the Jewish pastoral caregiver, for they are all doors to meaning.

Sod: The Soul Level

The fourth and final level of PaRDeS is *Sod* (mystery), which is the mysterious point of connection to the *soul*. When we are present on the most profound plane, we feel linked to the other's *neshamah*. Martin Buber described the listening person as "one who believes in the creative power of another and is able to demonstrate it by small signs such as a glance, a word, or a touch that he or she grasps the hidden latent unity of a suffering soul."[9]

It is difficult to articulate what makes possible a *Sod* level connection with another human being. We cannot catalog particular words or interventions that will necessarily get us there, for in a very real way, a *Sod* connection is a gift of *chesed* from the *Kadosh baruch Hu* (Holy Blessed One). Perhaps we can say of this connection that you know *Sod* when you *feel* it. Nonetheless, we can prod ourselves to investigate whether our connection has approached this level by asking:

- Do I understand this person as a whole?
- Do I *get* this person on an intuitive level?
- Do I honor the mystery of this soul and his or her journey?
- Do I see the image of the Divine in this person?
- Is this an I–Thou encounter?

Buber taught that we cannot live every moment, or even most moments, in I–Thou encounter. Similarly, our pastoral encounters will not consistently arrive at *Sod*. Indeed, the people with whom we work will not always seek or be open to such a deep encounter. But we can nonetheless keep ourselves open and available for the *neshamah* connection, and appreciate its blessing when we do arrive at it.

Another way of understanding *Sod* is that *Sod* is God's presence. When we are listening for God's "still, small voice," we are open to *Sod*. That voice may come in the electrical charge of a profound soul connection, or in our intuitive sense that we are being guided in the interaction by the Merciful One. We can't will *Sod*, but we can practice spiritual reflection and strengthen our faculties of discernment and openness to the Divine.

Perils of the PaRDeS

Opening ourselves to pastoral care at the deeper levels, entering the *PaRDeS,* is a perilous mission. As J. L. Cedarleaf reminds us, "Ministry of presence . . . means vulnerability to and participation in the lifeworld of those served."[10]

Our sages understood the dangers of the encounter with the Ultimate. We recall the account of the four who entered the *pardes*. They didn't fare so well, on the whole:

> Ben Azzai cast a look and died. [Of him Scripture says: Precious in the sight of the Eternal is the death of God's saints.] Ben Zoma looked and became demented. [Of him Scripture says: Have you found honey? Eat as much as is sufficient for you, lest you be filled with it, and vomit it.] Aher [Elisha ben Abuyah] mutilated the shoots. R. Akiba departed unhurt.[11]

Rashi explains that entry into the *pardes* was really a visit to the heavens, a sojourn in the immediate presence of the Divine. Most of us, he warns, are not prepared to meet the Ultimate. So, it behooves us to examine some hazards along the way of entering the pastoral *PaRDeS*.

Assumptions or Jumping to Conclusions

In the Talmud's account of the four who entered the *pardes*, Rabbi Akiba warned his colleagues before they set out, "When you arrive at the stones of pure marble, say not, water, water!"[12] Perhaps he meant not to come to conclusions about what you're seeing before you have evidence. Akiba's warning applies to the pastoral *PaRDeS* as well. It is too easy for us to assume we know what we're dealing with when we approach a person.

> A chaplaincy intern was working with a woman with severe dementia. The woman was obviously unhappy and kept repeating, "You can't give me what I need." The intern earnestly attempted to help her. "Do you need a glass of water?" "Can I get you a blanket?" Still, the woman repeated, "You can't give me what I need." The intern assumed that the woman, whose sense of reality was tenuous, was simply in another world. Then the woman said, "You can't give me what I need because what I need is love." The intern knew that the resident's husband, who visited much of every day, was away from her side for an hour, and now understood that this woman, broken in mind as she was, knew *exactly* what she needed.

Another example of false assumptions comes from the account of Rabbi Yochanan's bedside visit to Rabbi Eleazar, who was ill (BT Berachot 5a).

> Rabbi Yochanan enters the room and finds Rabbi Eleazar sitting in the dark. Thinking this is the problem, he quickly uses his unique abilities to provide a *tachlis* (practical) solution; he rolls up his sleeve and light radiates from his arm to illumine the room. Then he notices that this hasn't been terribly efficacious, for Rabbi Eleazar is crying. "Why are you crying?" he asks, in good pastoral form, and then goes on to answer his own question: "Is it because of Torah that you didn't succeed in learning? Don't worry, in the eyes of God it's not important how much you learned, but that your learning was *l'shem shamayim* [for the sake of Heaven]. Or perhaps you are crying because of your meager means? Not everybody is rich! Or perhaps you're crying because you don't have

children? Here's the bone of my tenth son!" [You think you have problems!]

Finally, Rabbi Eleazar interrupts his esteemed colleague: "[It's not because of any of these things that I'm crying], but because of this beauty of yours which will rot in the earth." In other words, "I'm crying because we're all going to die!" Now, Rabbi Yochanan responds, "This is certainly worth crying about!" and the two of them cry together. Then, Rabbi Yochanan is able to offer healing to Rabbi Eleazar and restore him to wholeness.

This is a powerful story, because even the great Rabbi Yochanan falls into the many traps of assuming, of jumping to conclusions, and of failing really to listen on the levels of *Remez, Derash,* and *Sod.* But when he is able to experience his own vulnerability, he is able to truly see and hear Rabbi Eleazar. Only then is he able to help and heal him.

Suffering and Pain Become Overwhelming

Assuming too much is a hazard that keeps us from offering our most useful pastoral presence. The other risks of the *PaRDeS* are more about our own well-being. Just as entering the *pardes* drove Ben Zoma mad and Elisha ben Abuyah to despair, so, too, the pastoral *PaRDeS* can take its toll. Encountering intense suffering and pain can easily become overwhelming. In every group of chaplaincy interns that I have supervised, there are always some who come in to see me early in the year with rings under their eyes. They tell me that they can't stop thinking about the people they work with. They dream of them, worry about them, psychically take them home with them. Of course, pastoral caregivers know we need to create and to maintain boundaries; most of us get better at it with practice. At times of intense workload or special personal stress, it can become hard to cope. In the face of tragedy and trauma, we might feel as though we have no affirming vision to lean on. It is frightening and devastating to confront horror on the deepest levels. Our work can shake us and challenge our faith.

Intensity of Real Connection Is Overwhelming

The final risk of the pastoral *PaRDeS* is not far from the *pardes* entered by the rabbis. Rashi understood the power and danger of the "four who entered"—into the Divine Presence. When we experience real connection in a pastoral encounter, the intensity of the experience can also be overwhelming. It is akin to seeing God's face, and we're not always prepared for it. There is a sense, as my colleague Rabbi Margaret Holub has said, that "nothing is more real than this."[13] There is a sensation of electrical charge, which can be exhilarating, but this can also make it hard to return to the mundane. How do we buy groceries, help children with homework, or watch mindless TV when our souls are still caught up with the most powerful spiritual encounters? We don't always know how to come back to earth, and the transition can be jarring, both for us and for those close to us.

Survival/Thriving Skills: What Do We Need to Enter the PaRDeS and to Emerge Whole?

Given these emotional risks, we need to think about what will help us to survive the *PaRDeS,* and also to thrive and to emerge whole, like Akiba, at the end of the day or career.[14]

Self-Awareness

Being present on the deeper levels of *PaRDeS* connects to our guts and our *neshomes.* Thus we need first to develop and constantly deepen our self-awareness. We can be present to the spectrum of others' emotions only to the degree to which we have access to our own. We need to hear our "counterstory," and at the same time be able to get it out of the way to truly make room for the other.

Emotional Support

Second, to enter the *PaRDeS,* we need emotional support. We all need a place to feel and to discharge the pain of the other as well as our own pain and brokenness. This place can be clinical supervision, therapy, spiritual direction, or talking to a close friend or partner. It doesn't matter what it is, as long as it is reasonably constant and totally safe.

Spiritual Nurture

Finally, and perhaps most important, to toil in the pastoral *PaRDeS,* we need spiritual nurture. We who are engaged in facilitating religious life for others need to be sure that we have a religious life that is engaged, growing, and nourishing. We need spiritual practice that comforts us, study that challenges us. We need opportunities to find affirmation and the means of expressing our despair, and we need to be in ongoing conversation with God in whatever way works for us.

Conclusion

By mobilizing our skills and sensitivity, by caring for ourselves and attending to our own well-being, we can meet those we serve on the deepest level of their being. We can truly be present with them *ba-asher hem sham* (in the place where they are).[15] We can, *b'ezrat haShem* (with God's help), make that place, barren although it may be, a *pardes*, a place of meeting the Divine.[16]

Notes

1. Sylvia Boorstein, *Don't Just Do Something, Sit There: A Mindfulness Retreat with Sylvia Boorstein* (San Francisco: HarperSanFrancisco, 1996).
2. C. V. Gerkin, *The Living Human Document: Revisioning Pastoral Counseling in a Hermeneutical Mode* (Nashville: Abingdon Press, 1984), p. 40.
3. Rachel Mikva, "Text and the Human Document: Toward a Model for Rabbinical Counseling," *Journal of Reform Judaism* 37, no. 3 (summer 1990), pp. 23–33.
4. Zohar Chadash, *Tikkunim*, 102d; also 107c. For an explication of this teaching, see Isaiah Tishby, *The Wisdom of the Zohar*, vol. 3 (Oxford: Oxford University Press, 1989), p. 1090.
5. Charles Taylor, *The Skilled Pastor: Counseling as the Practice of Theology* (Minneapolis: Fortress Press, 1991), pp. 19–20.
6. Taylor, *The Skilled Pastor*, pp. 21 ff.
7. Gerkin, *Human Document*, pp. 122–24.
8. Viktor Frankl, 1988 address to American Society on Aging Conference, Washington, D.C., based on my notes.
9. Martin Buber, cited in Richard C. Cabot and Russell L. Dicks, *The Art of Ministering to the Sick* (New York: Macmillan Company, 1952).
10. J. L. Cedarleaf, cited in Rodney J. Hunter, ed., *Dictionary of Pastoral Care and Counseling* (Nashville: Abingdon Press, 1990).
11. BT Hagigah 14b.
12. Ibid.
13. Rabbi Margaret Holub, personal communication.
14. For more information on spiritual nurture and self-care for pastoral caregivers, see chapter 9 of this book, "Spiritual Nurture," p. 172.

15. See Genesis 21:17, in which God is described as hearing the voice of Ishmael *ba'asher hu sham* (in all that he faces, exactly where he is). Interestingly, the text does not actually mention that Ishmael has spoken or cried. This offers us a model of listening and presence which meets people where they are, and that can hear and understand more than they are able to say about their troubles.
16. The material in this chapter is based in part on Dayle A. Friedman, *"PaRDeS:* A Jewish Model for Pastoral Listening and Presence," *The Jewish Chaplain* 3, no. 1 (spring 1988): pp. 3–9.

Bibliography

Gerkin, C. V. *The Living Human Document: Revisioning Pastoral Counseling in a Hermeneutical Mode.* Nashville: Abingdon Press, 1984.

Mikva, Rachel. "Text and the Human Document: Toward a Model for Rabbinical Counseling." *Journal of Reform Judaism* 37, no. 3 (summer 1990): pp. 23–33.

Taylor, Charles. *The Skilled Pastor: Counseling as the Practice of Theology.* Minneapolis: Fortress Press, 1991.

Rabbi Dayle A. Friedman, M.A.J.C.S., M.S.W., is the director of the Geriatric Chaplaincy program at the Reconstructionist Rabbinical College, where she also serves as a spiritual director. She has served for many years as a nursing home chaplain and as a supervisor to rabbinic and cantorial students in clinical internship programs.

SECTION II

Basic Tools for the
Jewish Pastoral Caregiver

Foundations of Jewish Pastoral Care: Skills and Techniques

Barbara Eve Breitman

Barbara Eve Breitman provides an accessible collection of basic pastoral tools. She offers guidance about effectively offering empathic presence and listening. She analyzes vitally important issues such as attending to boundaries, transference, and countertransference, and teaches the all-important art of referral.

The art of listening is the foundation of all forms of pastoral caregiving. For the Jewish pastoral caregiver, listening is both an essential skill and a spiritual practice. The *Shema*, the central statement of Jewish faith, declares that hearing is the quintessentially sacred act for Jews: "Hear O Israel, YHVH is our God, YHVH is One." Indeed, the *Shema* announces that listening is the spiritual discipline through which the Oneness of God can be known. Paradoxically, the name for God used in the *Shema* is precisely the one name that cannot be spoken, that is ineffable, exhorting Jews to listen precisely to that which cannot be spoken, to hear in the living silence that which unites us all.

What kind of listening is this? It is the listening that requires us to quiet the noise in our minds, listening that involves both the outer and the inner ear—the ear of the heart. Empathic listening involves hearing what others are communicating, with and without words. With such attentiveness, we begin to sense what is moving in the other's inner life. It is the kind of listening that enables others to come to speech, to find their own voice. As early feminists discovered, it is possible to "hear each other into speech," to listen in a way that literally enables a previously hidden or buried aspect of the speaker's self to emerge through articulation.[1] This is listening as a spiritual discipline, meant to be practiced with focus, commitment, and intentionality. This kind of listening is at the heart of pastoral caregiving. Such listening begins with presence.

Presence: Being with Another Person

> Rabbi Eleazar fell ill and Rabbi Johanan went in to visit him. [R. Johanan] noticed that [R. Eleazar] was lying in a dark room, and [R. Johanan] bared his arm and light radiated from it. Thereupon he noticed that R. Eleazar was weeping. (BT Berachot 5b)

One of the greatest mysteries of pastoral caregiving is the healing power of presence. When faced with a congregant in distress, a sick person who has been hospitalized for a life-threatening illness, or a college student concerned about a problem with her parents, an inexperienced pastoral caregiver might say, "I don't know what to do" or might ask, "What should I say?" Being told simply to be with the other person can be a mystifying answer. "How can that help?" wonders the pastoral caregiver. "I want to know what I can *do*!"

We all know that it is possible to sit across the table from another person or to sit at the bedside of an ill friend and not be present at all. It is possible to look another person directly in the eyes, and to be not behind our eyes, but a million miles away, distracted by extraneous thoughts, focused on our own agenda, or even consciously withholding ourselves, not wanting to let the other in. On the other hand, it is possible to bring ourselves into and to be behind our eyes, to open our hearts, to exude warmth, and to take the other in. For a healing relationship to begin, pastoral caregivers must bring their being to the encounter with the other person and open their hearts.

The mysterious image of light radiating from Rabbi Johanan's arm points to this mystery of healing presence. When we bring the fullness of our being into relationship, it is like bringing light into a darkened room. Once Rabbi Johanan was really present, he was able to discern his friend's weeping; before, he was in the dark and could not see the emotional distress of his beloved colleague.

The mystery of being is at the center of our holiest name for God. The ineffable name for God in Hebrew is an impossible declension of the verb *to be,* collapsing forms of the past, the present, and the future into one. This mysterious name points to the possibility of our finding a way of being that is so alive and imbued with presence that all dimensions of time as we know them are so full as to be transcended. Part of the mystery is that when we are fully present, it is as if we are bringing God into the space between people. As the Kotzker Rebbe said, "God is present where we let God in."

When people can be with one another, imbuing the time and space they share with presence, the possibility for holiness is manifest. Being with another creates the basic condition for healing or sacred encounter. As we offer and enable our being to touch another, we enable that aspect of God Who dwells among us, the *Shechina*, the indwelling presence, to become manifest. In a world in which medical healing has become split off from its roots in the mystery of being, the pastoral caregiver can be a reminder of the healing power of presence. This reminder is one of the unique gifts that chaplains and pastoral caregivers can bring into the highly technological settings in which many of the sick and elderly abide.

> A Jewish chaplain was asked to be an observer at an emergency ethics committee meeting of a major urban hospital. About twenty medical professionals were gathered to discuss whether to remove life support systems from a young man with a devastating spinal cord injury. In attendance were the young man, who was hooked up to breathing machines, his family, and the two doctors whose dissenting opinions had occasioned this meeting. All of the professionals understood the extreme gravity of the decision and had brought their intelligence, integrity, and knowledge to bear, and yet, as this young man and his family stood at the threshold between life and death, no prayer was uttered. No one in the room overtly acknowledged the sacredness of the moment. In the face of the hospital culture, the chaplain felt paralyzed; he was shaken to realize he was failing to bring his pastoral presence into this most liminal of spaces. He knew how powerful it would be even simply to ask for a moment of silence, to enable the "being" of those present to touch one another for just a moment before making their decision.

It is a challenge for pastoral caregivers to believe in the power of presence in a world that values doing and knowing over being, but that is precisely what we are called to do.

A rabbi is called to officiate at the funeral of a young man in his twenties who has committed suicide. At her first meeting with his parents and siblings, the most important gift she can offer is presence. Although she will gently ask questions about the deceased, drawing people out about their relationship with him, she knows that there are no words she can possibly say that will lessen their pain. At moments of such trauma, people's private worlds are shattered, creating a profound emptiness; into this void, the most sacred gift a pastoral caregiver can bring is presence. When the attachment to a loved one has been severed by death, the bereaved often feel temporarily cut off from the flow of life. Being with a family at such a time of loss, sitting with them, caring about them, allowing them to speak, to cry, to wail, to rage, reconnects them with the ongoing flow of life.

But presence is not only important at times of loss or trauma. Presence creates the bridge across which people can walk when they endeavor to communicate with one another. A college student comes to the Hillel director and needs to talk about his difficulties getting along with other students; a young Christian woman comes to talk with a congregational rabbi about the possibility of converting to Judaism; a grandmother tells the cantor that the distress she is experiencing over her daughter's divorce disrupts her ability to rejoice in her grandson's upcoming bar mitzvah. In all of these situations, a person seeking the counsel of a pastoral caregiver needs to speak from a place of vulnerability. If the pastoral caregiver is not fully present, the other person will have difficulty speaking, sensing that there is no bridge across the expanse between them. Pastoral caregivers' ability to transmit, through the energy and warmth of their presence, a sense of safety and availability make it possible for others to open up and share with them their inner lives.

Empathic Listening: Can Empathy Be Taught?

Do not judge your fellow person until you have come unto his or her place. (Pirke Avot 2:5)

What is empathy? In the 1980s, feminist psychologists at Wellesley College's Stone Center noted that empathy had often been "dismissed as a vague and [an] unknowable subjective state." They decided to study the nature of empathy in the therapeutic relationship. Along with Heinz Kohut, the so-called father of self psychology, the Stone

Center psychologists emphasized that empathy is a psychological nutrient that can be nourishing and healing. They also suggested that the capacity for empathy is a developmental milestone as advanced and critical to adult functioning as the capacity for autonomy.[2]

The researchers' description of the experiential process involved in empathizing is highly instructive: "Empathy always involves affective surrender and cognitive structuring. . . . Experientially, empathy begins with . . . a perception of the other's affective cues, verbal and non-verbal. This is followed by surrender to affective arousal in oneself—as if the perceived affective cues were one's own—thus producing a temporary identification with the other's emotional state. Finally, there occurs a resolution period in which one regains a sense of separate self that understands what has just happened."[3] It is important to note that empathy requires both a capacity to identify with others and a capacity to differentiate oneself from others. It also requires a capacity to move in and out of these psychological states with fluidity.

Over the past thirty years, a plethora of books and programs have taught active listening and effective communication skills for personal and professional relationships.[4] The most important message is that the ability to listen attentively can be taught and improved, and the capacity for empathy can be expanded. Although approaches and emphases may vary, most systems agree that there are several important components to developing astute listening and more accurate empathy.

First, and basic to empathic listening, is the ability of the person receiving the message to hear accurately the verbal content of a communication, the actual words being said. Although this sounds almost too obvious to state, it is well known that people often do not hear what is being communicated to them because their own reactions to, interpretations of, and feelings about what is being said interfere with listening. Internal noise, nervousness about being able to find the right thing to say in response, thinking about one's response while the other is still talking, or being flooded with emotion can literally drown out the words of the speaker in the mind of the listener. One of the ways to practice accurate listening is literally to reflect back to a speaker what the listener has heard and to allow the speaker to correct any errors. Practicing this mirroring technique can greatly improve basic listening. Even people who believe they are good listeners are often surprised to discover how inaccurately they hear when they attempt such a disciplined exercise.

Second, a listener needs to notice and to attend to the speaker's nonverbal cues. People communicate nonverbally in two ways: with body language, such as facial expressions, gestures, or posture; and also through spatial relationships, such as proximity, the distance between people. Often nonverbal cues hold more information about the real feelings or meaning of a communication than the words; body language almost always points the listener to the deeper truth of a person's inner experience. For example, a chaplain might ask a woman, "How are you feeling today?" She shrugs, looks down dejectedly, and responds, "Oh, I'm fine, Rabbi." A key to understanding nonverbal communication is noting whether there is congruence between the words and the body language. An empathic listener recognizes incongruence as a signal to probe more deeply.[5] "Are you really feeling fine? You seem somewhat down today."

Third, a listener needs to understand the meaning of what is being communicated from the perspective of the speaker. The discipline required of the empathic listener is to step temporarily inside the other person's universe of meaning, to look out at the world through their eyes, and to understand what they are describing.

> A mother says to a rabbi, "I know Jonathan is not able to keep up with the work at Hebrew school because he attends only every other week. I want you to know, Rabbi, that on the alternate Sundays he goes to soccer practice with his father, who is not Jewish. His father feels it is as important for Jonathan to have this father–son time together as it is for him to go to Hebrew school. I'm not really happy about the situation, but I have to honor my husband's feelings."

Although the rabbi probably has many complex feelings and opinions about these parents' choices, he cannot begin to frame a response to the mother until he stands in her shoes. The rabbi needs to understand that from the mother's perspective, this compromise with her husband is the best she can do to keep peace in the family and to ensure that her son can continue his Hebrew education. Any further pastoral care with this family must begin with this understanding.

Correlatively, to feel heard, a speaker needs feedback from the listener that is communicated clearly, that sends the message: "What you said makes sense to me"; this provides cognitive validation to the speaker. Unfortunately, listeners often confuse letting a speaker know that what they said has "made sense" with agreeing with them. In fact, these responses are very different. It is possible to understand what someone thinks and how they create meaning without actually agreeing with their interpretation of reality. To provide comfort or counsel, a pastoral caregiver must first understand how the speaker interprets their situation. The rabbi might respond to the mother, "I understand this is a very difficult dilemma for you. You want to avoid conflict in your family, and you want Jonathan to continue his Hebrew school education. I understand that, for you, this is an attempt at compromise."

Finally, listeners need to move what they have heard with their ears and have understood with their minds, into their hearts. Listeners need to imagine how the speaker might be feeling. Imaginatively projecting ourselves into another person's experience is not the same thing as merging with them, imitating them, or pretending to know what he or she is going through. Empathy requires that listeners go through the brief but complex process described by the psychologists at the Stone Center. The rabbi might respond to this mother, "I can hear how concerned and torn you feel about this situation. I even detect a note of sadness in what you're saying. I'm glad you felt comfortable enough to tell me about the complexity of your family situation. Perhaps I can be helpful to you."

For a pastoral relationship to begin, this mother needs to know that the rabbi can understand and empathize with her dilemma, even if he ultimately holds a different opinion about how things might be arranged for Jonathan's education. Clearly, there are many times when rabbis must take an ethical position, state clearly their value stance on a particular issue, or interpret the tradition's perspective on a situation. Nevertheless, such an interpretation is best received when the congregant or the sick person feels that the rabbi understands and empathizes with her or his reality. The beginning of a counseling relationship requires us to "start where the client is."

"Starting Where the Client Is" and Conscious, Intentional Use of Self

The king's son once went mad and decided he was a turkey. As a turkey, he had a need to sit naked under the table and gobble up crumbs. The doctors all despaired of helping him, and the king was distraught. Then a wise man came and announced he would heal the prince. He stripped naked and sat under the table alongside the prince, pecking at crumbs and bones. The prince asked him: "Who are you and what are you doing here?" He replied, "What are you doing here?" "I," said the prince, "am a turkey." "And I," said the sage, "am a turkey, too." So the two of them sat there together for some time until they got used to one another. Then, at the wise man's signal, a shirt was thrown down. "Do you think," said the sage, "that a turkey cannot wear a shirt? You can wear a shirt and still be a turkey." After a time, he signaled again, and trousers were thrown down. "Do you think that with pants you cannot be a turkey?" They both put on pants and other clothes. He signaled again and human food was thrown under the table. "You can eat this food and still be a turkey." And so they ate. "Do you think that a turkey can only sit under the table? You can be a turkey and sit right at the table." Thus, he went on with him, until he had cured him completely.[6]

Two basic concepts from social work practice can be very useful to the pastoral caregiver: starting where the client is[7] and the conscious use of self.[8] The basic precept of social work literature is to start where the client is. This concept suggests that assisting healing, growth, or movement toward change can begin only when the helper starts where the person really is, not where the caregiver wishes he or she would be. When people are suffering, or when they are making choices or behaving in ways that are unwholesome, unhealthy, or unethical, caregivers can only begin to provide comfort or to discern the reasons for such suffering or behavior by entering into the world of the other's experience. The doctors who failed to cure the turkey prince probably began their interventions by judging the prince's behavior as inappropriate. Perhaps they made it a precondition of relationship that the prince first sit at the table and talk with them like a man. Only the wise man understood that for healing to begin, trust had to be established with the prince, which could only be accomplished by starting where he literally was, under the table.

However, the wise man did not accept or agree with the turkey prince's interpretation of reality. By a very conscious and intentional use of himself in the relationship, the wise man developed a relationship of trust with the prince and then gradually shifted the prince's perspective and helped him change his behavior. To do so, the wise man needed to have a clear sense of purpose and intention.[9]

> A chaplain is told by the staff of a nursing home for the elderly that Mrs. Cohen is a very difficult, isolated, noncompliant resident. She is always complaining about how much she hates being in a wheelchair but refuses to do the physical therapy that might help her walk again. She isolates herself from others and focuses instead only on her appearance, demanding that staff do things for her she could do for herself, while she spends her time putting on makeup and perfume. Although the chaplain, too, is initially put off by Mrs. Cohen's demands and by the visage of this elderly woman with bright, poorly applied lipstick and smeared eyeliner, he visits her, draws her out, listens, and learns that when she was younger she had been a model. He begins to empathize with how difficult it is for her to cope with the loss of her beauty and mobility, and Mrs. Cohen begins to share her feelings of loneliness and fears of dying alone. She begins attending services, and although she still does not go to physical therapy, she makes better connections with the other residents.

The primary difference between personal and professional relationships lies precisely in how intentional and focused is the use of self. In friendships and love relationships, the purpose of the relationship is mutuality and intimacy. In professional relationships, professional mission determines the goal or purpose. The difference between psychotherapy and pastoral care lies in how the troubles of life are engaged. When a person in pain goes to a psychotherapist, the professional purpose is to reduce suffering by alleviating symptoms and solving problems. However, the pastoral caregiver understands that suffering is built into the fabric of life because much human pain arises from the vicissitudes of mortality, and mortality is not a problem that can be solved. Therefore, the troubles of life are seen as opportunities for spiritual growth; for examining one's life; for finding ways of sustaining hope and faith while avoiding bitterness; for responding to questions of meaning, purpose, and ethics; for understanding one's spiritual journey; and, perhaps, redeeming one's soul through *teshuvah*. For pastoral caregivers, the professional mission involves sustaining, comforting, helping, teaching, or guiding by connecting or reconnecting individuals, families, or communities with their own authenticity through the selfhood of the caregiver, and the wisdom, resources, and values of Jewish tradition, liturgy, texts, rituals, history, and community. To do so, pastoral caregivers need not only to have empathy and knowledge but also to be intentional in their interactions.

Jewish tradition has a wonderful word for sacred intention, *kavannah*, which has traditionally been applied to prayer. In that context, *kavannah* refers to a concentration of mind, direction of attention, intensity of purpose, and avoidance of anything that might distract the one who prays from closeness with God. It is useful to apply the spiritual practice of *kavannah* to the realm of pastoral relationship. When pastoral caregivers or chaplains are functioning in their professional roles, all interactions with others need to be done with *kavannah*. Even when rabbis, cantors, or other pastoral caregivers engage in what might appear to be small talk at an Oneg Shabbat or in a hospital waiting room, they need to do so with *kavannah*, with the sacred intention of establishing empathic connection, discerning where the other person is, listening with attention and focus, and thereby building a trusting relationship.

Intentionality should not be confused with manipulation, warmth with informality, or a conscious use of self with formality. This is the way in which the Hebrew concept of *kavannah* can be helpful. When caregivers approach a pastoral relationship with *kavannah*, it means that they are not engaging in a relationship in which the goal is mutual reward, intimacy, or manipulation. The goal is sacred service: It is to help bring congregants, the sick, or students, into a closer relationship with themselves, their loved ones, Judaism, Jewish community, the larger human community, nature, or God. Although pastoral caregivers may derive a deep sense of satisfaction and personal meaning from such service, the purpose of the relationship is not to meet the caregivers' needs but to be present for the other.

Another aspect of the conscious use of self is clarity about role and purpose in relationship. Is the pastoral caregiver's role that of comforter or caregiver, teacher or spiritual guide, prayer leader, facilitator of a life-cycle transition, or source of referral for other professional help in a crisis? Clarity about one's role shapes the direction of one's intentionality and one's use of self in professional relationship.

Peter VanKatwyk, director of training at an interfaith pastoral counseling center, developed a helping styles inventory that looks closely at the dimensions of use of self and the use of power in the helping relationship. His model, shown in Figure 1, is valuable in describing a varied repertoire of helping modes and postures that may be called for in different pastoral situations.[10]

The horizontal axis describes a range in the use of self on a continuum between focus on the person and focus on the task. One helping style is strong in empathy, on identifying with the person in the situation; the other is strong in resourcefulness, in providing guidance, advice, and information toward the end of accomplishing a life task.

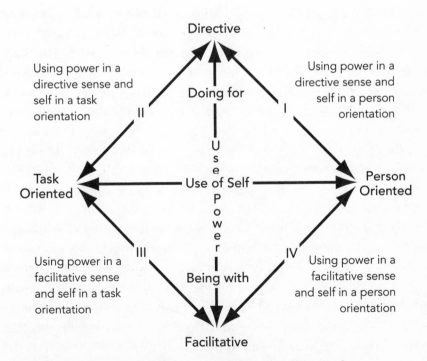

Fig. 1 Two Helping Modes; Four Helping Styles

The vertical axis looks at the continuum in the use of power where, at one end, the locus of power is in the authority of the helper (professional, charismatic, or symbolic) and the style is directive; at the other end of the continuum, the locus of power is within the person being helped, and the helper is primarily in a facilitative role. As these axes define quadrants, four different helping postures emerge, each with its own value and usefulness for different pastoral situations.

Quadrant I involves using power in a *directive sense* and using self in a *person orientation*. In this posture, the caregiver focuses on hearing a person's distress, attends with empathy to enter into the person's experience, but becomes directive in advising and guiding. The situation that exemplifies this helping posture is counseling a person in crisis—for example, a parent who comes to the pastoral caregiver for help with a deeply troubled or suicidal teenager. The pastoral caregiver needs to focus on hearing the distress in the inner life of the mother or father, and to make a good referral for further psychological treatment, which requires providing information, resources, and perhaps coaching or directing the parent to follow through on the recommendations.

Quadrant II involves using power in a *directive sense* and self in a *task orientation*. An example of this posture is that of a rabbi conducting a bar mitzvah ritual on the *bimah*. The rabbi has completed the teaching and the guiding as well as the work of pastoral counseling with the family in planning the ritual. Now, the rabbi needs to ensure that the ritual event on the *bimah* proceeds according to plan and within an allotted period. Although the moment is a sacred one, the rabbi's use of self and focus are now on task. The rabbi might switch to a Quadrant I posture when she addresses the bar mitzvah or his parents directly on the *bimah*, but her primary stance is directive and task oriented to ensure that the ritual proceeds well.

Quadrant III describes using power in a *facilitative sense* and self in a *task orientation*. A rabbi or cantor might use this posture in guiding a couple through premarital counseling focused on the planning of a wedding. The focus is on the accomplishment of a life task, but the style is facilitative. The rabbi or cantor draws out the couple as they talk about each other and their relationship, helping them explore what the ritual means to them and empowering them to use the ceremony to facilitate emotional and familial processes. All the information about the couple discerned through empathic listening is then channeled into creating a life-cycle ritual that will best serve this unique couple and family.

Quadrant IV is using power in a *facilitative sense* and self in a *person orientation*. Visiting a hospitalized person, comforting the bereaved, and being with the dying exemplify this posture. In these situations, the purpose is comfort, support, listening with empathy, and being with another. There is no task to accomplish, no change process to direct. A profound transformative process is already underway in the life of the ill, dying, or bereaved. The caregiver needs to attend with *kavannah* and empathy to what is unfolding in the inner life of the congregant, to listen to both the words and the silence, to flow with the process of transformation that is occurring beyond human control. The pastoral caregiver's function is to serve that process, to be guided by the mystery that is unfolding, and to touch the process only with presence and the sacred wisdom of the tradition. Matching one's breathing to the rhythm of a person who can no longer speak communicates presence. Focusing attention on the dying or bereaved, meditating, and quietly singing or praying with them creates a connection between caregivers and the souls of people who are momentarily suspended between worlds. Being with them makes God's immanence palpable and honors the holiness of these times of transition.

Everyone has differing natural abilities in these modes of helping. Pastoral caregivers may be called on to function in any of these varied situations, thus they need to know where their natural strengths lie and in which direction growth and skill development lie. The significance of VanKatwyk's model is that it can point caregivers to areas for expansion in the development of the pastoral self. A mature pastoral caregiver will ultimately develop the capacity to function in all four postures and the facility to switch modes with fluidity as each situation demands.

Basic Counseling Skills and Techniques: Prompting, Probing, Paraphrasing, and Summarizing

The wise person does not break into [another's] speech; he [or she] is not in a rush to reply; he [or she] asks what is relevant and replies to the point; [the wise person] speaks of first things first and of last things last; of what he [or she] has not heard he [or she] says "I have not heard"; and acknowledges what is true. (Pirke Avot 5:7)

Sometimes people speak to a pastoral caregiver freely and spontaneously, but sometimes it is necessary to encourage people to speak, to draw them out. *Prompts* and *probes* are simple, subtle, and gentle verbal encouragement that can take the form of questions or statements to help people explore their inner experiences.

When asking questions, there are two techniques that are the most important: asking open-ended questions and asking questions that serve a purpose. Open-ended questions are questions that require more than a yes or no answer. Rather than asking a recently bereaved widow, "Have you been thinking a lot about your husband?" frame the question as, "What thoughts and memories have been coming up about your husband?" Rather than asking teenagers, "Do you get along with your parents?" ask them, "How do you and your parents get along? What is your relationship like with them?"

It is also important not to ask aimless questions but rather to ask purposeful questions that enable people to explore the issues or feelings they have brought to the pastoral caregiver. Questions that begin with "what, how, in what way" are usually far better than questions beginning with "why," which tends to make people feel they have to justify or explain themselves. Questions that begin with "what" or "how" encourage people to explore their inwardness. Rather than asking "Why do you feel this way?" ask, "How are you feeling?" or "What might be giving rise to these feelings?" Rather than asking, "Why are you doing this?" ask, "What do you think might be motivating your actions?"

Statements can also be used as gentle probes. Statements that express the pastoral caregiver's interest, confusion, or desire to understand more usually encourage people to clarify and to speak further: "I hear what you are saying, but I'm not sure I understand what this means to you," "I'm confused by what you're saying; I want to understand better how this makes you angry," and "I see how sad you are, and I am really interested to know more about what happened" are examples.

By periodically paraphrasing, summarizing, or asking questions of clarification, pastoral caregivers can help people explore and organize their inner worlds, thus leading them gradually to understand themselves and to be able to communicate better with others. Paraphrases are brief reformulations in the caregiver's own words of the essence of what he or she has just heard. Paraphrases can be used to draw a person out further and to check the accuracy of one's listening. At the end of a paraphrase or summary, it is often useful to check the accuracy of one's listening by asking, "Am I hearing you correctly?" or "Is that close?" Summarizations are similar to paraphrases but attempt to cover more information. Summarizations are especially useful at the beginning or end of interactions when a pastoral caregiver wants to focus a conversation or bring closure to one, as well as for making transitions to a new topic. Most important, summarizing helps people reflect on their feelings and organize their thinking.

These basic counseling techniques are aspects of disciplined listening that are conscious and intentional as well as empathic.[11]

Boundaries

Ben Azzai said:
You will be called by your name;
you will be seated in your place,
you will be given what is yours.
No person touches what is meant for his [or her] fellow.
No kingdom touches its neighbor by so much as a hairsbreadth.
(BT Yoma 38a–b)

In the realm of interpersonal relationships, boundaries define the limits and the parameters of interaction. Boundaries exist in time, in space, and in the psychosocial dimension, referring to the degree of emotional expressiveness, self-revelation, or physical contact between people. Pastoral caregivers often meet with people in ambiguous settings and situations, such as in houses, in hospital waiting rooms, at bedsides, in college cafeterias, and at wedding receptions. In addition, people often share pastoral concerns during ambiguous times, such as during Oneg Shabbat after services, committee meetings, or even on the street, in restaurants, and in supermarkets. Both setting and timing

may be ambiguous, thus wherever a congregant bumps into a rabbi or
cantor, it is extremely important for pastoral caregivers to learn how
to maintain professional boundaries in subtle but clear ways, and how
to channel a person's concern into an appropriate pastoral context.

For example, at the Oneg Shabbat, a distressed congregant explains that the reason she is at services alone tonight is that her husband was just diagnosed with cancer and is too despondent to come to
synagogue as he usually does. Or, on the cantor's day off, as he is eating lunch at a restaurant with friends, a congregant comes over to his
table and interrupts, stating that his sister, who is sitting with him at
the next table, is going through a difficult divorce. He asks, "Could
you just offer her some words of comfort?" Or, after a committee
meeting, the president of the congregation asks for time with the rabbi
and tells him that he is having an extramarital affair. How does the
pastoral caregiver negotiate these difficult situations, create the
boundaries and context that will make it possible to function as an effective pastoral presence, and attend to his own self-care so that he
will not burn out?

When a situation requires pastoral counseling or a pastoral visit,
it is crucial to structure a context in which that important form of
service can be provided. It is not possible to engage in appropriate
pastoral care in the synagogue lobby, over coffee and pastry, where the
expectation is to be cordial and conversant in a social setting. On the
other hand, it would obviously be unconscionable to treat the information of a husband's cancer as small talk, regardless of the setting
chosen by the congregant for such a communication. The pastoral
caregiver needs gently to define the boundaries of the relationship:
"Miriam, this is such devastating news for you and Joe. I want to talk
with you further and, of course, visit Joe at home. I cannot give you
the attention you need here. Let's meet after the Oneg in my office
where it is private and I can give you my undivided attention." By
establishing different boundaries in time and place, the pastoral caregiver defines a context in which caregiving is possible.

The same is true of the second situation. Although the cantor may
pause for a moment in eating lunch to be introduced to the congregant's sister, he cannot provide pastoral care in a restaurant and does
not need to disrupt his day off to do so. The cantor can extend himself
and offer an opportunity for the sister to make an appointment when

he is in his office. Maintenance of good boundaries not only ensures that congregants receive the attention they need, but also ensures that pastoral caregivers can care for themselves. "Balancing healthy boundaries and living one's own life is often a challenge in ministry. . . . [B]oundary maintenance and . . . self-care are synergistic rather than competing principles of ethical action."[12]

The third example raises different issues and concerns the nature of overlapping relationships, which is one of the greatest challenges for contemporary pastoral caregivers and, at times, creates conflicting roles. Rabbis, cantors, and lay caregivers should not be passive victims of their multiple roles, but rather, acknowledge that such overlaps exist, be conscious of the possible impact these overlaps will have on their ability to function professionally, and find ways to act responsibly to protect themselves and their congregants. This stance requires the ethical management of overlapping relationships. There are many unavoidable dual relationships; for example, the rabbi at a fund-raising meeting who is disagreeing with the chair about the process of soliciting funds also recently performed a funeral for the chair's mother and comforted him in his bereavement. Some potentially overlapping relationships can be avoided, like the one in the third example, in which the congregational president confided in the rabbi about his marital infidelity.

The guiding principle is, whenever possible, to avoid engaging in different forms of relationship with congregants (such as counseling and administration) at the same time. Therefore, when the president of the congregation says that he or she is having an extramarital affair, it is better for the rabbi or cantor to make a good referral than to engage the president in a counseling relationship: "Although I am open to listening to your feelings, confusion, and guilt about this affair tonight, I do not think it would be best for me to become your primary confidant and caregiver. We would both be wearing too many hats in this relationship. What I want to do is find you a good person to help you sort this all out. You and I have a job to do together in providing leadership for this community." By setting these boundaries, the rabbi or cantor not only avoids potentially difficult overlapping roles with the president but also ensures that the greater responsibility of working with the president to provide leadership to the community is protected from unnecessary contamination.

Many rabbis, out of a desire to serve their communities, believe they need to be available to their congregants at all times and in all ways. They might even believe that having clear boundaries between home and work, public and private life, and between conflicting roles interferes with their ability to serve. As Katherine Clarke points out in her feminist approach to professional ethics for clergy, "[Although] ministers clearly are in as much need of support, nurturance, and attention as their parishioners, they are often socialized to neglect those needs."13

As pastoral care becomes an ever-expanding aspect of the contemporary rabbinate and cantorate, and clergy are increasingly called on to fulfill caregiving roles, self-care becomes a critical ethical issue. Pastoral caregivers can learn much about self-care from feminist therapists, such as therapy, clinical supervision, and spiritual direction as ethically mandatory.14 Pastoral caregivers are more prone to overextend their boundaries through abuses of power when they are not attending to self-care. To understand this complex issue more deeply, pastoral caregivers need at least an elementary understanding of the dynamics of helping relationships, of transference and countertransference.

Transference and Countertransference

And there we saw giants . . . who come of the giants; and we were in our own eyes as grasshoppers, and so must have been in their eyes. (Numbers 13:33)

Although human beings have always been susceptible to distorting interpersonal relationships by perceiving people differently than they are, it was not until the twentieth century that this process was named and systematically explored: The concept of transference, which was among Sigmund Freud's most significant contributions to our understanding of human psychology, refers to the fact that human beings are not capable of entering a new relationship as completely new. Instead, perceptions and experiences of people in the present are colored by experiences with people in the past and by recent or even current environmental influences and relationships. These distortions are an inevitable aspect of human relationships and can contribute to misconceptions and misunderstandings between people, as well as to healing, love, and erotic feelings. Transference is the term used in the field of psychotherapy to refer to a patient's or client's response to the therapist as imaged through his or her unique psychological lens, rather than to the person the therapist actually is. For example, a client might have had a particularly critical parent who was very difficult to please and, anticipating that a therapist will also be judgmental, will be on guard for the first signs of disapproval.

Countertransference, as used in psychotherapeutic literature, refers to the emotional responses and distortions experienced by a therapist toward a patient. The narrowest definition of countertransference refers to distortions made by the therapist from unresolved experiences in the therapist's past. Another aspect of countertransference refers to reactions a therapist may have to what a patient is transferring onto him or her. Although it is not the pastoral caregiver's responsibility to interpret transferences, as it is for a psychotherapist, it is nevertheless crucially important for pastoral caregivers to know what transference and countertransference are and how they might affect pastoral relationships. Although the psychotherapeutic literature on transference and countertransference is voluminous, very little has been written about the kinds of transference and countertransference that commonly arise in pastoral relationships.[15] This is a field ripe for future exploration.

According to psychiatrist Richard Schwartz, clergy are particularly susceptible to specific "preformed transferences." These fall into at least three categories: (1) transferences based on previous experiences with parents and other family members in positions of authority; (2) transferences based on previous relationships with clergy; and (3) transferences based on experiences of or relationship with God.[16] To this list, Jews must add transferences based on people's experiences with and attitudes toward Judaism, the Jewish community, and its authoritative representatives.

One rabbi provides an impressive and troubling list of a few such preformed transferences.

> Among the most severe of our challenges is that people expect from us nothing less than everything. We should know every answer. We ought to provide infinite time. We ought to attend every event and committee meeting, conduct every program, visit each

class in every school, participate in every communal institution. We are expected to spend all our time making phone calls to our congregants, visiting them in their homes and their hospitals, and always making time to grow and to learn so that we in turn are able to teach them. . . . And, of course, we are supposed to love every single person at every moment.[17]

Transference that perceives the rabbi as larger than life, capable of constant availability, and wise and loving at all times is based on a mixture of nostalgic fantasy, a wish for perfect superparent, and a hope for the rabbi to be the unifier of a community at an historical moment when liberal Jewish communities, with all their diversities, have no unifying practice.[18] As the symbol of Jewish tradition and continuity, the rabbi is expected to be all things to all people and to be a kind of superglue capable of holding everything and everyone in a community together.

Contemporary rabbis and cantors have many different counter-transference reactions to this symbolic function, depending on the vicissitudes of their unique personal psychology. Some try to be all things to all people, hoping that they will be loved, until they become resentful and burned out. Others might be angered by the unrealistic expectations people have of them, and relationships with congregants may become disrupted by expressed or unexpressed hostility. Some may be gratified by being seen as larger than life and allow an unrealistic sense of personal grandiosity to develop. Still others might so shy away from fulfilling congregants' temporary idealization that they withdraw at a time of crisis when the rabbi or cantor could provide a special kind of comfort or succor. It is crucial for rabbis to understand the nature and content of the variety of preformed transferences and their own idiosyncratic ways of responding to them so they can function effectively as pastoral presences in their communities.

Preformed transferences, based on the rabbi's symbolic function, often arise in counseling relationships as well as in relationship with the congregation as a whole.

An interfaith couple set up a meeting with the rabbi at the request of the Jewish wife. The wife has developed a trusting relationship with the rabbi and now wants her non-Jewish husband to explain to the rabbi why he does not like attending services. After being

coaxed by his wife to tell the rabbi about issues they have discussed as a couple, the non-Jewish husband explains that he finds
there are too many references in the liturgy to Jewish peoplehood
and to the Jews' unique relationship with God. He finds them ex-
clusionary and off-putting, and as a non-Jewish partner who has
agreed to raising his child as a Jew, he believes that his experiences
and differences are not recognized or valued. He had thought that
Judaism, being a monotheistic tradition, would be more welcom-
ing of him as a non-Jew. In an attempt to empathize with the husband who is feeling like an outsider, the rabbi says, "I understand
what you mean. There are times when I, too, even as a rabbi, find
some of the particularistic elements of Judaism to be problematic." As soon as the rabbi pauses, the wife, clearly disappointed
and disapproving, cuts him off, saying, "Now, rabbi, I am sure
you don't mean that!"

The wife clearly feels the rabbi has let her down, even betrayed her.
Through her transference, the wife had expected the rabbi would take
the same positions that she had had in conflicts with her husband. She
had never imagined that he, as a representative of the Jewish tradition,
would have any empathy for her husband's criticism of Judaism. Suddenly, the rabbi finds he has failed the wife in his symbolic function
and become triangulated in the couple's conflict. Had the rabbi de-
tected the wife's transference, he could have proceeded differently in
the counseling session. For example, he could have explored the nature of the disagreement between the husband and wife first, addressing the conflict between them before he offered his own interpretation
of aspects of Jewish tradition. In that way, he might have been a more
successful mediator of this couple's relationship to each other and to
the tradition.

Chaplains visiting people in the hospital often encounter a particular form of transference from Jews; as soon as the chaplain enters,
they may assume that he or she is a rabbi and will begin explaining
why they don't go to synagogue or how they are not "good Jews,"
imagining that authoritative representatives of Judaism will be judgmental about their level of observance. They need reassurance that the
chaplain is available as a comfort to all, regardless of their level of
participation in Jewish communal life or tradition.

Many contemporary Jews are also uncomfortable with personal prayer. Their lack of knowledge of Hebrew or familiarity with traditional prayers or rituals, leaves many contemporary Jews in a spiritual vacuum at precisely those moments when prayer might be comforting, regardless of their belief in God. The Jewish chaplain needs to enter such situations with great sensitivity, knowing that he or she may well encounter not only emotional distress about illness but also feelings of shame about prayer and a lack of knowledge about Judaism.

Women and gay or lesbian rabbis and cantors have to deal with additional complexities in the transferential relationship. For example, women rabbis report that authority issues are likely to arise with congregants who are uncomfortable with their gender as rabbis. Congregants will sometimes insistently challenge the rabbi's knowledge or position to decrease a sense of too much symbolic power for a woman. At other times, congregants may treat women rabbis like daughters, children, or even sexual objects, unable to see or to acknowledge their authority as spiritual leaders or teachers. Dress or appearance may become a focus of attention for congregants in relation to women rabbis in ways that might never be an issue with men rabbis. Gay or lesbian rabbis or cantors can become role models for homosexual Jews who have had difficulty integrating the Jewish and gay aspects of their identity. A homosexual rabbi may be idealized as a role model and put on a pedestal by gay congregants; conversely, if a gay cantor is perceived as a peer and member of the same stigmatized minority within the Jewish community by gay or lesbian Jews, they may have great difficulty accepting the necessary boundaries of the professional relationship. All of these transferences affect the clergy's functioning as pastoral caregivers. Women and gay and lesbian rabbis and cantors have only recently been ordained, thus there is much yet to be explored about how gender and sexual orientation affect transferences toward them.

It is beyond the bounds of this chapter to explore further the complexity of the ambivalence some Jews feel toward other Jews, Jewish authority figures, and Jewish communities. However, it is important at least to acknowledge that such ambivalence exists, and that it can profoundly affect relationships with pastoral caregivers and the Jewish community. Kurt Lewin, the prominent social psychologist, believed that ambivalence was a psychosocial fact of minority group membership.[19] Negotiating one's relationship between the minority and dominant culture can create conflict and ambivalence. Many liberal Jews have complex reactions and feelings about Jewish particularity and exclusivity and the ways in which that membership in Jewish groups can lead to isolation from or within the larger culture. Many of these conflicts may be played out through a transferential relationship with Jewish pastoral caregivers and can add increased complexity to pastoral relationships.

When and How to Refer?

The more counsel, the more understanding.

—PIRKE AVOT 2:8

The necessity for contemporary pastoral caregivers to have at least a rudimentary understanding of the dynamics of professional counseling relationships results from the changing role of the clergy in contemporary culture. Rabbis today are valued and sought after more for their pastoral presence and less for their ability to render decisions about Halacha. Increasingly, cantors, chaplains, and lay caregivers are called on for pastoral support, thus pastoral caregivers need to know when they can and should provide pastoral care, and when to refer a congregant for additional help. In a study of the counseling activities and referral practices of rabbis, researchers found that "members of the clergy are often the first helping professionals to be contacted by people experiencing psychological distress and personal or family problems."[20] This study notes that, in order of frequency, the top sixteen concerns brought to rabbis are: death and dying issues, marital problems, parent–child problems, adolescent concerns, depression, anxiety, guilt, premarital issues, job-related concerns, school-related problems, suicide issues, physical problems, pregnancy/birth control, alcohol/drug abuse, and sexual concerns. Clearly, most rabbis and cantors are neither trained nor able, given the demands of their work, to enter into long-term pastoral counseling for all of these concerns; thus, knowing how and when to refer is a critical pastoral skill.

The essential elements of making a good referral are knowledge of the resources available, and the counseling skills necessary to interpret those resources in a way that facilitates congregants in making contact with those resources. Pastoral caregivers need to develop and constantly to update a referral file of community resources, agencies, services, self-help organizations, and practitioners in a variety of helping professions. To evaluate the trustworthiness, competence, and effectiveness of an organization or professional, the best guide is either direct contact or observation of the outcome of referrals.[21]

In his chapter on referral counseling, Howard Clinebell outlines several steps in effective referral counseling that clearly define the process from beginning to end:[22]

1. Create the expectation. Mention referral as a pastoral function in any written material that lists the pastoral caregiver's availability for counseling.

2. Mention the possibility of referral early in the counseling relationships, if it is likely to occur. As Clinebell states, "The longer the pastor waits to plant the seed of the possibility of referral and the greater the dependence that has developed, the more likely referral will arouse feelings of rejection." It is often beneficial to create boundaries at the beginning: "I want to reach a good understanding of your situation, and then I think it will be best for you and me to make some decisions about where to go from there. If I can help you, I will. If I think you will be better helped by someone else, I will let you know that soon."

3. Start where people are in their perceptions of their problems and with the kind of help needed. This is an extension of the principle of "starting where the client is." If a congregant has a completely different idea than that of the pastoral caregiver about the help needed, the congregant will not accept the referral.

4. Work to bring a congregant's perception of his or her problems and their solutions close enough to the pastoral caregiver's perceptions to enable referral to be accepted.

5. Help people resolve resistance to the particular helping person or agency recommended. Trying to refer people without understanding their resistance to getting help often results in a failed referral. It is important to elicit a person's reasons for resisting a referral. Here are some common resistances and useful pastoral responses to facilitate a mental health referral:

- "I'm not crazy." "No, you aren't, but your situation may be."
- "What's the point, nothing will get better." "You owe it to yourself to feel better. You really don't have to suffer this much. Things look like this because you are depressed."
- "Rabbi, I don't trust therapists. I would rather just talk with you." "Actually, I don't trust all therapists either. But I have been compiling a list of therapists I do trust."
- "Cantor, I'm afraid to see a marriage counselor. I'm afraid if we start talking, my marriage will fall apart." "Actually, it sounds like there is more of a chance of your marriage falling apart if you don't get some help."

6. Interpret the general nature of the help the congregant is likely to receive, relating it to his or her own sense of need.

7. Establish a rapport strong enough to develop a bridge over which the congregants walk into another helping relationship. It is important for the pastoral caregiver to be a bridge, but not the one to make the appointment, unless there is a disability involved. The likelihood of appointments with mental health professionals being kept is increased if congregants make their own appointments, even if that means placing the call from the pastoral caregiver's office.

8. Strongly encourage referred congregants to try a given therapist or agency, even if they are only mildly willing.

9. Let people know that pastoral caring and concern will continue after the referral.

10. Make a follow-up contact with the congregant to find out how the referral appointment went and if any other help is needed.

Conclusion

Rabbi Hiyya bar Abba fell ill and Rabbi Johanan went in to visit him. He [R. Johanan] said to him: "Are your sufferings welcome to you?" He replied: "Neither they nor their reward." He [R. Johanan] said to him: "Give me your hand." He gave him his hand and he [R. Johanan] raised him.

Rabbi Johanan once fell ill and Rabbi Hanina went in to visit him. He [R. Hanina] said to him: "Are your sufferings welcome to you?" He replied: "Neither they nor their reward." He said to him: "Give me your hand." He [R. Hanina] gave him his hand and he raised him. Why could not R. Johanan raise himself? They replied: "The prisoner cannot free himself from jail." (TB Berachot 5b)

The tradition is clear. When people are physically, emotionally, mentally, or spiritually ill, it is not possible for them to raise themselves on their own. Although it is incumbent upon all Jews to perform acts of loving-kindness *(gemilut chasadim)*, pastoral caregivers can make a unique contribution. With consciousness, intentionality, skill, and presence, pastoral caregivers can draw on the depth of their own inwardness and the riches of the Jewish tradition to serve better the pastoral needs of their communities.

Notes

1. Judith Plaskow, *Womanspirit Rising* (San Francisco: HarperCollins, 1992), p. vii.
2. Judith V. Jordan, et al., *Women's Growth in Connection* (New York: The Guillford Press, 1991).
3. Ibid, p. 29.
4. For example, see Thomas Gordon, *Parent Effectiveness Training* (New York: New American Library, 1970); Gerald Egan, *The Skilled Helper* (Belmont, Calif.: Wadsworth Publishing Company, 1975); Matthew McKay, Martha Davis, and Patrick Fanning, *Messages: The Communication Skills Book* (Oakland, Calif.: New Harbinger Publications, 1985); Harville Hendrix, *Getting the Love You Want* (New York: Simon & Schuster Inc., 1990).
5. McKay, *Messages,* pp. 59–60.
6. Tale attributed to Rabbi Nachman of Bratzlav.
7. Howard Goldstein, "Starting Where the Client Is," *Social Casework: The Journal of Contemporary Social Work* 64, no. 5 (May 1983).
8. Alfred Kadushin, *The Social Work Interview: A Guide for Human Services Professionals* (New York: Columbia University Press, 1990).
9. What is missing from this story is any mention about whether the prince himself is suffering, or whether it is only the father who is in distress. One must read between the lines and assume that during the many hours the wise man and prince sit together under the table, the prince communicates his distress. Otherwise, the tale could be read as promoting trickery or manipulation rather than healing.
10. Peter VanKatwyk, "The Helping Styles Inventory: A Tool in Supervised Pastoral Education," *Journal of Pastoral Care* 42, no. 4 (1988): pp. 319–28. Diagram reprinted with permission.

11. This section draws heavily on concepts from chapter 6 of Egan, *The Skilled Helper,* pp. 105–29.

12. Katherine Clarke, "Lessons from Feminist Therapy for Ministerial Ethics," *Journal of Pastoral Care* 48, no. 3 (1994): p. 240.

13. Ibid.

14. Ibid.

15. Richard Schwartz, "A Psychiatrist's View of Transference and Counter-transference in the Pastoral Relationship," *Journal of Pastoral Care* 43, no. 1 (1989): pp. 41–46.

16. Ibid., p. 42.

17. Bradley Artson, "Who Heals the Healers?" *Jewish Spectator* (winter 1999), p. 14.

18. I am indebted to Rabbi Sheila Peltz Weinberg for the insight about rabbis being the unifier of communities at this historical moment when practice is so diverse.

19. Kurt Lewin, *Resolving Social Conflict* (New York: Harper Brothers, 1948), p. 177.

20. Barbara Lichener Ingram and Dennis Lowe, "Counseling Activities and Referral Practices of Rabbis," *Journal of Psychology and Judaism* 13, no. 3 (1989).

21. Howard Clinebell, *Basic Types of Pastoral Care and Counseling* (Nashville: Abingdon Press, 1992), pp. 310–20.

22. Ibid.

Bibliography

Adler, Rachel. "A Stumbling Block Before the Blind: Sexual Exploitation in Pastoral Counseling." *CCAR Journal: A Reform Jewish Quarterly* (spring 1993): pp. 13–43.

Clinebell, Howard. *Basic Types of Pastoral Care & Counseling.* Louisville, Ky.: Westminster John Knox Press, 1992.

Lester, Andrew. *Hope in Pastoral Care and Counseling.* Kentucky: John Knowles Press, 1995.

Levine, Aaron. *To Comfort the Bereaved.* Northvale, N.J.: Jason Aronson Press, 1994.

Young-Eisendrath, Polly. *The Resilient Spirit.* Reading, Mass.: Addison-Wesley, 1998.

Barbara Eve Breitman, M.S.W., L.S.W., teaches Pastoral Counseling at the Reconstructionist Rabbinical College and Advanced Practice at the University of Pennsylvania School of Social Work. She is a psychotherapist in private practice and a spiritual director contributing to the emerging field of Jewish Spiritual Guidance as a spiritual practice.

Jewish Spiritual Assessment

Rabbi Zahara Davidowitz-Farkas

Rabbi Zahara Davidowitz-Farkas presents a compelling case for the systematic evaluation and articulation of the needs of those whom pastoral caregivers serve. She offers Midrash as a Jewish framework for understanding the assessment enterprise. Rabbi Davidowitz-Farkas analyzes existing Christian and Jewish assessment tools and gives guidance on developing a personal approach to spiritual assessment.

The Need for Spiritual Assessment

As pastoral caregivers, we often encounter people who are in acute spiritual pain from loss or trauma. Whether they are enduring illness or other kinds of suffering, those with whom we work may find that their sense of identity has been battered, bruised, and reordered by outside forces over which they have had minimal or no control. The caregivers must meet the suffering individual in that place of challenge. This work must be done with intelligence as well as with heart. We must gather clear information about the individual's concerns, perspectives, and life story. We must understand, order, and interpret that information to see patterns and relationships and to provide meaningful support. Steven Ivy points out that when we approach this task only intuitively, we may fail to examine and understand important aspects of the situation. The limits of our experience and perspective may yield a view that is "prejudicial and unexamined . . . we all experience ourselves and others through habitual categories which lead us to attend to certain behaviors, feelings, and thoughts while not attending to others."[1]

Spiritual assessment is a tool to help us develop a thorough and useful understanding of the sufferer's situation, needs, and resources. The process of spiritual assessment leads to a pastoral diagnosis and treatment plan. It helps both the caregiver and the sufferer make sense of a difficult experience and clarifies what is needed for effective caregiving, providing an entrance into the pastoral task. Spiritual assessment is a tool that helps us give full attention and respect to the Holy of Holies of those whom we serve by exploring and interpreting with them the nature of their suffering, and the spiritual resources they can use to transcend it.

External Demand for Accountability

The contemporary practice of Jewish pastoral care moves beyond traditional concepts of *bikur cholim,* which form its roots. In part, this is because today's pastoral care involves much more than visiting the sick. A pastoral caregiver's work may involve the incarcerated, the developmentally disabled, the recovering addict, the mentally ill, the alone and sick at heart, or anyone suffering a serious loss. Furthermore, the conceptualization and delivery of pastoral care has changed dramatically in the current health care environment. Institutions increasingly hire only pastoral caregivers who have extensive training and professional certification. The Joint Commission for the Accreditation of Healthcare Organizations (JCAHO) now includes spiritual care among the services institutions are mandated to offer in order to be accredited. At the same time, many of these institutions are finding themselves in deep financial distress, causing them to scrutinize budgets and to cut services viewed as ineffective or nonessential. The combination of these pressures has caused institutions to demand unprecedented accountability of pastoral caregivers.

Evolution of Pastoral Care

Today's pastoral care is the product of an evolutionary process. Through the early twentieth century, the caregiver essentially set the agenda, which was to offer the sufferer hope, to pray, and to ensure the sufferer that "God will take care of you." After the mid-twentieth century, a new, psychological model has recently been adopted: The caregiver set no agenda, but rather "mirrored" the sufferer, reflecting what the caregiver was hearing.[2] There was no interpretation or imposition of self on the part of the chaplain. This reduced the pastoral caregiver to little more than a friendly visitor or an unlicensed therapist. Even worse, the language and metaphors for understanding the human experience of suffering and how to approach it were now couched in psychological terms rather than in religious and spiritual ones. Paul Pruyser's landmark 1976 book, *Minister as Diagnostician,* called pastoral caregivers to task for abandoning the language of faith.[3]

Pastoral caregiving has continued to mature since Pruyser's clarion call. Rather than trying to impose hope on another, we now strive to help individuals find their own hopefulness—or to be with them when they believe there is none. The "ministry of presence," the comfort that can be given by simply "being with" the sufferer, is still the cornerstone of pastoral care. However, we now appreciate that we must be actively therapeutic rather than passively assuming. We cannot be with people if we do not know where they are; we cannot know unless we ask. Spiritual assessment is part of the way in which we ask.

Growing Desire for Professionalization

All of this attention to spiritual care has sometimes been uncomfortable for Jewish pastoral caregivers. It has put the nature and quality of our work into a new and sometimes unwanted spotlight. It has shown our strengths as well as our weaknesses. We have discovered that it is no longer enough for us to simply make a friendly visit, offer good wishes, and make a quick *mishebarach*. Not only are institutions demanding more accountability, but so are the communities whom we serve. They want to know that we are willing and able to respond in ways that make a demonstrable difference.

Jewish pastoral caregivers are responding to the challenge. In the past ten years, the National Association of Jewish Chaplains has developed standards for certification of professional Jewish chaplains. Increasing numbers of seminary students are pursuing clinical pastoral training. Jewish pastoral caregivers aspire to be professional, effective, and responsive. Where appropriate, we want to integrate into the healing team and to know that we are competent and worthy of the responsibility we carry. This attention to the professionalization of pastoral care has fostered exciting growth and creativity in the field. The birth of spiritual assessment as a serious tool for care and treatment is one such example.

What Is Spiritual Assessment?

As Fitchett and Handzo state in *Psycho-oncology*, spiritual assessment "is the process of discerning the spiritual needs and resources of persons in various contexts where spiritual care is offered."[4] It offers caregivers a way to organize and to understand their observations about a person's spiritual life and helps them keep track while they listen. "A caregiver's spiritual assessment is their summary of key issues in the patient's spiritual needs and resources, formulated according to a specific model, often after an open-ended or semistructured conversation."[5]

Making Midrash: A Jewish Framework for Spiritual Assessment

As *Jewish* pastoral caregivers, we are committed to understanding the pastoral work we do as a Jewish spiritual enterprise. We need to know: how does Judaism challenge us to this endeavor? What makes it holy? What is our responsibility as caretakers of a human soul in partnership with God?

The Jewish tradition offers us a wonderful way to conceptualize the holiness of our task of assessment. However, during the Temple period, our people communicated with God through sacrifice. With the Temple's destruction in 70 C.E., however, this was no longer possible. Instead, prayer, text study, and the performance of deeds of loving-kindness served to maintain the relationship between the community of Jews and God. Midrash was one of the forms that this text study took. It may also be understood as an archetype for the work of spiritual assessment.

The word *midrash* comes from the Hebrew root *drs*, which means "to investigate," or "to search out." Midrash is the process of delving deeply into a text in order to plumb its many possibilities of meaning. We question our received texts; we wrestle with them, try to understand them and, by extension, ourselves. These texts invite relationship. They urge us to revel in their language and their meanings. They challenge us to uncover their depth and sacredness even as they insist that they are grounded in the everyday.

We presume that the text we study is at least partly hidden; and we are told to "turn it and turn it again" in our efforts to understand it.[6] Although Midrashic reading is creative and careful, parts of the text inevitably remain inaccessible. There will always be more to learn and to understand. The same text may elicit different perceptions and explanations in individual readers, based on the perspective of their own experience.

Every text can be read simultaneously on several levels. It can be studied for its literal, straightforward meaning or with the hope of discovering its hidden, implied, or mystical meanings. These many meanings are not mutually exclusive but coexist, enriching both the text and our understanding of it.

We are, each of us, a *living* text being written with our every breath and relationship. We are created in the image of God, thus the text of our being is, by definition, sacred. As text, our lives, stories, beliefs, dreams, hopes, and fears are open to the various understandings that are gleaned from respectful investigation.

"A single [person] was created to show the greatness of God, for a [person] stamps many coins from a single die, and they are all alike, but the Ruler of Rulers has stamped every [person] with the die of Adam, and yet not one of them is like his [or her] fellow [human being]."[7] It is the task of the pastoral caregiver to try to understand each unique human text as deeply as possible in its own right. We must study it well, turn it, and turn it again as we pursue its mysteries. We must also remember that we each bring our own idiosyncratic text to the process of study. The interaction between our text and the texts of those for whom we care is the fertile ground for the work of pastoral care. Spiritual assessment provides a means of understanding the sacred human text.

Functions of Spiritual Assessment

Understanding the Problem

To understand an individual requires more information than can be gleaned by simply intuiting the feelings of the moment. Just as physicians must first perform a physical examination before they can offer a diagnosis, so must caregivers of the soul conduct a spiritual review. Spiritual assessment provides a way for caregivers to organize their observations about the spiritual behaviors, beliefs, and relationships of the people whom they are striving to help. It offers a structure for understanding the intricacy of each person and helps prevent critical facets from being lost along the way. Furthermore, it helps caregivers make use of the wealth of our tradition and helps them focus on the spiritual nature of our task.

The process of spiritual assessment can often be therapeutic in and of itself. It can help a person clarify his or her spiritual response to a difficult situation and may facilitate immediately helpful understandings. Spiritual assessment may prompt people to connect to a spiritual practice that has been helpful in the past, or help them to see a gap between what they say they believe and what they actually believe.

> Hannah, an observant Jewish woman, professed faithfully that *HaShem* is just and merciful. Simultaneously, she desperately sought to find meaning in her painful struggle with end-stage cancer. The only possible justification she could think of was that she was being punished because she had failed to save two of her children from predeceasing her. In her heart, she rejected this answer. She was torn between her loyalty to God and the pain and loneliness of her terminal illness.
>
> Hannah felt betrayed and abandoned. This rift in a primary sphere of her life compromised her relationships with her family and caregivers and her own ability to find peace in her suffering. Her spiritual and emotional pain caused her to despair, which led to a wish to end her life. The task of the pastoral caregiver was precisely in this place of vulnerability and reckoning.
>
> The pastoral caregiver reached out to Hannah by bringing her a text from the tradition she so passionately embraced. Hannah found ease in a powerful confrontation with a text from the Talmudic tractate, Sanhedrin: "The human being was created as a single individual to teach us that anyone who destroys a single life is as though he destroyed an entire world; and anyone who preserves a single life is as though he preserved an entire world."[8] She came to realize that nowhere was it written that the life she saved could not be her own, and that in saving her own she could preserve the memory of her children. At the suggestion of the pastoral caregiver, Hannah recorded her love and her recollections on tape. She gave a tape of her reflections to her surviving daughter and her two grandsons.

Forging a Covenant Between
Caregiver and Sufferer

Spiritual care is not achieved in a vacuum. It is a joint enterprise between sufferer and sustainer. Assessment should allow both the caregiver and the one being counseled to develop a common language for the understanding of issues, the evolution of a pastoral plan, and the work of care itself. First, both the sufferer and the caregiver must agree that there is a problem: They need a mutual understanding about the nature of the problem and its implications. There should be a covenantal agreement between the individual and the caregiver, so that the pastoral plan is a mutual one in which each understands his or her role in the process and their mutual expectations. The language of the assessment tool can articulate the covenant of care established between the caregiver and the person being helped. It provides a metaphor for discernment and a basis for evaluation.

Self-Monitoring for the Caregiver

We spiritual sustainers are also sufferers. Therefore, it is important that we have a vehicle to guide us in monitoring our own reactions to the challenges we are confronting. The spiritual assessment tool helps us overcome our blind spots. It provides a means of self-supervision and the assessment of transference and countertransference. For example, if a pastoral caregiver had a positive relationship with a parent for whom she cared, she might assume that the daughter of a stroke patient is feeling sad because her mother can no longer speak to her. Perhaps she would learn through a spiritual assessment tool that the daughter is wracked by guilt and fears divine punishment because she and her mother had an argument right before her stroke. Self-conscious, deliberate, and intentional spiritual assessment provides caregivers with a way to guard against projecting our own assumptions, needs, and beliefs onto the person in our care.

The Content of Assessment

A spiritual assessment is a way to help individuals examine the meaning they are making of their experiences.[9] In doing a spiritual assessment, it is important to ask "What do you believe, practice, or both?"

and "How does this belief or practice help you cope with this problem?" The first of these questions addresses the *substance* or content of a person's belief and practice, whereas the second investigates the *function* of the person's belief and practice. This second approach looks at how a person finds meaning in his or her life. Different systems of spiritual assessment emphasize one or the other of these aspects of spirituality; both are important.

Using Spiritual Assessment to Guide Intervention

There is no one "right way" to do an assessment. It is a subjective process guided by intuition as well as intellect. There is no particular set of questions to pose; rather, there are general content areas that should be addressed. It is up to the caregiver to determine in the context of the relationship which topics to address, in what order, and at what depth. The choice and phrasing of questions and the interpretations that are generated depend on the overall nature of the growing relationship and the context of the encounter.

The details of *what* is being asked are less important than that caregivers have a general methodology to help them organize and understand what they hear, and a way to communicate this to the individuals with whom they are working. The best way to do an assessment is the way that feels most comfortable and authentic for the caregiver.

Relationship Between Identified Problems and Beliefs and Practices

The pastoral caregiver must analyze the relationship between the problem and the beliefs, values, and practices discovered in the assessment. He or she will consider whether they help or hinder the process of coping and healing.[10] Most important, the spiritual assessment should yield a plan for caring for the individual.

> Steven had suddenly become seriously depressed. His depression progressed swiftly into debilitating despair whereas before this occurred, he had felt blessed—happily married, the father of two young, healthy children, and content with his job. Fearing for his life, he admitted himself into a psychiatric hospital. He was

treated with electroshock therapy, which he believed was helping. In that year, 1986, Steven had just celebrated his thirty-seventh birthday. His depression made no sense to him.

In every assessment, it is important to investigate: Why is this happening to this person at this time? Steven considered himself a committed, albeit somewhat assimilated, Jew. He belonged to a congregation, spent free time on *tzedakah* projects, and sent his children to Hebrew school. He believed he was doing all the right things, but he could not shake an almost-subconscious belief that "it was not nearly enough."

> As the conversation between Steven and the caregiver deepened, he began to "connect the dots" of his life. As his pastoral caregiver probed Steven's life and family situation, Steven realized that his mother had been thirty-seven when she was deported to Auschwitz. Suddenly, it all made sense. Nothing he could possibly do would ever make up for his mother's suffering at the hands of the Nazis. Unknowingly, he had connected his thirty-seventh birthday with the beginning of his mother's slide into hell. Buried inside him was a flood of grief and mourning begging to be let out.
>
> With Steven's permission, the pastoral caregiver shared this new insight with his doctors; it became new material for his therapy sessions. Again with Steven's permission, the caregiver invited his congregational rabbi into the healing process. Together, they created a ritual which confronted the grief and, finally, offered release and renewal. First, Steven wrote a *Viddui* (confessional) for his mother, which he recited and then buried in a Jewish cemetery. He created a *Yizkor* (memorial) prayer in memory of his mother, which he offered after lighting a *yahrzeit* (memorial) candle. Steven now needed to heal his sadness with his blessings. He planted trees in Israel for his children and was called to the Torah for a special *aliyah* in his synagogue.

A pastoral caregiver may have understood and approached Steven's situation in any number of ways. Why did Steven's caregiver make certain decisions and not others? Since the caregiver listened to Steven's story with a focus on his spiritual needs and resources, she was able to avoid directing her efforts toward extraneous issues. For example, Steven's primary concerns did not appear to center around feelings of loneliness. Similarly, he did not appear to mistrust God's intentions and he was not despairing over the strength of his faith. Additionally, Steven did not present himself as disturbed over some deeply hidden sin or shame.

Based on her assessment of Steven and his narrative, the caregiver determined that his central concerns related to issues of meaning. Steven's current experiences did not fit into his understanding of the world or his place within it. Because he could not identify any purpose in his suffering, he was not able to approach it with any sense of hope. The pastoral caregiver helped him to discover meaning in this specific experience, and then guided him to integrate it into his global understanding of life and its purpose. The caregiver did not intend to help Steven find a reason for his suffering but, rather, hoped to help him find meaning within his suffering.

This assessment and evaluation resulted in the creation of a multi-layered intervention intended to help Steven find meaning in his experience. The caregiver's immediate concern dealt with finding a locus of meaning. Once this was accomplished to their mutual satisfaction, it became necessary to re-evaluate in order to create a further plan focusing on integration.

Understanding Steven's crisis, the caregiver was able to help Steven to mobilize his considerable spiritual resources. Steven's commitment to Judaism and his appreciation of its rituals and practices provided opportunities to support, enrich, and ultimately heal. His writing of a *Viddui,* his creation of a *yizkor* prayer, his lighting of a *yahrzeit* candle, his *aliyah* in his synagogue, and his planting of trees in Israel all resulted from Steven's search with his caregiver to find Jewish ways to address both his grief and his hope.

The caregiver's pastoral interventions also drew upon the support system Steven had in place. With Steven's permission, the caregiver turned to his family, his rabbi, and his psychiatrist and thus enlarged the healing opportunities available to him. This also assured that Steven would have compassionate spiritual, emotional, and physical support well past his discharge from the hospital.

Steven had come into the psychiatric facility with only the barest facts of his narrative available to him. Spiritual assessment allowed for the unfolding of the many layers of his story. The expression of his life and his beliefs, his values and experiences were studied as holy text, created in God's image. This shared reflection led to a mutual understanding of Steven's spiritual suffering and a pastoral plan to help alleviate it.

Developing a Care Plan

Spiritual assessment gives us the information we need to determine a plan of care. This plan includes goals and the means to reach them. At times, a spiritual assessment may produce a plan that involves silent presence as a core element of responding to an individual.

> Brian was a ten-year-old boy on life support. His chances of recovery were slim and deteriorated over time. A deep relationship developed between the pastoral caregiver and the parents, especially Brian's mother, who rarely left Brian's side. Much of their time together was spent quietly, as the caregiver held Brian's hand, his mother's, or both. No language was capable of describing the unfolding tragedy.

This case illustrates the importance of silence and presence. In this case, silence is a means of offering support and solace to Brian and his mother as he is dying. However, on occasion silence is used because caregivers are so preoccupied with their own unease that they are at a loss in what to say or do. Like any pastoral intervention, silence should be chosen consciously from among many possible responses.

This caregiver assessed that trust built through consistency of presence would provide the acceptance and safety necessary to help this mother through her unspeakable grief. The caregiver's pastoral style, personal and professional experience, comfort, and intuition generated this particular response over another. Another caregiver might have chosen to focus pastoral intervention on concrete tasks, on prayer, or on issues of faith. Regardless of the approach chosen, any pastoral intervention must be evaluated frequently to determine its appropriateness in the moment. Caregivers must be flexible enough to learn from this process and change their approach as necessary.

Silence and presence are some of the tools available to the pastoral caregiver. On the other hand, some spiritual assessments will yield a treatment plan that includes very concrete action.

> Rena, a young mother of a one-year-old child, was diagnosed with inoperable brain cancer. All her hopes and dreams were dashed.

She was devastated that she would not see her daughter grow up and would not be able to instill in her a love for Judaism. Rena did not want her child's only Jewish connection to her to be the *Kaddish* she would say as an adult. How could she pass on her own joy in Judaism along with the inevitable sadness? What in the tradition could she give to her child?

In order to help her, the pastoral caregiver first needed to understand the state of Rena's physical, emotional, intellectual, and spiritual health. Was Rena in great pain? How much time did she believe she had left? Was her thinking clear? Was she angry, bitter, full of regrets, despairing, hopeful, loving, grateful, or sad? What did she believe about her illness? How did she conceive of God's relationship to her and her illness? Did she have a history of growth through adversity? Who did she care about the most? In the inevitable narrowing of her world, what mattered most to her?

The pastoral caregiver found that Rena was fundamentally an optimistic person. Although she was deeply saddened by her situation, and acutely aware of her losses, Rena was still able to care and to love. She believed she had several months of functional time left. Her anger and regrets were appropriate to her situation and did not dominate her behavior. Rena loved her husband and daughter. She knew that her daughter would not remember her, so she chose to create memories for her daughter. Although Rena did not understand God's "plan" for her, and though she could find little meaning in her illness, she continued to love Judaism and wanted to impart its richness to her one-year-old.

The pastoral caregiver wove these insights into a fabric of care, which enabled Rena to devise several ways to pass her dreams on to her daughter. The caregiver's encounters with Rena gave her a safe place to grieve, as well as an opportunity to constructively reframe her loss. Rena experienced multiple losses in knowing that she would not have an opportunity to contribute to her child's psychological, emotional, intellectual, or spiritual growth. Rena chose to leave a tangible legacy in several ways, as one single approach could not address her many distinct losses.

With the help of her pastoral caregiver, Rena created an ethical will that expressed her faith in the world's goodness and her hopes and dreams for her daughter's life. She placed her sadness and experience of illness in the broader context of her life so that her daughter would know that her illness had not defined her.

Having cared for her daughter emotionally and intellectually through an ethical will, Rena then turned to her concerns about her daughter's spiritual well-being. Rena made a prayer book for her daughter, containing her favorite prayers and spiritual readings.

Last, to nurture her daughter physically, Rena decided to record six family recipes that had been passed down from mother to daughter through the generations. She had her husband promise to teach their daughter how to make the recipes when she was old enough.

The shared process of spiritual assessment gave Rena the opportunity to discover what tasks really mattered to her. As Viktor Frankl teaches, "Every human being has to have a task. If he can find his song, or his task—it doesn't matter what it is but it has to be his own—he can keep his dignity with a sense of hope and can transcend even the most desperate circumstances."[11] The plan of care developed by Rena with her pastoral caregiver also gave her the chance to use her new knowledge in meaningful and productive ways that might later be sustaining for her daughter. In finding her own song, Rena found her hope.

Models of Spiritual Assessment

Although scarce, some useful models for the gathering of information and the understanding of spiritual pain, disassociation, and injury do exist.

Paul Pruyser:
Seven Aspects of Religious Life

Paul Pruyser, a psychologist frustrated by clergy's reliance on psychological frameworks, articulated a way to describe an individual's religious state of being in his book, *The Minister as Diagnostician*.[12] In the absence of other available tools, his model became accepted practice; subsequent assessment models were patterned after his work.

Pruyser suggests seven areas to examine to understand a person's religious life. They include awareness of the holy, providence, faith, grace or gratefulness, repentance, communion, and sense of vocation.[13] In Pruyser's diagnostic tool, the spiritual caregiver poses questions and seeks to tease out several main themes. All of the questions investigate the person's capacity or inclination to cope with his or her situation, and also explore how the person will enter into relationship with the caregiver.

Pruyser's model of spiritual assessment speaks from a Christian perspective. The tone and language used, as well as the items he chooses to appraise, may feel foreign to a Jewish ear. Even so, there is much to learn from it. The assessment of explicit value and belief concepts and the determination to rely on more than ritual observance to help individuals find inner religious and spiritual resources are invaluable teachings. Also key is appreciation of the open-ended nature of the conversation that such an assessment can elicit. It leaves a great deal of room for caregivers to pose questions and responses in ways idiosyncratic to them, and thus that are comfortable for them and their own approach and style.

George Fitchett: 7 × 7 Model

Since Pruyser, others have produced different models for the assessment of an individual's spiritual experience. Many are meant to be appropriate for persons of various faith traditions. One such framework for spiritual assessment is the 7 × 7 model developed by George Fitchett. His widely used model presents a multidimensional approach to the process and is "concerned with how a person finds meaning and purpose in life and with the behaviors, emotions, relationships, and practices associated with that meaning and purpose."[14] Fitchett emphasizes the need to place the current crisis in the context of a person's entire life experience. Our physical, emotional, intellectual, and spiritual lives are interrelated, thus we must not ignore any one of them if we are to understand the meaning that individuals derive from their experiences. In Fitchett's model, a person's spiritual dimension is the seventh dimension considered in a holistic framework.[15] This dimension explores issues such as belief and meaning, vocation and obligation, courage and growth, ritual and practice, community, authority, and guidance.

Gregory A. Stoddard: Spiritual Triage

Gregory A. Stoddard has approached the question of spiritual screening and triage with his explication of levels of spiritual need. His instrument is intended to screen patients to determine which individuals are in need of spiritual care intervention. Since a pastoral caregiver is not always present or available, Stoddard's instrument is designed to be administered by direct care staff. Staff members can use the results of this assessment in deciding whether referral for pastoral care is indicated.

Spiritual Triage: Stoddard Referral Model[16]

No Spiritual Concerns

- No spiritual content expressed by patient or family regarding hospital stay

Spiritual Concerns: Mild

- Anxiety
- Concerns with God
- Anticipatory grieving
- Questions of meaning

Spiritual Distress: Marked

- Conflicting beliefs
- Searching for alternative beliefs
- Struggling to find meaning in life or death
- Seeking spiritual aid
- Disturbed God concept
- Ethical dilemma
- Moderate/severe anxiety
- Disturbed sleep
- Grieving

Spiritual Despair: Marked

- Social withdrawal
- Loss of affect
- Loss of belief
- Loss of hope
- Loss of meaning

- Severe depression
- Death wish

Davidowitz and Handzo

In the essay "Using Religious Resources in Clinical Ministry," David-owitz and Handzo identify areas that may be helpful for caregivers and those they care for to explore in partnership.[17] Davidowitz and Handzo suggest that caregivers and those in their care explore the following in the process of spiritual assessment:

- Meaning
- God
- Self in relationship to God
- Hope
- Religious praxis
- Community
- Authority

Spiritual Assessment Models from a Jewish Perspective

Jewish spiritual assessment entails a shared exploration of an individual's life—its structure, meaning, purpose, direction, challenges, and blessings—through the values, vocabulary, norms, and resources of Jewish tradition and community.[18]

The development of a body of tools for the formal spiritual assessment of Jews, either healthy or in crisis, has only recently begun. Jewish tradition affords some obvious ways to think about the categories a spiritual caregiver might use for assessment. God, Torah, and Israel provide thematic possibilities, as do Torah, *avodah* (prayer), and *gemilut chasadim* (deeds of loving-kindness).

Simkha Y. Weintraub: Descriptives of State of Spirit[19]

Rabbi Simkha Y. Weintraub created the "Intake Form: Jewish Spiritual Counseling" for his work with the New York Jewish Healing Center.[20] The form was developed for use in spiritual *counseling*, which may differ from pastoral *care*. It is a serious attempt to create an "operating Jewish spiritual profile" that can be used to diagnose differentially, determine an immediate Jewish spiritual response, set an agenda for care, and create and sustain an ongoing intervention.[21] Along with questions about observance and affiliation, Rabbi Weintraub asks individuals to reflect on their spiritual well-being. He invites them to indicate which descriptions accurately depict their "state-of-spirit."

Both the English categories and their Hebrew counterparts make this inventory powerful and helpful. Simply encountering the list may help people know they are not "crazy" and that their experience, indeed, can be named. The following are examples of states-of-spirit included:

> Vulnerable *(pagi'a)* and exposed *(meguleh, 'arom)*
> Strengthened *(hit'azer oz)* and shielded *(hugan)*
> Overwhelmed *(ayum)* and compressed *(dachus)*
> Awestruck *(maleh yir'at kavod)* and expansive *(rechav)*
> Withdrawn *(nesigah)* and imploding *(parotz penimah)*
> Exploring *(choker)* and overflowing *(shif'a, revayah)*
> Alienated *('ituk, harchakah)* and aberrant *(galuz, soteh)*
> Familiar *(mukar)* and normal *(bari b'ruach)*

Shulevitz and Springer: Assessment of Religious Experience

Rabbis Marion Shulevitz and Mychal Springer created the "Assessment of Religious Experience: A Jewish Approach" in response to the overwhelming Christian idiom of their clinical training model.[22] Although it was created for use with pastoral education students, it has a place as a more general tool for the assessment of Jewish experience. The topics covered in this instrument are included here.

God in the World[23]

Experiencing God
Approaching God

- *Tefilah* (prayer)
- Torah (study)
- *Ma'asim* (deeds)
- Sin, Justice, and Mercy
- Living in Community

This model enriches the whole assessment enterprise with deeply Jewish language, thought, and essence, using Max Kadushin's exposition of traditional rabbinic value concepts as its spiritual and religious assumptive base.[24] It implies a certain way of being Jewish within which there is room for movement. This model also presents a question: How can this assessment tool be used with an individual whose stance is not traditional and whose theological center revolves around personal autonomy and informed choice?

Bonita Taylor: Identifying Laments

The early beginnings of another model of spiritual assessment may be found in the clinical pastoral education work of Rabbi Bonita Taylor. Using the Book of Lamentations as illustration, she works with her Jewish students to help them identify the lament in what their patients are saying. She challenges them to uncover the depths of spiritual injury in what might otherwise be perceived or experienced merely as a complaint, sigh, or *"kvetch."*[25]

Evaluating Models of Spiritual Assessment

Any model of spiritual assessment should be evaluated on the basis of questions such as these: Is the model flexible? Is it easy to use and to interpret, and does it provide insight for the development of a pastoral plan? Can it adapt to new information and the growth of the pastoral relationship? Does it provide for a wide range of beliefs and practices, or does it presuppose a right and a wrong? Does it offer room for the so-called unaffiliated or the non-believer to wrestle with spiritual concerns? What are the assumptions inherent in the instrument? What is its underlying theology and conception of spirituality? Are they fixed or do they allow for inquiry and change?[26] With these guidelines as a base, caregivers can use one of the spiritual assessment models already developed, or choose to create one of their own.

Challenges to Integrating Spiritual Assessment into Our Professional Approach

The notion of spiritual assessment is a difficult one for caregivers. The two terms, *spiritual* and *assessment*, feel mutually exclusive; they elicit cognitive dissonance. We consider our pastoral task to be largely intuitive: How can work that is so subjective be consigned to detached analysis? Caregivers rebel against the idea of quantifying a person's inner being, and recoil at the image of doing pastoral care while performing research with clipboards, impartially and impersonally intruding to measure responses to a specific set of questions on our own agenda. The gathering of such intimate information raises concerns about confidentiality. We worry as well about spending more time recording what we learn than in being present to those we serve.

An additional challenge is how to assess spiritual needs and resources if a person's belief system or observance is very different than our own. As Fitchett and Handzo[27] point out, we tend to think of religious traditions as being either right or wrong, with what is right being what we ourselves believe. Some religious adherents not only maintain that those who believe otherwise are wrong, but that their God will punish others' faithlessness. This intolerance puts caregivers in a precarious position, for even if we are not as absolute in our beliefs, difference can be provocative. How can we affirm another's faith without implying that our own is wrong? Caregivers need to take the posture that both can be right.[28] To be truly open to another, we must adopt the attitude that each person has a right to his or her own belief and that it is possible to affirm that belief while not doubting one's own.

Conclusion

Spiritual assessment does not mandate any one way of ordering the perceptions and observations of caregivers or of those whom we are striving to aid. A spiritual assessment tool is meant to be just that—a tool. The models presented in this chapter are some of the very few that have been actually published. The specifics of the assessment tool are less important than the fact that it exists. It is crucial that there be a formal method for the organization of observations, which can then lead to a diagnosis and the development of an agreed-on pastoral care plan. Effectively performed pastoral care is a creative art form, not a set of techniques blindly followed. Assessment is intended neither to constrain caregivers, nor to shackle their inventiveness or elegance of style.

Caregivers are often fearful that they will be required to document intimate spiritual details in the lives of those they are serving. This is not the case. An assessment is meant to inform and to aid those directly involved in the pastoral relationship; it is not meant for general consumption. The instrument is intended to be a familiar, open-ended companion and guide, not a checklist of questions to torment the sufferer. If it hinders the establishment of pastoral relationships or limits self-revelation on the part of the one cared for, something is amiss. Spiritual assessment should open the potential for relationship, not shut it down.

Before he died, Rabbi Zusya said, "In the world to come they will not ask me, 'Why were you not Moses?' they will ask me, 'Why were you not Zusya?'" Pastoral caregivers are devoted to the human spirit, and we strive to support those who are trying to make sense of the world in difficult circumstances. We should remember that we must not attempt to make them over in our own image or to ask them to be other than they are: It is significant enough that they have been created in the image of God. Rather, through our shaping of a holy relationship, we move both them and ourselves to an encounter with that which is at the heart of meaning. We are each moved to discover our own Zusya.

Notes

1. Steven S. Ivy, "Pastoral Diagnosis as Pastoral Caring," *The Journal of Pastoral Care* 42, no. 1 (spring 1988), p. 81.

2. George Handzo, personal communication.

3. Paul Pruyser, *The Minister as Diagnostician* (Philadelphia: Westminster Press, 1976).

4. George Fitchett and George Handzo, "Spiritual Assessment, Screening, and Intervention," in *Psycho-oncology*, ed. Jimmie C. Holland (New York: Oxford University Press, 1998), pp. 790–808.

5. Fitchett and Handzo, *Psycho-oncology*, p. 791.

6. Pirke Avot 5:22.

7. Mishna, Tractate Sanhedrin 4:5.

8. Ibid.

9. For research on the impact of meaning-making on coping, see Susan Folkman and Crystal L. Park, "Meaning in the Context of Stress and Coping," *Review of General Psychiatry* 1, no. 2 (1997): pp. 115–44.

10. Gary Ahlskog and Harry Sands, *The Guide to Pastoral Care and Counseling* (Madison, Conn.: Psychosocial Press, 2000), p. 339.

11. Quoted in Pesach Krauss and Morrie Goldfischer, *Why Me? Coping with Grief, Loss, and Change* (New York: Bantam Books, 1988), p. 73.

12. Pruyser, *Minister*.

13. Ibid.
14. Fitchett and Handzo, *Psycho-oncology*, p. 793.
15. Fitchett and Handzo, *Psycho-oncology*, p. 796.
16. Fitchett and Handzo, *Psycho-oncology*, p. 801.
17. Ahlskog and Sands, *Guide*, pp. 323–59.
18. Simkha Y. Weintraub (from unpublished presentation to the National Association of Jewish Chaplains Conference, February 2000).
19. Ibid.
20. Ibid.
21. Ibid.
22. Marion Shulevitz and Mychal Springer, "Assessment of Religious Experience: A Jewish Approach," *The Journal of Pastoral Care* 48, no. 4 (winter 1994).
23. Ibid., pp. 399–400.
24. Ibid., p. 402.
25. Bonita E. Taylor, personal communication.
26. Fitchett and Handzo, *Psycho-oncology*, p. 797.
27. Fitchett and Handzo, *Psycho-oncology*, p. 802.
28. Ibid.

Bibliography

Ahlskog, Gary, and Harry Sands. *The Guide to Pastoral Counseling and Care*. Madison, Conn.: Psychosocial Press, 2000.

Fitchett, George. *Assessing Spiritual Needs: A Guide for Caregivers*. Minneapolis: Augsburg, 1993.

Pruyser, Paul. *The Minister as Diagnostician*. Philadelphia: Westminster Press, 1976.

Shulevitz, Marion, and Mychal Springer. "Assessment of Religious Experience: A Jewish Approach." *The Journal of Pastoral Care* 48, no. 4 (winter 1994), pp. 399–406.

Rabbi Zahara Davidowitz-Farkas, M.A.T., is the Director of the Jack D. Weiler Chaplaincy of the New York Board of Rabbis and a staff member of The Jewish Institute of Pastoral Care of the HealthCare Chaplaincy. She previously served as Dean of Hebrew Union College–Jewish Institute of Religion in New York, and as Coordinator of Jewish Chaplaincy at the New York Hospital–Cornell Medical Center under the auspices of the HealthCare Chaplaincy.

Prayer and Presence

Anne Brener

Anne Brener explores one of the central spiritual tools of the Jewish pastoral caregiver. She analyzes the impact of prayer in pastoral care and its healing power. Brener offers a caregiver's toolbox of specific prayers and rituals from Jewish tradition, investigating their meaning and outlining practical methods for using them most effectively. She also examines the use of prayer to support pastoral caregivers in remaining whole in the face of their sometimes wrenching work.

One who visits a suffering person and does not pray for that person has not fulfilled the obligation of bikur cholim *[visiting the sick].*

—Isserles on Shulchan Aruch Yoreh Deah 335:4

Pastoral care is a different modality than counseling, psychotherapy, or advice from other professionals or friends because of its acknowledged spiritual component. It is to the essence of this distinct mission that this chapter is addressed. That essence is most purely represented through prayer.

Prayer is conversation. It uncovers the authentic inner conversation of the self and places it in dialogue with the timeless, universal conversation of the infinite. This connection can promote healing whether physical cure or the resolution of a painful situation is possible or not. According to Halacha, prayer is an essential component of any pastoral visit. A Jew is obligated not only to visit the suffering but to pray for them. Visits must be timed so that those who visit will be moved to pray on behalf of those who are suffering. So essential is prayer to pastoral care that visiting is permitted neither in the early hours of the morning when the ill person might be feeling better, leading the visitor to feel prayer is unnecessary, nor in the late evening, when the ill person might appear so sick that the visitor would give up hope that prayer could help.[1] These guidelines for prayer ground pastoral prayer in tradition and affirm its importance as a component in pastoral care situations.

Prayer can be used by pastoral caregivers to cut through what is superfluous and to address the essential concerns of those whom they seek to help. Whether in the words of traditional liturgy, through spontaneous outbursts of emotion, or in silence, prayer can be used to harness pained voices, to clarify direction, to affirm values, and to enable connection with the Holy. Despite obstacles, prayer can be a primary source of comfort to those who suffer. Through prayer, they can find the strength to make peace with a universe in which *hatov* (the good) and *hara* (the bad) often seem meted out in an arbitrary manner.

What Is Prayer?

If, as Rabbi Abraham Joshua Heschel asserts, Shabbat creates a cathedral in time, prayer creates a cathedral in soul.[2] No matter what mode is chosen for prayer, it can build word by word, and breath by breath the Place of connection between those who suffer and the Source of Healing. Appropriately, *HaMakom*, which literally translates as The Place, is the name of God invoked on behalf of those facing life challenges.[3]

The Holy Place of prayer is built by reaching in and by reaching out. Those engaged in prayer descend into the deepest part of the self, then reach deeper, daring to confront their most troubling feelings. From that Place, they reach out to the holy and mysterious Source of Healing.

Obstacles to Prayer

The two great obstacles to using prayer to construct a Holy Place in which God can dwell are none other than God and prayer. During a time of turmoil, God's availability and prayer's usefulness frequently appear obscured. Many people, particularly those who are suffering, are uncomfortable with any mention of God or prayer.

> Annie was unprepared to rely on spiritual sources of healing. Her cancer had metastasized, and her prognosis for physical healing was poor. At the suggestion of the nurse who had attended her

during one of her late-night moments of despair, Annie spoke to the chaplain assigned to the hospital's cancer unit. Although uncomfortable about seeking pastoral help, Annie confided her fear and lack of faith. She told him that she had been a so-called red-diaper baby. Annie's socialist parents had had complete faith—in the Communist Party. When they became disenchanted with the Soviet Union, they turned their concerns to progressive political organizations. They were professional union organizers who claimed to be atheists, and they considered people who turned to God in prayer during times of hardship as naive fools.

So many doubts come before the pastoral caregiver. So many people are uncomfortable with the word *God*, which evokes in them rigid childhood concepts that may not have matured with them. Although they may feel a connection to something greater than themselves that they can tap into as they work toward healing, they may remain uncomfortable calling it God. The need to pray is stifled by the limited concept of God that has been given to them. Prayer may feel nothing short of impossible.

Prayer can be intimidating to the caregiver as well. The pastoral caregiver may feel self-conscious about encouraging a person to reach from the depth of need, to bare the self to the universe, and to wait for an answer. The caregiver may be humbled when help is sought at moments of great difficulty and may feel it audacious to speak words of faith. The caregiver may fear that the offer of prayer will be rejected or seem ridiculous. The caregiver may not know what to pray for in the face of a seemingly hopeless situation.

However, caregiver and sufferer can be reassured in remembering that prayer is contingent neither on receiving an answer nor on faith that an answer will come. It does not even require a clear picture of what the answer to a prayer may look like; acknowledging a need and reaching out are enough. Prayer exists in the struggle to burst open the self and to enter a larger world that holds more possibility than the world from which healing is sought, but it is not the responsibility of the caregiver to make that transition happen. The caregiver might want to reassure the suffering person that there may be outcomes that he or she cannot imagine at this time, but it would be a mistake for the pastoral caregiver to try to convince someone of God's caring or the efficacy of prayer.

Know Before Whom You Stand

Some people come to challenging times with well-constructed dwelling places of soul to fall back on. They have been sustained by faith, prayer, and spiritual connection in the past and can draw on the foundation that those experiences have built for them. These people can derive comfort from traditional liturgy and are likely to be receptive to healing services and to respond to the use of known blessings and prayers. The pastoral caregiver can comfortably share with them familiar modes and words of prayer.

Other people may find that the spiritual tools that have worked for them in the past are insufficient for new challenges. Pastoral caregivers must assist them in transforming their shattered structures of belief into grander constructions capable of holding more complex understandings of existential questions.

However, those beset by trying times have often built few spiritual structures. They may have had limited or dissatisfying experiences with prayer. They need help in building, from the ground up, spiritual structures strong enough to contain the unfolding of their current spiritual healing. This task is particularly daunting for pastoral caregivers as they struggle to speak words of faith to those for whom such words are a foreign language. The art, for the pastoral caregiver, lies in knowing when to speak God's name and when to let God's name remain silent.

> "Get outta here, Rabbi," Sam said, ranting from his hospital bed. "Keep your prayers to yourself. I don't want any part of you and your God." Sam was speaking to his long-time rabbi from the bed where he lay with a shattered pelvis and two broken legs following the car accident that took the life of his wife.[4]

> Ms. S., a divorced mother of a drug-addicted teenager, looked across the desk and prepared to say what she presumed to be anathema. In a small, apologetic voice, she confided to her rabbi, "I am angry at God. I feel as though Gabriel and I have been abandoned."

Although some are buoyed by their faith during difficult times, many find that during extreme suffering the concept of God that has sustained them in the past has been shattered and is no longer viable. It is not unusual for people in extreme turmoil to feel abandoned by God. Those who are afflicted may feel angry with God or with the way in which the universe appears to be unfolding, victimized by whatever power it is that runs the universe, or incredulous that a universe that can present such horrors could have any organizing force at its core.

Sam and Ms. S. may have felt as if their cathedral had turned into a hovel bereft of holiness. They could no longer embrace the God who had had meaning for them earlier in their lives, nor did they feel embraced by that God. Their healing journey would call for the reconstruction of their theology into a wider understanding of holiness, one that could accept that the poles of pleasure and horror coexist in the world. This move from what kabbalists call *mochin de katnut* (the contracted mind) to *mochin de gadlut* (the expanded mind)[5] represents an expanded understanding of healing that might enable them to find peace while simultaneously acknowledging life's paradoxes.

With affirmation and skillful direction from the pastoral caregiver, anger and doubt can become tools for finding the voice of prayer on the path to transformation. The caregiver's acceptance of the angry feelings gives permission for the full expression of feelings and thereby promotes growth. The meeting with Sam, which took place in the hospital after his devastating accident, was the first in a series of arguments between Sam and his rabbi that lasted for years. Sam accused his rabbi of working for an evil God; he attacked the rabbi's belief system, his choice of profession, and sometimes even his intelligence. Through it all, the rabbi continued to initiate meetings and to respond to Sam with respect, attention, and caring. Each time they met the rabbi would greet Sam with a hearty, *"Baruch haba, Sh'muel"* (Welcome) and would end their time together by saying, *"Shalom aleichem, Sh'muel"* (Peace unto you). By calling Sam by his Hebrew name and framing each session with blessings, the rabbi communicated to Sam that this ongoing conversation with the rabbi was in the realm of holy ritual.

The rabbi knew that Sam's attacks were not personal, but were directed at a concept of God that had been shattered by Sam's tragedies. He saw Sam's anger as a profound God-wrestling after the dissolution of the underpinnings of his world.[6] The rabbi turned Sam's anger into prayer, helping him unburden his soul without Sam's even knowing that he was praying!

Meeting congregants amid their doubts is challenging for the pastoral caregiver, particularly those who believe that they must defend God's reputation. This situation presents interesting transference issues, such as those which arose in the interaction between Sam and his rabbi.[7] When a congregant is angry at God or filled with doubt, the rabbi or other pastoral care professional often ceases to be a person and comes to represent God. The anger at God often gets transferred onto the caregiver, just as Sam transferred his anger onto his rabbi. As difficult as this situation may be, it is an opportunity for caregivers to encourage articulation of the emotional and existential issues that accompany major life changes and, with it, the expression of a deep, prayerful healing voice.

Prayer and Healing

The pastoral caregiver uses prayer to evoke hope, but not to raise false hopes. Prayer is sometimes a tool of transformation and sometimes a means to "avert the bitterness of a severe decree," bringing peace but not cure.[8]

The *Misheberach* prays for a *refuah shelema* (complete healing) of body *and* soul. The concept of dual realms of healing encourages an understanding that *refuat haguf* and *refuat hanefesh* are at once distinct and interrelated, and this awareness helps those who suffer confront the erroneous notion that healing and cure are synonymous. Promoting this understanding teaches that sometimes the body's symptoms ameliorate but the soul continues to ache, and other times the body does not heal but there is a transformation and healing of the soul. In addition, sometimes the expanded view of the meaning of *refuah shelema* must in some cases include the difficult truth that relief will come only with death and that this, too, is a form of healing. By offering the *Misheberach* or other prayer and sharing these insights, the caregiver promotes the belief that even in the absence of a cure, healing is still possible. This shift in understanding is a healing in itself.

For many people who suffer, healing may initially be imagined only as cure. People want an absence of symptoms or a return to an earlier level of functioning, and they come to pastoral caregivers demanding to have their former lives back. In the process of denial, they narrow their sights and demand the impossible. They want their family to function as it did in the past. They want their deceased loved one back in their arms. Their conception of what healing will look like is not congruent with what is possible. When one is the midst of pain, one cannot conceive of the possibility of healing. To seek healing through the use of prayer is to aim toward the unimaginable. One must suspend the intellect and call out that holy phrase, "I don't know." By helping those who suffer to reach beyond the limits of their understanding, the pastoral caregiver helps to reframe the definition of what healing might look like. This opens the one who suffers to an unknown picture of the world. Prayer is a step into this unknown and a surrender to the possibility that life is much larger than might have been imagined. The following analysis of traditional prayers and creative application of the *Amidah* offer ways of entering the understanding. The thoughts that enable one to open up to an unknown world are a form of prayer.

The Caregiver's Toolbox:
Prayers for Pastoral Encounters

Jewish tradition includes many prayers that are natural resources for pastoral encounters. In the section that follows, we examine several central liturgical modalities from a pastoral perspective.

Spontaneous Prayer and
Mixed Spontaneous–Liturgical Prayers

Prayer is a conversation with God. That conversation can rely on the words of traditional prayers or on spontaneous words of prayer, and sometimes the two can be combined. The themes of traditional prayers explored in the following guided conversations can facilitate a transforming encounter with the Divine.

> When Henry described to his rabbi a harrowing drive through a teeming rainstorm in which he could not see the cars immediately in front of him, his rabbi interrupted his anguished tale. Together, they recited the *gomel* blessing that is traditionally recited when one has survived a life-threatening situation. As they came to the

end of the prayer, Henry burst into tears. His anxiety dissolved and he was overwhelmed by gratitude for his survival.

Just as many of the prayers of today's liturgy are substitutes for the sacrificial practices of the Temple, there is a parallel between the process of healing and the Temple rites. As the ancients watched their offerings go up in smoke, they made the transition from matter to spirit and connected with an invisible and omnipotent God. Healing, too, begins with the concrete—a fixed idea of what needs to be ameliorated. Through the process of healing, it is redefined as a connection with a larger and less rigidly defined understanding of wholeness, as in the shift from *mochin de katnut* to *mochin de gadlut* described earlier. Facilitating that shift is one of the goals of prayer.

Soul-searing suffering often provides the opening that brings a person to that which is eternal, just as the *esh tamid* (eternal fire maintained on the Temple's altar) transformed the Temple sacrifices into the smoke that reached toward God (Leviticus 1:17). It is the deep voice of prayer that is the personal *esh tamid*.

> I will not speak with restraint, I will give voice to the anguish of my spirit; I will complain in the bitterness of my soul (Job 7:11).

> I have been pouring out my heart [before God]. I have only been speaking all this time of my great anguish and distress (1 Samuel 1:15–16).

For many, that transforming fire is found not in the existing liturgy, but in the spontaneous expression of uncensored, deep feelings. It can be helpful to find role models for prayer. Job, who refused to be censored, and Hannah, who spoke from a place of such uncommon depth that she was taken to be drunk, are models to encourage crying out without restraint, for accosting the workings of the universe from the depths of the soul.

The pastoral caregiver must help each person find the language through which his or her unique heart and soul can speak. Speaking of these role models for prayer gives congregants (like Sam, previously) permission to open up their full range of feelings in addressing God, even if the feeling is anger directed at God.

Sometimes existing prayers can provide the words. The congregant might be encouraged to cry out familiar words of prayer or to tuck personal petitions within passages of those prayers, such as the *gomel*, *Misheberach* blessing, or personal words added to the petitions of the *Amidah*. Alternatively, the pastoral caregiver might craft and offer a spontaneous prayer in which feelings, hopes, and wishes of the suffering person are expressed. Hearing one's strivings articulated in the form of prayer is affirming, and can help the individual feel connected to the caregiver and to God.

Spontaneous words coming from the individual may well provide a more direct line between the suffering heart and the source of healing. Rebbe Nachman of Bratzlav taught his students to speak out to God from the depths of their being, saying exactly what was in their hearts, through a prayerful practice called *Hitbodedut*.[9] He encouraged his followers to go to a secluded place in the woods and give voice to a spontaneous, uncensored flow of words. Addressing God in their own language, they would shout out whatever they were feeling, even if what they were feeling was distance from God. Although today's pastoral caregivers may not always be able to direct those receiving pastoral care to a secluded place in the woods, they can encourage those who seek help to talk to God. The question, "What would you say if you found yourself face-to-face with God?" might be asked. It might be suggested that they write letters to God in which they "shout out" what is in their hearts. Some people have been known to lift their voices in passionate, spontaneous prayer in the shower, into their pillow, or in their car!

The *Shema*

The *Shema* is a prayer that is most likely to be familiar to even the most assimilated Jew. For those who know little else, the sound itself may be efficacious because its Hebrew words fall on the ears like a magic elixir. The recitation of the *Shema* can pull forth a primal connection with another time or place, tapping a well of feeling inside one who suffers and helping to dissolve some of the emotional defenses that intensify the pain.

The *Misheberach*

May the One Who blessed our ancestors Abraham, Isaac, Jacob, Moses, Aaron, David, and Solomon (Sarah, Rebecca, Rachel, and Leah)[10] . . .

In connection there is healing, and the *Misheberach* is a potent tool in the caregiver's tool box. The prayer connects the sufferer in the present to those who have suffered in the past, to those who currently suffer, to his or her own past, and to the caregiver. In the first line of the *Misheberach*, the person who is sick is connected with "the early ancestors and great figures of Jewish history."[11]

This connection to the large, historic community is an invocation of hope. For prayer to be efficacious, there must be the sense that it is a tested, healing modality: If our ancestors have been worthy of blessing, perhaps we are as well. Drawing on ancestors through words of prayer is a way of renewing faith. When they are placed in the context of the community and its ancestors, sufferers are likely to feel less isolated or singled out in their suffering.

Shifting a sufferer's focus to a communal context from an individual one gives him or her a broader perspective on the healing process by recognizing that others are also in pain. There is a Chasidic injunction that one should always wear a garment with two pockets; each pocket should contain a note. The first note should say, "I am a speck of dust in the universe." The second note should say, "The universe was created just for me." Each day one is told to choose between the two notes, depending upon whether it is one's grandiosity or one's humility that needs to be either nurtured or checked. The first part of the *Misheberach*, which mentions by name the ancestors of the Jewish people, puts the individual and his or her difficulties into a larger context.

> . . . bless and heal this ill one, (insert the name) son/daughter of
> (insert the mother's name) . . .[12]

The communal connection is made more potent by use of the Hebrew name, which stirs up a spiritual association that can have power on its own.

> One never knows what might be triggered when prayer enters a helping interaction. A hospital chaplain had spent a frantic half hour with a woman who had just received a dire diagnosis and was preparing for emergency surgery. They spoke briefly of her fears, but spent most of their time together anxiously making phone calls and attending to the arrangements that had to be organized before the surgery could proceed. As he was leaving, the

chaplain spontaneously asked, "What is your Hebrew name? I would like to pray for you." She looked at him quizzically and said, "My Hebrew name? I haven't said my Hebrew name in years. It has been decades since anyone has asked me my Hebrew name." As tears fell, she told a story of rejection by her family after her marriage to a Roman Catholic thirty years earlier. She described a life of yearning in the wake of that loss. An hour later, when the hospital orderlies came to take her to surgery, she reached for the chaplain's hand. In the midst of her terror, the request for her Hebrew name had shifted her attention to other parts of the self that needed healing. She went to the critical surgery looking serene and ready to face the unknown.

After its opening line, the focus of the *Misheberach* shifts from the community to the individual, as is seen in the perspective of the second note in the previous Chasidic text. This selective attention conveys the message that the one who is suffering is deserving of attention and has a right to focus on their own suffering. However, this attention does not suggest that the individual is alone; rather, the person is referred to in the prayer as "the son/daughter of . . . "—a person who, at least in the ideal world, has been loved and cared for. Traditionally, the *Misheberach* names the individual by his or her mother's name instead of by the father's name, which is traditionally used whenever a person is called to the Torah. Although this happens less frequently in our more egalitarian times, it is interesting to speculate on the reason that the mother's name was used for healing prayers. Perhaps it is because suffering regresses us and frequently evokes yearning for maternal caring: Even mature adults may "want their Mommy" when they are in pain. Acknowledging this through the prayer's use of the name of the mother is especially appropriate because of the prayer's petition for mercy/compassion—*Rachamim*, a Hebrew word that is a cognate of the word for womb.

. . . and on whose behalf we pray and offer *tzedekah*.[13]

Being able to pray and offer *tzedekah* suggests the ability to take action in the face of one's suffering. It empowers the sufferer, encouraging the fight for healing. This can be a turning point in attitude as one shifts from the stance of victim to that of fighter.

> May the Holy One of Blessing be filled with mercy upon him/her,
> to cure and heal, strengthen and sustain him/her; and may God
> send quickly a complete healing from Heaven to all his or her
> limbs and nerves.[14]

The petitions in the middle section of the *Misheberach* as well as the
places where the names are inserted in the prayer provide an opportunity to mix words of tradition with those of spontaneous prayer. Into
this envelope the caregiver can insert an understanding of the hopes
that have been expressed during the encounter. The caregiver can seize
the moment to express his or her own hopes on the person's behalf or
to summarize the needs that have been disclosed. This moment can be
one of powerful intimacy between the caregiver and the recipient of
the blessing. In this moment, a soul connection that transcends the intellectual meaning of the words can give a sense to the one who suffers
that he or she has been heard. Feeling heard can often bring a sense of
healing and peace.

> Among all the other sick of Israel [may it be] a cure of soul and a
> cure of body.[15]

By placing the one who seeks blessing within the context of others
who are suffering, the prayer merges the one who suffers with the
Jewish past and with those "among all the other sick of Israel" who
are currently suffering. Viewing the self within this context helps
break through isolation, once more linking the individual to a larger
group, breaking through the loneliness of the sickbed[16] and promoting the larger perspective affirmed by the note in the first pocket in the
Chasidic tale related earlier.

The *Amidah* as Rubric for Petitional Prayer[17]

Another prayer that can be a resource in pastoral encounters is the
Amidah (literally, standing prayer). The centerpiece of the prayer service, the weekday *Amidah* includes a prayer for healing among its nineteen petitions. The *Amidah* has a fixed liturgy that has evolved over
the centuries. Much of the *Amidah* is recited quietly, allowing for a
private conversation with God. With this spontaneous, individual
expression as precedent, the *Amidah* can be used as a template
through which even the most secular Jew can find a voice of prayer.

The different sections of this prayer can be worked into a conversation or can take on the form of a guided meditation to be read to one receiving care, who can then respond in writing or in discussion.

Step One. Salutation:
Welcoming the Divine Who Has the Power to Heal

The *Amidah* begins with a salutation. One can address an energy or a force (what may be called a face of God) that is imagined to have the power to heal the person's specific wound, thus allowing the suffering person to imagine what healing would look like. Again, belief is not required. Sometimes, the sufferer's willingness to participate in an imaginal experience and to conceive of such a helping energy can bring about a shift in the situation.

Step Two. Ancestors:
Looking for a Precedent on Which to Build Faith and Hope

Like the *Misheberach*, the *Amidah* invokes *zechut avot* (the merit of the ancestors) when asking for favors. The person asking for help is placed in the midst of a centuries-old conversation, hoping to derive benefit from the good deeds of others by aligning with those deeds and with God's past accessibility. The memory of our forbears' survival of past difficulties ensures that there is a precedent for healing. Perhaps the sufferer can recall getting through another challenging time, or can think of a person who has made it through a difficulty similar to the one that the sufferer is facing. Recalling those times of Presence, whether on behalf of the patriarchs and matriarchs, other role models, or oneself, the person asserts, "As it worked in the past, let it work for me now." This exercise can build faith.

Step Three. Reaching Out: Petitioning the Divine

Now is the time for pleading the case. In a practice similar to the Chasidic meditative practice of *Hitbodedut,* the sufferer is encouraged to speak out passionately, raising his or her voice to appeal to the Source of Power for exactly what is needed.[18] If it is true that God hears the prayers of the brokenhearted, this is the moment to make prayer heard.[19] This deep expression targets doubt, complacency, and depression. Its aim is to pierce stagnation and to energize dormant, life-affirming healing potential.

Step Four. Reaching In:
Listening in Silence for the Divine Voice

Silence should follow this overflow of feeling. Silence is a form of surrender, cultivating receptivity to the subtle effects of the preceding petition. Change often follows deep expression. By waiting and silently observing, one keeps the space open for the unknown. The expressive phase of prayer frequently activates emotion or insight. Silence may give rise to tears, anger, or relief; these reactions can be transformative.

Step Five. Closing: Expressing Gratitude

Having created a meeting place for God and the human partner in the quest for *shalom,* this exercise can be brought to an end with a simple statement of gratitude and farewell.

The *Viddui:* A Thematic Approach

Another prayer that can be a powerful pastoral resource is the *Viddui,* the final confession. Although the *Viddui* is traditionally recited by the dying person, the themes raised by the prayer are not of concern only to those at the end of life. The *Viddui* deals with issues that are on the minds of everyone facing profound turning points. The Shulchan Aruch enjoins us to offer *Viddui* whenever someone is seriously ill. To avoid terrifying the person asked to recite it, we are taught to say, "Many people have not said the *Viddui* and died, and many people have said the *Viddui* and lived."[20]

The *Viddui* prayer has three parts: There is a prayer of repentance asking God to forgive sins, a petition for the protection of the surviving family, and an affirmation of faith in God, including a recitation of the *Shema.* The *Viddui* addresses concerns appropriate to all who confront mortality, regardless of their proximity to death or their beliefs about God and the afterlife. It invites an internal conversation that enhances life's depth and endows those who dare to probe its concerns with sustaining wisdom. The *Viddui* stimulates discussion about life's profound concerns. One who does pastoral work cannot serve effectively without the self-examination suggested by the prayer. Others will be fortified by the self-knowledge that comes by examining its themes.

By approaching the prayer thematically, pastoral caregivers can begin the essential conversation that is at the heart of pastoral care: the conversations about the deepest concerns humans face.

Step One. Life Review: The Sacred Trust

My God and God of my ancestors . . . let my prayer come before You . . . do not ignore my plea. . . . Forgive me for all the wrong I have done in my lifetime. . . . May it be your will . . . I sin no more. With your great compassion cleanse me of my sins . . . may my death atone for all the wrongdoings which I have committed before You.[21]

The first part of the *Viddui* suggests a life review. The person receiving pastoral care might be asked to imagine the moment of death as preparation for accounting to God about one's life—its meaning, achievement, and failures. One might be asked to reflect upon how he or she has fulfilled God's sacred trust of life, the promises kept or the potential wasted. This is an opportunity to examine feelings about fulfillment and achievement, and to evaluate one's behavior over the course of a lifetime. The prayer speaks of sin and repentance. When using the words of the actual prayer, it is important to explain Judaism's compassionate view of sin as a missing of the mark rather than as an inherent, evil quality or permanently staining transgression.

Step Two. Concern with Relationships

God: Parent of orphans, defender of widows, protect my beloved family, with whose soul my own soul is bound.[22]

The second part of the prayer brings the expanded mind to the relational area of healing, an important focus of much of pastoral caregiving. The *Viddui* expresses concern about people whom the dying person will leave behind and provides an opportunity to reflect on any unfinished business in relationships. These issues are even more important to consider when more life lies ahead and there is an opportunity to bring healing to relationships. What concerns the person about significant people in his or her life? Are there words that need to be said, apologies due, regrets to be spoken?

Jewish tradition teaches that sins committed against other people cannot be forgiven by God but must be confronted directly. This can motivate the direct healing of relationships. The context is one of gravity—the deathbed, real or imagined. The prayer places existing difficulties in a larger context, one that encompasses the entire lifetime (and possibly beyond). It encourages one to ponder the relationships of his or her lifetime with sincerity and generosity. If someone has come to a pastoral caregiver seeking guidance in a difficult relationship, the second part of the *Viddui* may provide perspective on the healing that is needed.

Step Three. Turning Toward God

Into your hand I deposit my soul. You have redeemed me, God of truth. *Shema Yisrael Adonai Elohenu Adonai Echad.* Hear, O Israel, Our God is One. *Adonai Hu Ha Elohim. Adonai* is God. God the Judge is God the compassionate. God the Judge is God the compassionate.[23]

The third part of the *Viddui,* which includes the *Shema,* addresses theological questions. It speaks of belief in God and of the destiny of the soul. It is an opportunity for a person to articulate his or her feelings about these weighty issues. The *Viddui* expresses the traditional belief that confession will bring redemption and forgiveness. The final *Shema* is recited, giving the dying person one more opportunity to affirm God's presence and unity.

The God of the *Viddui's* final paragraph is a God of truth, judgment, and compassion. How does the suffering person see God? What does he or she imagine will be the fate of the soul after death? This final paragraph of the *Viddui* implies that "death is a destination" and possibly a gateway to another kind of healing.[24] Within this context it may be possible to explore hopes and fears of life after death, and to speak frankly about the nature of death (and of life). For those who are suffering greatly, there is the possibility that this conversation can make the difference between dying in terror and dying in peace. For those who are not imminently facing death, this conversation opens up the possibility of a more spiritually rewarding life.

Spiritual Medicine: Using Focal Verses or Phrases for Affirmation or Guidance

In the treasure-house of Jewish literature the pastoral caregiver can find words of comfort that can penetrate the souls of those they seek to help and provide spiritual balm. It has been shown that through the repetition of sounds and movement, prayer creates what is known as the relaxation response that reduces stress and produces calm.[25] This soothing effect is one of the reasons people pray.

Jewish texts and liturgy provide an infinite supply of phrases that can be repeated to create this relaxation response. These lines, repeated over and over, are spiritual medicine directed at focusing and relaxing the soul. They can also be used as affirmations designed to cultivate and to reinforce qualities that individuals need to develop and to internalize as part of the healing process. These phrases can be read, written, chanted, or repeated out loud. They can be used as a focal mantra for silent meditation.

> A middle-aged woman was plagued with depression after her youngest child left for college. She had spent twenty-five years identified primarily by her role as Supermom, as she was called by her kids and their friends. She felt at a loss to figure out what to do with the rest of her life and could see no value in herself. Without her children to "do for" she felt that she was unworthy of love. Affirming that God can see the strengths that we may not be able to see in ourselves, her rabbi suggested that she repeat the phrase *ahava rabba ahavtanu* (with a great love God has loved us) whenever she was overcome by these feelings.

> Parents who had struggled for years with their son's drug addiction and the consequent behavior had made rescuing him the center of their lives. Their caregiver had them repeat the phrase *Adonai melech, Adonai malach, Adonai yimloch, le'olam va'ed.* (God rules, God ruled, God will rule forever and ever). He hoped they would recognize that their son's fate was beyond them and in the hands of God. These words became the springboard for the wrenching work of separating from their son, creating boundaries between themselves and their son and his disease. They undertook this difficult journey with the help of their spiritual caregiver and with a psychotherapist. They also received support from Al-anon, a twelve-step program targeting those who care for addicted persons.

Jewish literature provides a vast spiritual pharmacopoeia, with "words of medicine" for every ailment. Prayer used in this way can implant and reinforce values. By encouraging those who seek pastoral caregiving to study Jewish texts and to participate in Jewish liturgy, pastoral caregivers provide the access to prayer and the healing that prayer can bring.

In addition to supporting private prayer, it is important to encourage those who suffer to participate in communal prayer. One of the most consistently healing of all Jewish practices has taken place over the centuries as a mourner sits day after day, three times a day, in a formal service in order to recite the *Kaddish* prayer. Repeatedly hearing the words of the liturgy engraves the values of Judaism on the broken hearts of those present, restoring meaning and direction to their lives.

Giving Blessings

Giving spontaneous blessings can be a particularly effective tool for pastoral caregivers. A blessing is a communication involving an I and a Thou.[26] The person who receives a blessing from another is reminded that he or she is not alone. Blessing another person is a reminder that any human interaction includes the third presence of Holiness. This thought can inspire more compassionate and daring interaction.

> A rabbi meeting with a young couple to plan their wedding ceremony taught them the art of blessing. At first, they giggled with awkwardness but soon transcended their discomfort. The blessing form gave them permission to express hopes and fears they had previously held back. As the bride-to-be blessed her husband, she expressed both her admiration for him and the concerns she had about how their marriage might be affected by negative patterns they had observed in their families of origin. She blessed their union and their ability to create something that did not mirror the memories they each carried from childhood. Her groom-to-be affirmed her concern and shared his vision of an egalitarian and affectionate marriage in which both partners had spaces of solitude. Using the format of blessing they spoke honestly about subjects that had been hard to broach in normal conversation because each had been afraid of bringing fear and negativity to the union. By framing their blessing with the traditional blessing format, beginning with the words, *baruch ata Adonai* (blessed are You), and ending with an Amen, they brought their concerns to a larger arena

and felt less isolated in them. They were reminded that they were embarking on a sacred journey with Holiness as a companion.

A rabbi demonstrated yet another approach to blessing when she met with a long-married couple as prelude to preparing their *get* (decree of divorce). Both feeling they had been wronged by the other, they had concluded that divorce was the only possibility. Fearing that the unresolved resentments would harm them and their children as they moved on with their lives, the rabbi announced, "I will prepare your *get* when you are capable of giving each other a genuine blessing." Despite resistance, both returned to the next meeting with a carefully constructed blessing. However, the blessings had continued the couple's acrimony: Both had used the assignment as an opportunity to reiterate their dissatisfaction and resentment. Husband and wife both asked that the other be blessed with a quality that he or she felt the other person was lacking; the blessings were actually curses. The rabbi repeated the assignment. Over time, the tone of the blessings shifted from vindictive to compassionate. Blessing became a vehicle through which the couple could acknowledge their differences and express regret, forgiveness, and generosity. The blessings were a means of *teshuvah* in a place where healing had seemed impossible.

It is sometimes helpful to ask what blessing a person feels they need. It helps them focus their intention and can be a good way of ascertaining what they garnered from the time spent with the pastoral caregiver. Feeding back what the client has said while delivering the requested blessing allows the caregiver to highlight the ultimate concerns raised in the interaction. The caregiver can reframe the issues, share insights, and give direction, while once more affirming the spiritual dimensions of healing. Blessings can provide a succinct statement for reflection after the encounter.

When asked what blessing he felt he needed, Mark, who was suffering from depression, wished that he were able to hold on to the affirmation of others, a theme that he had mentioned repeatedly throughout the interaction. The chaplain expressed Mark's wish in the form of a blessing, adding her own emphases.

"Dear God," she chanted, "please help Mark to see the strength and creativity with which you have endowed him—attributes that are so evident to all who have come to know Mark. When he is blind to his own beauty, help him to rely on the eyes of others so that he can have a more accurate vision of himself . . . and can come to trust and to use more effectively the gifts you have given to him." Mark called out, "Amen." The chaplain's blessing heightened Mark's learning and gave him something to hold onto after the interaction was over.

A caregiver can also receive a blessing, empowering the recipient of assistance and leveling the inequality that occurs when one person is a helper and the other a recipient.

A young chaplain spent several hours speaking with an elderly woman who was to undergo surgery to remove a growth that was likely to be malignant. At the close of the interaction the chaplain asked the frail, older woman to bless her. "Live a long happy life . . . and get married," said the woman. By inviting the older woman to offer blessing, the chaplain gave respect and honor to the woman, her age, and her accumulation of wisdom and experience.

One additional form of blessing has a particularly poignant power. When a caregiver offers to pray for a person after leaving that person's side, the encounter and the concern intrinsic to it is extended beyond its boundaries in time. This act imparts a message of genuine caring that can be a potent agent of healing.

Prayer as a Spiritual Resource for the Pastoral Caregiver

Prayer is as useful for those who seek to help as for those who need help. Pastoral caregivers must be attuned to the effect of pastoral encounters on their own spiritual, emotional, and physical health. Specific prayers can be tools through which rabbis, counselors, cantors, or chaplains can maintain clarity and openheartedness while protecting against the dissolution of boundaries.

Each pastoral encounter can be considered as an act of prayer. Preceding each encounter with prayer can help the pastoral caregiver hold this sanctity in mind. Several prayers appear to be epigrams of the values of Jewish pastoral caregiving and can be used by pastoral caregivers to focus their attention, to align themselves with the values of Jewish pastoral care, and to prepare for the pastoral encounter.

Kavannah to Create The Place of the Pastoral Encounter

> I will betroth you to Me forever, I will betroth you to Me with justice, and with law, loving-kindness and compassion. And I will betroth you to Me with faithfulness and you will know God.[27]

Preparing to enter a pastoral encounter is similar to putting on *tefillin* each morning in preparation for prayer: Both acts need to be approached with great care and reverence. Just as putting on *tefillin* helps one to get ready to pray, so the pastoral caregiver needs a way to prepare for the holy work of encountering another human being.

The words of the prayer recited daily when wrapping the leather straps of the *tefillin* are a microcosm of the ideal pastoral interaction. Each of Hosea's seven attributes describing the qualities with which God is betrothed to the Jew on a daily basis characterizes a discrete part of the pastoral encounter. These are words that caregivers can recite to themselves as preparation for the pastoral interaction and to focus attention, become grounded in the encounter's mission, experience partnership with the Divine, and be reminded of the values of pastoral care. Reciting this phrase is also an opportunity to acknowledge and to accept the limits of what pastoral caregivers can do, for the human healer affirms God as the ultimate healer. Each of the words carries important messages for the pastoral caregiver and are examined in turn.

Le'olam (universe, world, forever): The pastoral caregiver enters the meeting as a representative of the Divine Healing Process that is at the core of the universe. He or she is a *shaliach* (messenger) from that infinite, unknowable world. *Le'olam* introduces the eternal truth that is the Holy Process of Healing and reminds us that healing is rooted in worlds that are unfolding beyond our understanding.

Tsedek (righteousness) and *mishpat* (law): Values shape the encounter. The contract between the caregiver and those receiving pastoral attention must be clear. Its nature is made explicit, whether or not it is spoken, in these two words. *Tsedek* stands for the qualities of righteousness and justice that undergird the pastoral encounter. The caregiver comes with skill and with the intention of bringing focused attention for the good of the client. The encounter is geared to relieve suffering through honest interaction. That impeccability is further represented in the word *mishpat,* which states that there are rules governing the behavior of the parties in the encounter and the ethics that derive from those rules will not be violated. These include respect for the boundaries of the interaction. The time together will focus only on the needs of the one receiving pastoral care and not the needs of the caregiver. There is a guarantee of the inviolability of personal, professional, and sexual boundaries. The encounter is to be a place of safety where the client's story will be treated as sacred, with respect, and in confidence.

Chesed (loving-kindness) and **rachamim** (compassion): These exquisite attributes are at the core of the pastoral encounter and describe the quality of presence the caregiver is called to manifest. *Chesed* is the graceful loving-kindness that enables the caregiver to listen with generous attention, lack of judgment, and unconditional positive regard. *Rachamim* adds the attribute of compassion to the encounter. The caregiver is encouraged to listen with the heart and, in the literal meaning of *rachamim,* with the *womb*, bringing the deep wisdom of embodied spirit to bear on what is being shared.

Emunah (faithfulness/trust): With this word, the caregiver begins to disengage from the pastoral interaction. Sharing a root with the word *Amen, emunah* seals the encounter with a statement of faith. The positive regard expressed earlier is echoed, affirming the caregiver's belief in the person's potential for growth, the process of healing, and in the power of the True Healer.

The caregiver's withdrawal from the encounter is described by the words *v'yada'at et Adonai* (and you will know God). This is a further statement of faith, declaring confidence in God's wisdom. The phrase creates a boundary that formally ends the interaction and yields to the True Healer. It acknowledges that one cannot and need not do it all. The *shaliach* departs and the healing process that he or she has represented returns to the Source of Healing.

Concluding Pastoral Encounters

Ending a session of pastoral care requires a shift from the particular, focused awareness of caregiving to the normal attention of regular life. This shift from sacred to mundane is a frequent concern in Jewish life.[28] A blessing is a good way to end an interaction with a congregant, using the familiar format of a blessing to bracket a summary of the time spent together and the hope for the future, as described earlier. In addition, the values of the *Kaddish* underscore what is necessary to move on.

Despite the fact that a formal *Kaddish* is not traditionally said without the presence of a *minyan*, the *Kaddish* addresses a theme that can serve the person receiving care and the caregiver as well. A traditional way of punctuating the end of a session of study or prayer, when recited in a prayer community, the *Kaddish* marks the transition between the sublime and the ordinary. It grounds spiritual intensity so that it is safe to move back into daily routine. When the *Kaddish* speaks of suffusing the world with *The Great Name*, it allows those who have touched holiness to find their way back into the mundane world without losing their connection to what is holy. In ending a session, it can be useful for a practitioner of pastoral care to be mindful of these themes of the *Kaddish*. The consciousness of the meaning of the *Kaddish* enables pastoral practitioners to step from the rarefied encounter of the caregiving meeting back to solid earth to continue their work of *tikkun olam*.

Notes

1. Isserles on Shulchan Aruch Yoreh Deah 335:4.
2. Abraham Joshua Heschel, *The Sabbath: Its Meaning for Modern Man.* (New York: Farrar, Straus & Giroux, 1951), p. 8.
3. The blessing for mourners, which in the time of the Jerusalem Temple was extended to others at profound turning points, refers to God as *HaMakom* (The Place).
4. All examples are composites drawn from my own experience and that of my colleagues with names and details altered to protect the confidentiality of those involved.
5. Dov Ber of Lubavitch, *Kuntres Hitpalut: Maamorei Admur Hoemtzaee Kintresim* (Brooklyn, N.Y.: Kehot Publication Society, 1991).

6. Waskow, Arthur, *Godwrestling—Round 2: Ancient Wisdom, Future Paths* (Woodstock, Vt.: Jewish Lights Publishing, 1998).

7. See Breitman, supra, pp. 94–99 for discussion of transference issues.

8. From the High Holiday liturgy, which states that *tefillah* (prayer), *tzedakah* (acts of generosity and righteousness), and *teshuvah* (repentance) can avert the severe decree.

9. Arthur Green, *Tormented Master* (Woodstock, Vt.: Jewish Lights Publishing, 1992).

10. From the *Misheberach*.

11. Quote from Joseph S. Ozarowski, private communication. I am indebted to him and to Rabbi Dayle A. Friedman for insights into the *Misheberach*.

12. From the *Misheberach*.

13. Ibid.

14. Ibid.

15. Ibid.

16. Joseph S. Ozarowski, personal communication.

17. Adapted from Anne Brener. *Mourning & Mitzvah: A Guided Journal for Walking the Mourner's Path through Grief to Healing* (Woodstock, Vt.: Jewish Lights .Publishing, 1993), pp. 166–71.

18. Green, *Tormented Master,* pp. 32, 145–148, 161, 324.

19. Psalm 34:19, God is close to the broken-hearted.

20. Shulchan Aruch Yoreh Deah 338:1.

21. Brener, *Mourning & Mitzvah,* pp. 166–71.

22. Ibid.

23. Ibid.

24. Alvin Fine, "Birth Is a Beginning," in *Rabbi's Manual* (New York: Central Conference of American Rabbis, 1988), pp. 138–40.

25. Herbert Benson, *The Relaxation Response* (New York: William Morrow, 1975).

26. Martin Buber, *I and Thou* (New York: Charles Scribner's Sons, 1970).

27. This prayer of affirmation, which is recited daily when putting on the *tefillin,* is taken from Hosea 2:21–22. The author is grateful for the teaching of Rabbi Shefa Gold on this prayer.

28. This is evident in the priestly rituals for purification that are described in the Bible as well as in the *Havdalah* ritual for separating Shabbat from the rest of the week and in the use of the *Kaddish* to mark transitions.

Bibliography

Benson, Herbert, with Miriam Z. Klipper. *The Relaxation Response.* New York: Wings Books, Avon Books, 1992.

Blanchard, Tsvi. *Joining Heaven & Earth: Maimonides and the Laws of Bikkur Cholim.* San Francisco: The Jewish Healing Center, 1994.

Brener, Anne. *Mourning & Mitzvah: A Guided Journal for Walking the Mourner's Path Through Grief to Healing*. Woodstock, Vt.: Jewish Lights Publishing, 1993.

Buber, Martin. *I and Thou*. New York: Charles Scribner's Sons, 1970.

Cutter, William. "Entering the Medical Voids." *CCAR Journal* (summer 1992), pp. 35–41.

Green, Arthur. *Tormented Master*. Woodstock, Vt.: Jewish Lights Publishing, 1992.

Greenbaum, Avraham. *The Wings of the Sun: Traditional Jewish Healing in Theory & Practice*. Jerusalem/Monsey, New York: Breslov Research Institute, 1995.

———. *Garden of the Souls: Rebbe Nachman on Suffering*. Jerusalem/Monsey, New York: Breslov Research Institute, 1990.

Hammer, Reuven. *Entering Jewish Prayer: A Guide to Personal Devotion and the Worship Service*. New York: Schocken Books, 1994.

Handler, Jane, and Kim Hetherington, with Rabbi Stuart Kelman. *Give Me Your Hand: Traditional and Practical Guidance on Visiting the Sick*. 2nd ed. Berkeley, Calif.: Congregation Netivot Shalom [1841 Berkeley Way, Berkeley, CA 94703], 1997.

Levine, Aaron. *How to Perform the Great Mitzvah of Bikkur Cholim*. Toronto, Canada: Alger Press Limited, 1987.

Levine, Stephen. *Who Dies? An Investigation of Conscious Living and Conscious Dying*. Garden City, N.Y.: Anchor Books, 1982.

Ochs, Carol, and Kerry M. Olitzky. *Jewish Spiritual Guidance: Finding Our Way to God*. San Francisco: Jossey-Bass, 1997.

Ram Dass and Paul Gormin. *How Can I Help? Stories and Reflection on Service*. New York: Knopf, 1985.

Schachter-Shalomi, Zalman M. *Spiritual Intimacy: A Study of Counseling in Hasidism*. Northvale, N.J.: Jason Aronson, 1991.

Wiener, Shohama Harris, and Jonathan Omer-Man. *Worlds of Jewish Prayer*. Northvale, N.J.: Jason Aronson, 1993.

Anne Brener, M.A.J.C.S., M.A., L.C.S.W., is a Los Angeles-based psychotherapist and the author of the acclaimed book *Mourning & Mitzvah: A Guided Journey for Walking the Mourner's Path Through Grief to Healing* (Jewish Lights Publishing). She lectures and leads workshops on the connection between psychology and spirituality and is a founder of the Jewish Healing Center at Metivta in Los Angeles, California, where she is on the faculty.

From the Depths: The Use of Psalms

Rabbi Simkha Y. Weintraub

Rabbi Simkha Y. Weintraub mines the riches of the Book of Psalms as a spiritual resource. He suggests seven basic modalities for using psalms in pastoral care: ritual, prayer, song, study, meditation, community, and conversation. Rabbi Weintraub describes each of these means of using psalms, and offers concrete guidelines for effectively employing this resource. He assists the reader in understanding the functions of psalms in pastoral care and provides techniques for creating bridges to them.

A major New York City building was being dedicated, and among the many dignitaries present was Chancellor Louis Finkelstein of the Jewish Theological Seminary, sitting next to a noted Jewish philanthropist. The opening invocation–blessing was offered by a Protestant minister, who included in his words a stirring reading of a psalm, in English translation. When he had finished, a woman who was a communally involved philanthropist leaned over to Chancellor Finkelstein and whispered, "Wasn't that moving? I wish we had that in our Bible!"

This anecdote may be "apocryphal," or it may have involved someone other than Dr. Finkelstein, but it does reflect a real or imagined lack of connection between many contemporary Jews and the Book of Psalms. To be sure, for some Jews, the psalms are simply foreign, unexplored territory, *terra incognita,* but even this author, with an Orthodox day school background, decades of daily *davvening*, a major in undergraduate Judaic studies, rabbinic studies, and ordination, didn't really turn to the psalms as a source of personal spiritual support until some bridges were built. Even Jewishly educated and traditionally observant Jews, who know many chapters of the Book of Psalms by heart, may need to approach them in a new light, with new tools offered and new possibilities opened. The purpose of this chapter is to explore possible approaches to enable Jews to draw solace, strength, and support from the remarkable spiritual treasure that is *Sefer Tehillim*.

Illness, suffering, and loss *mute* us—they leave us without words. Whether overwhelmed, confused, distraught, despairing—or profoundly grateful, reflective, renewed, attuned—whatever our state, we are often left speechless, feeling that words fall flat or do not convey what we want, need, or intend. In the face of these challenges, those who are in pain, as well as those who care for them, may need new ways of communicating, new tools for talking, and new modes of relating.

Enter the Book of Psalms

For centuries, Jews and others have turned to the biblical Book of Psalms for solace, guidance, catharsis, renewal, and much more. The 150 psalms that constitute this important component of the Writings section of our Bible reflect a wide range of experience and expression—anger and acceptance, blunder and bravado, complaint and comfort, despair and delight, exhaustion and exhilaration, frustration and faith, and so on. In approaching this body of ancient spiritual or sacred poetry, many people have found words or images that work for them, or that help uncover words of their own, that were obscure or inaccessible. Even though some of the language or many of the images of the psalms may seem alien, when one digs deeply enough one may find wellsprings of great value.

Psalms pervade the established Jewish liturgy of morning, afternoon, and evening prayer services, but our tradition has made the psalms into a very flexible resource. Tradition encourages us to turn to them when we need them and not to be bound by any strictures related to time or number of people present, as with prayers requiring a *minyan*, a quorum of ten. Therefore, although certain psalms are, indeed, assigned to certain moments, we may always turn to the Book of Psalms as an ad hoc source of support.

The Levites sang the psalms in the ancient Temple, and many congregations welcome Shabbat on Friday night by chanting their way through six psalms (Psalms 95–99 and Psalm 29), praising the beauty of nature (corresponding to the six days of Creation) and culminating in the Psalm for Shabbat. Psalms may be heard at many moments in life: at the bedside of those who are ill, at the beginning of the blessing after meals, at funerals, when visiting a grave, and in many other settings. Psalms are there to help express our great joy *and* devastating despair, our gratitude *and* our distress, life's ups and, of course, its downs.

Over the centuries, certain psalms became associated with particular moments or transitions in life, for example:[1]

- For times of communal distress: Psalms 20, 28, 85, 86, 102, 130, 142
- For recovery from illness: Psalms 6, 30, 41, 88, 103
- For thanksgiving: Psalms 9, 21, 57, 95, 116, 138
- On a wedding day: Psalm 19
- At the birth of a child: Psalms 20, 139
- On the day of *brit milah*: Psalm 12
- When traveling: Psalm 91
- When seeking repentance: Psalms 51, 90
- When visiting a gravesite: Psalms 33, 16, 17, 72, 91, 104, 130

Some have identified thirty-six psalms as particularly suited to the spiritual needs of a sick person and concerned relatives and friends: 2, 6, 9, 13, 16, 17, 18, 22, 23, 25, 30, 31, 32, 33, 37, 38, 39, 41, 49, 55, 56, 69, 86, 88, 89, 90, 91, 102, 103, 104, 107, 116, 118, 128, 142, and 143.[2]

This list is not exhaustive, and different communities and individuals have developed variations responsive to their own needs and understandings.

How Might Jews Offering Pastoral Care Approach and Use Psalms?

To answer that question, it would be helpful to identify and explore seven functions that psalms have served in Jewish life:

Ritual

Psalms serve as a source of structured expression, to mark certain moments and give a container for feelings, ideas, and values, either in an established, traditional, communal context, or in one's own personal, innovative time and place. One recent example is a Jewish support group that began each meeting with a psalm of despair or complaint (such as 10, 13, 37, 73, 77, 82, 88, 92, or 94), and ended with a psalm of gratitude or acceptance (such as 9, 18, 21, 57, 91, 95, 116, 118, or 138).

Many people come to pastoral caregivers with a thirst for something to do, a craving for words to say. A wonderful gift to those who want and need such practice is to open up and read a psalm (or two or three) for their personal devotion, the private service of their heart. Read a well-chosen psalm with them, and then explore how to work it into their day.

A woman, aged forty-two, who was dealing simultaneously with a divorce, a serious medical diagnosis, insensitive rejection by a community, and an adolescent daughter who was acting out, was looking for "a Jewish place to retreat." She spoke at length with her rabbi who, as a pastoral caregiver, worked with her to explore and more clearly to articulate what she was seeking. They decided together that her home and her workplace had to become that "retreat," and as part of that project she began to say, study, and chant Psalm 30 three times a day, in a quiet, private space.[3]

Adonai, my God
    I extol You
        for You have lifted me up
            and not allowed enemies to rejoice over me!
Adonai, my God
    I cried out to You
        and You healed me
Adonai
    You lifted my *nefesh*/my being from *She'ol*
        You revived me from descent into the Pit
Shema/Hear, Adonai,
        have mercy on me!
        Adonai—be my help!
You turn my lament into dancing;
    You undo my sackcloth and gird me with joy!
So that my whole being sings praises to You
    so I am not silent
        Adonai, my God,
            I will thank/praise You forever.

For many people, a psalm explored with a rabbi or pastoral caregiver can become a portable, sacred space, an opportunity for meaningful self-care and devotion, long after and far from the pastoral encounter.

Prayer

As with other forms of Jewish prayer, psalms provide a range of opportunities. Psalms allow us to give words to hopes, fears, and wishes; they help us to experience pain and transcend it. Psalms are effective for "taming-by-naming" one's distress or for locating and articulating a sense of gratitude. They also can enable an individual to reconnect to tradition, to community, or to a basic inner sense of wholeness.

In Jewish pastoral care, some meetings—notably with people with whom we have an ongoing relationship and whose spiritual state and personal character we understand—might well begin with a psalm–prayer. This psalm–prayer might serve to dedicate the moment (Psalm 112), to form an alliance (Psalm 50), to free up expression (Psalm 148), or perhaps to name the struggle, or to shape the agenda (Psalm 139). In many Chasidic counseling models, a counseling session ends with a blessing, which might well include a psalm (Psalms 46, 112).[4]

Some people are unable or unwilling to tackle a whole psalm; for them, it is helpful to select a line, a phrase, or even just a word from a psalm to carry in their hearts. For example, since Jewish tradition assigned psalms from the biblical Book of Psalms to each of the seven days of the week, one approach is to focus in on certain lines within the designated psalms. These lines can become marker–prayers that help locate where one is in the week's work, and help shape one's conduct:

Sunday (from Psalm 24)

Who may ascend the mountain of Adonai?
Who may rise in God's sanctuary?
    One with clean hands and a pure heart,
        who has not used God's name in false oaths,
        who has not sworn deceitfully.

Monday (from Psalm 48)

In Your Temple, God, we meditate on Your *chesed*/loving-kindness.
Your Glory, like Your Name, reaches to the ends of the earth.
Your Right Hand is filled with *tzedek*/righteousness.

Tuesday (from Psalm 82)

Rescue the weak and the needy,
Save them from the grip of the wicked.

Wednesday (from Psalm 94 and Psalm 95)

When my foot slips, Adonai, Your *chesed*/loving-kindness supports me;
When I am filled with concerns, God's comfort soothes my soul.
Let's sing out to Adonai, acclaim the Rock of our deliverance!
Let's greet God with praise and sing songs in joy!

Thursday (from Psalm 81)

I heard a voice I never knew:
"I removed a burden from your shoulder;
freed your hand from a heavy load. . . .
I will feed you with the richest wheat,
with honey from the rock I will satiate you."

Friday (from Psalm 93)

Rivers rise and rage,
Waters rush and roar,
Floods swell and storm. . . .
But above the crash of the sea and its breakers,
awesome is Adonai!
Your decrees are most enduring, Adonai,
Kodesh/holy dedication befits Your house, for endless days!

Shabbat (from Psalm 92)

The righteous will flourish like a palm tree;
thriving like a cedar of Lebanon.
Planted in Adonai's house,
they will flourish in the courts of our God.
They will yield fruit even in old age;
they will always be fresh, fragrant!
To proclaim,
"Adonai is just!
My Rock, without flaw!"

Finding one's prayer voice in the psalms is, of course, a process. Doing so may well involve rejecting certain images or ideas, linking verses from different psalms, or interweaving one's own words of praise or protest. This process entails a dialogue between ancient, well-worn sacred poetry and the individual's unique and emerging expression of hopes, fears, values, and quests. For Jewish pastoral caregivers, it is this *process,* rather than a "Here, read this!" *product,* that enables people to reach in to their inner selves, to reach out to others in community, and to reach up to God in their times of need.

Song

He who stands on a normal rung weeps;
he who stands higher is silent;
but he who stands on the topmost rung
converts his sorrow into song.

—ABRAHAM JOSHUA HESCHEL[5]

So many wonderful lines of psalms have been put to music, and every decade new melodies emerge that enable us to reach deeply into the verbal and metaverbal impact of these verses. Often, just calling on the melody, the *niggun,* without the words can have the greatest impact.

Here are eighteen examples of lines from the psalms that may be called Jewish healing songs because of their evocative words or music:

1. *Lo ira meirevevot am*
       asher saviv, saviv
       shatu alai
   Kumah Adonai ve'hoshi'eini!
   I do not fear the thousands of people
       that have set upon me, all around.
       Rise up, Adonai! Save me, my God!

—PSALM 3: 7–8

2. *Va'anachnu lo neda mah na'aseh*
       ki alecha eineinu
   Zechor rachamecha, Adonai
       vachasadecha
           ki me'olam heimah.
   We know not what to do—
       Our eyes are upon You.
   Remember Your mercy, Adonai,
       and Your *chesed*/loving-kindness,
           for they are eternal.

—II CHRONICLES 20:12; PSALM 25:6

3. *Achat sha'alti, me'et Adonai*
    Ota avakesh
        Shivti b'vet Adonai
        Kol yemei chayai
        Lachazot benoam, benoam Adonai
        U'levaker behechalo.

  One thing I ask of Adonai,
    One thing I seek:
        To dwell in the House of Adonai
        All my days,
        To behold Adonai's pleasantness
        and to meditate (experience/visit)
        in Adonai's Sanctuary.

                        —PSALM 27:4

4. *Kave el Adonai*
    Chazak veya'ametz libecha
    Vekavei el Adonai.

  Have hope (trust) in Adonai
    Be strong and your heart will be strengthened.
    Have hope (trust) in Adonai.

                        —PSALMS 27:14

5. *Elecha, Adonai ekra*
    v'el Adonai etchanan
        Sh'ma Adonai, vechoneni
        Adonai, heiye ozer li.

  To you, God, I call,
    And to Adonai I appeal:
        Hear, God, and have compassion on me,
        God—be my Help.

                        —PSALM 30:9,11

6. *Ke'ayal ta'arog al afikei mayim*
    Ken nafshi ta'arog elecha
        Tsam'a, tsam'a, tsam'a nafshi
        Tsam'a nafshi leEl chai!

  Like a hind crying for springs of water,
    so my soul cries out for You. . . .
        My soul thirsts for God,
        for living El/Almighty!

                        —PSALM 42:2–3

6. *Lev tahor bera li, Elohim*
   V'ruach nachon chadesh bekirbi
   Al tashlicheini milfanecha
   V'ruach kodshekha al tikach mimeni.
   Create for me a pure heart, God;
   And the right spirit renew within me.
   Don't cast me away from Your Presence,
   Don't take Your Holy Spirit away from me.

   —Psalm 51:12–13

7. *Va'ani tefilati, lecha, Adonai*
   Et ratzon
   Elohim berov chasdecha
   Aneini be'emet yish'echa.
   May my prayer to you, Adonai,
   be at a favorable time;
   God, in your abundant kindness,
   Answer me, with the truth of your deliverance.

   —Psalm 69:14

8. *Ki hu yatzilcha mipach yakush*
   Midever havot.
   God will save you from the fowler's trap,
   From a plague that devastates.

   —Psalm 91:3

9. *Im amarti matah ragli*
   Chasdecha Adonai yisadeni.
   Whenever I have said, "My foot has slipped,"
   Your kindness/loyalty, Adonai, has supported me.

   —Psalm 94:18

10. *Or zarua latzaddik, uleyishrei lev simcha*
    Simchu tzadikim b'Adonai, vehodu l'zecher kodsho!
    Light is sown for the righteous, joy for the upright-in-heart;
    Rejoice in Adonai, righteous ones! Give thanks to God's Holy Name!

    —Psalm 97:11–12

11. *Ivdu et Adonai besimcha! Bo'u lefanav birnana!*
    Serve God with joy! Come before God with exultation!

    —Psalm 100:2

12. *Min hameitsar karati Yah*
    Anani vamerchav Yah.
    Out of narrow straits (distress) I've called out to God,
    God answered me with wide open spaces (by setting
      me free).

—P<small>SALM</small> 118:5

13. *Pitchu li sha'arei tzedek*
        Avo vam
        Odeh Yah.
    Zeh hasha'ar l'Adonai
    Tzadikim yavo'u vo.
    Open for me the gates of righteousness;
        I will enter them,
        I will give thanks to God.
    This gate is Adonai's,
    The righteous enter it.

—P<small>SALM</small> 118:19–20

14. *Esa einai el heharim*
        Me'ayin yavo ezri?
    Ezri mei'im Adonai
    Oseh shamayim va'aretz.
    I lift up my eyes to the mountains:
        Where will my help come from?
    My help comes from Adonai,
    Creator of heaven and earth.

—P<small>SALMS</small> 121:1–2

15. *Hinei lo yanum*
        velo yishan
        Shomer Yisra'el.
    Behold, the Guardian of Israel
        neither slumbers nor sleeps.

—P<small>SALM</small> 121:4

16. *L'ma'an achai verei'ai, L'ma'an achai verei'ai*
    Adabrah na, adabrah na
    Shalom bach!
    For the sake of my kin and my companions,
    I wish that peace be with you!

—P<small>SALM</small> 122:8

17. *Malchutcha malchut kol olamim*
Umemshaltecha bechol dor vador
Somech Adonai lechol hanoflim
Vezokef lechol hakefufim.
Your Kingdom is an everlasting kingdom,
and Your Dominion endures from generation to generation.
Adonai supports all those who are falling,
And straightens up all who are bowed down.
—PSALM 145:13–14

18. All of Psalm 150!

Singing *with* and singing *to* Jews is an important resource in Jewish pastoral work. It can be a critical way of joining, of relating; it may facilitate the expression of pain and sorrow, or trigger the experience of joy and gratitude, or both. Of course, singing lines from psalms can be a critical asset in the pastoral caregiver's own self-care and refueling. Immediately before or right after an encounter, words of the psalms may provide comfort, strength, focus, solace, or helpful distraction. In the repertoire of Jewish spiritual and pastoral resources, songs and *niggunim* are certainly at or near the top of the list.

Study

Study of the psalms can be challenging because many laypeople are unfamiliar with the text. In addition, the Hebrew is often obscure or otherwise hard to "crack," after centuries of less-than-accurate recopying. We can see this difficulty more as an opportunity: It means that there is a lot to explore, to uncover, to recover. For example, compare how different editions translate the same lines. In Jewish pastoral work, as in Jewish life in general, Torah study is key to growth and to life, and delving into the meanings of an ancient psalm is no exception! To be sure, Torah study may at times be heavily cognitive and intellectual, drawing on the left brain. However, its eternal, life-giving dimension certainly stems from the integration of ideas with feelings, relationships, values—the whole person, the spirit.

Reb Nachman of Bratslav (whose *Tikkun HaKlali*/Complete Remedy included Psalms 16, 32, 41, 42, 59, 77, 90, 105, 137, and 150) taught that the psalms can have minimal value in mere recitation.[6] One must grow to identify with their contents in a deep and meaningful way, and seek to apply the words to oneself, to find oneself in the psalm. For those who have not explored a psalm before, here is one approach to doing so in Jewish pastoral care:

Out of the Depths: One Approach to Exploring a Psalm

1. Read the psalm through once out loud—and then once to yourself, quietly.
2. Look for a section, sentence, phrase, or word that speaks to you, and circle it.
3. Chart the psalm's meaning:
   a. Can you identify two, three, or four distinct sections? Please mark and label them.
   b. Are there distinct voices (psalmist, God, enemies, others)? Please label them.
   c. Can you summarize the "flow" of the psalm (e.g., "from pain to despair to searching to reaffirmation")? If so, please describe briefly:

   _____

   _____

4. Do you experience something that is familiar? Where?
   Verse(s) _____

   _____

5. Where do you encounter difficulties in the psalm's meaning?
   Verse(s) _____
   a. What is foreign to you? What needs clarification?

   _____

   _____

   b. What would you eliminate (which words, verses, ideas)?

   _____

   _____

6. If you were asked to amplify or to develop one piece of this psalm, what might you write? Feel free to offer two or three lines.

   _____

   _____

   _____

7. Last, if you had to entitle this psalm, as you would a poem, what would you call it? (Feel free to use something from the psalm or from outside it.)

Meditation

Many people seeking Jewish pastoral care want and need an authentically Jewish and a deeply personal private spiritual practice to complement (and, perhaps, to reinforce) the more interpersonal, public, outer-directed observances and traditions. Not all Jewish pastoral caregivers need to be able to teach meditation, but they should be able to guide those interested in this dimension of a Jewish spiritual life. The pastoral caregiver should be prepared to refer to helpful publications, programs, and people.

Words of the psalms can be valuable tools in refocusing, centering, and quieting oneself, by using them as a kind of Jewish mantra. Some people post a verse, phrase, or even just a word from a psalm on their office computer screen so they can easily turn to it in the course of a workday. Others make their own audio recording of a psalm, or a piece of a psalm, to play back while sitting in a quiet, undisturbed setting, or even while jogging, driving, or shopping. More than just another stress-reduction technique, these meditative practices bring the sacred into the everyday, marrying text with context, bringing Torah into life and life into Torah.

People dealing with illness, suffering, and loss often turn, quite naturally, to the resources of the world around them for spiritual healing. They seek to restore a damaged connection to nature, to reassert that despite everything they are still *ba'alei chayim* (active possessors of life), and to renew precious moments of life within Creation. To name, to concretize, to sanctify these activities, and to bridge the world of the senses to that of the spirit in a conscious manner, *pesukim* (verses) may be joined with the actions before, during, and after the experience.

Eighteen healing activities follow, each paired with a relevant *pasuk*. These verses from the Book of Psalms represent possible focal meditations meant to accompany, not replace, traditional blessings connected with many of these activities. For some of these activities, there may be no traditional blessing, and the verse may serve as a *kavannah* (dedication).

For hand washing:

Erchatz benikayon kappai, va'asovevah et mizbachacha Adonai!
I wash my hands in purity, and encircle Your altar, Adonai!

—PSALM 26:6

For candle lighting:

Ki ata ta'ir neri, Adonai, Elohai, yagi'ah choshki.
It is You who lights my candle; Adonai, my God, illumines the
    darkness.

—PSALM 18:29

For planting seeds or nurturing plants:

Vehayah ke'etz shatul al palgei mayim,
Asher piryo yiten be'ito,
Vi'leihu lo yibol,
Vechol asher ya'aseh yatzliach.
Like a tree planted alongside streams of water,
which will yield its fruit in season,
whose foliage will not fade,
and all it undertakes succeeds.

—PSALM 1:3

While stroking a pet:

Tov Adonai lakol, verachamav al kol ma'asav
Adonai extends Goodness to all;
Adonai's Compassion reaches all creatures.

—PSALM 145:9

While breathing slowly:

Kol haneshamah tehallel Yah
Kol haneshamah tehallel Yah!
Let every breath praise *Yah*/God,
Let every breath praise *Yah*/God!

—PSALM 150:6, TWICE

With baking or cooking:

Noten lechem l'chol basar,
Ki le'olam chasdo!
God gives food to all flesh
with steadfast love that is eternal!

—PSALM 136:25

With walking:

Horeini Adonai darkecha
Ahalech ba'amitecha
Yached l'vavi lir'ah shemecha.
Teach me, Adonai, Your Way,
I will walk in Your truth;
Make my heart one/whole, in awe of Your Name.

—PSALM 86:11

While chanting, singing, playing musical instruments:

Shiru lo, Zamru lo, Sichu bichol niflotav!
Sing to God, compose songs, play instruments for God—
Tell all about God's wondrous acts!

—PSALM 105:2

While walking through the woods:

Ya'aloz saddai v'chol asher bo,
Az yeranenu kol atzei ya'ar!
Let the fields and everything in them exult;
All the trees of the forest will shout for joy!

—PSALM 96:12

While taking in rain, snow, climatic shifts:

Ata heitzavta kol gevulot aretz,
Kayitz vachoref ata yetzartam!
You fixed all the boundaries of the earth,
Summer and winter—You made them!

—PSALM 74:17

While watching clouds roll by:

Hashamayim shamayim l'Adonai
Veha'aretz natan livnei adam.
The heavens belong to Adonai
but the earth Adonai gave to humankind.

—PSALM 115: 16

While enjoying bodies of water:

Asher lo hayam vehu asahu,
V'yabehshet yadav yatzaru.
God's is the sea, God made it;
The land—God's hands fashioned.

—PSALM 95:5

While witnessing sunrises or sunsets:

Mimizrach shemesh ad mevo'o
Mehulal shem Adonai!
From the east, where the sun rises, to where it sets
Adonai's Name is praised!

—PSALM 113:3

While handling or exploring rocks:

Even ma'asu habonim hayta lerosh pinah!
The stone rejected by the builders became the chief cornerstone!

—PSALM 118:22

While touching items of tactile import:

Poteach et yadecha umasbi'a lechol chai ratzon.
You open Your Hand, and satisfy the desire of every living thing.

—PSALM 145:16

While looking at art and architecture:

Im Adonai lo yivneh vayit, shav amlu vonav bo;
Im Adonai lo yishor ir
Shav shakad shomer.
Unless the Lord builds the house, those who build it labor in vain;
unless the Lord watches over the city, the watchman stays awake
   in vain.

—PSALM 127:1

While painting, sculpting, doing crafts:

Veyehi noam Adonai Eloheinu aleinu
Uma'aseh yadeinu konena aleinu
Uma'aseh yadeinu koneneihu!
And let the beauty of Adonai our God be upon us;
and establish the work of our hands upon us;
O prosper it, the work of our hands!

—PSALM 90:17

While gazing at crowds and passersby:

Odecha bikahal rav, be'am atsuv ahalelcha.
I will give You thanks in the great congregation;
I will praise You among a great many people

—PSALM 35:18

Jewish pastoral caregivers play an important role in guiding seekers in articulating their quests by identifying meaningful meditative opportunities in their surroundings, thus helping infuse the world with healing activity using words from our tradition.

Community

The prisoner cannot free himself from jail.

—BABYLONIAN TALMUD, BERACHOT 5b

Community is central to Jewish life, and thus to Jewish healing and Jewish pastoral care. The Jewish pastoral caregiver has a unique responsibility to and a special resource in Jewish community. He or she helps people (re)locate their place in it and clarify their relationship to it.

Over the centuries, the Book of Psalms has emerged as a rich tool for the development and enhancement of spiritual community. One profound Jewish practice organizes members of a Jewish community into a *chevrah tehillim*, a Psalms Fellowship that gathers regularly to study/chant psalms together. In some places, when an individual is ill, the community divides the 150 psalms among its members so that the entire Book of Psalms is read and dedicated daily to healing, strength, solace, and recovery.

Some *chevrot tehillim* explore in depth three psalms a week, studying the entire Book of Psalms in the course of a year. Some chant the psalms out loud, sometimes antiphonally. Some create art based on the images developed in *tehillim*. Some begin by mentioning out loud the names of people who are ill or bereaved, dedicating their fellowship and service to their healing. Recently, *chevrot tehillim* have even been created over the Internet, and 150 individuals dispersed around the world take on a commitment to recite a particular psalm daily as a prayer for the recovery of someone who is ill. Some *chevrot tehillim* are led by laypeople, others are directed by rabbis, cantors, educators, or other professionals. All have at heart the desire to reach into the spiritual wellspring of the psalms for the benefit of the community.

The work of Jewish pastoral caregivers can relate to these psalm communities in any number of ways. Caregivers can be catalysts for new groups and efforts to get underway, or send individuals who are coping with illness or loss to a psalm group that is open to including new members or visitors. Alternatively, they may simply inform existing groups of the names of people to keep in mind as they pray and study. Sometimes, simply letting a person know that such fellowships exist and are praying for those who suffer is a source of solace, comfort, and inspiration.

Conversation

When we consider all of the preceding, we begin to appreciate, really to *experience*, what Jewish tradition means when it so consistently affirms that the Torah is our Tree of Life. Torah can help us navigate and tolerate life. Torah helps us savor, uplift, and deepen life. Torah enables the Jew to live life. The psalms embody all of these.

Over time, as certain words or phrases from psalms become especially meaningful to those being helped, the pastoral caregiver can encourage the integration of these into daily speech so that the ancient words bolster the ability to heal and integrate. This happens primarily through role modeling, through the caregiver's own conscious linking of Torah words with otherwise mundane conversation.

Here are examples of seven such verses from psalms:

- Psalm 26:11. As for me, I will walk in my wholeheartedness; redeem me, favor me!
- Psalm 68:20. Blessed be the Eternal, who daily bears our burden.

- Psalm 71:5 5. For You are my hope, O Eternal God; You have been my Trust from my youth.
- Psalm 86.12. I thank you, O Eternal my God, with all my heart.
- Psalm 90:12. So teach us to number our days, that we may get a heart of wisdom.
- Psalm 118:5. In distress I called upon the Eternal; the Eternal answered me, and set me free.
- Psalm 119:143. Trouble and anguish have taken hold of me; yet Your commandments are my delights.

Mention must be made of "the psalmist in *you*." Readers may be familiar with the remarkable writings of Debbie Perlman, Psalmist-in-Residence of Beth Emet–The Free Synagogue in Evanston, Illinois. Through her various challenges in life, Debbie has blessed us all by turning pen to paper and creating contemporary psalms that bridge the tradition with an intimate, first person, contemporary voice.[7]

The strength of psalms lies substantially in you—in what you, the reader, bring to the words and infuse in them. Psalms are a container for our fears and hopes, a catalyst for the freeing up, and offering up, of our profound and deep wishes, prayers, desires, and insights.

Integrating Psalms in Spiritual Support and Pastoral Care

In one-on-one or group pastoral caregiving, psalms can be a profound and powerful tool. Here are some functions that these kinds of texts might serve in the work of pastoral care:

- Joining with people; normalizing problems or issues
- Naming or articulating challenges; revisiting issues
- Triggering questions; challenging people; facilitating movement
- Reframing problems; placing problems in a context; packaging issues
- Encapsulating or highlighting a dispute
- Offering guidance; suggesting a way to go

- Offering new perspectives on old *tsuris* (troubles); making new connections
- Encouraging; supporting; giving hope
- Consolidating gains
- Distracting; offering or drawing out humor; entertaining

Although Jewish education may be therapeutic, and counseling may have a significant educational component, it is important to know what the goals of a meeting are, what the balance of "information" and "transformation" is. In pastoral care, so much is related to timing and relationship that it is important to remember that *any text must come out of the context* and be not a barrier to but a support for human connection and relatedness.

A woman who was wracked with self-doubt and obsessive second-guessing about her mother's serious illness found a resonant voice and empathic support in Psalm 41. A man who was physically cured but not spiritually healed after his recent bout with cancer found great meaning in and direction from Psalm 139.

Sometimes we must take risks and make mistakes. The key is to see texts as special mirrors, tools, and assets for exploration. The guidance of our tradition is tremendously sensitive to speech and language: It urges us to be present and not to overdo verbiage; this also applies to textual exploration. We must be as sensitive and attuned to our fellow *Tzelem Elohim* (image of God) as possible, also trusting that our deep care and concern, aided by growing insight and learning from experience, will carry the day.

How we segue into a text depends on many factors—including the situation, the person, the particular juncture, our comfort, experience, and outlook, for example, but here are a few possibilities:

- "Your recent comment about XYZ reminded me of this text."
- "Some people have felt that XYZ . . ."
- "There is a Jewish text that deals with some material related to XYZ."
- "I thought you'd appreciate this perspective, from a Jewish text."
- "As I thought some more about XYZ, a perspective from the Jewish tradition came to mind."

- "I would like to give you a gift that might be helpful in some way to you."
- "I wonder what your reaction is to this material?"
- "I came across this text; see how your experience is or is not reflected in it."
- "Even though it's from another time and another place, this Jewish text seemed to be speaking to the problem of XYZ."
- "I heard an echo of your challenge in this Jewish text."
- "Look at this!"

Conclusion

To practice what has just been preached, this chapter concludes with words from the Book of Psalms, offered as a prayer for guidance, empowerment, and support in the life-affirming work of Jewish pastoral care:

O Lord, open my lips; and my mouth shall declare your praise.

—PSALM 51:17

Hear my prayer, O God; give ear to the words of my mouth.

—PSALM 54:4

Turn to me, be gracious with me;
Give of Your strength to Your servant,
Save the son of your maidservant!

—PSALM 86:16

As you provide pastoral care for God's children, may the words of the psalms become your words, and may your words, too, become psalms.

Notes

1. Many prayer books and traditional editions of the Book of Psalms provide this kind of chart; see for example *The Metsudah Tehillim* (New York: Metsudah Publications, 1983) or in the back of the Judaica Press edition of *Psalms* edited by Rabbi A. J. Rosenberg (New York: The Judaica Press, 1991).
2. See Avraham Yaakov Finkel, *In My Flesh I See God: A Treasury of Rabbinic Insights About the Human Anatomy* (Northvale, N.J.: Jason Aronson, 1995), p. 300.

3. All translations of the psalms are by the author.
4. See Zalman Meshullam Schacter-Shalomi, *Spiritual Intimacy: A Study of Counseling in Hasidism* (Northvale, N.J.: Jason Aronson, 1996), pp. 302–7.
5. Abraham Joshua Henschel, *A Passion for Truth*, quoting a Chasidic teaching about mourning and loss (New York: Farrar, Straus & Giroux, 1973), p. 283.
6. See the Introduction in the author's *Healing of Soul, Healing of Body* (Woodstock, Vt.: Jewish Lights Publishing, 1994).
7. Her most recent book is called *Flames to Heaven: New Psalms for Healing and Praise* (distributed by Independent Publishers Group: 800-888-4741).

Bibliography

Feuer, Avrohom Chaim. *Tehillim Treasury: Inspirational Messages and Uplifting Interpretations of the Psalms of David*. Brooklyn, N.Y.: Mesorah Publications, 1994.

Hirsch, Samson Raphael. *Sefer Tehillim: The Psalms*. Jerusalem/New York: Feldheim Publishers, 1978.

Levine, Herbert J. *Sing Unto God a New Song: A Contemporary Reading of the Psalms*. Bloomington, Ind.: Indiana University Press, 1995.

Polish, Daniel F. *Bringing the Psalms to Life: How to Understand and Use the Book of Psalms*. Woodstock, Vt.: Jewish Lights Publishing, 2000.

Rosenberg, A. J., trans. *Psalms* (three-volume edition with Rashi and commentary). New York: The Judaica Press, 1991.

Sarna, Nahum M. *On the Book of Psalms: Exploring the Prayers of Ancient Israel*. New York: Schocken, 1993.

Weintraub, Simkha Y. *Healing of Soul, Healing of Body: Spiritual Leaders Unfold the Strength and Solace in Psalms*. Woodstock, Vt.: Jewish Lights Publishing, 1994.

Rabbi Simkha Y. Weintraub, C.S.W., is the Rabbinic Director of the New York Jewish Healing Center and the National Center for Jewish Healing at the Jewish Board of Family and Children's Services in New York City. He is the author of *Healing of Soul, Healing of Body: Spiritual Leaders Unfold the Strength and Solace in Psalms* (Jewish Lights Publishing).

Spiritual Nurture for
Jewish Pastoral Caregivers

Rabbi Nancy Flam

The work of Jewish pastoral care is demanding. The Rabbis say *Rachmana liba ba'ei* (God wants our hearts); certainly this endeavor requires our very hearts and souls. Rabbi Nancy Flam reminds us that we cannot do this work of caring for others without also caring for ourselves. She helps us understand the costs and demands of our work and offers strategies based in Jewish tradition for maintaining our own well-being by knowing our place, knowing our limits, doing our own grief work, obtaining supervision, and creating balance in our lives. Rabbi Flam urges pastoral caregivers to pay attention to their own spiritual lives and offers concrete suggestions about how to do so.[1]

It is a privilege to provide pastoral care for those who are ill. As rabbis and chaplains, we often have a profound intimacy with the people with whom we work. We are invited into people's lives at a time when they are deeply vulnerable. We witness their suffering and struggle, their grief, sadness, anger, and pain. We move with people through their existential questions and concerns. We get to know their hearts and minds, the yearnings of their souls. We grow to know their families and loved ones. As care providers, our pastoral relationships often bring us a level of human connection and communication that we cherish.

At the same time, working with the ill can take its toll. As hospital chaplains, hospice workers, *bikur cholim* volunteers, or congregational rabbis or cantors dedicated to helping people meet their spiritual needs at times of illness, we find ourselves day after day in the presence of human pain and suffering. Good pastoral care providers open themselves to seeing and knowing the reality that the other person is experiencing. Good listening and true presence require empathy: Although the pain or sadness we witness is not ours, the care we feel for the other person opens our heart to listen empathically. Such attention to pain, grief, sadness, or anger in the lives of those about whom we have grown to care can be depleting; there is no way around this. As Francis Peabody wrote, "The secret of the care of the patient is caring for the patient."[2] The basis of the work we do is the care we provide. Caring means that we will, from time to time, become exhausted or experience burnout.

There is no magic formula for guarding against burnout, but there are ways of doing our work and of caring for ourselves that will help us continue to provide the love and the attention that is at the heart of pastoral care.

Knowing Our Place

One essential element in taking care of ourselves as care providers is to make sure that our conceptual understanding of ourselves and our work is a good one. The images we hold of ourselves as care providers influence the way we work, and in so doing, contribute either to our spiritual health or to our depletion and burnout. Among many possible positive images, I have found those of midwife, holy vessel, and partner to be especially helpful.

As Jews, we know from our tradition that God is the source of all healing, *Rofeh hacholim*. Doctors, nurses, psychologists, social workers, and rabbis are not themselves the source of healing; rather, they aspire to influence conditions so that healing may occur. Pastoral care providers, like all those who practice the healing arts, can be midwives in the work of healing. We can stand by another's suffering, witness another person's soul-labor toward release, clarity, acceptance, or understanding. Our words, touch, glance, or attention may help the soul-labor along, but ultimately, this process is not in our control. We witness, ease, and accompany, but we must be careful not to interfere inappropriately.

The classical Jewish law codes hint at the role of the human healer in relation to the divine. The codes say that when a person is sick, the *Shechina* (God's presence) dwells at the head of the bed.[3] For this reason, the human visitor should not sit at the head of the bed. This image reminds us that we should be very careful not to take the place of the *Shechina*. We should not get in the *Shechina's* way. We should make sure that our own ego needs or false understandings of our role do not obscure the Divine. We should know our place. Or as the tradition teaches, *"Da lifnei Mi atah omed'* (Know before Whom you stand).

Along with the image of midwife, another image that can help us remember our role is to think of ourselves as striving to be *klei kodesh*, vessels for the Divine. We are vessels for God's love and care, servants to the Divine. Rabbi Rami Shapiro writes in his poem about the partnership between God and humanity:[4]

> We are loved by an unending love.
> We are embraced by arms that find us
> even when we are hidden from ourselves.
> We are touched by fingers that soothe us
> even when we are too proud for soothing.
> We are counseled by voices that guide us
> even when we are too embittered to hear.
> We are loved by an unending love.
> We are supported by hands that uplift us
> even in the midst of a fall.
> We are urged on by eyes that meet us
> even when we are too weak for meeting.
> We are loved by an unending love.
> Embraced, touched, soothed, counseled . . .
> Ours are the arms, the fingers, the voices;
> ours are the hands, the eyes, the smiles.
> We are loved by an unending love.

We can learn something about our role as healers from wisdom that has emerged from the twelve-step recovery movement. People who are involved in twelve-step programs reflect on God's role in their healing and recovery. They come from different backgrounds and hold all kinds of beliefs about who or what God is. Although the recovery program is built on a spiritual foundation, there is no elaborate twelve-step theology. People involved in twelve-step communities say that the only thing you really have to understand about God or one's Higher Power is that "you're not it."

As care providers, it can be hard to remember that "we're not it." In working with individuals and families, we often witness amazing moments of insight, gratitude, forgiveness, acceptance, or peace. Often, these moments of grace are enabled by our own love and attention, our words, silence, and prayer. It is easy to forget that we are not the source of healing. At such times of confusion, forgetting the divine source of all good, we are at risk of distorting our role in the healing process. Quite subtly, we begin to identify with the Divine, our ego taken up in the humming energy of God that passes through us. We must be aware of this danger. Keeping a solid model of healing and perspective about our role in the healing process can help.

In addition, as Jews we have been taught that our actions can make a tremendous difference. We can heal the world; we have the power to bring the Messiah. All of this is true, but at the same time we must nourish a healthy sense of humility, perspective, and knowing ourselves in relationship to the Infinite.

Rabbi Jonathan Omer-Man describes the healing relationship as triangular—the one seeking healing, the one hoping to help with the healing, and God.[5] There are *three* partners in healing. This image of partner, along with those of midwife and holy vessel, can help us stay on course.

> Several years ago, I worked with a man who had had a serious back injury. After several surgeries he found, to his great disappointment, that he was worse off after the surgeries than he was before them. After a long period of recuperation, he was about to see yet another doctor. He asked me if there was a prayer he might say as he would began yet another relationship with a medical professional. I suggested that he offer the *Asher yatzar* prayer from the morning liturgy, which thanks God for the miraculous functioning of our bodies. The prayer ends with a blessing that acknowledges God as "the Healer of all flesh who works wonders." This young man told me that he and his new physician offered this prayer together at the end of their first meeting. The last line reinforced for both the patient and the doctor that there were three partners in the healing process. The shared understanding guided their work together.

On a practical level, meditating on verses from the tradition can help us to remember our place as we prepare to enter the room of the person we are visiting, and as we leave when the visit is over. As we enter, we might stop for a minute at the door, take a breath or two, become aware of the sensations in our body, relax into them, touch the *mezuzah* (where there is one), and say to ourselves, *Shiviti Adonai l'negdi tamid* (I set the Eternal before me always).[6] This simple ritual may be all we need to remember our place, our role, our hope, and our Ground.

As we walk out of the room when the visit is over, we might say to ourselves: *B'yado afkid ruchi* (Into God's hand I place myself,[7] or less literally: I acknowledge that I have done my best; the rest is up to God). An exit ritual such as this may help us to acknowledge that the visit is over, that we have given our best, and that we are not in control of the outcome. It may help us, once again, to gain perspective and to touch our faith.

Knowing Our Limits

Closely connected to knowing our place is knowing our limits. Care providers must be aware of the impulse, buried within all compassionate souls, to fix another person's ills. We long to remove the source of physical pain or disease, to provide conclusive answers to troubling existential questions, and to take care of matters that fill the heart with anxiety. Some problems are, indeed, fixable: Sometimes, surgeons can cut out disease; internists can prescribe a medication that cures; caseworkers can discover solutions for difficult situations; pastoral caregivers can comfort or illuminate.

However, some problems are not fixable: The disease is too advanced, the body does not respond to medication, or the soul is unable to find solace. Such situations can be painful for care providers if we have not reckoned with the limits of our own efforts and abilities.

It can be painful to work with someone who is unable to escape his or her suffering. Sometimes we sit with people week after week, month after month, and find that their anger never dissipates; their souls do not know even the least liberation. Our words, our prayers, our wisdom, our caring do not help the bitterness go away. Such relationships can be frustrating, especially when we have forgotten our place in the healing process. We can grow frustrated with our own impotence and the limited repertoire of what we have to offer. Sometimes, it does not seem that our visits help. In fact, they may not help. Sometimes, the good they bring may be so small as to escape measurement. At such times, amid a sharp understanding of our inability, it can be hard to nourish our own hopes and prayers for the person who is suffering. Sometimes, hope and prayer is our best offering.

In the Talmud, we read that Rabbi Abba son of Rabbi Hanina said, "One who visits the sick takes away one-sixtieth of the sick person's pain."[8] The Sages replied, "If this is true, why not let sixty people visit him and restore [the sick person] to perfect health?" Rabbi Abba clarified that each visitor removed one-sixtieth of the remaining illness, so that even sixty visitors would not eliminate the illness altogether.

It seems that the rabbis are saying that one person's compassionate presence to another at a time of illness and suffering can bring a very small but real measure of relief. Sixty people all at once could not really take away all of the pain (although another opinion says that, under the right conditions, they could). No amount of love and attention could entirely heal another person's pain, but each person has the ability to make a small difference in the experience of another. However, we cannot always gauge our impact.

Professional care providers need to be aware of another aspect of our own limits. We need to accept that we can only provide a finite amount of care without using ourselves up entirely. One of my colleague's students had an interesting question about the one-sixtieth story. If each visit takes away one-sixtieth of the pain, she wondered, where does that pain go? Perhaps it may be useful to imagine the pastoral caregiver absorbing, with her exquisite empathy, an immeasurably small but real part of the suffering that those she cares for shed. If so, then there is only so much pain and suffering that any care provider can witness. There are only so many people for whom a caregiver can care.

Each of us needs to adjust the balance differently. Some pastoral care providers are able to work full-time and still take care of themselves; some need to work part-time. Some choose to work with the ill and dying only for a discrete period in their life. All of us have quantitative limits vis-à-vis our work. Those of us who work full-time need to make sure to protect weekend or evening or other important times; there will be occasions on which we will have to say no in order to do this. We need to be aware that the quantity of our work will itself have an effect on our well-being. Therefore, we need to remember the sage advice we find in Pirke Avot: "Rabbi Tarfon used to say, 'It is not your obligation to complete the task, but neither are you at liberty to desist from it'"(Pirke Avot 1:14).

Doing Our Own Grief Work

> Brenda, a woman who works with the dying, called me up this fall in a panic. "I had three deaths in the past ten days. I thought I was completely fine. But this last one threw me over the edge. I woke up two days ago and could not get out of bed. How do I go on?"

Brenda had been working with terminally ill women for the past five years. She loved her work, loved many of the women, and worked hard. Strangely, although she herself was perfectly healthy, she realized at a recent retreat she attended that she had entirely stopped planning her own future. She had identified so strongly with the women she was serving and had so dismantled her own denial of death that she was living as if she were going to die any day.

In conversation, it became clear that Brenda had failed to grieve the deaths of many of the women with whom she had worked. The last woman who had died had been particularly dear to her: Something about the woman's keen wit, dark humor, and the poignancy of her care for her dependent sons touched Brenda deeply. With the loss of this client, Brenda felt the full weight of her accumulated grief.

Professional care providers need to process their own grief. A physician I knew in California designed a monthly grieving and remembrance ritual for his office staff to help them process their feelings of loss. Knowing that they had this monthly ritual and the support of one another helped them open to their own capacity for love and care toward those whom they served. Rachel Naomi Remen, a physician who works with Commonweal, a retreat center for cancer patients in northern California, now spends half her time working with burned-out physicians. In part, she helps them acknowledge and express their grief. She teaches them that grief "mobilizes life energy and helps move it forward."[9]

Pastoral care providers need ways to grieve their losses and to experience emotions like sadness and fear that may arise in working with the ill and dying. We often find that our work grows heavier when we bear it in isolation. We are often not even aware of our own feelings until we take the time to process them in a journal or with a friend, a support group, a therapist, or another community. We need to speak the truth of our own sadness, fear, or maddening sense of impotence as we work with those who are ill and dying.

Some Jewish communities organize community-wide healing services of remembrance, in part to help the helpers in the community acknowledge their losses. Unattended feelings of loss might require periodic work with a grief counselor, as I suggested to Brenda. It is important to know that grief is a natural part of what we experience when we work with those who are ill, dying, or both.

As we work with the ill and the dying, we sometimes hear the echoes and feel the tremblings of our own past losses and threatened losses. To work as pastoral caregivers means that we will periodically revisit and re-examine our own legacies of loss. We know that our own significant losses are never forgotten; at best, we are able to integrate them into our own life stories and life paths. We must be willing to explore painful memories and feelings as they resurface for us through our work.

In addition, it sometimes happens that we become deeply attached to particular clients or congregants because of the depth of their soul, the light of their laughter, the way they remind us of someone we love, or maybe, even particularly, of ourselves; we find that we care especially deeply, that we love them with the love of the soul. However uncomfortable or unfair it may seem to us, it is nonetheless natural that we will have a greater soul-connection with some of our clients than with others. My colleague and friend, Rabbi Amy Eilberg, and I used to call such people "one of those." In our peer-supervision, as we noticed the way the other's soul was moved in talking about a particular client, we would help each other see that that person had surely become for us "one of those." Our hearts had opened and would not be closed.

Just as working with such people brings an added dimension to our lives, losing such people or watching them suffer aggrieves us deeply. Sometimes the full weight of our accumulated grief will hit us when we experience such losses, just as it happened to Brenda. I heard about a physician who had cared particularly deeply about one of his patients, a young rabbi who eventually died of cancer. When she died, he knew that he could not pretend that he was unaffected. He could not simply go back to work as if nothing had happened. He decided to do something he had never done before: He decided to attend her funeral. As he sat in the last row of the synagogue and heard the chanting of the prayers, his face became wet with tears. Before his mind's eye he saw the faces of dozens upon dozens of patients who had died. His heart had cracked open and out of it flowed both his love and his grief.

In the "one-sixtieth" text, there is a minority opinion that says that sixty people could indeed take away all the ill person's pain "if they loved him like themselves" (Lev. Rabbah 34:1). Another text says that they could do so if they were *ben gilo,* which is variously understood as the same age or the same astrological sign. That is, the closer the identification with the person, the greater the love. Were we able to love so fully, according to this minority opinion, we might make miracles happen. Miracles do happen when we love fully, but such loving is rare. Furthermore, as professional caregivers, this is not part of our job description! We wouldn't last long if it were, but sometimes it just happens. We need to know when we are working with "one of those." We need to acknowledge that at such times we may need more support, more nurturance, and an ongoing way to express our emotions.

The Need for Supervision

Another cause for burnout is isolation: Not only do we need the support of others, but we also need their wisdom. It is essential to have regular meetings with a supervisor or peer-supervisor, to speak one-on-one, in a group, or both.

All of us are prone to falling into the competence trap. We do not want to admit to ourselves or to others that a particular case is confusing, that our own buttons are being pushed, or that we really do not know what to do. The competence trap can be especially dangerous for those of us who have been providing pastoral care for a number of years. We knew that we needed supervision when we were young and fresh out of school, but we sometimes fail to remember we still need supervision when our skills increase. Although we may not need supervision to do our basic work, we do need a place to check in. Without that structure, it is easy to lose track of ourselves, to fail to notice where we may be fraying due to burnout, and to miss out on important wisdom. Without that structure, and under the illusory veil of our competence, it becomes harder for us to recognize and to admit those times when we do need help. This isolation, itself, may then lead to burnout.

Striving for Balance

To provide pastoral care for those who are ill is compelling and sometimes consuming work. By comparison, the rest of life can seem unimportant, even trifling. It is not uncommon to find ourselves neglecting to take care of our own needs for rest and recreation. This neglect can be the result of our sense that such realms of life are unimportant, of an unconscious guilt about our own relative health and well-being as compared to those with whom we work, or of sheer exhaustion.

As pastoral care providers, we must be aware of this tendency to neglect our own care and we must work to create balance in our lives. Not only do we need proper rest, but we need to engage in other kinds of activities—movies, books, socializing, and so forth. We must organize our lives to leave room for rest, recreation, and exercise. It may be helpful to think of oneself at the center of a wheel with different spokes bringing different kinds of nourishment. We need food, exercise, friendship, love, learning, fun, prayer, and laughter. With any essential spoke bent or missing, the wheel is likely to become unbalanced.

It may be helpful to ask yourself these questions: What elements do you need to create a balanced life? What new resources might you draw on this week, month, or year that you haven't drawn on recently or perhaps ever? Where do you know yourself to be particularly weary and in need of nourishment?

Paying Attention to
Our Own Spiritual Lives

A critical part of caring for ourselves as pastoral caregivers is to make sure that we are nourishing our own souls. For each of us, spiritual nourishment takes different forms. The nourishment may come in the form of Jewish communal activity, of intentional retreat from the world, of artistic expression, of intimate relationship, of listening to or making music, of body work, from an infinite number of sources. We need to know ourselves well to discern whether we are receiving the kind and amount of spiritual care that will sustain us. We need to take a step back every month or so and evaluate where we are and what we need.

Most of us need regular structures for our own spiritual care, activities that we do not have to organize for ourselves but that are scheduled into our lives. Without such structures, we often find that at the times when we most need such care, we are too depleted to figure out how to go about getting it.

For instance, our regular participation in Jewish communal life can bring important nourishment. The peace and depth of Shabbat, taking one day away from work to recharge the batteries, can be tremendously powerful. Regular study of Jewish sacred texts or other inspirational literature with a *chevruta* partner or group of people can also water the soul, as can celebrating the holidays.

It is also important to pay attention to individual practices that nourish the spirit. For instance, it helps to build in regular times for prayer and meditation, for connecting with one's intimate friends, for walks in nature, for spiritual direction, for massage, for exercise. Our personal combination of such habits and commitments keeps the *shefa*, the flow of divine abundance, moving through us.

Although all people need to pay attention to the quality of their spiritual lives and the nourishment it brings them, those who work with the sick and dying need even more. The bottom line is that we can't give what we don't have. Or in the words of Rabbi Hillel, "If I am not for myself, who will be for me?"(Pirke Avot 1:14).

A Prayer for the Caregiver's Nurture

May we all learn to take care of ourselves. May our intention be to turn ourselves into a resting place for the *Shechina*. May the light of the Divine shine through us and help others to know love, acceptance, joy, peace, beauty, and strength. *Ken yehi ratzon:* May all this, too, be God's desire.

Notes

1. A version of this chapter will appear in the forthcoming work, *The Jewish Book of Healing* (Jewish Publication Society), by Rabbi Nancy Flam and Rabbi Amy Eilberg.
2. Quoted in a presentation by Rachel Naomi Remen.
3. Tur, Yoreh Deah, Section 335.
4. Rabbi Rami Shapiro, "Unending Love," based on the *Ahavah Rabbah* prayer in the morning liturgy. Reprinted with permission.
5. Rabbi Jonathan Omer-Man, personal communication.
6. Psalm 16:8.
7. *Adon Olam* prayer, daily and Shabbat liturgy.
8. BT Nedarim 39b.
9. Audiotape of presentation by Rachel Naomi Remen.

Bibliography

Boorstein, Sylvia. *Don't Just Do Something, Sit There.* San Francisco: HarperSanFrancisco, 1996.

Buxbaum, Yitzhak. *Jewish Spiritual Practices.* Northvale, N.J.: Jason Aronson, 1990.

Davis, Avram, ed. *Meditation from the Heart of Judaism: Today's Teachers Share Their Practices, Techniques, and Faith.* Woodstock, Vt.: Jewish Lights Publishing, 1997.

Shapira, Kalonymus Kalman. *Conscious Community: A Guide to Inner Work.* Andrea Cohen-Kiener, trans. Northvale, N.J.: Jason Aronson, 1999.

Other Resources

The Spirituality Institute at Metivta, 2001 S. Barrington Avenue, Suite 106, Los Angeles, CA 90025; 310-477-5370.

Elat Chayyim: A Jewish Spiritual Retreat Center, 99 Mill Hook Road, Accord, NY 12404; 800-398-2630. www.elatchayyim.org.

Rabbi Nancy Flam, M.A., is Cofounder of The Jewish Healing Center and a pioneer in the field of Jewish healing. She writes and teaches about healing, spirituality, and social justice, and is the editor of *LifeLights: Help for Wholeness and Healing,* a series of pastoral care booklets to help those in need. She is currently the Director of The Spirituality Institute at Metivta in Los Angeles, a retreat-based learning program for rabbis and other Jewish leaders.

SECTION III

*Jewish Pastoral Care for
Specific Needs and Settings*

Jewish Spiritual Care in the Acute Care Hospital

Rabbi Jeffery M. Silberman

Rabbi Jeffery M. Silberman addresses spiritual issues in the acute care setting. He offers a profound analysis of the acute care environment, and the ways in which it challenges dignity and well-being. He explores the emotional and the spiritual needs of Jewish patients and their families. Rabbi Silberman provides guidance on practical aspects of pastoral care in the acute care hospital. He explores four aspects of the role of spiritual caregiver in that context: the priest, the chaver/spiritual companion, the rabbi, and the prophet.

Mr. R. was waiting to be taken into surgery. The chaplain found his name on the presurgery visit list and stopped by to see him before surgery. In the first several exchanges, Mr. R. made it clear that he was fine and that he had no use for a chaplain.

Mr. R.: "You're a chaplain, right? You probably want to offer some comfort or solace or engage me in a conversation. Well, no thanks."

Chaplain: "Those are some of the things that we do, but sometimes, we simply sit with someone, just to keep them company. Would you mind if I sat with you for a few minutes?"

Mr. R.: "Suit yourself."

After a few minutes of silence, curiosity and a bit of anxiety began to stir in Mr. R.

Mr. R: "You know that I am waiting for surgery?" (Pause.) "They are going to do a coronary bypass."

Chaplain: "I understand that."

Mr. R.: "Do you know what it is like to face open heart surgery?"

Chaplain: "No, I don't. Why don't you tell me about it?"

At this, Mr. R. poured out his fears and anxieties. He was able to tell his story and, at the end of a twenty-minute visit, he

received a *Misheberach* prayer from the rabbi before being
wheeled from his room to surgery.

This chapter begins with an examination of the nature of the contemporary acute care hospital, followed by an analysis of the
needs of hospitalized Jewish patients and their families. Next, we address practical aspects of spiritual care in the acute care setting.[1] Finally, we analyze the various roles of the Jewish spiritual caregiver in
the hospital. Our focus in this chapter is primarily on Jewish spiritual
caregivers serving as professional chaplains in acute care hospitals.
However, congregational rabbis, cantors, and lay volunteers may find
this material helpful in guiding them in their hospital visits.

The Acute Care Environment

The exigencies of health care finances, combined with the highly
technological nature of medical care, have made the contemporary
acute care hospital a rather inhospitable environment for patients
and families. The realities we describe here make the need for spiritual care more pressing, also making it more challenging to provide
it appropriately.

Few institutions in our country have undergone as radical a
transformation as acute care hospitals. The last century brought remarkable advances in the medical technology for prolonging and improving life. At the same time, health care institutions have
experienced a transition from economic abundance to scarcity; currently, many if not most hospitals' viability is challenged by uncertain
or reduced reimbursement.

Prompted in large measure by the demands of third-party payers,
medical centers place a priority on cost-effectiveness, even when quality of patient care consequently suffers. The modern hospital typically
is not a very warm environment. Staff and resources are stretched well
beyond reasonable limits. There is constant pressure to do more with
less. The ultimate victim of this pressure too often is the patient, who
is sometimes seen as a diagnosis rather than as a whole person. The
dignity and uniqueness of the individual can be lost. The average patient encounters scores of caregivers, most or all of whom are
strangers. It is likely that even the physician will be unfamiliar to the

patient. The result of the complexity of technological treatment modalities and the confusing jargon that describes them is that patients and their families often may not understand treatment decisions presented to them by their physicians. The hospitalized patient often feels like a stranger in a strange land.

While hospitalized, patients may confront boredom and loneliness. Patients frequently spend long, painful, and empty hours in hospital rooms. Apart from short daily visits of the physician and brief stopovers of nurses and various therapists and technicians, the patient often suffers alone. Frequently, access to the medical center is difficult for family and friends coping with multiple responsibilities of childcare or work. Assaulted by sounds from the television or the stranger in the next bed, patients have few positive things with which to occupy their time. Feeling poorly to begin with, patients may ruminate on their fears, hopes, and questions of meaning, and very likely have no one with whom to share these concerns. The spiritual caregiver can pierce this isolation, providing solace as a caring presence and a representative of the Jewish community.

An additional problem for patients is the ever-decreasing length of hospital stays. Although patients used to stay long enough to allow both complete diagnosis and recuperation, only patients with the most severe illnesses are today granted more than a minimal hospital stay. Insurers and managed care organizations, following the lead of Medicare, have predetermined the normative length of stay and the standard forms of treatment required for most illnesses. A stay of more than a few days in the hospital is an uncommon occurrence except for those who are gravely ill. Patients report that they feel like they are on a medical assembly line, shuttled out the door almost as fast as they came in. Even worse, many patients are released from the hospital although they still require significant care, and they and family members are often unprepared emotionally, physically, or financially for this reality.

The brevity of hospital stays is challenging for spiritual caregivers because they have a very narrow window in which to connect with patients. They are often lucky to meet with a patient one time before discharge. Obviously, this time constraint limits the depth and the breadth of the spiritual care relationship.

Patients who are hospitalized for longer than a few days are kept because of the complexity and the severity of their illness. In these cases, patients are often heavily sedated or connected to machines that render them incapable of coherent communication; they may be existing in a frightening zone between life and death. If they are aware at all, they may struggle to gain a sense of where they are and what is going on around them. Their family members may be engaged in a long vigil waiting for death, or a confusing morass of one wrenching treatment decision after another.

A final consideration regarding contemporary hospital experience is that patients today are significantly older than ever before because of increased longevity. Older patients may suffer more demanding challenges as they live with multiple chronic illnesses, often for decades on end. Family members may be caring for dependent elderly persons for extended periods, straining family resources emotionally, financially and spiritually. These realities raise serious ethical dilemmas in the course of hospitalizations. Families are regularly confronted with decisions about life and death because of what medical science *can* do, not necessarily because of what it *should* do. Jewish spiritual caregivers have an important role to play in these decisions by supporting and caring for individuals and families through the maze of healthcare decision-making.

The Emotional and Spiritual Needs of Jewish Patients and Their Families

To provide Jewish spiritual care, it is essential for caregivers to be aware of the needs of Jewish patients and their family members.

Confronting Loss

A primary aspect of the experience of acute illness and hospitalization is loss. Being a patient creates a sense of loss of control and dignity. The following scene is not uncommon.

> Dr. A., a male doctor who is a total stranger to the elderly female patient, enters the room with a resident and a medical student. Without saying hello or introducing himself and his colleagues, he addresses Ms. J. by her first name. He asks how she feels, her medical history, and about her symptoms, including recent bowel

movements. Dr. A. then tells Ms. J. in very technical language about
a potentially life-threatening diagnosis and about the tests he plans
to order. Ms. J is totally caught off guard and says nothing.

Is it any wonder the patient feels a loss of personal dignity? The emotional responses to the loss of control and dignity can include fear,
anxiety, anger, and helplessness. Some people cope by reading complex medical literature or by questioning medical staff about details of
every diagnosis and test, hoping to regain a sense of control. Others,
even normally assertive individuals, become passive and submissive.
This loss of control and dignity presents challenges to one's spiritual
life. When a person cannot exert normal, self-directed behavior, the
foundations of life's meaning or one's relationship to God may be
called into question.

Older patients may experience particular kinds of loss during illness. The aging process inevitably includes a series of losses of roles, relationships, and capacities. The dependency experienced in illness and
hospitalization can reawaken other losses, resulting in great emotional
and spiritual pain. Older patients may focus upon the loss of youth, the
loss of various physical or mental abilities, or the loss of hope for the future. The limitations imposed by an acute or a chronic illness may evoke
grief or anger. As they engage in life review, some elderly patients may
experience regrets about decisions or actions of their youth.

For older patients in particular, the aggregation of losses may result in a profound existential crisis. Among people in their seventies,
eighties, or nineties, who may have lost a spouse, most of their friends,
or both, the difficulties of hospitalization can give rise to a feeling that
life no longer holds much appeal. This crisis of meaning can become a
focus for Jewish spiritual care intervention. The chaplain responds by
exploring with the individual patient his or her options and choices,
affirming the person's unique value, offering a spiritual connection, or
seeking for ways in which the person might find hope.

Family and Relationship Concerns

For some patients, the experience of acute illness evokes concern
about relationships in their lives, especially with a spouse, children,
or parents. They may find new appreciation of the blessings these
ties bring, or they may note with sorrow the ways in which their

relationships are broken or unsatisfying. They may wish to make specific efforts to repair relationships. Alternatively, instead of addressing their own immediate health, patients may direct their attention toward solving problems of people close to them. For instance, an older woman may worry about how her grandchild is being raised, while her own medical condition remains uncertain.

Understanding both family dynamics and the spiritual distress of hospitalization, the Jewish spiritual caregiver can offer a sounding board for this concern. The spiritual caregiver might explore the nature of the specific family concerns and determine whether the patient is in denial about her condition. The spiritual caregiver can help her both cope with her situation and continue caring for her family.

Jewish chaplains serve the spiritual and practical needs of the patient's family as well. When a loved one is hospitalized, family members usually want information to help understand their relative's condition and their treatment decisions. The family may also require help in facing the changes in the person they knew because of his or her increasing frailty or disability. They may need support in coping with their helplessness in the face of a loved one's suffering or have to prepare for new or ongoing caregiving responsibility or to face the death of a dear one. The chaplain's task is sometimes to help the family begin to let go when death is inevitable. Spiritual care to the family of an acute care patient is an important aspect of the role of the spiritual caregiver.

The Need for Presence and Connection

In the midst of their isolation and pain, Jewish patients need Jewish presence, compassion, and connection. The Jewish spiritual caregiver represents the community's concern for the patient and family. By being present at their bedsides, the spiritual caregiver affirms patients' connection to the Jewish community.

Another way in which the spiritual caregiver may foster connection is to link patients to their rabbis and congregations. With the patient's permission, the spiritual caregiver can notify the rabbi and congregation that the individual is in the hospital so that the rabbi, the *bikur cholim* committee, or both, can visit. Some professional spiritual caregivers may also coordinate and supervise lay volunteers, who can bring warmth and comfort through their visits.

The spiritual caregiver's compassionate presence can offer solace in a time of pain. The nature of this presence is articulated in the Shulchan Aruch's summation of the *mitzvah* of *bikur cholim*: "The essential feature in the religious duty of visiting the sick is to pay attention to the needs of the invalid, to see what is necessary to be done for his benefit and to give him the pleasure of one's company, also to consider his condition and to pray for mercy on his behalf."[2]

The trained spiritual caregiver's presence is distinct from that of caring friends and family. Although loved ones bring their own emotions and needs into the encounter, the spiritual caregiver is called to be present *with* and *for* the patient and the family, to be grounded, to offer a nonanxious, open, and caring presence. The spiritual caregiver might listen for the deep, unspoken concerns borne by the patient, or serve as a neutral person as conflicted family members express their divergent views about an agonizing treatment decision. Being present for the individual might also mean assisting with concrete concerns, such as helping a patient's family to coordinate children's transportation, or making sure that a dying patient who is unable to eat has ice chips to bring her comfort. The Jewish spiritual caregiver is a visible representative of the Jewish community's care and concern. No other member of the health care team focuses exclusively on the spiritual side of caring.

Religious Needs of Jewish Patients

As they face uncertainty and suffering, Jewish patients need to have continuity of Jewish religious observance. Whatever one's level of observance, being able to continue practicing those customs and traditions creates a tangible connection to normal life. The complexities of life in modern medical centers can obstruct this religious connection. The spiritual caregiver may have to act as an advocate to assist in patients' observance, or to take creative measures to facilitate it. For example, it is common for hospitals to prohibit lighting candles anywhere in patient areas. This restricts the lighting of Shabbat candles, unless approved electric candles are available. Jewish spiritual caregivers can stock the standard Orthodox-approved electric Shabbat candles and ensure that there is a procedure for patients who wish it, to have them.

Religious observances create a bridge to normal life for patients.

Recent clinical studies have repeatedly shown that a positive emotional and spiritual attitude contributes to patients' healing process.[3] Certainly, *kashrut*, the observance of Shabbat and the festivals are beneficial to the Jewish patient. Even the nonreligious Jew may enjoy a *ta'am* (taste) of Judaism. From the good wishes of a fellow Jew to the opportunity to light the Hanukah *menorah*, most Jews welcome a Jewish connection in the hospital. One very positive example of such efforts is the growing movement of Jewish volunteers around the country to bring *chalah* to Jewish patients to enable them to participate in observance of Shabbat. In addition, Jewish spiritual caregivers, volunteers, or both can conduct holiday ceremonies in individual patients' rooms, or in common areas throughout the hospital. Familiar symbols and practices such as these help hospitalized Jews feel cared for and more human in a setting that by its very nature is alienating and impersonal.

Enabling Jewish patients to pray can be a powerful aspect of spiritual care. Making available necessary liturgical resources such as a *siddur, machzor,* or *haggadah*, as well as selected Jewish readings and reflections on illness and suffering, can also be supportive for patients.

In facilitating the observance of Jewish patients in the modern medical center, the Jewish spiritual caregiver must educate staff about Jewish practices and observances. Instructing the food service staff about *kashrut* and medical staff about community resources for *taharah* (the ritual cleaning of the body) are examples of such teaching. In effect, the Jewish chaplain becomes an advocate for all Jewish patients in the institution, explaining religious practices and Jewish sensibilities to non-Jewish staff.

Religious Needs of Traditionally Observant Jews

For traditionally observant Jewish hospital patients, there are a myriad of halachic concerns and considerations regarding both religious observance and the provision of medical care. In addition to the normal anxiety associated with being a patient, the traditionally observant Jew may also worry about maintaining the standards of religious behavior that are part of his or her normal life. Jewish spiritual care to traditionally observant Jews in an acute care hospital requires attention to these needs.

Concerns about diet may be a challenge for the traditionally observant Jew and for the institution trying to meet those needs. Obtaining food that meets the particular standard of *kashrut* the patient observes is of great importance. It can be a further source of distress when the institutional dietary department does not pay careful attention to details. In one hospital, a Jewish patient received a fresh roll along with her strictly Kosher for Passover meal tray, the gift of a well-intentioned but misguided staff person. With in-service training, the Jewish chaplain eventually helped the dietary staff to direct their generosity in a more appropriate manner.

Being able to adhere to Shabbat observance, an essential aspect of Jewish life, is another important need of the observant Jewish patient in the acute care setting. The patient needs to observe the positive ritual aspects of Shabbat, such as lighting candles and saying kiddush and *ha'motzi,* and to be able to avoid prohibited behaviors, such as writing or riding in an elevator. This can be difficult because the hospital operates on its own time schedule, twenty-four hours a day, seven days a week. Decisions made by staff about treatment, surgery, and discharge can interfere with observance of Shabbat. For example, a traditionally observant patient may refuse to sign in when admitted on Shabbat. This religious behavior, reasonable when understood from a traditional Jewish perspective, may become an annoyance for hospital staff when they need to register a new patient. A professional Jewish chaplain may help resolve such matters by educating hospital administrators to create reasonable options. Also, managed care providers require that the patient be discharged from the hospital as soon as possible, thus there may be resistance to an observant Jew's request for delays in procedures or discharge until after the end of Shabbat.

The spiritual caregiver can help the institution respond sensitively to the observant patient's religious needs. At times, what is needed is an explanation of the patient's concerns to staff members who may be unfamiliar with the dictates of traditional Jewish observance. In other cases, it may be necessary to bring the matter to the attention of hospital administrators who have the power to make exceptions to rules. Beyond specific cases, the spiritual caregiver might also advocate changes in institutional policy. In addition, the chaplain may work to develop special resources to meet those needs, such as a Shabbat elevator, or a Shabbat apartment for family members of observant patients who would otherwise be unable to be with the patient over Shabbat.

Along with matters of ritual observance, traditionally observant Jewish patients have special concerns about some treatment decisions. For instance, questions about the appropriateness of a treatment or the cessation of mechanical life support may require consultation with a patient's rabbi or a *posek* (Jewish legal decisor). Traditionally observant patients will routinely refuse autopsy and will agree to organ donation only in limited circumstances. Although staff usually perceive the involvement of local clergy as helpful, it is possible that rabbinic interventions in these issues may challenge hospital routines and may be seen as interference in the patient's treatment plan. The spiritual caregiver's support in educating staff and administration about the nature of authority in traditional communities and about particular concerns can be invaluable.

The needs of the traditionally observant Jew are an important focus of Jewish spiritual care in the modern acute care setting. A professional Jewish chaplain who is integrated into the fabric of the hospital organization can work from within to educate and to inform an institution about Jewish religious needs.

Practical Aspects of Spiritual Care in the Acute Care Hospital

Deciding Which Patients Will Be Seen

Most acute care institutions with Jewish patients have limited spiritual care resources. A ratio of more than one Jewish chaplain to one hundred Jewish patients is a luxury, thus a system of prioritization becomes essential because it is seldom possible to see every Jewish person who is in the hospital.

One model of priorities focuses on the critical care and emergency areas, where the need is the most evident. Another model relies on patient requests for chaplains. A third option is for the non-Jewish chaplaincy staff to make referrals of Jewish patients whom they encounter. If none of these systems is in place, the Jewish spiritual caregiver must devise a strategy for triage and must find ways of coping with the reality that he or she can never address the spiritual needs of all of the Jewish patients in the institution. Above all, it is important that the Jewish spiritual caregiver remain flexible to respond to calls and referrals throughout the institution.

Collaboration with the Health Care Team

Collaboration with medical and nursing staff is an essential feature of spiritual care in an acute care hospital. Hospital staff members frequently make informal referrals to the chaplain of patients whose spiritual distress is most evident. Even when patient records are available to the chaplain, conversations with the patient's nurse are usually the most efficient way to obtain a picture of his or her current condition. Physicians can also inform the chaplain about patients' needs. Input from professional caregivers aids in planning an effective spiritual care intervention. In addition, staff members frequently use chaplains to support them, too. The intense pressure of modern hospitals affects everyone and the chaplain provides an easily accessible resource for nurses, doctors, and other staff to discuss their own religious and personal concerns.

Respecting patient confidentiality is always an issue in acute care settings. On one side of the issue, hospitals usually consider chaplains as staff and thus chaplains have full access to patient records. The newest Standards from the Joint Commission for the Accreditation of Healthcare Organizations (JCAHO), which surveys all accredited hospitals every three years, includes a requirement that chaplaincy documentation be integrated into the medical records. A question may be raised about limits on what the chaplain should share with the health care team about needs or concerns the patient has discussed in the spiritual care encounter. If the patient says anything that indicates that he or she is a danger to himself or herself or to another person, it is the chaplain's duty to report that information. With the patient's permission, a spiritual caregiver may choose to share other information about the patient's needs and concerns with other caregivers to foster better care and enhance well-being. Otherwise, matters of personal faith, struggle, or confession can and should be held in confidence.

The Role of the Jewish Spiritual Caregiver

The task of professional Jewish chaplains is in many respects unique. Although not all professional Jewish chaplains are rabbis or cantors, the majority are. This official religious status affords certain authority to the chaplain role, which encourages the trust of the Jewish patient. The patient may disclose to the Jewish chaplain fears and concerns that he or she would not share with a volunteer or even a family member. Telling one's story is one way in which spiritual healing begins. Attending to the personal midrash (story) of a patient entails a sacred responsibility for the professional Jewish chaplain. The spiritual connections that a Jewish chaplain fashions with a patient can have a profound impact upon an individual life. Helping another Jew to face fear, loss, and even death is a sacred and singular task.

The symbolic power of the chaplain's role resides *uniquely* with that role. A kind of mystery surrounds the living presence that chaplains bring to their patients. Christian writings about pastoral care view this special nature as the incarnational aspect of chaplaincy. Rabbi Jack Bloom calls this dynamic in the rabbi's role the *symbolic exemplar*.[4] In effect, it is a power and authority from religious heritage that we embody in the chaplaincy.

We can further understand the chaplaincy role as a unique combination of professional functions and leadership models rooted in Torah and rabbinic tradition. The contemporary spiritual caregiver fulfills the functions of the priest, the *chaver*/spiritual companion, the rabbi/teacher, and the prophet. Jewish chaplains claim all four roles as fundamental aspects of who we are.

Priest

In the role of priest, Jewish chaplains use ritual and ceremony in the spiritual care of patients. In ancient Judaism, priests were the principal functionaries in divine services; their special role was to engage in ritual ceremony. Chaplains may fulfill this role in the modern context by offering a formal prayer, such as the recitation of the *Viddui*, the confessional prayer near death, or by constructing a creative ceremony to meet the unique needs of a particular patient or family.

> Mr. S., sixty-six years old, whose left side was paralyzed by a stroke, tells the Jewish chaplain that he feels angry over the circumstances in which he finds himself. It is evident to the chaplain that Mr. S. does not allow himself to be angry at God. The

chaplain suggests that Mr. S. may feel connected to the words of psalms. The chaplain offers a reading from Psalm 13, which surprises Mr. S. He is then able to express his anger at God and to open up the possibility of a renewed relationship. The chaplain helps Mr. S. to pray to God, voicing both his anger and his longing for connection and solace.

The Jewish chaplain functions as a priest, forging connections to God, Jewish tradition, and the Jewish people using the healing power of ritual. Our participation in these religious or spiritual events allows Jewish chaplains to enter the world of an individual as a priestly figure, coordinating mythic and symbolic events and helping to navigate times of transition or uncertainty.

Prayer is a powerful tool for the Jewish spiritual caregiver. Both as a vehicle for the patient's religious and spiritual expression and as an entryway into a deeper spiritual care relationship, prayer offers a special means of connection to personal meaning and healing. Prayer opens the possibilities of a closer relationship with God, with the Jewish community, and with the chaplain.

Another important dimension of the priestly role is the expiation of guilt. Facing illness or death may prompt a person to feel guilt for past errors; responding to this guilt is an important aspect of the professional spiritual caregiver's role. Whether enabling an individual to voice his or her regret over failings in life, creating a ceremony of reconciliation, or praying for forgiveness, the spiritual caregiver can help to relieve a patient of some of the burden of guilt.

Ms. C. was a patient with a recent diagnosis of cancer. In her mind, the illness was brought on by her history of reckless and irresponsible behavior. The Jewish chaplain invited her to relate her story, to explore her sense of sin, and, eventually, to be blessed by a prayer for forgiveness that the rabbi offered.

Chaver: Spiritual Companion

A *chaver* is a companion, friend, or colleague; we use the term in this context to refer to the spiritual caregiver's role as spiritual companion to those he or she helps. The role of the spiritual companion conveys the sense that Jewish chaplains bring a listening ear, a compassionate presence, and a caring heart. The *chaver,* or spiritual companion, accompanies someone on life's journey. Companioning suffering or dying people is at the core of Jewish spiritual care. The qualities associated with this model include active listening, support, consolation, and compassion. Spiritual companions care for the human spirit by reaching out to the divine spirit. When we commit to being present with a patient, not fixing or doing something, professional Jewish spiritual care professionals offer trust, compassion, and empathy.

Pirke Avot (Sayings of the Fathers) presents the model of spiritual companion. Yehoshua ben Perachya said: "Provide yourself a teacher, get yourself a companion, and judge all people favorably."[5] We all need a faithful companion to walk with us as we face the rough and painful parts of life's journey. The Jewish spiritual caregiver is a *chaver* who aids, counsels, and gives support and help to another person. Indeed, the Jewish chaplain serves as a *chaver* not only to the sick and dying, but to families, friends, and hospital staff as well. As a spiritual companion, the Jewish chaplain provides solace through presence and serving as witness to the struggles and triumphs of the souls he or she meets.

Every professional spiritual caregiver is trained to listen to feelings of self and others. This self-awareness is integrated with psychological insights and theological understanding toward the goal of appropriate spiritual care interventions.

> Ms. F., forty-five years old, sits alone in a darkened room with no cards, no flowers, and no visitors. When the chaplain arrives, the feeling of sadness is palpable. "Having a tough time?" begins the chaplain. "No one seems to care," says Ms. F. "I would like to hear what is going on. Tell me, please," replies the chaplain. "I am so alone," states Ms. F. The chaplain sits down on a nearby chair, reaches out and takes her hand, saying nothing. Ms. F. then tells the chaplain that she is divorced, has no children, and has just had a hysterectomy because of uterine cancer. She grew up in a city 800 miles away, and all her relatives are there. She talks about her fear, sorrows, and hopes. After listening with sensitive concern, the chaplain offers a prayer and asks Ms. F.'s permission to

contact the rabbi of the congregation Ms. F. has recently joined to let him know of her situation.

Professional Jewish spiritual care includes a caring and compassionate dimension that is fulfilled through our companionship. The Jewish chaplain's work derives from this accessible symbolic role of spiritual companion. Functioning as *chaver*, the spiritual caregiver is able to respond to issues of personal need and faith.

Rabbi/Teacher

In the role of the rabbi or teacher, the Jewish chaplain serves as teacher, religious authority, and moral compass; the cantor or trained lay Jewish chaplain also fulfils this role at times. These functions have an important place in the delivery of professional Jewish spiritual care. The rabbinic role carries authority, based on the professional's knowledge of Jewish literature and wisdom. Like traditional rabbis, Jewish chaplains can provide a moral foundation to guide patients and families seeking direction in the face of complex ethical decisions. The Jewish spiritual caregiver does not use the rabbinic role to teach in a didactic way, but rather offers guidance in response to the needs and questions of patients, family members, and hospital staff. The spiritual caregiver uses both specific halachic dicta and the values embedded in aggadic tales in teaching about Jewish tradition's perspectives on the issue at hand.

> Mrs. P., an elderly woman who lives alone, resists the help that her family offers her while she is incapacitated. "I don't want them to come here to the hospital. They have their own lives, their own *tzuris* (troubles)." The rabbi asks her if she believes in doing *mitzvot*. "Of course," she replies, "even though I can't do many of them. But I do what I can." The rabbi says, "So, then, you need to realize that by not letting others help you, you are preventing them from doing the *mitzvah* of *bikur cholim*." This framing of her plight offered Mrs. P. a lens for understanding her situation. With this perspective, she was able to agree to let her family take care of her.

When Jewish chaplains articulate *what they believe*, not to judge others, but as leaders and symbols, they offer patients and staff valuable moral direction. Another aspect of the rabbinic role of Jewish spiritual caregivers is addressing theological questions provoked by patients' and family members' encounters with illness and mortality. It is critical to respond to the spiritual and emotional pain that is present in these questions, not just to teach what Jewish text or tradition has to say. People who are suffering seek comfort as well as information or knowledge.

Jewish spiritual care includes a dimension of teaching and moral authority. In the rabbinic role, Jewish spiritual caregivers can use Jewish text and tradition to offer moral guidance and to support patients and family members struggling for faith and comfort.

Prophet

Lastly, the Jewish chaplain may also assume the traditional role of prophet. In Jewish tradition, the prophet is endowed with the divine gift of both receiving and imparting the message of God. Although the prophets' mission came from God, they also remained unique individuals whose own personalities and sense of priorities was manifest in the messages they conveyed. The prophets' messages for Israel were often difficult and upsetting. In this same sense, the Jewish chaplain may become an advocate for the patient as person. Whether it is obtaining a kosher meal or helping a patient to deal with an uncommunicative physician, this paradigm of prophet may be useful.

> The family of Mr. H. called the chaplaincy office, saying that they felt that he was not being treated appropriately. The rabbi went to visit the patient to explore the issue. It became clear that the patient was uncomfortable with some of the nurses' aides who did not speak English very well. Mr. H was anxious when they brought his kosher food and it was already open. He feared that they were tampering with it in some way. It was relatively easy for the rabbi to speak with the head of the dietary services department to make sure that the dishes remained covered until they were served.

The Jewish chaplain comes to visit patients and families as a messenger of the institution who has credibility with both sides. As a kind of intermediary between hospital and patient, the Jewish chaplain functions as a prophet in facilitating the communications that are often difficult for others to say and to hear. At times, this mission will require the chaplain to take a stand that goes against norms or policies of the institution.

Conclusion

Being hospitalized is a time of spiritual transition. Patients go through many emotions, traumas, and surprises while lying in a hospital bed. This experience can be one of great despair or great insight. There may be no more fertile time to connect with one's true inner self, with what we hold dear, and with God than when we are hospitalized.

The professional Jewish chaplain serves a critical role. As one who cares and as one who understands the issues and dynamics of hospital life, the Jewish chaplain simultaneously links the patient to Jewish community and to tradition through presence and compassion and navigates the bewildering and uncaring sea of modern medical centers. Many patients have described Jewish chaplains as a beacon of light in the darkness of their hospital experience, bringing a sense of spiritual healing and hope to the bedside. This is the role of the Jewish spiritual caregiver in acute care hospitals—to stand between the medical technology and the patient, on holy ground.

Notes

1. I prefer the term "spiritual care" to "pastoral care" because it is a more apt description of our task. The caregiver is also referred to here as the "chaplain," the professional engaged by an institution to provide spiritual care within it.
2. Shulchan Aruch. Yoreh De'ah 335:8.
3. See, for example, Harold G. Koenig, *Is Religion Good for Your Health? The Effects of Religion on Physical and Mental Health* (New York: Haworth Press, 1997).
4. Jack H. Bloom, "By the Power Invested in Me: Symbolic Exemplarhood in the Congregational Rabbinate," in *Conservative Judaism* 50, no. 4 (summer 1998): pp. 59–66.
5. Pirke Avot 1:6.

Bibliography

Krauss, Pesach. *Why Me? Coping with Grief, Loss and Change.* New York: Bantam Books, 1988.

Schur, Tzvi G. *Illness and Crisis: Coping the Jewish Way.* New York: NCSY/Orthodox Union, 1987.

Wolpe, David. *The Healer of Shattered Hearts: A Jewish View of God.* New York: Henry Holt Books, 1990.

Rabbi Jeffery M. Silberman, D. Min., is Director of Pastoral Care and Education at Beth Israel Health System in New York City. He holds degrees from the University of Dayton, Hebrew Union College–Jewish Institute of Religion and Andover Newton Theological School. In 1988, he founded the National Association of Jewish Chaplains and became its first President. He continues his involvement as Chair of the national Certification Committee. Previously, he was Director of Spiritual Care and Pastoral Education at UCSF–Mount Zion Medical Center in San Francisco and also served as Codirector of Pastoral Care and Education at Lenox Hill Hospital in Manhattan.

Preparing for the Chupah:
Premarital Counseling

Rabbi Ellen Jay Lewis

Rabbi Ellen Jay Lewis guides readers in the crucial area of pastoral premarital counseling. She offers several distinctly Jewish theological frameworks for the task of premarital counseling. She walks the reader through the process of premarital counseling and suggests strategies for using the experience within it to foster growth in the couple. She examines the challenging area of the pastoral caregiver's emotional reactions. Lastly, Rabbi Lewis presents situations that require special sensitivity or skill on the part of the pastoral caregiver, such as same-sex marriages.

"When three sit together and study Torah, it is accounted as though they have formed a bond with the Holy One of Blessing."[1]

The rabbi had been ordained only two months when she first sat with a newly engaged couple in her office. Although one of the congregation's senior rabbis would be officiating at the ceremony, the couple had come to ask her if she would bless them on the Shabbat before their wedding. The rabbi readily agreed, and then, not knowing what else to say, asked if there was anything else they wanted to discuss. "Yes," said the groom. "My parents had a terrible marriage and I worry we might end up divorced." In that moment, the rabbi's mind went completely blank. Surely premarital counseling had been discussed in rabbinical school, she thought desperately, but if so, why couldn't she remember a thing? What should she say? And why, oh why, she wondered, were they seeking help from her, of all people?

This story is the stuff of which pastoral caregivers' anxiety dreams are made. Although not everyone's first meeting with a couple ends with the groom's blurting out his fear of divorce, most rabbis and cantors remember the first couple who made them ask themselves, "*Now* what do I do?" This chapter is geared toward helping rabbis and cantors find an answer to that question by becoming comfortable in working with "the healthy premarital couple" who come in not to resolve conflict but for assistance in getting married.[2] Whether by choice or by circumstance, clergy still do the bulk of the premarital counseling that occurs in the United States.[3] Approximately two thirds of all first-marriage couples have premarital discussion with clergy.[4]

Establishing a Theoretical Framework

Effective pastoral counseling has never been more urgently needed. It is general knowledge that the divorce rate in both Jewish and non-Jewish communities in the United States has climbed rapidly in recent years; no one disputes that marriages bear increasing burdens in a rapidly changing world. Why not educate couples before marriage so that they can anticipate obstacles to their relationship and overcome them? Therapists joke that it is easier to get a marriage license than it is to get a driver's license.[5] Although research has not established that premarital counseling can prevent failed marriages, premarital counseling clearly can be beneficial for couples approaching the *chupah*.[6]

It is essential that the rabbi or cantor preparing a couple for the *chupah* have realistic objectives for the three-or-so sessions to be spent with a given couple. One attainable goal is helping the couple make good decisions together by educating them emotionally so they are able to approach the premarital process at a deeper level. This education begins by responding to the issues that the couple presents, however minor their questions might seem. By showing interest in what concerns them, the rabbi or cantor begins to develop an emotional alliance with the couple and to demonstrate that marriage differs from other commitments they have formed in the past. In so doing, the clergy member teaches by example the nature of covenant as a reciprocal context in which conflict can be addressed and mutual needs can be met without threatening the basic bond. Like God and Israel, both parties remain independent yet mutually dependent, while sharing a sense of reciprocal obligation.[7]

However, before beginning this process of emotional education, it helps to understand the nature of the engaged couple. Although the interplay of individual and family issues make the so-called normal transition from singlehood to couplehood one of the most difficult transitions in the family life cycle, most couples seem oblivious to the enormity of the task.[8] The typical premarital couple lives happily ensconced in their own cocoon. They may be interested in the world outside solely as a mirror reflecting their self-absorbed joy. In fact, everyone but the happily engaged couple seems to be aware of the pitfalls of marriage.[9] Despite the evidence that the seeds of later marital discontent are present during the courtship period, most engaged couples themselves do not see it. No matter how sincere the attempt to open the couple's eyes to future reality, such an effort is unlikely to succeed and will result in the frustration of couple and clergy alike.

As part of understanding the nature of the engaged couple, it is important for the rabbi or cantor to clarify a basic difference between the couple who comes to the clergy for help in getting married and the couple who goes to a therapist for help in resolving conflict. The usual incentive for people to enter any kind of therapy stems from their desire to stop the pain they are experiencing. This is not usually the case for a couple coming to the rabbi or cantor for premarital preparation. Herein lies one of the primary issues in premarital counseling: the healthy couple is not presently experiencing pain in their relationship, thus they are not inclined to be receptive to any kind of externally imposed premarital counseling that focuses on conflict or future marital pathology.

Therefore, to be realistic, clergy should determine premarital counseling goals with this dual awareness: First, the couple has come voluntarily to plan their wedding; and second, the premarital couple may not yet be interested in acknowledging significant differences or confronting major conflicts. However, with encouragement, they will ask for help with conflicts that are bound up in the task of accomplishing the wedding. The rabbi or cantor who can join with them in helping them resolve their stated issues and achieve their goals has already begun to introduce emotional education and to reinforce the idea that Judaism has wisdom to offer them in their marriage.

The process involved in achieving emotional and spiritual preparation for marriage is threefold: (1) to help the couple feel comfortable talking about emotional issues with a third party; (2) to help them communicate effectively with each other; and (3) to do both of these in a Jewish context. By helping the couple achieve their stated goals and not imposing on them other goals, premarital counseling can plant seeds for the future and pave the way for the couple to seek out subsequent counseling after their marriage.[10] Although a postwedding follow-up meeting might be suggested, the couple may or may not be interested in keeping that appointment, but their memory of the rabbi or cantor's ability to be with them and talk about what interests them now can facilitate their choosing to talk to a third party when they encounter obstacles in the future.

Establishing a Spiritual Context

Just as it is necessary for rabbi and cantors to work within a theoretical framework of premarital counseling, it is equally important for them to operate within a spiritual context. Jewish tradition offers many different conceptual models for relationship. The individual preference, comfort level, and belief system of the particular clergy determine which model is most appropriate. Whichever model is chosen, however, the rabbi or cantor becomes the embodiment of that model in working with the couple. Although it is not necessary for the clergy member to explain explicitly his or her spiritual framework to the couple, it is crucial that those spiritual ideas be communicated and modeled through mature interaction with the couple.

The three models presented here do not exhaust the possibilities, but are included to encourage each individual rabbi and cantor to develop his or her own theological perspective. The first model, the concept of the Jewish home as a *mikdash me'at* (a miniature sanctuary), encourages the couple to invite the Divine Presence into the routine of their daily lives. The second model, Martin Buber's I–Thou theology, offers the example of partners truly listening to each other and respecting that each was created *b'tzelem Elohim* (in the image of God). The third paradigm, the Sinaitic covenant, presents a model for establishing boundaries and expectations for the couple's relationship with each other and with the larger Jewish world. Each of these models attempts to help the couple integrate the personal with the spiritual.

Mikdash Me'at

Since the destruction of the second Temple in Jerusalem when the symbols of Temple worship were reconceptualized and incorporated into the individual home, Jewish tradition has considered the home a *mikdash me'at*. One's home is one's Temple, the marital partners assume the role of the priest, their table becomes the altar on which they offer the sacrifice of their hearts, and all that goes on within that tabernacle, including human relationships, has the potential to be holy. The goal of marriage is to recreate this *mikdash me'at* every day, to infuse what would otherwise be profane with holiness. In the same way, the clergy's office comes to represent its own *mikdash me'at*, carving out a corner of sacred space in an otherwise mundane world. If the rabbi or cantor can create an environment in which mature communication is encouraged, anger is constructively verbalized and differences are explored, that interaction demonstrates how the couple might do the same in their own home. The office becomes more than just an office, just as their home should be more than just a home. Therapists speak of creating a holding environment in which a mother maintains a safe space for her child's growth and expression.[11] For that hour of meeting with the premarital couple, the rabbi or cantor's office is transformed into a holding environment that can contain all of the couple's excitement, anxiety, fear, joy, love, and hate. Insofar as the clergy functions as a symbolic representative of Judaism for the couple, they come to appreciate the idea that Judaism itself is a holding environment that can accept and value them for who they are. Couples feel valued when they have the experience of being listened to and understood.

I–Thou Encounter: Real Meeting

Pastoral premarital counseling requires the rabbi or cantor to "listen with the third ear."[12] Although there are times when it is appropriate to answer couples' questions, more often than not, they need to be listened to more than they need to be responded to or answered. In listening for what is said as well as what is not said, in being truly present with them, the rabbi or cantor can help them aspire to "real meeting." Martin Buber says that such real meeting occurs between people when they enter into genuine relationship with each other, when they fully accept one another, and when there is "mutual confirmation of their separate selves."[13] According to Buber, every time one enters into such an "I–Thou" relationship, one also discovers

God: "In each Thou we address the Eternal Thou."[14] The rabbi or cantor who can be fully present with a couple will have helped them to connect, if only for a moment, to the Divine Presence. By sitting patiently and attentively with a couple, rabbis and cantors can educate the couple to the idea of relationship as a dynamic process and can demonstrate that marriage as *kiddushin* (a holy covenant) requires time and talk if it is to become a unique relationship set apart from all others.

The Sinaitic Covenant: Reciprocal Love and Obligation

This uniqueness of the couple's relationship reflects the special relationship between God and Israel. The time the Jewish people spent in the Sinai Desert before the revelation is, for all intents and purposes, the premarital period of God and Israel. Their love knows no limits but it is not yet reciprocal. The people themselves possess a childlike idea of love, in which they expect to receive love unconditionally from God but not to give it in return. Not until the covenant at Sinai are the people introduced to the idea of mature reciprocal love in which there are new conditions and rules that require sacrifice on the part of both partners for their mutual benefit. Although the threat of infidelity (the Golden Calf) always lurks in the background, the covenant is a reminder of the marital commitment between God and Israel. The Torah becomes the *ketubah* (marriage contract) that legitimizes their union.[15] Just as Israel needs the rules of Torah to live in holy relationship, married couples need rules of relationship to sustain them in the times when romantic love does not. In this way they are taught that whereas love is the basis of covenantal relationship, love without rules and limits is not enough to sustain a relationship. The developing relationship between clergy and couple becomes a model for the couple's developing with each other a similar contract of mutual obligation and reciprocation.

Whether the rabbi or cantor selects one of these three models of Jewish relationship or a different one, the caregiver's office itself implicitly comes to represent that model and to function as a spiritual laboratory for living and demonstrating Torah. The chosen theological perspective should permeate all interchanges with the couple.

Beginning the Premarital Counseling Relationship: Preparing Oneself

Rabbis and cantors who prepare themselves emotionally, practically, and spiritually before meeting with a couple convey to the couple the dual message that their upcoming marriage is deserving of the clergy's respectful consideration and that, similarly, they as a couple need to prepare themselves seriously for marriage. Before seeing the couple for an initial appointment, even the seasoned rabbi or cantor should spend some time thinking about what he or she needs to feel comfortable relating to them. The more at ease the rabbi or cantor feels, the greater will be the comfort level of the couple. The couple will be relying on the clergy to create the spiritual context for the relationship and to guide them in their religious decision making.

Rabbis and cantors should thus prioritize their own need for information. Most rabbis and cantors develop a wedding information form that lists the information they will need for the ceremony and includes other topics relevant to Jewish premarital counseling. How many meetings should be held with the couple? What does the rabbi think about couples who might want to write their own vows or couples who are interviewing a number of rabbis as candidates for their wedding? How does the cantor feel about couples who want to marry on the beach or elsewhere outdoors? Does the rabbi have a halachic objection to a wedding ring with cutouts or stones or to a double-ring ceremony altogether? Does the cantor require the couple to provide their own *ketubah* or is he or she willing to provide one? When should Tay-Sachs disease testing be mentioned?

There will be many other areas the rabbi or cantor needs to consider in creating a comfortable environment; these preliminary suggestions are intended to help rabbis and cantors think about what makes them comfortable and to assist them in developing their own style. Newly ordained and invested clergy who are just beginning to work with couples cannot be expected to know in advance what will increase their comfort level or how they feel about every issue. These answers will be discovered through supervision, experience, and discussion with colleagues. The rabbi or cantor who is comfortable with his or her own preparation will feel free to be with the couple, to listen to them, and to enjoy them.

The premarital counseling relationship begins before the couple ever enters the rabbi or cantor's office. It starts with that first phone call: "We're getting married." "*Mazel tov!*" Now what? The clergy's own goals, implied or otherwise, will inform what happens next.

Setting the First Appointment

Other than preliminary calendar-checking, it is best to try to avoid discussion of other wedding details over the phone so that, in keeping with the *mikdash me'at* model, such conversation can occur inside the rabbi or cantor's study. Once the initial congratulations are over, the couple is invited in to discuss their plans: "When would you like to come in?" Their response to this invitation will indicate something about them. There is the eager couple who cannot wait to come in and share their happiness with the rabbi. There is the apprehensive pair who may be looking forward to the meeting with the cantor but are feeling unsure about what to expect. There is the disinterested couple who acquiesce to what is required but do not feel they have anything to learn from talking to either rabbi or cantor. There is even the couple who are resentful and hostile at having to take yet more time out of a busy schedule already overloaded with prewedding obligations.

Here, too, it helps to develop a spiritual conception of how to respond appropriately to each of these couples. In its discussion of the four children, the Haggadah offers a useful paradigm for how to respond.[16] Each child asks a question that reflects his or her own understanding at that moment; each child is to be responded to in kind. The intelligent child asks a thorough question and thus is to be given a detailed answer. The wicked child asks a hostile question and thus should receive an equally aggressive response. The simple child asks a short straightforward question and should receive a similar answer. For the child who does not know how to ask, the parent must begin the conversation. Engaged couples run a similar gamut. Some seem to be sophisticated in their knowledge of what they want, interested in researching wedding traditions and in seeing whether they want to integrate particular traditions into their ceremony. Others will have no questions and will need the rabbi or cantor to stimulate them enough to get them started.

The way in which each couple reacts to the setting of an

appointment will begin to offer clues as to which type of couple is on the other end of the phone. Some couples will need help to come in. Often, one of them is willing to be available at any time but the other always seems to be in the "busiest season" at work. In this case, maintaining a sympathetic attitude toward the couple ("Our schedules keep us so busy, don't they?") will help them to feel understood. However, that does not mean that the rabbi or cantor should agree to an inconvenient appointment time. Exploring scheduling problems with them so that they can come in at a mutually convenient time begins to educate them in making their relationship a priority and in recognizing the clergy as a partner in mutuality. Establishing boundaries in this way conveys an unspoken message to the couple that just as the relationship between God and Israel is defined by the covenant of Torah, so do all relationships require boundaries to function and so, too, do they need to respect boundaries in their relationship with the rabbi or cantor.

The Initial Interview and Beyond

The act of walking into the rabbi or cantor's study usually causes the couple's defenses to lock into place. This is a new experience for them; even if their initial visit excites and intrigues them, they cannot help but experience some apprehension. The way to help them to feel comfortable is to support these defenses, not challenge them. The session should last no longer than one hour. At the start of that hour, it is best to ask them friendly questions that are just personal enough to encourage them to talk but not so personal as to probe or create discomfort: How did you meet? How long have you known each other? Where are you from? How did you get my name? It is then appropriate to ask if they have any questions or any particular expectations of what they would like to see accomplished in this or other sessions.

By approaching them in this careful and respectful way, the rabbi or cantor communicates that they have some control over what they discuss and that they do not have to discuss everything in that first meeting or even at all. Most newly engaged couples will have questions relating to the logistics of the wedding ceremony (when, where, how long, and getting the marriage license). How quickly these questions are dealt with will depend on the couple and the clergy. If there is information the rabbi or cantor needs to obtain in that first session, a good question to ask them is, "Would this be a good time for me to ask some questions or would you prefer that I wait until later?" If they ask a difficult question whose answer is not clear or which puts the clergy in an awkward position, it is always possible to respond, "Would it be all right if I gave that some thought and we discussed it next time?" Some couples will spend all their time on logistics; others will skip the logistics and move right to the issues that concern them.

The couple is encouraged to begin with the topics that interest or concern them most, thus the majority of couples become engaged in the process immediately. They will then be more relaxed and willing to discuss subjects introduced by the rabbi or cantor. One can gain not just practical information but also an enormous amount of emotional information from asking the objective questions included on the wedding information form. Questions related to the ceremony can be expanded to address larger questions related to their marriage. When the rabbi or cantor asks about when the couple plans to get their marriage license, he or she can also suggest their being tested for Tay-Sachs on the same day as any testing required for the license. After hearing an explanation that Tay-Sachs is a Jewish genetic disease, the bride might explain that she was adopted and her birth parents were of Irish heritage, so she is unlikely to carry the worrisome gene. The groom might volunteer that he had cancer as a child and is unable to have children. This allows the rabbi an opening to discuss their ideas about having children. A question about the honorarium for the rabbi or cantor can move into exploration of how the couple handle their finances. A request for their Hebrew names might elicit the information that the groom was circumcised in a hospital and never received a Hebrew name or that the bride is a convert. Such a discussion leads naturally into talking about their respective religious backgrounds and their religious plans for their own family. The rabbi or cantor might then use this opportunity to begin to teach the couple about living a Jewish life and creating a Jewish home, about observing Shabbat, studying Torah, or making *tzedakah* a part of their married life.

Some clergy like to draw genograms with the couple to raise their awareness of historic family patterns to which they might be susceptible; others use a written premarital inventory to gather information about the couple, their background, and their ideas about marriage.

Still others prefer to receive the information in the way in which the couple wants to give it as the session unfolds. In any case, despite whatever desire the clergy may have for order, it is hard to predict what issues couples will raise and when. Being prepared for anything puts them at ease and allows them to comfortably disclose more information about how they relate to each other. This approach allows the clergy and the couple to become partners in a joint search for important information.

Any item on the wedding information checklist, no matter how mundane it might seem, can become a window into the couple's Jewish past and their emotional present. In the following case, a question about who would be walking down the aisle in the processional opened up a new area for discussion.

> The couple, both in their sixties, were trying to incorporate all of their children and grandchildren into the wedding processional. Both had been widowed—he once, she twice—and they couldn't believe their luck at finding each other. The bride was meticulous in assigning the processional order and in making sure everyone was included until it became clear that she had not included herself. She was not planning to walk down the aisle, she said; she was planning to sneak in under the *chupah* from the side right before the beginning of the ceremony. Her husband-to-be was horrified; his first wife had not been Jewish and he had been looking forward to watching his new bride walk down the center aisle of the sanctuary. After gentle, nonjudgmental questioning from the rabbi, the bride at last confessed that a friend had said to her, "It's not fair that you are so lucky. I can't even find one decent guy and you find three!" That comment dovetailed neatly with her own feeling that she was unworthy of being loved a third time. She was able to voice this concern, and thus her fiancé was able to reassure her of her worthiness and his love. She regally walked down the aisle at her wedding.

A routine question about who will participate in the processional may not fall into the category of strictly "religious" preparation for the ceremony, but it does fall under the category of emotional dynamics, and thus offers the clergy an opening for exploring and deepening the relationship.

Clergy and the Couple: Understanding and Managing One's Own Emotional Reactions

Counseling premarital couples will evoke a range of feelings in the clergy. Because couples can induce a variety of strong feelings, rabbis and cantors need to stay as self-aware as possible so that they can distinguish between their feelings and those of the couple. A rabbi who finds herself feeling anxious during a meeting with a couple should ask herself whether that anxiety is emanating from her or from the couple. A cantor who finds that he is feeling inordinately sleepy during a session but wide awake the minute the couple leaves might wonder whether the couple was hiding some important information. If a normally clear-thinking rabbi feels confused when talking with a couple or if a usually mild-mannered cantor feels angry in session with a couple, those feelings should be honored as an indication of unexplored emotional undercurrents. In any of those situations, it is best for the clergy to ask a neutral question that is linked to the particular feeling: Is there something confusing here? Am I doing what you need me to be doing? Is there something uncomfortable about this discussion? For rabbis and cantors to keep their own personal issues separate from those of the couple, they should find a supervisor or therapist who can help them talk and thus become more aware of their own feelings.

Couples automatically transfer onto the rabbi positive or negative feelings they had or have for their own parents; this phenomenon is commonly referred to as transference. When the rabbi or cantor in turn experiences particular feelings in response to the couple, those feelings are called countertransference.[17] While transference and countertransference operate in all relationships, they can become heightened in a premarital counseling environment. Some couples want the rabbi or cantor to fix their problems so they can avoid personal responsibility and mature relationship; in that case, the rabbi or cantor will often feel a strong desire to take action on the couple's behalf. The couple will benefit if the clergy chooses to restrain himself or herself from repairing the problem and instead helps the couple develop the skills to resolve their conflict themselves. When a couple with a desire to be "fixed" meets up with a rabbi who has a desire to be a "fixer," it is the rabbi who must resist the impulse to take inappropriate action and remember the advice, *"Shev ve'al taaseh"* (Sit and do nothing).[18] If rabbis and cantors can sit and tolerate the feelings raised in them by the couple, that tolerance, by example, will help the couple tolerate their own feelings.

The following two examples illustrate the transference–countertransference dynamic.

> The couple expressed a desire to come in as soon as possible but rejected every possibility the cantor suggested. The cantor felt that she had offered them every conceivable meeting time and had exhausted the possibilities. When they asked to meet with her outside of her usual office hours, the cantor realized that she was feeling tense, resentful, and cornered. She felt conflicted about what to do.

This couple has transferred onto the cantor an infantile fantasy that the cantor should gratify their every need; the cantor, in turn, is likely to experience countertransferential pressure to accommodate them. It is better in the long run for both cantor and couple that the cantor not rush to gratify their wish. If she decides reluctantly to meet with them at their time on their terms, she will be assuming the burden of their schedule as if it is her own and solving their problem at her own expense. The cantor is likely to feel angry with the couple for their lack of consideration and angry with herself for allowing it to happen; such anger will interfere with her ability to develop a good relationship with the couple. Additionally, she will be depriving them of the opportunity to make choices as a soon-to-be-married couple. If she can instead help them resolve the obstacles that stand in the way of their coming to see her, she will be demonstrating the idea that problems in scheduling are normal and can be resolved through effective communication. She will be educating them to function in a world that will make many conflicting demands on their time. Her behavior will be consistent with her own theoretical perspective because she believes that their spiritual needs take precedence over the secular. Most couples take time off from work to choose a ring, find a photographer, rent a reception hall, hire a band, and interview a florist. The cantor needs to reinforce the religious message that if they can take a day off from work to rent a tuxedo, they can take a day off from work to meet with her. She is educating them to begin creating their own *mikdash me'at.* In a case like this, if they cannot find a mutually convenient meeting time, she may need to tell them that she will look forward to hearing from them after they have had a chance to sit down and consult their schedules again.

> The couple had originally scheduled their wedding with a different rabbi: the wedding had been canceled. Six months later, they called and came in to see him, her parents' rabbi. The couple seemed nervous. The rabbi felt anxious and, after trading pleasantries, asked: "What was the cause of the cancellation of the earlier date?" The groom had been seriously ill, they said. The rabbi waited, tempted to fill the silence as they looked at each other for what seemed to be an interminable amount of time. The groom made his decision: "We had not planned to tell you the truth," he said, "but I have AIDS [acquired immune deficiency syndrome]." The rabbi felt temporarily paralyzed by the feelings that flooded over him. How could he marry a couple where the marriage might mean a death sentence for the bride, no matter how careful they were about contraception? What kind of marriage could be developed under the cloud of impending death? How could he ever look into their eyes under the *chupah* and conduct their ceremony? The rabbi held those questions in his mind, took a deep breath, and continued talking with them as if they were any other engaged couple coming in for an initial meeting.

Having the feelings and asking himself these questions is a necessary first step for this rabbi. The fact that he felt anxious even before he knew the truth would indicate that the couple, too, had had similar doubts and equally strong feelings. In this case, the rabbi struggled to practice a personal *tzimtzum* (voluntary constricting of self) and not allow his emotions to get in the way of the task. He respected the idea of his office as a so-called holding environment in which all feelings could be expressed, accepted, and tolerated.

When feelings become intolerable, people often consciously or unconsciously seek to find a way of eliminating those feelings. The problem is that feelings cannot be erased; they just lodge somewhere in the psyche or in the soma doing insidious damage while awaiting their reappearance. In this case, as in all such cases, it is more productive and healthier for the rabbi and the couple to explore and to experience those feelings together. In this case, the rabbi felt a strong desire to save the bride from the danger of contracting AIDS and from the death of a young husband. He wanted to say, "Why don't you find someone to marry who is healthy, with whom you can bear children?" but after careful and gentle exploration, he understood that this couple had made their choice.

> The couple did marry; the rabbi chose to officiate, although he experienced strong emotions while standing under the *chupah*. The bride's father wore sunglasses during the indoor ceremony to conceal his tear-filled eyes. The groom became seriously ill and died two years later. He lived long enough to experience the usual early-marriage conflicts of any normal relationship. Before he died at age forty-three, he said that those two years of marriage had been the best two years of his life. His wife was glad that they had had this time together as a married couple.[19]

Commonly Encountered Issues

The Triangulated Couple

The prospective bride and groom called and came in to see the rabbi. She was vibrant; he was sullen. She was barely nineteen; he was twenty-nine. Her family was thrilled with the match. His father, a member of the rabbi's congregation, called to tell the rabbi that both bride and groom were too immature to marry and to ask the rabbi to discourage them.

In this situation, the rabbi who feels caught in the middle is having the right feelings. The father of the groom has created a neat relational triangle involving himself, the rabbi, and the (thus-far) unsuspecting couple. The creation of such a triangle is no accident but probably reflects that family's habitual way of regulating distance and intimacy. The father may be having difficulty with his son's moving outside of the family orbit and into a new family constellation. It may be that the son until now has been one leg of a triangle that has stabilized his parents' relationship over the years. It may be that the relationship between father and son has become too intense (positively or negatively) for the father to tolerate. Whatever the reason, by involving the rabbi, the father unconsciously acts to take the pressure off his relationship with his son and place it onto the relationship between his son and the rabbi.

The rabbi who will be most tempted to accept this scenario will often turn out to have been the peacemaker in his or her own family. Ironically, the "peacemaker" rabbi usually ends up becoming the lightning rod for everyone's anger in this kind of case unless the rabbi knows enough to "detriangulate" him or herself. The rabbi needs to keep in mind his or her own theoretical framework in determining what is best long-term for the couple and what is best for the rabbi. The rabbi also needs to recall and rely on his or her own spiritual framework. After their initial premarital bliss, Israel and God needed boundaries in order to define a bilateral relationship in which growth could occur and in which conflict could be resolved. So, too, this couple needs to define their own boundaries as a new family despite the resistance from the groom's father. The family will not be helped to solve their problems if the rabbi assumes the role of fixer. Rabbis will find themselves victims of "clergy burn-out" or worse if they take on the burdens of the families they counsel.

In this case, the rabbi might ask the couple, "Were you aware that I received a call from your father?" Depending upon the couple's reaction, the rabbi might then ask why the father might want to discourage the marriage. Should anything be done about that? Do they have similar concerns of their own? Would they like to bring the father in for a family session? Does the mother agree with the father? Even if the couple does not have the answers to these questions, they will be stimulated to think and will be strengthened as a couple separate and distinct from their families of origin.

The Jewishly Alienated Couple

> Both members of the couple were Ph.D. computer scientists who worked in research for a large corporation. Neither believed in God, although he was more adamant than she. They wanted a ceremony that did not mention God's name. They also asked the rabbi for a copy of the ceremony he used, so they could rewrite the ceremony in their own words.

Although it might be tempting to argue with this kind of couple, such action would be unproductive and frustrating. The rabbi must not allow himself to be seduced into focusing only on the content of their question. Rather, he should try and create a Buberian sense of "real meeting," in which he accepts and tolerates their ambivalence. Although they give the arrogant impression that they know better than the rabbi, the rabbi must remain open to the possibility that something deeper lies behind their request.

In this case, it turned out that the couple was afraid that their wedding would not feel sufficiently personal because they would be constrained by traditional Jewish ritual. They believed that the only way to ensure intimacy was to insert their own words. This admission gave the rabbi an opportunity to educate them about intimacy, both by being emotionally present to them in that moment and by describing the role of ritual. He explained that the intimacy of a ceremony does not come from the words but from the relationship of the people standing under the chupah, much like the difference between reading a script of a play and then seeing a live performance of that play. What makes the performance more or less effective is not changing the script but changing the cast; what makes a wedding special depends more on the uniqueness of the couple than on the liturgy. Once the three of them got to know each other better, that intimacy would be reflected in the ceremony. He also told them that he planned to ask them what they wanted him to say in his wedding sermon to them. In encouraging them to have a dialogue with him, he demonstrated how they might have an emotional dialogue with each other.

Although this approach raised the couple's comfort level when it came to the basic ceremony, it still did not resolve the issue of including God's name. Again, the rabbi accepted their ambivalence and explored the issue with them: Did they know where in the ritual God's name appeared? Would it be acceptable if the rabbi said God's name but they did not? Did they prefer one term for God to another (i.e., would referring to God as The Divine or Eternal One be more acceptable)? If they so objected to including God's name, what made them come to a rabbi rather than a justice of the peace?

Through this kind of exploration, clergy and couple usually can come to a mutually satisfying resolution that allows them to proceed with the wedding plans. However, there are times when a compromise cannot be reached and the rabbi or cantor cannot accommodate what a couple wants. Couples will sometimes insist that there be no Hebrew in the ceremony or that the wedding last only fifteen minutes, that it begin before sunset on a Saturday night or that the photographer be allowed to take pictures at will during the service. Talking long enough might lead either couple or clergy to the conclusion that this clergy member is not the right person to officiate at their ceremony and that they would be better off in a more secular environment. Whether the issue can be resolved to mutual satisfaction or whether clergy and couple choose to part ways, the rabbi or cantor will have demonstrated that complex issues can be discussed and resolved in a mature fashion. He or she will also have helped them to clarify their mutual goals as a couple.

The Cohabiting Couple

A couple declared with confidence that they were fully aware of what they needed to know about each other and could predict no surprises in the future; after all, they had lived together for years and knew each other's idiosyncratic ways. They did not want their relationship to change.

Like the Jewish people before accepting the tenets of Torah, this couple is living in an unmarried, precovenantal state. God and the Jewish people, too, had long lived in a loving but uncommitted relationship. They realized that they could not stay that way indefinitely. Israel and God then chose to relate to each other in a new way, based on covenant. That way was designed to elevate and alter their relationship forever. In the same way, the couple's willingness to enter into the legally binding commitment of marriage changes their relationship.

It is best not to argue with their fantasy. This couple is not yet ready to know that marriage will serve as a crucible for their relationship, that problems which could be avoided before will require a different kind of attention now. They probably do not realize that, although it appears that only two persons are marrying, they also carry within their psyches an emotional legacy from their respective families. The fact is that, no matter how long a couple has lived together, certain unconscious ideas do not bubble up until people are officially married. That does not mean that no discussion is warranted, just that the topic must be approached with care and respect for their opinion. The rabbi or cantor might join the couple's feelings by saying, "You could be right that your relationship will stay the same; but could you entertain the possibility that it might change? What if it does change?"[20]

The rabbi or cantor might also ask a couple like this if they would like to hear an observation about marriage gleaned from his or her experience. If they do not seem interested, the rabbi should wait until another opportunity presents itself. If they do seem interested, he or she can introduce the idea that they are marrying because they want to make a change, because they are ready to deepen their relationship. Couples generally like the idea that *kiddushin* represents a greater spiritual commitment to each other. If they seem receptive to the clergy's continuing, he or she might mention that another difference is that *kiddushin* requires sexual fidelity, a legal condition that may or may not have been part of their premarital living arrangement. Therefore, after marriage, the physiological act of sex is also raised to a higher level, both because it is within the context of the *mikdash me'at* and because it contains within it the potential for producing children and raising a family together.

> The story is told about the bride, newly married after two years of living with her fiancé, who came downstairs on the first morning after the honeymoon to find her new husband sitting at the breakfast table reading the paper: "What's for breakfast?" he asked. The bride stood aghast. Before their marriage, he had been the one who made breakfast. She had turned into a wife for him without his realizing he was doing anything differently.

This kind of problem cannot be addressed successfully premaritally because the couple has not yet experienced the conflict. It takes getting married for those unconscious fantasies to manifest themselves. When they do, the rabbi or cantor may have planted the seeds that will enable them to seek professional help.

The Enmeshed Couple

> To the cantor's surprise, the couple arrived for their appointment with the bride-to-be's mother.

The arrival of a threesome where the cantor expected two might alert her to the possibility that psychological separation is an issue for this couple. It would not be surprising for her to wonder, "If they are old enough to be getting married, why is her mother here?" Her external reaction should be to accept the family as they present themselves. No separation should be forced upon the family before the cantor has a chance to study the situation. She might ask the couple if they want Mother to join in the session with them and Mother whether she would like to join them. If not, would Mother mind waiting in the other room? If so, is there anything in particular they should discuss with Mother there before they excuse her and talk about other private matters? In this way, the cantor is modeling respect for the parental relationship while at the same time modeling separateness for the couple. The late Rabbi Jakob Petuchowski captured this notion of the couple's newfound separateness when he translated "*Harei at mekudeshet li*" (Behold, you are consecrated unto me) as, "Behold, I am taking you out of circulation." Parents and children both need to become educated to the process of being separate as well as being together. The couple has the task of creating their own *mikdash me'at*, of forging their own unique family, still linked to their families of origin but free to make their own choices.

The Conflicted Couple

> They came in fighting about the guest list. He wanted his family to invite as many guests as her family was inviting; she was sympathetic but said that because her family was paying for the wedding, they had the right to tell him how many guests he could invite.

Occasionally, a couple will arrive in the throes of premarital conflict. If the cantor can accept their conflict calmly and help them to work on it, he will be conveying the message that having both loving and hateful feelings is a normal part of human existence. His office represents a holding environment that can contain their feelings. The additional subliminal instruction teaches that if the cantor can handle those feelings, so can they. The cantor can also help them learn that, although it is important to express these feelings, it must be done in a way that lets the other partner hear them without feeling hurt or attacked. When people love each other intensely, their feelings of hatred for each other are likely to be equally as intense. The Rabbis tell us that two basic human impulses, the *yetzer ha-ra* (evil inclination) and the *yetzer ha-tov* (good inclination), are both interdependent and necessary for human survival. Without both instincts, they said, "No man would build a house, marry a wife, or beget children."[21] Just as within each individual lies the potential for instinctual conflict, so too will conflict appear of necessity in every relationship. Even if a particular conflict cannot be resolved by the time of the wedding, the cantor can help educate them to the healthy process of working on conflict.

The Interfaith Couple

They were an interfaith couple who had resolved that the children would be raised as Jews. After hearing of their engagement, the groom's mother suddenly began to attend daily mass and to talk with him about baptism and salvation. Now he was no longer sure he could accept that initial agreement; the bride was frantic. They suffered though a few premarital counseling sessions before the bride called up and said, "We know we have a conflict but we know we love each other. We have both invested too much in this relationship to end it now. We want to enjoy our engagement instead of arguing all the time. We are going to stop seeing you until after the wedding."

A major difference between interfaith and same-faith couples becomes apparent the minute the engagement is announced. A Jewish couple is offered a hearty *mazel tov*! An interfaith couple often is greeted with disapproval, rejection, or questions from family and friends: "Is he going to convert? Who is going to officiate? How will you raise the children?" The couple may also have called area synagogues in their search for a rabbi and discovered that they cannot get past the secretary, who has informed them that "the rabbi doesn't do intermarriages." Unlike most Jewish couples, an interfaith couple has already experienced conflict with the outside world, if not with each other; paradoxically, this fact may be to their advantage. The couple needs a place to do the work, and they need a guide who is willing to be with them and assist them.

Even rabbis and cantors who do not officiate at interfaith

ceremonies can make themselves available to meet with any interested interfaith couple. Again, all premarital discussion should take place in person in the rabbi's or cantor's study, in keeping with the concept of the clergy's office as a *mikdash me'at*. That environment allows the rabbi or cantor to make the couple comfortable, to find out what they want, and to explore options with them. It often happens, for instance, that the Jewish partner has not raised the question of conversion with his prospective spouse: "I couldn't ask her to convert." The rabbi or cantor can then facilitate the conversation they have been unable to have alone by asking interested questions: Are there conditions under which he would ask her if she were interested in conversion? What makes this different from other requests he might make of her or she of him? Is there something that gets in the way of her considering becoming a Jew? The rabbi and cantor should be aware that the decision to "marry out" may be a complex one rooted in emotional family dynamics; some couples, for instance, marry out in a dramatic but unconscious attempt to separate from their families.[22]

After understanding the couple better, the clergy can make recommendations that are in keeping with his or her theological perspective. One might recommend that the couple enroll in an Introduction to Judaism class where they can explore what it means to create a Jewish home. Rabbis and cantors who officiate at intermarriages might discuss their requirements; those who do not officiate might say, "I officiate at weddings when a conversion takes place." Although many couples will not choose the path of conversion, this framing of the clergy's position may be experienced as less rejecting. It is good to find ways to keep the door open for future contact, even if the clergy will not be officiating at the wedding.

The rabbi in this case, who was not the officiating rabbi at their wedding, told the bride that they deserved to enjoy their engagement and that he understood their decision not to continue working on this problem at this time. He also recommended that they come in for one more session before the wedding so that the three of them could develop a plan for the future. They came in and talked about how to proceed. They wanted to behave like responsible adults, they said, but they just could not handle the conflict now; they wanted to be sure that at some point in the future they could meet again with the rabbi. They set up an appointment then for six months after the wedding.

Although it is easier if a couple (whether interfaith or same faith) can agree in advance about how to raise their future children, such agreement is not always possible. Even if they can come to an agreement before the wedding, there is nothing to prevent people from changing their minds later. If the rabbi or cantor can establish a positive relationship with the couple and encourage a healthy dialogue, he or she will have opened the door to them for continuing relationship within the context of the Jewish community.

The Gay or Lesbian Couple[23]

Sarah and Leslie approached their commitment ceremony with both enthusiasm and dread. They were thrilled to be affirming their love with a public ritual but worried about how their families might respond. Their anxiety turned out to be well founded. When Sarah had first told her parents about her relationship with Leslie, Sarah's parents had said, "You might as well lie down on a train track; you are destroying your life!" As a result of this earlier reaction, Sarah decided not only not to invite her parents but not even to tell them the ceremony would be held. Leslie, on the other hand, was determined to invite both her siblings and her parents. Her parents refused to come, saying that it was "just too public, it would be too hard for us." Her sister said that attending the ceremony would force her to explain their lesbian relationship to her young daughter and she was not prepared to do so. Her brother cited Jewish law as the reason same-sex couples could not be married. In the end, neither partner's immediate family members were present at the ceremony.

The homosexual couple's announcement that they plan to wed is often greeted with shock, disapproval, rejection, questions, and even revulsion. The shock factor is greatest when the wedding invitation also serves as a "coming out" announcement, making the family aware for the first time that their son or daughter is gay. While the public announcement might be liberating for the couple burdened by secrecy for so long, it is not without its risks. Many parents experience an intense grief reaction as they realize that they must give up their fantasies about their child and his or her future. Although even parents who respond initially with rejection or upset may eventually come to accept their children's sexual orientation, this process can take time. Although the rabbi or cantor might have a role in helping the various family members come to terms with the new situation, it might not be possible to effectuate a happy outcome in time for the scheduled ceremony.

In light of the often painful and conspicuous absence of, or conflict with, the couple's immediate family, the couple might have more need for the support of the rabbi or cantor, the Jewish community, and their extended family of friends. Couples whose parents have yet to make peace with their children's homosexuality might use their premarital sessions to prepare themselves for the disappointment and rejection they may feel when parents refuse to attend the ceremony. The rabbi or cantor first needs to explore what the couple wants vis-à-vis their family members. Do they want to try to effect reconciliation with their parents? If so, how would they want that to happen? What do they think might work? What do they think would not work? What have they already tried? Is there a compromise that would allow their family members to attend? What will the couple do if their strategies fail? If they want the rabbi or cantor to intercede, what do they want done? Why do they think the rabbi or cantor would be any more likely to succeed than they are?

These questions imply not just respect for the couple's commitment but also a willingness to create a holding environment for their pain. The rabbi or cantor's attitude, perhaps more in this case than others, symbolically represents the attitude of Judaism. From the initial precommitment counseling session to the ceremony itself, the rabbi or cantor's feelings and interventions can take on an unusual intensity since the spiritual and emotional stakes are so high. On the other hand, the couple may well have been together for many years and may evidence a higher degree of stability and experience than an average heterosexual couple coming to the rabbi or cantor for premarital counseling. The committed gay or lesbian couple has managed to maintain a lasting relationship despite the pressures of living in a culture that does not give civil or social recognition to their love.

For the couple themselves, there are advantages and disadvantages to the lack of a civil parallel. On the one hand, their relationship has been marginalized by secular and Jewish society and they lack basic legal protections and social benefits. On the other hand, because of this ostracism, they may have thought through their commitment on a more profound level than most heterosexual couples. They can talk more readily about the spiritual message they want their wedding to convey because they have had to consider why they should ritually celebrate their union. No one has pressured them to meet with a rabbi or cantor to discuss their ceremony; it is likely that no parents have demanded that they have a Jewish wedding.

Gay or lesbian couples who venture to meet with a rabbi or cantor usually have already researched whether he or she will be receptive to who they are and what they want to do. The rabbi or cantor may become an important bridge between the couple and the Jewish world from which many gays and lesbians become alienated upon becoming aware of their sexuality. The rabbi or cantor who meets with a gay or lesbian couple may be sitting down with two people who themselves never dreamed that they would be able to marry the person they loved. They may also never have dreamed that there might be a way to reenter the Jewish community and to be accepted for who they are. Gay and lesbian couples often have been unable to make even the most basic assumptions about their lives, much less their wedding ceremony.

Given the lack of civil recognition of gay and lesbian unions and the concomitant legal issues, the rabbi or cantor should encourage the couple to execute legal documents (such as wills, healthcare proxies, power of attorney arrangements, and guardianship arrangements for existing or future children) to protect their rights.[24] If the couple has not considered the legal implications of their union, the rabbi or cantor should refer them for legal advice to an appropriate social agency or a knowledgeable private attorney.

As with heterosexual couples, the questions about the ritual of the ceremony will lead directly into emotional and spiritual issues. In discussing the plans for the ceremony with the couple, the rabbi or cantor will discover how much of the traditional heterosexual ceremony is bound up in traditional gender roles. The couple may want to fundamentally reframe the ceremony outside of the construct of *kiddushin*.[25] Even if they want to include the traditional elements of a heterosexual Jewish wedding, the couple may worry that those elements will look different when done by two women or two men and that they will be misunderstood. What should they wear and how will that be seen? Who should arrive at the *chupah* first (if anyone)? Who should step on the glass and what might the guests infer from that about the nature of their relationship? What terminology should replace *chatan* (groom) and *kallah* (bride) in the *sheva berachot* (seven wedding benedictions)? Should they transvalue some or all of these elements, or replace them with other elements that better capture the essence of this union? The couple may need assistance from the clergy in conveying to the congregation the seriousness and meaning of commitment ceremony.[26] As with every premarital couple, the goal of meeting with the gay or lesbian couple is to educate them emotionally so that they can communicate effectively with each other, can resolve conflicts constructively, and can deepen their relationship.

The Couple with Divorced Parents

Although the groom's parents had long been divorced, he continued to maintain the fantasy that on his wedding day they would put aside their differences and together escort him to the *chupah*. However, they angrily refused, claiming that even if they walked on either side of their son and held his hand, it would be as if they were holding hands with each other. The groom was distraught. In his profession as a chef, he attempted to make people happy, yet somehow he had failed when it came to his parents. His bride offered to help but he rejected her involvement, saying he was worried that the contagion of his parents' poisonous relationship would affect her. The bride felt miserable that her fiancé would not accept her help. The rabbi offered to intercede with the groom's parents, inviting them to his office individually and urging them in no uncertain terms to cooperate with their son's wishes and warning of the dire consequences of failing to do so. The parents were furious but did icily escort their son to the *chupah*; they refused to make eye contact during the ceremony.

It is always wise to begin by asking the couple what their goal is and what role they envision for the clergy in this situation. This encourages the bride and groom to think of themselves as a couple with mutual goals, although they might not begin with a clear vision of those goals. Their confusion should not prevent the rabbi from asking himself, "What should my goal be?" Should he concentrate on the

short-range goal of the ceremony or the longer-range goal of the marriage? Should he offer to mediate between the groom and his parents?
Should he guide bride and groom to resolve their resistance to operating as a couple in confronting this issue? Should he help the groom explore his relationship with his parents and his need for having
his fantasy fulfilled? Should the goal include all of the above? Do any
of these alternatives cause the rabbi to experience discomfort or
apprehension?

The rabbi might have begun by calmly investigating the groom's
insistence on having both parents walk him down the aisle. What
would happen if they did not walk him down? What would it mean if
they did? Would it ruin his wedding? Why would the groom be willing
to allow his parents to ruin his wedding and to bring disharmony into
his relationship with his bride? At the same time, the rabbi might explore the impact of this conflict on the bride and groom's relationship
and teach them how to relate to each other, thereby using the family
strife as an opportunity to help the couple learn the nature of reci-
procity in relationship. Has the groom noticed how his bride feels
about his rejecting her involvement? Is the bride aware of how
strongly the groom feels? If the rabbi alternates asking each partner
how the other is reacting to something that has been said, those
questions will help to train them to think about each other's responses.[27] Does the only solution require that one of them loses and
the other wins, or can they both win? By asking these kinds of questions, the rabbi models the idea that marital partners have to work together to produce a good marriage and that they can be trained to
work as a team.[28]

If the bride and groom choose the goal of having both of his parents walk him down regardless of how poorly the parents might behave, that leaves the rabbi with several options. Depending on his own
comfort level, he might determine that any intercession on his part
would be inappropriate and thus leave them to fight their battle without his aid. Alternatively, he might choose to help them to further
their goal themselves. He might even intercede directly with the parents, as this rabbi did, in a Minuchin-like therapeutic intervention intended to "confront and challenge a family in the attempt to force a
therapeutic change."[29] Only a highly skilled, experienced rabbi should
make this kind of intervention, in which the rabbi knowingly chooses

to escalate the family's stress. There is no one right way to handle a volatile situation like this, other than for the rabbi to remain calm and retain his position of leadership.

Choosing Not to Officiate

The rabbi observed that the couple seemed depressed throughout their engagement. They showed no joy but expressed many fears. She married them and they separated within three months. The rabbi felt that she should have told them what she had seen before they married.

There are times a rabbi may observe even in a first meeting that the partners do not seem to have the requisite skills to function in a mature relationship. What would it feel like for the rabbi to officiate at a wedding that seems likely to end in divorce? Does the rabbi have any responsibility to make the couple aware of her feelings? A rabbi with serious concerns certainly is entitled to ask if the couple has considered couples' therapy and to recommend it as an option. Whether the rabbi should refuse to officiate unless the couple agrees to enter therapy is a different question, however. It is true that no rabbi or cantor should have to officiate at any wedding if she feels uncomfortable about doing so. In most situations, however, the likelihood is that the couple will just find someone else to marry them.

The metaphor of marriage between God and Israel can offer a useful analogy in this case. Israel had been enslaved and had never grown beyond a childlike way of relating to God; no one would have predicted a successful covenantal relationship, yet somehow they were able to forge a partnership. God actually commands the prophet Hosea to marry a woman destined to be unfaithful; in the same way, God betroths Israel knowing that Israel, too, will violate their covenant. Just as the marriage between Hosea and his notoriously unfaithful wife is no accident, so it is no accident when two people find each other; a rabbi or cantor cannot determine in a few brief sessions why the couple has chosen each other. It is not the business of the rabbi or cantor to discourage the marriage because he or she cannot make sense of the couple's choice. People choose partners whose personality and marital style permit them to reexperience early relationships.[30] This choice is both powerful and necessary; it can neither easily be changed, nor should it be. Usually people make the best choice of which they are capable at the time. It would be better for the couple if they can be helped to relate to each other during the time they are in the rabbi or cantor's office.

If the couple asks specifically what the rabbi or cantor thinks about their relationship, the couple's relationship will be strengthened if their questions can be reflected back to them: What makes them ask this question? Do they themselves have doubts? What kind of doubts do they have? What would be a good reason to get married? What would not be a good reason to get married? If the rabbi told them not to marry, would they listen? If the rabbi told them to marry, would they heed that advice? These questions encourage them to clarify their own thinking and to realize that their marriage results from their decision alone. It is not the clergy's purview to predict failure or success or to deprive the couple of the opportunity to marry.

Conclusion

If one thinks of three sessions with a couple as a mere 180 minutes relative to months of lengthy engagement, those three sessions may not seem enough time to nurture a serious relationship. However, if one can reframe those three sessions as sacred time spent in the sanctuary of the rabbi or cantor's office, one will come to appreciate the religious potency of a mere 180 minutes. When the threesome moves from office to *chupah*, the relationship that has been nurtured moves with them. The space beneath the canopy becomes transformed into a holding environment for all the feelings that arise during the wedding. The comfort that has developed between couple and clergy will expand to include the surrounding congregation of friends and family. As the three of them stand together beneath the *chupah* in that brief but eternal moment, everyone present will witness the convergence of the *mikdash me'at*, the primordial union of Adam and Eve in the Garden of Eden, and the marriage of God and Israel at Sinai. Once the glass is broken, that transcendent moment will go with them as they leave the *chupah* for the four walls of their own *mikdash me'at*. The rabbi's or cantor's part in their sacred journey has ended for now, but both clergy and couple will continue to carry that shared experience of the Eternal that is the foretaste of redemption.[31]

Notes

1. Avot d'Rabbi Natan, nusach a, chap. 8.
2. Robert F. Stahmann and William J. Hiebert. *Premarital Counseling: The Professional's Handbook,* 2d ed. (Lexington, Mass.: Lexington Books, D.C. Heath, 1987), p. 13. "Premarital counseling is typically done with relatively healthy persons and is designed primarily as an experience to enhance and enrich growing relationships and secondarily to treat pathological ones."
3. Norma Schweitzer Wood and Herbert W. Stroup, Jr., "Family Systems in Premarital Counseling," *Pastoral Psychology* 39, no. 2 (1990): p. 111.
4. D. H. Olson, "How Effective Is Marriage Preparation?" in *Prevention in Family Services: Approaches to Family Wellness,* ed. David R. Mace (Beverly Hills: Sage Publications, 1983), pp. 65–75.
5. Ibid., p. 65.
6. Stahmann and Hiebert, *Premarital Counseling,* 1987.
7. Hyman Spotnitz, "The Marriage Partnership," *Modern Psychoanalysis* 2, no. 1 (spring 1977): p. 14.
8. Monica McGoldrick, "The Joining of Families Through Marriage: The New Couple," in *The Changing Family Life Cycle,* eds. B. Carter and M. McGoldrick (Boston: Allyn & Bacon, 1989), pp. 209–34.
9. Wood and Stroup, "Family Systems," p. 112: "The couple comes to a pastor, rabbi or priest expecting to celebrate their relationship by marrying, not really to examine its future. Positive that their love surpasses any other, the two sit before a pastor, anticipating a wedding, but not the full reality of married life. It is usually difficult to get the two to touch this reality, as they sit, wrapped up in each other (sometimes literally), yet strangely insulated from the world around them. To entice the couple into a consideration of mundane aspects of future living when compared to their immediate aura of romantic love is not at all easy."
10. Walter R. Schumm and Wallace Denton, "Trends in Premarital Counseling," in *Journal of Marital and Family Therapy* 5, no. 4 (1979), p. 26. "The most important goal of premarital counseling may become the establishment of a positive relationship with the counselor as a prelude to several post-wedding meetings at which time the counseling/enrichment process may be genuinely facilitative of the couple's relationship development."
11. D. W. Winnicott, *Babies and Their Mothers* (New York: Addison-Wesley, 1987), pp. 96–97.
12. Theodor Reik, *Listening with the Third Ear: The Inner Experience of a Psychoanalyst* (New York: Farrar, Straus & Co., 1949), p. 146: "It can catch what other people do not say, but only feel and think; and it can also be turned inward."
13. Daniel B. Syme and Rifat Sonsino, *Finding God: Ten Jewish Responses* (New York: UAHC Press, 1986), p. 89.
14. Martin Buber, *I and Thou,* 2d ed. (New York: Charles Scribner's Sons, 1958), p. 101.

15. Jakob Petuchowski, *Ever Since Sinai* (Milwaukee: B. Arbit Books, 1979), p. 3.

16. Based on Mishnah Pesahim 10:4.

17. See p. 77 chapter 5 of this book, "Foundations of Jewish Pastoral Care," for more about transference and countertransference.

18. Talmud Eruvin 100a.

19. Rabbi Maurice Lamm, in *The Jewish Way in Love and Marriage* (Middle Village, N.Y.: Jonathan David Publishers, 1991), p. 16, writes: "If a man wishes to marry a woman he loves, although she is seriously ill, more power to him. The Sages affirm this in reference to the prophetess Miriam, the sister of Moses and Aaron, who was called *azuvah* (abandoned) because all the young men abandoned her when she became sick. But Caleb the son of Chezron did marry her, and because he nursed her through her illness he was considered her 'father' (I Chronicles 2:18); and it was accounted a marriage for the sake of heaven and much praised."

20. Dr. Eugene Kalin, private communication, 1999.

21. Cited in Francine Klagsbrun, *Voices of Wisdom* (Middle Village, N.Y.: Jonathan David Publishers, Inc., 1980), p. 409.

22. Edwin Friedman, "The Myth of the Shiksa," in *Ethnicity and Family Therapy*, ed. Monica McGoldrick, John Pearce, and Joseph Giordano (New York and London: The Guilford Press, 1982).

23. This section was written based largely on the advice and professional experience of Rabbi Yoel Kahn, Rabbi Nancy Wiener, Rabbi Joan Friedman, Rabbi Sue Levi Elwell, and Rabbi Linda Holtzman. The author acknowledges with gratitude their irreplaceable contribution. See also an unpublished book manuscript by Yoel Kahn, "Kiddushin: A Guide to Commitment Ceremonies for Gay and Lesbian Jews," Congregation Sha'ar Zahav, San Francisco, 1992.

24. See *Legal Guide for Gay and Lesbian Couples* (San Francisco: Nolo Press) at www.nolo.com. See also Susan Saxe, "Legal Protections for Same-Sex Couples—More Than a Checklist," *The New Menorah* 59 (spring 2000): pp. 9–10.

25. See Rachel Adler, *Engendering Judaism: An Inclusive Theology and Ethics* (Philadelphia: Jewish Publication Society, 1998). Adler proposes replacing *kiddushin* with a *brit ahuvim* ceremony, which she calls "a marriage between subjects." See also Sue Levi Elwell, "Honor the Holiness of Lesbian and Gay Marriages," *The New Menorah* 59 (spring 2000): pp. 11–14; and Eyal Levinson, "A Covenant of Same-sex Nisu'in and Kidushin," pp. 15–18.

26. For further assistance to clergy in preparing gay or lesbian commitment ceremonies, see *The Rabbi's Manual*, published by the Reconstructionist Rabbinical Association, available at 215-576-5210 or RRAAssoc@aol.com.

27. Phyllis Meadow, "The Treatment of Marital Problems," *Modern Psychoanalysis* 2, no. 1 (spring 1977): p. 22.

28. Spotnitz, *The Marriage Partnership*, p. 12.

29. Salvador Minuchin, *Families and Family Therapy* (Cambridge, Mass.: Harvard University Press, 1974), p. 138.
30. Meadow, "Marital Problems," 1977, p. 25.
31. The author would like to thank Rabbi Kim Geringer for her careful reading of earlier versions of this chapter and for her valuable suggestions.

Bibliography

Aleph: Alliance for Jewish Renewal. *New Menorah* 59 (spring 5760/2000). Issue devoted to same-sex marriage. See especially Nancy H. Wiener, "Pre-marital Counseling for Same-sex Couples: Highlights for Rabbis and Cantors." Also, *Points to Consider in Counseling Same-sex Couples for Marriage/Commitment Ceremonies.* Philadelphia, Pa.: Aleph, 2000.

Clinebell, Howard. *Basic Types of Pastoral Care and Counseling: Resources for the Ministry of Healing and Growth,* rev. and enl. Nashville: Abingdon Press, 1984.

Kahn, Yoel. "Kiddushin: A Guide to Commitment Ceremonies for Gay and Lesbian Jews." Unpublished manuscript. Congregation Sha'ar Zahav, San Francisco, 1992.

Kornfeld, Margaret. *Cultivating Wholeness: A Guide to Care and Counseling in Faith Communities.* New York: Continuum, 1998.

Wiener, Nancy. *Beyond Breaking the Glass.* New York: CCAR Press, spring 2001.

Rabbi Ellen Jay Lewis, N.C.Psy.A., is a psychoanalyst in private practice in New Jersey and New York. She received her analytical training at the Center for Modern Psychoanalytic Studies in New York. Since her ordination at Hebrew Union College–Jewish Institute of Religion in 1980, she has served congregations in Dallas, Texas, and Summit, New Jersey, where she was named Rabbi Honorata. She is currently the spiritual leader of the Jewish Center of Northwest Jersey in Washington, New Jersey. Rabbi Lewis has a particular interest in developing models of clinical supervision for rabbis and cantors.

Responding to Domestic Violence

Gus Kaufman, Jr.
Wendy Lipshutz
Rabbi Drorah O'Donnell Setel

Dr. Gus Kaufman, Jr., Wendy Lipshutz, and Rabbi Drorah O'Donnell Setel provide a practical manual for helping victims of this often invisible but deadly scourge. Their contribution defines the problem and examines classical Jewish perspectives on it. They suggest ways of responding to both victim and perpetrator, with concern for practical and spiritual needs. They describe Jewish spiritual resources for caring for battered women and children in families plagued by violence. The authors also direct pastoral caregivers in their roles as educators and advocates.[1]

Dedicated to the memory of Rabbi Julie Spitzer, *z'l* (of blessed memory), who pioneered contemporary awareness and intervention to stop wife battering in the Jewish community, and who inspired this chapter.

"Rabbi, I'm in trouble," said the voice on the other end of the phone. "During the sermon you gave Friday night on abuse, I felt as if you were speaking directly to me. I never knew there were other Jewish women living in this kind of hell."

Bernice, forty-one, a Jewish woman with three children aged fourteen, ten, and six, has been married for sixteen years. While in nursing school, she met her husband, Sam, a medical student, and quickly fell in love with him. Once, shortly after they met and while Bernice was talking on the phone to her former boyfriend, Larry, Sam grabbed the phone out of her hand and hung it up. He shoved her against the wall with a menacing look, his face right in hers, and said, "You don't need to be talking to Larry anymore." Bernice was terrified; she had never told anybody about this.

Sam and Bernice married within a year of meeting each other. When Bernice got pregnant, Sam insisted that she quit school, although her parents encouraged her to finish her nursing degree. Sam told her, "Just stay home. I'll take care of you." They moved from city to city for his medical training. Bernice stayed home to raise the children. When her youngest turned six, Bernice wanted to go back to school to complete her degree so she could finally begin her nursing career. Sam insisted that she stay home, saying, "You don't have to work. I make plenty of money and I'll take care of you."

As the years went by, Bernice and Sam built a life in the city where he had grown up. Sam worked hard and was involved in the Jewish community. It sometimes seemed to Bernice that everyone got some of Sam but her, or rather, that the only part that she got was the back of his hand. Bernice felt that she should be grateful for what she had: she and Sam were prospering. Yes, he sometimes hit her, but she thought that she must have provoked it by getting so angry at him. Yes, she had been feeling down and had been on antidepressants for the past three years. It was just that Sam had such a mean mouth: How often she had heard him say, "You were nothing when we met and you would be nothing if I left." What especially hurt her was that Max, the fourteen-year-old, had begun yelling at her the same way Sam did.

What's the Problem?

At this point, the rabbi might be saying to herself, "Maybe they just need a little couples' counseling." Very seldom does someone call you and say, "Rabbi, I am being abused," and even less often, "Rabbi, I am battering my wife and I want to stop." Therefore, how will the problem emerge and how will it be labeled?

How We Define the Problem Determines How We Respond

What is abuse? Why is it so confusing when we actually face real situations? One way of asserting and maintaining power over others individually and collectively is to appropriate the power to define reality. Therefore, the description of what has happened is very much in question. The person who yells, throws things, and hits says, "I just lost it," and perhaps, "You provoked me." But these acts are not the result of an abuser striking out uncontrollably. Abusers clearly choose when and whom they abuse. They do not usually strike their employers, the mail carrier, or the rabbi; they do not usually attack in public places, such as the synagogue. This kind of control is illustrated in the title of the first book on woman-battering, Erin Pizzey's *Scream Quietly or the Neighbors Will Hear,* published in 1974.[2] Abusers usually choose how much they are going to hurt their partners, though they sometimes miscalculate.

Abusers certainly do not label their own behavior as abuse. Rather, they refuse to talk about their behavior, deny or minimize the abuse, or blame the victim or other factors ("I was tired, drunk, stressed"). If we take them at their word and excuse their behavior, they feel permission to do it again, and it will very likely escalate. Limits, sanctions, and negative consequences are a necessary part of intervention to stop abusive behavior.

What Does Jewish Tradition Say About Abuse?

In Psalm 55 we are taught the following:

> It is not an enemy who reviles me—
> I could bear that;
> it is not my foe who vaunts himself against me—
> I could hide from him;
> but it is you, my equal,
> my companion, my friend;
> sweet was our fellowship;
> we walked together in God's house.[3]

In her groundbreaking book, *When Love Is Not Enough: Spousal Abuse in Rabbinic and Contemporary Judaism,* Rabbi Julie Spitzer mined the Talmud and commentaries and uncovered an ongoing debate concerning acceptable behavior in marital relations and the appropriate response to transgressions of these norms. This conflict appears to reflect a battle between Judaism's strong emphasis on justice, on the one hand, and the legacy of patriarchal culture, in which the husband had absolute authority over the household, on the other.

A teaching by Maimonides highlights this struggle: "Any woman who refrains from doing her household chores as she is required to do, the *Bet Din* (rabbinic court) should compel her, even by using the rod."[4] Rabbi Spitzer notes that Maimonides also quotes the sages who "commanded that a man should honor his wife more than he honors himself, and love her as he loves himself."[5] In fact, the permissibility of beating one's wife was hotly debated by the sages. For example, Simchah b. Samuel of Speyer wrote in the twelfth century that not only is a man forbidden to beat his wife, but that "if such an abusive husband refuses to submit to it, the court may appeal to Gentile authorities in order to have them compel him to do as the law of Israel prescribes."[6] On the other hand, Rabbi Simchah's contemporary, Rabbenu Tam, taught, "Wife beating is unheard of among the children of Israel," reflecting a denial of the problem that persists in some quarters even today.[7]

In the next century, Rabbi Meir of Rothenberg responded to a question about a man who frequently struck his wife: "A Jew must honor his wife more than he honors himself. If one strikes his wife, one should be punished more severely than for striking another person, for one is enjoined to honor one's wife, but is not enjoined to honor the other person."[8] Ultimately, whether or not the Bible, Talmud, or other ancient texts address the specifics of violence that we encounter, we can rely on underlying principles of human dignity and our imperative to choose life to support and to advocate for victims of abuse.

Key Jewish Values

Shalom bayit (peace in the home), *pikuach nefesh* (preserving life), *lo ta'amod al dam re'echa* (Do not stand idly by the blood of your neighbor), and *lashon hara* (defamatory speech) are values that shape the classical rabbinic response to cases of suspected abuse. Excellent work has been done by Rabbis Spitzer, Dorff, Dratch, and others in summarizing the application of these principles to marital abuse.[9] We will not attempt to summarize this work, but only to point to two particular concerns. First, the concept of *shalom bayit* has sometimes been used to hold women responsible or to silence them in the face of abuse.[10] Secondly, the prohibition of *lashon hara* need not be understood as preventing reporting or speaking out about abuse.

> Ann, who was physically battered by her husband, asked her rabbi for help. The rabbi sent her home to preserve *shalom bayit*.

The abuse continued, and eventually, without the rabbi's support, Ann left her husband and began to lead a violence-free life. Years later she ran into her rabbi. By this time, the rabbi had learned that his own daughter had been battered and he apologized to Ann.

Of this use of the notion of *shalom bayit* Rabbi Spitzer says:

> We are exhorted by the psalmist, "Seek peace and pursue it." We must consider not only peace among nations, not only peace between neighbors, but *shalom bayit,* peace in the household as well. *Shalom bayit*: We must recognize that not every household is one of peace and harmony, that violence exists in the Jewish community as much as it exists in the general population. The end to such violence is expedited by awareness of the signs of a troubled home, and by obligating ourselves not to turn away or pretend the problem doesn't exist. *Shalom bayit* must be held up as an ideal—not as a trap but as a release. Keeping peace in the home is not a reason to stay in an abusive situation. It is a reason to leave one.[11]

But what about *lashon hara*? Is reporting suspected abuse a case of inappropriately speaking ill of another person? Rabbi Dorff reminds us of the very clear exceptions to the prohibitions against (otherwise) defamatory speech: "When failure to disclose the abuse to the proper authorities will result in continued abuse, the abused person, and for that matter anyone who notices the abuse, are obligated to reveal the abusive facts."[12]

Perspectives from the Battered Women's Movement

The contemporary response to the beating of women began in the early 1970s with the birth of the battered women's movement. Drawing on the women's movement and the civil rights movement of the 1960s, women who had suffered rape, battery, and incest began to speak their truths and to make common cause. These women realized for the first time that other women were also being beaten and that they could support each other by inviting other battered women into their homes for safety. These battered women's shelters were testimony to the failure of the civil and religious community to provide battered women with safety. As in the black struggle for liberation, these women often drew inspiration from biblical sources. For example, one of the early shelters (in Baltimore) was called The House of Ruth. The first national grassroots domestic violence organization, the National Coalition Against Domestic Violence, was organized in 1978. Today, there are almost 2,000 community-based battered women's shelters and programs in the U.S.

These women disclosed truths about their situations. They listed common tactics used to subjugate them. In their support groups, they saw through the veils of rationalizations surrounding abuse. They uncovered the common thread—the systematic exertion of power and control over another.

These pioneering women taught us that abuse is:

- Physical: Pushing, hitting, shoving, grabbing
- Sexual: Use of force, refusing to take no for an answer, unwanted touching
- Financial: Controlling the money, making all the big decisions
- Psychological/emotional/verbal: Putdowns, name-calling, denigration of the victim, claiming the truth, being the authority

Abuse is not:

- Losing control
- Lack of communication or merely marital conflict
- Merely an anger management problem
- One so-called sick person striking out at another

Abuse is one person choosing to control another person.

By and large men have more power in society and learn to control others. In a 1998 national survey sponsored by the National Institute of Justice and the Centers for Disease Control and Prevention, 8,000 men and 8,000 women were questioned. The survey found that most violence perpetrated against adults is perpetrated by men: Ninety-three percent of women and eighty-six percent of men who were raped, physically assaulted, or both, after the age of eighteen were assaulted by a man. For this reason, in this chapter we refer to the perpetrator as "him" and the victim as "her." Of course, when a woman is abusing a man, it is wrong, but a careful assessment of claims by men that they are abused is essential, because men who batter often claim that *they* are being abused.

Abuse occurs in homosexual as well as heterosexual relationships. Gay, lesbian, bisexual, and transgendered people have great trouble getting help when being abused. They have reason to fear not only the abusers, but also society and the authorities' discrimination and persecution.

Intimidation is especially effective as a means of maintaining control and power once the abuser has attacked his victim physically. This issue must be looked at quite carefully; a man hitting a woman may not have the same effect as a woman hitting a man. Batterers will often say, "She hit me first," but if you ask, "Are you afraid of her?" or, "Are you terrified?" the true balance of power is likely to be disclosed. Men are so much more trained in the use of force that it is far more common for them to intimidate women than vice versa. In addition to the use of threats, other forms of intimidation include blocking the door, standing over her, using one's size or yelling to intimidate, and threatening or attacking children, other family members, and pets.

Those who deal with abuse on a regular basis report that both the abuser and the abused deny and minimize. Whatever abuse is divulged may be only the tip of the iceberg. Contrary to popular belief, most victims do not flaunt their victimization: They hide and minimize it from shame, fear, and guilt.

How Should the Pastoral Caregiver Respond?

Responding to the Woman

- *Listen to her.* You may be the first person she has ever told. Your response may make the difference in whether she continues to seek the help she needs.
- *Believe her.* Typically, her abuser has repeatedly told her she exaggerates and lies, making her question her reality. Your belief in her can help her to believe her own experiences and continue to seek support. She may fear that you or others in the community will not believe her, especially if her abuser is a community leader.
- *Acknowledge her courage in seeking help.* Her abuser has likely kept her isolated from those who could help her,

and may have threatened to hurt or discredit her if she tells anyone.

- *Acknowledge her strengths.* It takes a very strong person to survive an abusive relationship. She can use these strengths to begin to live free of violence and abuse.

- *Safety planning.* Addressing a woman's safety is an essential first step. Refer her to a domestic violence program to begin this process: This could truly save her life. Her safety planning may include deciding whom she wants to tell about her domestic situation; preparing those she tells to call the police if necessary; finding a secure place to leave extra money, car keys, clothes, and important papers; and obtaining a legal protective order.[13]

- *Avoid questions that seem to blame her for the abuse,* such as "What was your part in it? What do you think you could do to keep him from getting so mad?" Most abused women already feel like the abuse is their fault because abusers tell them so over and over again. Tell her the abuse is not her fault and that she does not deserve to be abused.

- *Support her in exploring her options and making her own choices.* Don't tell her what to do. Part of living in an abusive relationship is having the abuser tell her what to do. Being told that *she* can best figure out how to take care of herself may give her the strength to move forward.

- *Support her even if she wants to stay.* While not forgetting safety, recognize that most women who eventually leave make an average of seven attempts before they can finally get away. There are some indications that it takes Jewish women even longer.[14] In addition to their keen awareness of how punitively their husbands will treat their leaving, women must juggle their responsibilities as primary caretakers of the family. Women may seek help when they are not planning to leave, and as helpers, we have to work on our feelings of helplessness, frustration, and fear for them so that we can be supportive. Trusting that the victim is the best authority on her own situation can be difficult for those of us who are used to being consulted as authorities. It is all too easy to feel annoyance or anger in the face of this sense of powerlessness. It might be safer to get angry with the least powerful party, yet our tradition requires that we side with those who are least powerful. In addition, keep in mind the fact that the period after separation between partners can be extremely dangerous for women. Many men experience this loss of control as both intolerable and degrading. They can be motivated to take ever more extreme actions to regain a sense of authority and control over their partner, including threats, stalking, severe assault, rape, murder, and suicide.

- *Recognize your limitations.* You play a vital role in meeting her needs, but you are not alone. It is important to recognize you cannot fix her situation by yourself.

- *Know your community resources.* Keep a list of battered women's shelters, support groups, hotlines, rape crisis centers, women's resource centers, and programs specifically for lesbian, gay, bisexual, and transgendered people.[15] Battered women report that the people who are most helpful are those who have been through battering. Therefore, the best resources are grassroots organizations whose programs have been shaped by women who have survived abuse. These organizations include battered women's shelters, state domestic violence coalitions, and Jewish domestic violence programs. Professional training programs usually have included minimal instruction in the area of domestic violence, thus a professional degree does not necessarily indicate that a caregiver is an expert in domestic violence.

- *Make referrals.* If you are not sure if she has been abused, or if she does not define herself as having been abused, suggest that she call a community resource number for help sorting through her situation. If the woman is willing for you to do so, it may be helpful for you to make an initial telephone call to the domestic violence program to say that she may be calling. Although it may feel difficult to go outside the congregation for help, it may be necessary because abuse thrives on secrecy. Both you and she are faced with the tension caused by the desire for privacy and the necessity for intervention (and thus some exposure) if the abuse is to be stopped.

- *Provide her with ongoing support.* Beginning a life free from violence usually takes a long time, and can be a protracted and complicated process. Standing by her during this process can be frustrating and even scary; recognize that it is even more frustrating and frightening for her. She needs you to remain patient and not give up.

Responding to the Abuser: Hard Choices

Back in her study, the rabbi began to reflect on Bernice's dilemma. "What am I going to do?" the rabbi thought. "Sam is on my synagogue's board." She realized, "Bernice has a dilemma, but so do I."

Those of us who are called to intervene in domestic violence quickly realize that we must consider our own position in society and in the Jewish community and how we are going to live our professed values. The patriarchal nature of violence against women requires us, if we are going to intervene effectively, to speak truth to power, to borrow a phrase from Quaker writers. Why do we say this? Abuse is a means for one person or group of people to take or maintain power over another. Each and every act of abuse reinforces this power.

- *When we intervene, we must confront the one who is more powerful.* It is not our job, and is actually contraindicated, to ask the victim to change to make the abuser stop. Of course, it would seem easier for us to just tell her to change because we wouldn't have to go against him and rock the boat. We also want to avoid facing an angry, cunning, manipulative, and powerful man, but he is the cause of the abuse, and it is his responsibility to stop, not hers.
- *Hold him accountable.* Abusers don't stop unless they experience negative consequences for continuing to abuse. To call the powerful to account is dangerous work and takes courage. It requires coordinated efforts with others

in the community. The courage it takes for you, the rabbi or cantor, to speak out may help you understand the courage it takes a battered woman to defy the batterer. She is in greater danger because she is his chosen target. He is neither likely to go after you physically, nor is he likely to isolate or to terrorize you. Confronting the abuser does require care because abuse might well intensify once it has been brought into the open. Of course, rabbis or cantors also need to protect themselves. For example, a woman pastoral caregiver may want to have another professional or lay leader present with her in meeting with or confronting a suspected abuser.

- *Let him know you expect him to do whatever is necessary to create safety and justice for those he has damaged.* Moving out of the home may be a necessary first step so that she and the children can begin to feel safe. If he is the only one working outside the home, he will need to provide her with money. This may need to happen before any legal arrangements have been made.

- *Help him develop a plan to restore justice now and over the long term.* This plan must include honoring her wishes about the relationship, and granting her a *get* (divorce decree) if she wishes.

- *Rely on battered women's advocates, including any local batterers' intervention program they recommend, as allies.* To do this you must acknowledge the limits of your knowledge about abuse.

- *Help the abuser to network with other men who are working to be non-abusive.* This happens in the context of a supervised, certified batterers' intervention program. In this setting, men can begin to turn to other men rather than expecting those they have abused to meet all their emotional needs. Abusers will not readily accept these referrals; their instinct is to remain private about abuse as a family matter; in fact, it is a social and a public safety issue.

- *Offer to work in alliance with the batterers' intervention program.* Perhaps you can go with him to an initial orientation session. Doing so provides him with support and accountability and educates you, allowing you to become familiar with an important community resource.

- *Help the synagogue to respond appropriately.* It may again be tempting to collude in pretending nothing is going on, but this is not just. What he really needs is not for his community not to turn its face away, but to call him to account. Therefore, you may have to insist he tell others (if she gives permission) in a way that does not make himself out to be a victim. You may need to let him know that until she has been treated justly he cannot receive honors such as having an *aliyah* (being called to the Torah). One rabbi refused to allow a man who he knew had battered his wife to serve as an officer of the synagogue. If the man who has been abusive is a rabbi, his community should suspend his rabbinic duties until he has set things right. Protocols developed by Kehilla Community Synagogue in Oakland, California, discuss reinstituting the tradition of *cherem* (formal expulsion from the community), by forbidding a batterer to be a member of the synagogue.[16] Rabbi Drorah O'Donnell Setel suggests he go to another synagogue to do his *teshuvah* and to work with a team of educated congregants who can help him be accountable. The testimony of many battered women makes clear that they are not safe in the same congregation as their abusers. Who can do this sanctioning and holding accountable? We recommend that a special committee be developed that would include members of the community and battered women's advocates. Committee members should receive specific training in this area, and work in consultation with the rabbi or cantor.

Two Models of Clergy Intervention with Abusers

1. **The clergy member approaches the abuser.**
   It is possible for the rabbi or cantor, with the permission of the victim, to confront the abuser directly, getting him to seek help voluntarily or to grant both a *get* and secular divorce or such other relief

that she wishes. Unfortunately, this almost never happens unless there is a strong sense of support for actively confronting batterers in the community. In one traditional community, a woman went to her rabbi and said, "I am being abused by my husband and I want a *get*." The rabbi called together a *Bet Din* and went to the husband, insisting that he appear. The man resisted (indirectly, by always having another commitment) but eventually showed up at the *Bet Din*, which ultimately persuaded him to give his wife the *get*.

2. **The abuser comes to the clergy member.**
A man who has abused his wife typically does not come to talk to the rabbi or cantor unless and until his wife has left him and taken the children. He certainly has been experiencing problems, but his socialization and belief have been that he needs to handle them himself by controlling and blaming her and, often, the children. When he does go to see the rabbi, he is likely to present himself as the victim who no longer gets to see his children. He wants to enlist the rabbi as an agent of social control—to get "his" wife back in "her place." He wants to head off any possibility of her getting community support.

A batterer may approach a clergy member when he has been ordered to a batterers' program as a consequence of an arrest or as part of custody arrangements after divorce. He may complain that the program is in a bad neighborhood or that no one there is like him. This is a way abusers attempt to use clergy and the Jewish community to avoid taking responsibility for their actions. If the clergy member gives in, the abuser does not have to work on justice, safety, and restitution for his partner, the children, and society. The rabbi or cantor would do well to be in contact with those batterers' intervention programs recommended by women's advocates. Clergy can be valuable members of the team working to hold batterers accountable.

Responding to Suspected Abuse

A rabbi or cantor often hears about battering from congregants. Clergy and community members are then in a difficult position—caught between obligations and injunctions concerning *lashon hara* and *pikuach nefesh*. Given the dangers of battering (thousands of women are killed in North America every year), intervention clearly has the potential to save lives.

A suspicion of abuse can occur by reading between the lines, or what one therapist has called "listening with the third ear."[17]

> A rabbi got a phone call from a woman saying she needed help with problems with her husband. And she added, "The children are so difficult, too." The rabbi had had experience with the children in Hebrew school and they seemed fine. As he drew her out about the problems, she reported she felt suffocated. Her husband seldom let her out of the house. When he allowed her to go to the store, he demanded to know what she was going to buy and only gave her enough for those purchases. He called her ten times a day to check on her activities and say he loved her. She felt bad that his attention didn't feel good. He insisted she be available and that he know where she was twenty-four hours a day, seven days a week. He checked the mileage on her car. Although some of this behavior might seem to be signs of caring, the effect on her was that she felt obsessively controlled.

Learning about abuse from talking to advocates and reading battered women's stories can help develop a so-called third ear. Signs of possible abuse include frequent illness, sudden change in attendance and other behaviors, and, of course, visible injuries. In some instances, abuse of one's partner follows alcohol or other drug abuse. When this is the case, it is unlikely the abuser will stop his controlling and violent actions as long as he is abusing substances. In the presence of substance abuse there may be a dual cycle of increasing tension, blaming, abuse, and remorse. It is highly unlikely that the spousal abuse will stop until the substance abuse is addressed. Physical abuse does not cause substance abuse, and vice versa; addressing one does not address the other.[18]

Spiritual Counseling for Jewish Battered Women

Although clergy are not qualified to act as legal or strategic advocates for battered women, they can provide invaluable help as spiritual counselors. First and foremost, listening deeply and acknowledging and validating the victim's experience can help her heal.

> After a severe beating by her husband, Pnina was angry and frightened. She felt vengeful toward her husband. She questioned whether it was okay to feel the anger and to wish for revenge. She struggled with the conflict between how she truly felt and her need to be nice. She went to her rabbi and asked if it was okay to have these feelings. He not only validated her feelings but also quoted a passage from the Torah that showed that it was justifiable to have such feelings after the abuse she had suffered. Pnina took comfort in this and was able to move forward.

Domestic violence raises profound questions about the nature of God, the experience of human suffering, individual responsibility, and the role of the Jewish community. It also challenges historical attitudes toward marital commitment, *teshuvah*, and the relationship between justice and compassion. Naturally, rabbis, cantors, and other spiritual leaders will already have faced situations in which they have had to formulate their personal beliefs about many of these issues. Be open to the probability that working with battered women will challenge some of those beliefs. For instance, what does it mean to assert God's omnipotence when you are talking to a woman whose husband held their children at gunpoint while threatening to kill her? Avoid victim-blaming platitudes that minimize the trauma and the violence experienced by victims. Asserting that their experience is "part of God's plan" or that "there are no accidents" can be taken by battered women as a suggestion that they deserve abuse. In addition, at a time when battered women most need spiritual support and connection, such images of God serve only to shut them off from these resources.

Jewish tradition teaches many positive theological models that can be helpful to battered women. Rabbinic ideas of human partnership with God acknowledge that the nature of our world is imperfect and incomplete. In this context, emphasizing God as the source of healing, compassion, and justice can provide a sense of hope. The kabbalistic concept of *tzimtzum* (God's withdrawal from part of creation so that human beings could exercise free will) helps place the responsibility for abuse with the perpetrator, not God. It is essential to give a clear message that violence and abuse are never God's will.

One view of suffering in Jewish tradition has seen it as an instrument of judgment and punishment. In the aftermath of the Holocaust, Jews have more and more found it repugnant or impossible to accept blame or responsibility for their oppression. A similar process has begun on an individual level, in which victims of abuse reject shame or responsibility for what has been done to them. Battered Jewish women can be greatly helped by understanding this connection and hearing that they are in no way to blame for the violence against them.

Wrestling with the meaning of their suffering can be excruciatingly painful for victims of abuse. Spiritual counselors must be prepared to witness that pain rather than trying to shut it off. Some individuals experience an extended or even lifelong process of grief. At the same time, victims can be encouraged to find meaning in their experience. Some choose to become advocates for themselves and other battered Jewish women; some act to challenge abusive power relationships, working politically for social change; others use creative expression (movement, writing, or fine arts) to tell their stories and to encourage others to do the same.[19]

Hillel's injunction "Do not separate yourself from the community" can be especially difficult for battered Jewish women. As Jews, we hold a fundamental belief that we can be wholly human only in relationship with others. Our synagogues, community centers, and other Jewish organizations are essential contexts for becoming our fullest Jewish selves, yet it is precisely these places where battered Jewish women often experience fear, isolation, and shame. Batterers use the pretext of needing to come to services or wanting to see the children at religious school as a means to have access to their victims. When battered Jewish women do not hear spousal abuse discussed or condemned, they hesitate to let their abuse be known to those who should be offering them support. Even those women who are brave enough to disclose their situation are frequently given the message that they have done something shameful in even raising the topic.

The issue of shame in the Jewish community is a complicated one. So vulnerable to the random violence of surrounding cultures for so long, Jews still have the fear of looking "bad" to others. Throughout our history, Jews have often dealt with community dysfunction by flatly denying that problems such as spousal abuse, addiction, and incest even existed within Jewish communities. We idealized our homes as refuges from a hostile, anti-Semitic world. For generations of Jewish women and children, the abuse suffered within those families was hidden or even viewed as acceptable. Now that victims and survivors have demanded these issues no longer be ignored, they are sometimes blamed for "airing dirty laundry" or bringing shame on the community. Sadly, women victims often have a similar experience: When they take the courageous step of leaving an abusive relationship, they may be perceived as betraying Jewish ideals of family and marital fidelity.

Those in the position of offering spiritual guidance must be sensitive to the shame many abused women carry. They must emphasize that violence and the controlling of one partner by another is a sin, and breaks the marriage bond. A victim's willingness to name the transgression should not in any way be confused with the actual transgression committed by the perpetrator: It is the batterer who has acted shamefully.

Jewish community can be an essential context for battered women to engage in the process of spiritual healing. For that to happen, a number of conditions must be met.

1. The theological messages addressed previously must not only be discussed with the victim but also with the congregation or organization as a whole. Spiritual leaders play a crucial role in setting the tone of that discussion.
2. Establishing policies and procedures concerning abuse provides an important opportunity for educating and engaging community members on this topic.[20]
3. Although all agree that synagogues should be sanctuaries, places of safety and refuge, it takes serious, consistent effort to approach that goal. Clergy and lay leaders must understand the long-term and arduous nature of that process.
4. As more synagogues and Jewish agencies develop protocols for dealing with violence and abuse on the part of their members and leadership, a time may come when there will be an area-wide *Bet Teshuvah* (crisis intervention and accountability team). Such a group would be composed of a mixture of clergy and laypeople with experience in working with sexual and domestic violence. Community-wide group supervision of the *teshuvah* process for perpetrators would remove some of the personality issues that can

arise when a single congregation or agency needs to judge one of its members. In addition, the pooled resources of a *Bet Teshuvah* relieve the expectation that each community group must provide enough individuals with expertise to handle matters on its own. In this model, representatives of each part of the community would implement the Jewish principle that "to save a single life is to save an entire world."

5. Victims must experience a sense of advocacy from their rabbis, cantors, and other members of their Jewish communities. Just as battered women's advocates help them create a safety plan, spiritual advocates can help them construct a "justice and healing plan." The victim must be the one to determine what she needs to feel safe within the community. As explained earlier, she may need the batterer to associate with another congregation. Clergy can be especially helpful in making such arrangements.

The process of justice and healing may also include rituals, speaking out about the violence, and creating symbols that provide the community with a consistent reminder of each person's responsibility to live nonviolently. Traditional Jewish prayers and ceremonies will be meaningful because the struggle for freedom from oppression is at the core of the Jewish experience. In addition, new prayers and rituals have been created for and by survivors of battering and abuse to explicitly articulate these links. Rituals can help to bring a sense of justice, healing, closure, or all three, to battered Jewish women. Examples of such rituals are a Passover prayer that connects Jews in Egyptian slavery with Jews enslaved in their own homes[21] and a Women's Healing Service for Jewish battered women, which uses the *Sukkah* as a symbol of the haven from domestic violence.[22] Marcia Cohn Spiegel's article "Spirituality for Survival: Jewish Women Healing Themselves"[23] and Rebecca Schwartz and Naomi Tucker's "A Jewish Spiritual Response to Domestic Violence"[24] provide frameworks to develop creative Jewish rituals for healing. Professor Laura Levitt and Rabbi Sue Ann Wasserman created a contemporary transformation of the ancient practice of *mikvah*, ritual immersion, as an act of renewal following sexual assault.[25] Rabbi Lynn Gottlieb also draws on the tradition of *mikvah* and suggests new rituals. Her book, *She Who*

Dwells Within: A Feminist Vision of a Renewed Judaism, is an excellent resource for women who wish to consider personalizing or creating new rituals for their healing process.[26] Those who desire public affirmation of the injustice done to them may seek help convening a *Bet Din,* a group of three community leaders, to announce formally a judgment and sanctions against the perpetrator of abuse. The desired ritual could be as simple as reaffixing a *mezuzah* as an affirmation of reclaiming her own home as a place of safety and well-being.

Justice is a prerequisite for healing. "Forgive and forget" are not Jewish principles. On the contrary, accountability and remembrance are key elements in Jewish observance, liturgy, and ethics. The sages of the Talmud taught that the world exists in a constant tension between justice and compassion: Too much of the former demands an impossible perfection, too much of the latter absolves individuals of their responsibility to one another. Although the term *teshuvah* is often translated as repentance, it can also be understood as the process through which we integrate seemingly contradictory mandates of justice and compassion. Traditional Jewish ethical writings concerning *teshuvah* are clear that the perpetrator must first acknowledge and take responsibility for his harmful actions. Next, he must give an account of his wrongful actions to another person and take whatever actions are possible to make amends to his victim, including financial restitution.[27] In the case of spousal abuse this should include extended involvement in a certified batterers' intervention program, parenting classes (where applicable), accepting and complying with the legal consequences of his behavior, and accepting the victim's assessment of his behavior toward her. In addition, the perpetrator must prove that his transgression will never be repeated. One standard for determining this is that when faced with exactly the same situation he responds in a different, appropriate way. Only after all these steps have been completed is the transgressor allowed to ask forgiveness, and even that must be without any expectation that it will be forthcoming.

For her part, the victim must never be pressured to forgive someone who has abused her. For the victim, forgiveness is not the goal of her healing process. If it happens at all, it is a byproduct of that process.[28] Even if she does choose to reconnect or reconcile with the batterer, the idea of forgiveness must never be confused with condoning abusive behavior or saying that it had no effect or didn't matter. Forgiveness, in the more Jewish sense of finding balance, is rooted in the victim's ability to feel outrage at the injustice done to her, grieve her suffering, experience acknowledgment and justice, develop her own interpretation of the meaning of her suffering, and feel spiritual wholeness.

The spiritual counselor for a battered woman must not simultaneously work with the abuser who battered her. She needs someone who will be her sole advocate; if the same person counsels both of them, that caregiver may have conflicting obligations. Ideally, rabbis and other Jewish spiritual leaders in a community would coordinate efforts so that victims remained in their own synagogues and batterers attended and received spiritual counsel in another.

Response to Children
When Violence Has Occurred

The spiritual community has a special obligation to children in a family in which violence has occurred. There is a high correlation between spousal abuse and child abuse, both physical and sexual. In addition, any child who has witnessed violence is, by definition, a victim of trauma. Even children who may not have actually seen the abuse are damaged by the tension, their parents' distress, and the subsequent loss of a secure home. These children must be assisted not only by therapists, but also by spiritual mentors who are willing to discuss what has happened in their families. In this context, the Jewish concept of all people being created with both a *yetzer hatov* (good nature) and *yetzer hara* (bad nature) may be helpful in explaining why the father they love hurt their mother or why the mother they love failed to protect them from their father. They can be reassured by knowing that we all have a mixture of good and bad and that we can work to make the good part stronger. In addition, Jewish tradition distinguishes between an evil action and an evil person. Just as the Talmudic sage, Beruriah, taught that one must pray for an end to the sin, not the sinner, so too can we condemn an action as wrong without negating the personhood of the one who committed it.[29]

Given that abused adults have great trouble reconciling traditional ideas about God with their experience, it can be even more difficult for children not to feel abandoned by God or responsible for the abuse that has occurred. The theological concerns of a child who has been raped, beaten, denied food or comfort, has witnessed the injury or death of a loved person or pet, or lived with a constant sense of terror must be answered with extreme care. For example, the notion that God is everywhere can be frightening to a child who has lived with abusive surveillance. A child might wonder what "God loves you" means when the people who love you are violent. Experiencing the world as a place of safety, meaning, and well-being can be a lifelong struggle for children whose families were the opposite. Children who have experienced violence in their homes can be reassured when helped to see God in the courage to tell the truth, the comfort of friendship, the joy of playfulness, and the strength to survive and to grow. As much as any child, and perhaps even more, they need to hear that their lives have purpose, that they do not have to be perfect or to perform to deserve love, and that their unique self is holy.

Children are powerless in response to family violence, thus they often construct an explanation for themselves that involves their own behavior. They try to understand what they might do to stop or mitigate the abuse and blame themselves when it continues. In addition, they feel it is their role to placate or to nurture their parents so that they will have no "cause" for further violence.[30] Ironically, this mirrors a strain of traditional Jewish belief that suggests that the sufferings of the Jews resulted from their own misdeeds and could be ended only if they perfected their obedience to God's will. Children must hear that they do not have power over the adults in their lives and are not responsible for the adults' actions. On the contrary, it is the parents' job to take care of the child, not the other way around. In this context, it may be useful to discuss the reasons we name God as a father or mother (creating life, nurturing, unconditional love, comforting) and distinguish this idealized version from real parents and their imperfections.

What You Can Do to Raise Awareness of Domestic Violence and Abuse

- **Speak out** in bulletin articles, sermons, and adult education courses. Giving a sermon that acknowledges wife battering (or child abuse, including child sexual abuse) may evoke some negative responses and denial, but will also prompt a response from people who have never had anyone to turn to. Be prepared to offer resources and referrals.

- **Educate yourself about the issue and resources before you face a crisis.** By now it should be clear that to respond well to a crisis, a lot of work needs to be done in advance. Get to know the people in your community who intervene; find out about the availability of battered women's shelters, support groups, and other services for battered women. Find out if providers are aware of the special needs of Jewish women, men, and children. Refer to providers even if they are not, and offer suggestions to make services more supportive of those who are Jewish. Examples of such support include providing a *Shabbat* kit with candles, prayerbooks, and so forth to the shelter; offering to bring kosher food when needed; recruiting Jewish women who are knowledgeable about family violence to provide training for shelter staff. Recognize that some Jewish women will not use Jewish agencies for fear of their plight being known in the community. Other women will hide their Jewishness from shelter staff because of fear of anti-Semitism.
- **Educate the community.** Hold conferences about abuse at your synagogue or organization. Many Jewish women's organizations have made this issue a priority and are looking for partners in the community. The long-term, positive effects of organizing such events for conference attendees and for the community are enormous.
- **Make use of the excellent resources available.** Many of them are listed in the bibliography. Stock these books, journals, and videos in your library. The videos and the play, *Not So Happily Ever After,* make powerful programs.

Karen's story provides evidence for how helpful rabbis can be. She told her rabbi and other synagogue staff about her ex-husband's abuse toward her. They listened to her, provided her with emotional support, referred her to a battered women's support group, and maintained contact with her to assess her well-being and that of her children. They made a point of looking to her for guidance in decisions made about the family. Three years after her divorce was finalized, her ex-husband continued to harass and scare her so much that she feared for her life. Even as she began to reestablish her life and socialize, she had to be careful about how much information she shared with her adolescent children because of her fear of retaliation from her ex-husband. Whenever there were synagogue events involving her ex-husband and the children, synagogue leaders put safety first and checked with her to make sure she was okay with his involvement.

The rabbi's and congregation's support allowed Karen to heal, and to do so in the context of a caring, supportive spiritual community. Karen's story is evidence that every action not only makes a difference but may also save a life.

Notes

1. In this chapter we do not delve either into the important issues of child abuse, including emotional, physical, and sexual abuse by strangers, neighbors, and family, or issues of abuse of congregants by rabbis. For information on child abuse, see Rabbi Mark Dratch, "The Physical, Sexual and Emotional Abuse of Children" in *Resource Guide for Rabbis on Domestic Violence* (Washington, D.C.: Jewish Women International, 1996). For clergy abuse issues contact the Center for the Prevention of Sexual and Domestic Violence, Seattle, www.cpsdv.org.

2. Erin Pizzey, *Scream Quietly or the Neighbors Will Hear* (Short Hills, N.J.: R. Enslow Publishers, 1977).

3. Jewish Publication Society, 1985, quoted in Julie Ringold Spitzer, *When Love Is Not Enough: Spousal Abuse in Rabbinic and Contemporary Judaism* (New York: Women of Reform Judaism, 1995), p. 14.

4. Sefer Nashim, Hilchot Ishut 21:10, quoted in Spitzer, *Spousal Abuse*, p. 18.

5. Sefer Nashim, Hilchot Ishut 15:19, quoted in Spitzer, *Spousal Abuse*, p. 18.

6. The Code of Maimonides, trans. Klein (New Haven, Conn.: Yale University Press, 1972), p. xxvi, quoted in Spitzer, *Spousal Abuse*, p. 19.

7. *Spousal Abuse*, p. 18.

8. Responsa Even haEzer, #297, cited in Spitzer, *Spousal Abuse,* p. 19.

9. Spitzer, *Spousal Abuse,* pp. 34, 57–60, as well as the Resource Guide, pp. 45–47, 95–101, 102–107.

10. Naomi Graetz, *Silence Is Deadly: Judaism Confronts Wifebeating* (Northvale, N.J.: Jason Aronson, 1998), pp. 78, 155–56.

11. Spitzer, *Spousal Abuse,* p. 59.

12. Rabbi Elliott N. Dorff, "In God's Image: Aspects of Judaism Relevant to Family Violence," in Spitzer, *Spousal Abuse,* p. 99.

13. A legal protective order may direct an abuser to refrain from acts of violence and may specify that perpetrators cease contact, leave the family home, and/or forfeit temporary custody. Protective orders are available through the courts. Specific information about obtaining a legal protective order differs from one locality to another. For specific information contact your local domestic violence program. Call the National Domestic Violence Hotline at 800-799-SAFE (800-799-7233) to find the domestic violence shelter or program in your area.

14. Perhaps because of the myths surrounding Jewish families, some Jewish women report that they do not receive support or encouragement to leave their abusive partners when they confide in family members. Having been told to take responsibility for improving the situation or fearing that they will meet with rejection, Jewish women may be particularly reluctant to take any action that might be seen as breaking up their families.

15. For information about local emergency shelters and resources for battered women, call the National Domestic Violence Hotline at 800-799-SAFE (800-799-7233).

16. Kehilla Policies and Protocol on Abuse Prevention (Shalom Bayit, 3543 18th St., #10, San Francisco, CA 94110, Kehilla Coalition Against Abuse, 510-654-3015).

17. T. Reik, *Listening with the Third Ear* (New York: Farrar, Strauss & Co., 1948).

18. Gus Kaufman, Jr., "Intervention with Abuse of Alcohol, Drugs and Women," *Uptake: A Journal for Ending Violence Against Women* (July 1994). Also available from the author, gkaufmanjr@aol.com.

19. Judith Lewis Herman, *Trauma and Recovery: The Aftermath of Violence—From Domestic Abuse to Political Terror* (New York: Harper Collins, 1992).

20. Kehilla Policies and Protocol on Abuse Prevention.

21. The Shalom Bayit Program of Jewish Family & Career Services in Atlanta, Georgia, offers the following prayer to include in a Passover seder:

A Prayer for Your Passover Seder

Each year at this time, it is our responsibility as Jews to look upon ourselves as if we had actually gone forth from Egypt.

The struggle for freedom is ongoing, and in every age there are new freedoms to be won. On this night our hearts turn to those among us who suffer the pain of homes in which shalom has been shattered. We have been reluctant to confront this violence and to join in the effort to liberate those in pain.

There are Jewish children who are sexually, physically and/or verbally abused; there are Jewish adults who cower in fear of their partners; there are Jewish elderly who are ignored or imprisoned in their own homes. All are victims of a violence tearing at the very essence of their beings. This night when we celebrate the miracle of liberation, it is incumbent upon us to grasp the meaning of this enslavement; to hear their cries and to aid their struggle for liberation.

Some of us around this table are survivors; others know survivors—and victims—of domestic violence. We must come to know the silence and sadness; the loneliness and embarrassment; the bitterness and the craving for liberation experienced by Jews terrorized in their own homes.

As we celebrate the memory of that first Exodus which unfolded in the heart of Egypt, let us actively, and with clear intention, chart a new path, so that those bound in the chains of domestic violence may be freed of their shackles and come to know in their lives the taste of liberation, the meaning of redemption and the experience of shalom.

If using this prayer, please credit the Shalom Bayit Program of Jewish Family & Career Services, Atlanta: 770-677-9322; www.jfcs-atlanta.org.

22. Adrienne Affleck, "Women's Healing Service Sukkot 5759: In recognition of Domestic Violence Awareness Month" (Atlanta: Shalom Bayit Program of Jewish Family & Career Services, 1998) www.jfcs-atlanta.org.

23. Marcia Cohn Spiegel, "Spirituality for Survival: Jewish Women Healing Themselves," *Journal of Feminist Studies in Religion* 12, no. 2 (fall 1996): pp. 121–137.

24. Rebecca Schwartz and Naomi Tucker, "A Jewish Spiritual Response to Domestic Violence," *NCADV Voice* (fall 1996) (P.O. Box 18749, Denver, Colorado 80218).

25. Laura Levitt and Sue Ann Wasserman, "*Mikvah* Ceremony for Laura," in *Four Centuries of Jewish Women's Spirituality: A Sourcebook*, eds. Ellen M. Umansky and Dianne Ashton (Boston: Beacon Press, 1992): pp. 321–25.

26. Lynn Gottlieb, "Ceremonies for Women's Lives," in *She Who Dwells Within* (San Francisco: HarperSanFrancisco, 1995), pp. 135–45.

27. *The Journey of the Soul: Traditional Sources on Teshuvah*, ed. Leonard S. Kravitz and Kerry M. Olitzky (Northvale, N.J.: Jason Aaronson, 1995).

28. Ellen Bass and Laura Davis, *The Courage to Heal: A Guide for Women Survivors of Child Sexual Abuse* (New York: Harper & Row, 1994).

29. BT Berachot 10a.

30. Alice Miller, *For Your Own Good: Hidden Cruelty in Child-Rearing and the Roots of Violence* (New York: Noonday Press, 1990).

Bibliography

Jewish Books on Domestic Violence

Graetz, Naomi. *Silence Is Deadly: Judaism Confronts Wifebeating.* Northvale, N.J.: Jason Aronson, 1998.

Jewish Women International. *Resource Guide for Rabbis on Domestic Violence.* Washington, D.C.: Jewish Women International, 1996.

Russ, Ian, Sally Weber, and Ellen Ledley. *Shalom Bayit: A Jewish Response to Child Abuse and Domestic Violence.* Los Angeles: Jewish Family Services of Los Angeles, Family Violence Project, 1993.

Twerski, Abraham J. *The Shame Borne in Silence: Spouse Abuse in the Jewish Community.* Pittsburgh: Mirkov Publications, 1996.

Spitzer, Julie Ringold. *When Love Is Not Enough: Spousal Abuse in Rabbinic and Contemporary Judaism.* New York: Women of Reform Judaism, The Federation of Temple Sisterhoods, 1995.

Other Essential Books on Family Violence

Adams, Carol J. *Woman-Battering* (Creative Pastoral Care and Counseling Series). Minneapolis: Fortress Press, 1994.

Bass, Ellen, and Laura Davis. *The Courage to Heal: A Guide for Women Survivors of Child Sexual Abuse.* New York: Harper & Row, 1994.

Herman, Judith Lewis. *Trauma and Recovery: The Aftermath of Violence—From Domestic Abuse to Political Terror.* New York: Harper Collins, 1992.

Middleton-Moz, Jane. *Children of Trauma: Rediscovering Your Discarded Self.* Deerfield Beach, Fla.: Health Communications, 1989.

Miller, Alice. *For Your Own Good: Hidden Cruelty in Child-Rearing and the Roots of Violence.* New York: Noonday Press, 1990.

Other Resources

Jewish Materials Clearinghouse. Center for the Prevention of Sexual and Domestic Violence (CPSDV), 936 North 34th Street, Suite 200, Seattle, WA 98103. 206-634-1903; www.cpsdv.org.

Kehilla (Synagogue) Policies and Protocol on Abuse Prevention. Shalom Bayit, 3543-18th St., #10, San Francisco, CA 94110. Kehilla Coalition Against Abuse, 510-654-3015.

National Coalition Against Domestic Violence Jewish Women's Task Force Information Packet. P.O. Box 18749, Denver, CO 80218-0749, 303-839-1852.

Spiegel, Marcia Cohn. *Bibliography of Sources on Sexual and Domestic Violence in the Jewish Community.* www.umn.edu/minicava/bibs/jewish.htm.

Videotapes and Multimedia

Broken Vows: Religious Perspectives on Domestic Violence (videotape and study guide). Seattle: CPSDV 1994, www.cpsdv.org.

Hirsch, Mira. *Not So Happily Ever After . . . the Very Real Stories of Some American Jewish Families* (dramatic presentation based on true stories). Atlanta: Shalom Bayit Program, Jewish Family & Career Services (JF&CS), 1996, www.jfcs-atlanta.org.

Russian-language domestic violence video. Atlanta: Shalom Bayit Program, JF&CS, 1993, www.jfcs-atlanta.org.

To Save a Life: Ending Domestic Violence in Jewish Families; videotape and study guide. Seattle: CPSDV, 1997, www.cpsdv.org.

Journals and Newsletters

Journal of Religion and Abuse. Binghamton, NY: Haworth Press.

Working Together to Prevent Sexual and Domestic Violence (quarterly news journal). Seattle: CPSDV, www.cpsdv.org.

Wendy Lipshutz, L.M.S.W., is Program Director of the Shalom Bayit Program and Project Connect at Jewish Family & Career Services in Atlanta, Georgia, and a member of the Jewish Advisory Committee of the Center for the Prevention of Sexual and Domestic Violence. An activist, battered women's advocate, and licensed social worker, she has worked to end violence against women since 1983.

Gus Kaufman, Jr., Ph.D., is a clinical psychologist, speaker, trainer, and social activist in Atlanta, Georgia, who has been working since 1982 to end male violence toward women. He cofounded the Jewish Advisory Committee of the Center for the Prevention of Sexual and Domestic Violence in Seattle in 1992 and in 1983 was one of the founders of the Shalom Bayit Committee of Atlanta's Jewish Family & Career Services.

Rabbi Drorah O'Donnell Setel, M.T.S., served from 1992 to 2000 as the founding cochair of the Jewish Advisory Committee of the Center for the Prevention of Sexual and Domestic Violence. In addition to her work as an advocate and a trainer on issues concerning abused Jewish women and children, she serves as the rabbi of Congregation Kol Ami and Kadima-Kehillah in Seattle, Washington.

Confronting Addiction

Marcia Cohn Spiegel
Rabbi Yaacov Kravitz

Marcia Cohn Spiegel and Rabbi Yaacov Kravitz address substance and
other forms of abuse. They depict the extent of addiction within the Jewish
community, offer definitions for the problem, and outline three key aspects
of the pastoral role in working with addictions: gateway to help, ongoing
support, and spiritual nurture. Spiegel and Kravitz explore Jewish spiritual
resources especially helpful to addicts, address particular challenges for the
pastoral caregiver in working with addicts, and suggest ways that synagogues can be involved in supporting recovery and preventing addiction.

Let us bless the Source of Life in its infinite variety,
which creates all of us whole, none of us perfect.

—JUDY GLASS, "AFTER BIRTH," FROM *LIFECYCLES, VOL. 2:*
JEWISH WOMEN ON BIBLICAL THEMES IN
CONTEMPORARY LIFE

For centuries, Jews have taken pride in their reputation for sobriety
and moderation in the use of alcohol and other drugs. This belief
was so widespread that in the late eighteenth century Immanuel Kant
taught that "women, ministers, and Jews do not get drunk. . . . Their
outward worth is based merely on the belief of others in their chastity
and piousness."[1] The first studies of alcoholism in the United States
compared low reported rates of alcoholism in the Jewish community
with high rates in the Irish American community. One such study concluded that the Irish drank in an atmosphere of joyous conviviality,
whereas Jews associated drinking with ritual, and thus did not drink for
the effects of alcohol.[2] This belief was supported by the popular Yiddish
tune "A *Shikkur* Is a Goy" (A drunk is a non-Jew). Rabbis and community leaders lauded Jewish sobriety from the pulpit and in the press.

In the 1960s, when George was drinking excessively, suffering
blackouts, and passing out, his wife, Miriam, did not identify

the problem as alcoholism. When she turned to her rabbi for help, he reassured her that Jews are not alcoholics, thus she should examine her own behavior to see what she was doing to make George drink. It was many years before Miriam finally found the help she needed, and it was outside of the Jewish community. If she were to return to that same rabbi today, he would probably refer her and George to a Jewish program for alcoholics, addicts, and their families. He might give them a book to read to help them understand addiction from a Jewish perspective, and suggest that she and George attend a spiritual retreat to help them in recovery. He would certainly not deny the existence of the problem in the Jewish community.

The lack of reliable statistics regarding the incidence of addiction in the Jewish community makes historical comparisons difficult. Only in the last thirty-five years has addiction begun to be recognized as a significant problem among Jews. The Jewish pastoral caregiver has a vital role in supporting addicted Jews and their families. To play a part in the recovery process, pastoral caregivers need to understand the incidence of addiction, the nature of the disease and recovery, and the unique contribution that they can make to the healing of individuals and their loved ones.

The Extent of Addiction in the Jewish Community

Jewish tradition has always understood that excessive use of alcoholic beverages could cause serious problems. "Rabba Anna, son of Cahana, observes, 'Wherever wine is mentioned in the Bible, some sorrow is connected with it.'"[3] Noah's drunkenness (Genesis 9:20–28) brings shame on him and punishment on his sons. Lot's drunkenness is directly related to incest with his daughters (Genesis 19:30–38). The elderly Isaac's mistake in giving Jacob the blessing he intended for Esau could have been due to the wine he had consumed with his meal of game (Genesis 27:18–40). Aaron and his sons are abjured from using wine or strong drink when going into the tent of meeting (Leviticus 10:8–9). The Book of Isaiah (5:11–12, 5:22–23, 28:1–8) relates the consequences of drunkenness. Proverbs (23:19–35) contains an accurate description of addiction to alcohol. Midrash describes the progression from benign use to harmful. "If a man drinks properly, he becomes as strong as a lion whom nothing in the world can withstand. When he drinks more than is proper, he becomes like a pig that wallows in mire, and when he becomes drunk, he dances like an ape, and utters folly before all, and knows not what he does."[4] A common thread throughout our sources is that overindulgence can have negative consequences not only to the drinker but also to other family members.

Despite Jewish tradition's awareness of the dangers of substance abuse, and despite popular beliefs to the contrary, it is clear that Jews have suffered from addictions in the past and continue to do so in the present. Estimates of the incidence of alcoholism in the American Jewish population are difficult to come by. Approximately 8 to 14 percent of adults have been diagnosed with alcohol dependence at some time in their lives.[5] The rate of alcoholism among Jews appears to be less than that among the general population.[6] This difference is probably a product of both cultural and genetic factors.[7]

In addition to alcohol abuse, other forms of addiction affect the Jewish community today. Although the rate of use of illicit drugs by Jews appeared low early in the twentieth century, by midcentury drug use among Jews was reported to be equal to that of non-Jews.[8] Young Jews are at high risk for problem encounters with marijuana and cocaine. A 1985 survey of the National Cocaine Telephone Hotline found that 18 percent of callers were Jewish.[9] Addiction to gambling afflicts between 1 and 3 percent of the population,[10] but those who treat addictions report that Jews are overrepresented.[11]

Although accurate statistics on the incidence of food addiction and eating disorders in the Jewish community have not been gathered, leading professionals believe that eating disorders are more frequent in the Jewish community than in the general American population.[12] Some theorists speculate that this disproportionate rate of food addictions may be a reflection of unique significance given to food and eating in Judaism and Jewish life. Special foods are prepared for each Sabbath and holiday. Permitted and forbidden foods are governed by distinctive laws and customs, the mixing of milk and meat products is prohibited, and specific blessings are prescribed for every substance consumed. The plea of the stereotypic Jewish mother, "*Ess ess, mein kind"* (Eat, eat my child) conveys a sense of the equivalence of eating with well-being. Some professionals in the field of eating disorders maintain that these cultural norms and predispositions increase the risk of eating disorders for Jews.[13]

Problems of addiction cut across the Jewish community. Participants in Jewish recovery programs for addiction, such as L'Chaim and JACS (Jewish Alcoholics, Chemically Dependent Persons, and Their Significant Others), range from the most secular to the most observant.

What Is Addiction?

An excellent description of addiction is elegant in its simplicity:[14]

> You are a teenager, or a middle-aged housewife, or a successful businessman, or a retired professional. You have just messed up, or have successfully completed your latest project, or have met an exciting new person, or have lost someone or something very important to you. You feel emotionally out of balance, so you drink or take drugs or eat or gamble or log onto the Internet. You take a substance that alters your brain chemistry, or you get your body and brain to manufacture those chemicals in response to the way you think or act. You become an addict when you can no longer stop yourself from going down that path. You become an addict when you do one of these things more than or longer than you planned, when there is a compulsion to continue it, when you try to cut down and you can't, and when you continue to abuse the substance or experience despite your knowledge that it is going to cause you significant difficulty with school, work, your emotions, or your family.

Mental health professionals currently view addiction as a multifaceted phenomenon. It is "a complex, progressive behavior pattern having biological, psychological, sociological, and behavioral components . . . [there is] overwhelmingly pathological involvement in or attachment to it, subjective compulsion to continue it, and reduced ability to exert personal control over it."[15] According to this view, people can become addicted to *substances* (alcohol, drugs, caffeine, nicotine, or food) or to *experiences* (gambling, spending, work, sex, or the Internet). There are three primary routes to addiction: through genetic predisposition, a learned response to coping with stress, or long-term use or experience.

The American Psychiatric Association's *Diagnostic and Statistical Manual of Mental Disorders,* fourth edition (DSM-IV), distinguishes between substance abuse, substance dependence, eating disorders, and impulse control disorders.

The DSM-IV defines substance dependence as:

a maladaptive pattern of substance use, leading to clinically significant impairment or distress, as manifest by three (or more) of the following, occurring at any time in the same [twelve]-month period:

1. Tolerance.
2. Withdrawal.
3. The substance is often taken in larger amounts or over a longer period than was intended.
4. There is a persistent desire or unsuccessful efforts to cut down or control substance use.
5. A great deal of time is spent in activities necessary to obtain the substance, use the substance, or recover from its effects.
6. Important social, occupational or recreational activities are given up or reduced because of substance abuse.
7. The substance use is continued despite knowledge of having a persistent or recurrent physical or psychological problem that is likely to have been caused by or exacerbated by the substance (e.g., depression, ulcer).[16]

Substance abuse is defined as:

a maladaptive pattern of substance use, leading to clinically significant impairment or distress, as manifest by one or more of the following, occurring within a twelve-month period:

1. Recurrent substance use resulting in a failure to fulfill major role obligations at work, school, or home.
2. Recurrent substance use in situations in which it is physically hazardous.
3. Recurrent substance-related legal problems.
4. Continued substance use despite having persistent or recurrent

social or interpersonal problems caused or exacerbated by the effects of the substance.[17]

The categories of dependence and abuse apply to alcohol, amphetamines, caffeine, cannabis, cocaine, hallucinogens, inhalants, nicotine, opioids, phencyclidine (PCP, angel dust), sedatives, and other addictive substances (steroids, nitrous oxide, over-the-counter medications).

Food addiction is not technically substance abuse, but disorders including anorexia, bulimia, and binge eating disorder can function similarly to other addictions. Impulse control disorders include pathological gambling and addictions to experiences such as sex, spending, work, and computer use.[18]

Addiction is a family disease. When a person suffers from the disease, all of the other members of the family are affected. Addicted persons may not only abuse substances but also be emotionally or physically abusive to their family members. They may destroy the family's financial security by spending precious funds on their addiction, or by losing jobs because of addiction-related irresponsibility. They very likely disappoint their spouses and children repeatedly. Family members might alternately chastise or protect the addict. In so doing. they unwittingly become enablers. An enabler is anyone who prevents the addict from experiencing the full consequences of his or her behavior. Coworkers, friends, medical or psychosocial professionals, and clergy can also be enablers. They rationalize the problem rather than risk anger and rejection. They make excuses and cover up the behavior of the addict. A family member cannot control a loved one's substance abuse. Accepting the limits of one's power to change another person may be one of the most painful aspects of living with the addicted individual.

Treatment for Addictions

The prognosis for untreated drug or alcohol addiction is disability or death. There is hope for recovery, but the addict cannot do it alone. Admitting the need for help is actually a sign of strength. Recovery always involves others in religious, medical, and social support roles. Frequently, recovery begins when a family member asks for help. A change in the attitudes of family members may be the impetus, at last, for the addict to acknowledge the problem.

Addiction has biological, psychological, sociological, and behavioral components, thus treatment must address each of these aspects. Nutritional and biochemical therapies address the basic biochemical imbalances caused by addictions. Some substance abusers may use drugs or alcohol to relieve symptoms of depression, bipolar disorder, anxiety, or other mental disorders.

Definitively identifying these complex situations is extremely difficult. It is important that a pastoral caregiver refer the individual to a physician if a dual diagnosis is suspected, so that appropriate treatment can be arranged. The psychological and behavioral aspects are addressed in psychotherapy and specialized support groups. Addicts often have to adjust their lifestyles to address the sociological components of their illness. These adjustments usually involve replacing the people, places, and things associated with addiction with new people, places, and things associated with a healthy lifestyle.

Twelve-step groups are the most popular support groups for those in recovery from addiction. These groups provide peer support while urging the addict to change the people, places, and things that supported his or her addiction. Belief in a Higher Power is seen as essential in helping the addict stay on the path of recovery. Twelve-step groups view addiction as a chronic, progressive disease over which the addict has no control, and as a behavior that the addict can change by "working the twelve steps." Alternatively, SMART Recovery (Self Management and Recovery Training) support groups provide a humanistic approach based on the rational–emotive therapy of Albert Ellis. Cognitive–Behavioral Therapy and Motivation Enhancement Therapy are two widely used approaches for the therapeutic treatment of addictions for those who reject a spiritually based approach.[19] Whatever approach is used, the addict will learn both to identify situations that trigger her addiction and to develop alternative coping strategies.

The Role of the Pastoral Caregiver

A pastoral caregiver must be judicious in counseling an addict or the family of an addict. Unless the counselor understands addiction, he or she can easily become an enabler rather than a healer. Professional counselors for addicts should be trained in the field, and it is important that they understand the disease and methods of treatment.

Rabbis, cantors, or pastoral caregivers can be gateways helping an individual move into recovery by serving as an ongoing support for the family and providing spiritual nurture and resources. An examination of each of these roles follows.

Gateway to Help

When there is a strong suspicion that an addiction problem exists, the pastoral caregiver might arrange a telephone contact or meeting to give the family or the abuser an opportunity to discuss their concerns. The pastoral caregiver can initiate such a meeting by simply inquiring, "I haven't seen you for a while and wondered if everything was okay?" Or, "You seem to be under a great deal of stress. I am concerned about you and I want to make sure that we have an opportunity to talk." It is important to convey concern for the well-being of the individual without any accusation of wrongdoing.

Often a family member, not the addict, is the person who comes forward to ask for help. The pastoral caregiver's role is to listen attentively and sympathetically. After offering support, he or she might place a call to a treatment program, agency, or an appropriate professional to set up an appointment. Although the caregiver can dial the call and introduce the addict or family member, the person asking for help must be the one to make the appointment to begin treatment. The simple act of setting up an appointment is a major step in taking personal responsibility for the addiction.

When a family member comes for help but the addict continues to deny that there is a problem, the pastoral caregiver can help to arrange an *intervention,* during which the addict is lovingly confronted by a team, which may include family members, friends, employers, and the pastoral caregiver. Under the guidance of a trained professional, participants in the intervention express their concern and love for the individual and describe incidents when they have been emotionally hurt or disappointed by the behavior of the addict. They express their desire to support the addict and present a plan for the addict to enter recovery immediately. The intervention process embodies the concept of *tochecha* (rebuke), as described in Bereshit Rabbah

(54:3), R. Yosi bar R. Hanina, when he teaches: "Love unaccompanied by *tochecha* (rebuke) is not love."

It is not the role of the pastoral caregiver to try to cure the addict, but rather to direct and to encourage the addict or the family to seek help. To give this direction, the rabbi or cantor should be familiar with local programs and professionals and maintain an up-to-date list of possible referrals. Local family service agencies or the National Council on Alcoholism and Drug Dependence can provide information about local recovery programs, addiction counselors, hospital and detoxification centers, medical professionals, and twelve-step meetings. They may conduct training sessions for pastoral caregivers or be able to recommend qualified institutions where such training is given. JACS (see Other Resources list) has developed training materials for rabbis and pastoral counselors who work with addicts. They also maintain lists of Jewish recovery programs across the country.

A pastoral caregiver can help the addict or family to recognize that addiction is present. Even people who have been jailed or hospitalized because of their abuse may cling to the myth that they are still in control of their behavior and deny that they are injuring others by their addiction. The pastoral caregiver should carefully review the individual's substance use history and the way in which it has affected the person, family, friends, and work. He or she should inquire into any possible medical or psychological problems, difficulties with other people, work or school difficulties, financial and legal problems, and loss of control. Addicts often admit problems such as being late to work when asked directly, but deny that it is important or truly a problem. Pastoral caregivers will find it useful to familiarize themselves with some of the basic screening tools for substance abuse.[20]

Before any recovery can begin, the addict must take responsibility for his or her own actions. It is particularly hard for families not to protect the addict from the consequences of what he or she has done. They may fear that the drug addict will wind up living on the street or overdose, or that the gambler will lose everything. Well-meaning assistance will delay the addict from finally accepting the truth. The pastoral caregiver can play an important role in giving support to the family as they allow the addict to take responsibility for the consequences of his or her actions. Helping the family to find and participate in an appropriate support program is an important part of the counseling.

Even when addicts come for help, they may cling to the notion that they can change without outside help. Repeated pledges of abstinence may be broken before they can accept that they cannot do it alone. The pastoral caregiver can be of assistance in demonstrating that there is no shame in asking for help. He or she can remind the addicted individual that having free will allows us to choose to reach out to others to recover. The pastoral caregiver can help to reframe seeking help as an act of strength rather than an admission of weakness or defeat. As part of their opening ritual, members of L'Chaim Alcohol and Drug Workshop read: "We believe that people are neither all good nor all bad. We must constantly make choices between good and evil—between life and death. We are a people of survivors so we choose life. L'Chaim."

Ongoing Support for the Addicted Person and Family Members

Those entering the recovery process may require both concrete and emotional support. In entering treatment, problems may arise with a person's work or childcare. The pastoral caregiver can help the person brainstorm solutions to any anticipated difficulties. Identifying helpful family members, friends, and communal resources is essential. Encouragement may be necessary to ensure that the individual will ask for help from others and follow through with planned treatment. Community members who attend twelve-step groups are often willing to accompany the newly recovering addict to his or her first twelve-step meeting. The pastoral caregiver can be instrumental in facilitating such contacts.

Once the addict has begun a program of recovery, whether in one of the anonymous programs or with medical and psychotherapeutic supervision, there is always the possibility of relapse. One of the pastoral caregiver's most important roles is to encourage the addict to continue treatment and participation in a recovery program. Short periods of sobriety often lead to a false sense of confidence, which may lead the recovering person to drop out of treatment. The pastoral caregiver can encourage and support continued treatment by asking frequently about the individual's progress. Recovering individuals may also need help with anticipating stressful situations that might trigger a relapse, and with brainstorming ways to deal with any problems.

Spiritual Nurture and Resources

Treatment for the multifaceted problems of addiction focuses on the thinking and the behavior of the addict. The pastoral caregiver is the professional best able to address the *spiritual* aspects of addiction. His or her task is to frame the problem of addiction in a spiritual context and to help the addict replace an addictive pattern with spiritually oriented thought patterns and behaviors.

The pastoral caregiver can frame addiction in a spiritual context by using biblical and midrashic images. For example, the pastoral caregiver might present the story of the Exodus of the children of Israel from Egypt as a model for the journey from addiction to recovery.[21] Egypt (*mitzrayim* in Hebrew) literally means the double narrow place; it is the place where the Hebrews were given over into slavery. Addiction comes from a Latin root meaning "to give oneself over." Addiction to substances or experiences is slavery; addiction is a state in which one is powerless and out of control. The story of the Exodus from Egypt is also the personal story of each addicted Jew emerging from his or her narrow place, tempted repeatedly to backslide, but struggling always to reach the promised land of recovery, serenity, and spirituality.

The great Chasidic master Rabbi Nachman of Bratslav taught that cravings and addictions destroy our awareness of God, and destroy the awe of God that every Jew has deep within his or her heart. Addictions are at one end of a continuum. Every day, each of us has thoughts and behavior we don't want, such as anger, jealousy, or cravings for food, wealth, or sex. We can become enslaved to any of these experiences because they appear to offer pleasure, prestige, or salvation from what we think ails us. Our normal, everyday cravings can become addictions when influenced by the right combination of genetic predisposition, unusual stress, or extended consumption.

Rabbi Nachman teaches that the way to rectify our cravings is to bring our knowledge of God into our hearts. Our goal is to create a constant awareness of God. This spiritual awareness is incompatible with addictive thinking and behavior. Addiction says, I need, I want, I can't cope with this. Recovery and spirituality say, I am in God's presence. I am here to do God's will. Anything I can't handle, God will. Our tradition provides many means of improving our connection with God and of understanding God's will for us.

The key to recovery, prevention, and self-mastery is to develop a strong set of healthy responses to stress and to those situations that trigger craving as well as addictive thinking and behavior. One role of the pastoral caregiver is to teach the recovering person how to respond to people, situations, and stress in a spiritually directed way. The pastoral caregiver can help the addicted person develop spiritual resources, using tools such as prayer, *mitzvot* (commandments), and *tzedakah* (charity).

Prayer and meditation are perhaps the most obvious tools that the pastoral caregiver can give to the recovering person or family member. The pastoral caregiver can help the individual use the reading and the singing of prayers as a means of expanding awareness and understanding of God. It may be particularly helpful to assist the individual in taking on specific daily practices, such as reciting prayers on awakening and before going to sleep, or to beginning to recite *birchot hanehenin,* the blessings assigned by tradition to mark both ordinary and extraordinary experiences of daily life. Similarly, the pastoral caregiver might help the individual develop meditation practices to expand the immediate awareness and experience of the holy, and how to use that experience in the service of mastery of feelings and cravings. Persons in recovery may be strengthened and encouraged by meditating regularly on particular verses, the divine name, or chants from tradition.

In addition to prayer and meditation, connecting the recovering person or family member to the practice of *mitzvot* can provide a spiritual anchor. The Book of Proverbs teaches, "Know God in all your ways." Keeping God constantly in mind is a spiritual discipline that has great value in the treatment and prevention of addictions. Regular performance of *mitzvot* accomplishes this. Although *mitzvah* is usually translated as "commandment," we see *mitzvah* as a deed connecting us to our Higher Power, and thus every *mitzvah* is a spiritual deed.

For example, *mitzvot* connected to eating help enhance a person's awareness of God. As part of recovery from food addiction, the pastoral caregiver might teach the use of the *berachah* (blessing) to change the experience of eating. In pausing to say a *berachah*, the person cultivates an awareness and experience of the Source of all food, thus transforming a mundane act into a holy experience, a moment of connection with God. Regular recitation of the *berachah* is a spiritual discipline that can bolster the spirit of the addicted person.

The language of spirituality alienates some Jews. For example, many Jews in recovery feel that step three in the twelve-step program—turning one's life and one's will over to God—seems more "Christian" than Jewish. The Jewish pastoral caregiver needs to address this issue. Torah, psalms, and rabbinic and Chasidic literature all stress the concept of surrender to God's will. For example, Pirke Avot teaches, "Do God's will as if it was your will."[22] In addition, Jewish practices can also be a means of turning one's life over to a Higher Power. For example, Shabbat is a dramatic practice of doing God's will. On Shabbat, we stop doing what we want to do, and do what God wants us to do. We simply rest and allow ourselves to be in tune with creation, enjoying food, family, and community; praying; and studying. Through Shabbat, a recovering person might find an opportunity to experience turning himself or herself over to God in a very positive, and Jewish, context. Pastoral caregivers can help people in recovery begin to embrace Shabbat observance and connect them to community as they do so.

Offering a Jewish Understanding of the Twelve Steps

One valuable role a pastoral caregiver can play in working with addicts and their families is to help familiarize them with the twelve steps, to understand them from a Jewish perspective, and to set up a program to practice these steps. The twelve steps are:

1. We admitted we were powerless over alcohol (or drugs, or gambling)—that our lives had become unmanageable.
2. We came to believe that a Power greater than ourselves could restore us to sanity.
3. We made a decision to turn our will and our lives over to the care of God as we understand [God].
4. We made a searching and fearless moral inventory of ourselves.
5. We admitted to God, to ourselves, and to another human being the exact nature of our wrongs.

6. We were entirely ready to have God remove all these defects of character.
7. We humbly asked [God] to remove our shortcomings.
8. We made a list of all persons we had harmed, and became willing to make amends to them all.
9. We made direct amends to such people wherever possible, except when to do so would injure them or others.
10. We continue to take personal inventory and, when we were wrong, promptly admitted it.
11. We sought through prayer and meditation to improve our conscious contact with God as we understand [God], praying only for knowledge of [God's] will for us and the power to carry that out.
12. Having had a spiritual awakening as the result of these steps, we tried to carry this message to alcoholics (or drug abusers, or gambling addicts) and to practice these principles in all our affairs.

Many Jews might feel initially alienated by the language and concepts of the twelve steps, and sense that they represent a spiritual approach distant from Judaism. In fact, the process outlined in the steps is harmonious with basic Jewish values and perspectives.[23]

A useful definition of spirituality in Judaism is found in the rabbinic teaching, "The world is based on three things: Torah, *avodah* (service to God), and *gemilut chasadim* (deeds of loving-kindness)."[24] Torah is the instruction book for relating to others and to God. Torah teaches how to rectify things when we have missed the mark, and how to cultivate the traits of a *tzaddik*, a righteous person. Steps four through ten reflect a process similar to the Jewish process of *teshuvah* (repentance).

The pastoral caregiver can help the recovering person see the twelve steps as a process of *teshuvah*. Like the twelve steps, *teshuvah* requires confession of one's sins, regret for the wrongs one has done, resolution not to repeat the wrong, the making of amends, and a turning to God in prayer and deed.[25] Individuals participating in twelve-step programs should be strongly encouraged to "work the twelve steps" because this spiritual aspect of the program may not be a significant part of the meeting that the individual attends.

The role of the pastoral caregiver is that of guide to the Jewish dimension of this process. Many Jews struggle with discomfort because the only twelve-step groups in their community meet in churches where the closing circle includes the recitation of the Lord's Prayer. The pastoral caregiver can creatively help the addict to overcome this discomfort, perhaps by suggesting a Jewish prayer that could be recited by her or him at that time.

The pastoral caregiver must be ready to respond to questions such as whether or not specific steps are compatible with Jewish beliefs (this comes up most often with step three), when and how it is appropriate to make amends, how to pray in the Jewish tradition, and how forgiveness enters this work. Familiarity with the traditional sources on *teshuvah* and the contemporary sources cited earlier is essential. Even more important is the quality of humility that comes from having worked through the process of *teshuvah* on a personal basis. Addicts are frequently expert in distinguishing those who are relating what they have learned in books from those who have actually walked a similar path. Caregivers may need to restrain their desire to teach and to give direction so they can hear and to respond to the very specific needs of the recovering person.

Avodah refers to service to God, to having a relationship with God and finding meaning and purpose in life. Steps one through three and eleven also address our basic orientation to God. Many addicts have disclosed that at first they did not believe in God, but that their peers in the twelve-step program told them to "fake it until they make it." Acting as if there is a God and that what one does really matters can be transformative. The rich variety of Jewish images and conceptions of God offer a person in recovery options for shaping a relationship to the Divine. For example, those in recovery who are alienated by masculine images and terms for God may be comforted to learn of other Jewish ways of describing and relating to God. They may be supported to grow in expressing views of God that are appropriate to their unique spirits and experiences. The pastoral caregiver can guide the person in recovery to embrace a life of purpose, and can teach about Jewish spiritual practices that can deepen the person's relationship with God.

Gemilut chasadim are deeds of loving-kindness, the way in which we relate to the members of our community and humanity. *Gemilut chasadim* points to the fact that recovery is not done in isolation but must occur in the context of a loving community. This concept of community and responsibility is found in step twelve. A pastoral caregiver can help connect the recovering person to Jewish community. *Gemilut chasadim* also points to the importance of making a contribution, which can be enormously valuable to recovering addicts coping with shame and guilt about their past hurtful behavior. Helping the individual devise ways in which he or she can give to others through *tzedakah* and *tikkun olam* work is also an important pastoral role.

Challenges in Providing Pastoral Care for Addicted Persons

Working with addicts is often frustrating because of their denial of the disease, their lying or dissembling to protect their self-image, and the possible unconscious collusion of family members with addicts in covering up their addictive behavior. In addition, some addicts and their families truly don't understand what addiction is. Addicts want to believe that they can set limits for themselves and control their behavior. Repeated failures to maintain those limits add to their shame and denial. Lastly, they can be so charming in their lies and manipulation that it is hard to identify when it is happening.

It is important that pastoral caregivers accept their own limitations. They must recognize that they cannot fix the problem of addiction. They *can* encourage, support, and comfort the addict and family. It is essential to maintain an open, nonjudgmental attitude to support addicts in healing and in taking responsibility for their actions. When pastoral caregivers feel in doubt, they should refer to outside experts rather than try to counsel these individuals beyond their skill. They should examine themselves for any tendencies toward addiction, and recognize and seek help for any such issues. Clinical supervision and peer support can also be invaluable. Attendance at Al-Anon meetings might offer another framework for developing acceptance of one's limits.

The Role of the Synagogue

Troubled individuals often seek out clergy to help them with their problems; it is important that the synagogue staff be prepared to respond to such requests for help. Training on addictions can enable the staff to feel competent in their responses, help them understand addiction, and integrate this information into synagogue policy and curriculum. The local professional or agency conducting such training can become an ally to assist in the creation of a plan when a case arises.

The rabbi, cantor. or educator can assist the board of directors in establishing a policy on drinking, drug use. and gambling by students and staff at all synagogue-sponsored events. Teenagers sometimes try to sneak drugs or alcoholic beverages into youth group retreats or social activities. Staff procedures should be set up before an incident arises. Factors to consider are the following: What type of action will the staff be authorized to take? If a child is using drugs or alcohol, will the parents be contacted to come and get them immediately? Will the child be suspended from activities? What kind of counseling or treatment will be suggested? What kind of follow-up will be available? Once the policy is set up, the staff must be assured that the board will support them when they follow the established policy. The adopted policy must be applied equally to all offenders.

A congregation may want to review its approach to serving wine for kiddush. A simple way to demonstrate that the synagogue is aware that some members do not use alcohol is to ensure that grape juice is available at all events where kiddush is recited or wine is served. Some synagogues serve only grape juice for kiddush. A congregation could serve white grape juice on the same tray with red wine so that congregants can choose what they prefer without calling attention to themselves. It is illegal in all states for minors to be served alcoholic beverages, thus children should always be served grape juice instead of wine. If the synagogue hosts catered events, the bar should be monitored so that youngsters do not take advantage of the merriment to sneak drinks. Those moments are powerful; many Jewish alcoholics report that their first episode of drunkenness was at such festivities.

The pastoral caregivers can raise consciousness about addictions. For example, the rabbi or cantor can use sermons or teaching to highlight Jewish tradition's view of the potential destructive impact of alcohol, and the value of moderation. A lesson from the pulpit enables the entire congregation to learn about the disease. Those who are suffering will find special significance in it and may feel impelled to examine their personal situation. In the classroom, texts from Jewish tradition can provide an opportunity to understand issues of addiction and allow students to express their own attitudes and concerns about drugs and alcohol.

Conclusion

Miriam and George might have entered recovery much sooner if they had been aware that they were not the only Jews to suffer from addiction and its consequences. If they had known of a twelve-step meeting at a synagogue or Jewish community center, they might have felt more comfortable attending. If they had encountered a knowledgeable and sensitive pastoral caregiver, they would have been encouraged by the spiritual sustenance available within Jewish tradition.

The Jewish pastoral caregiver can contribute to spiritual healing from addiction and be inspired and transformed by the encounter with individuals walking the twisted path toward recovery. When recovering addicts return to Judaism, they often do so with a renewed eagerness to learn, study, and participate. When they say at a twelve-step meeting, "I am a grateful alcoholic/addict," they truly mean it, for in recovery they have been given a new life and opportunity for continuing change and growth. Their courage and their enthusiasm in embracing Jewish life can be inspiring. Pastoral caregivers who recognize, support, and encourage recovery from addiction may find that the unanticipated benefit of this work is to strengthen their own practice, faith, and belief in Judaism and to expand their own spiritual life.[26]

Notes

1. E. M. Jellinek, "Immanuel Kant on Drinking," *Quarterly Journal of Studies on Alcohol* 1 (1941): pp. 777–78.
2. R. F. Bales, "Cultural Differences in Rates of Alcoholism," *Quarterly Journal of Studies on Alcohol* 6 (1946): pp. 480–99.

3. Midrash Rabbah, Genesis 43:7.

4. Tanchuma, Noah, 13:21.

5. American Psychiatric Association, *Diagnostic and Statistical Manual of Mental Disorders,* 4th ed. (Washington, D.C.: American Psychiatric Association, 1994), p. 202.

6. Leslie Katz. "Experts Debunk New Depression Study on Jewish Male Despondency," *Jewish Bulletin of Northern California Online* (June 2, 1995).

7. Debra Nussbaum Cohen, "Study: Jews Drink Less, More Likely to Get Drunk," *Jewish Telegraph Agency Weekly News Digest* 64–2 (Jan. 15, 1999): p. 4. Genetic studies reported that Jews carrying a specific genetic mutation were very light drinkers, and hypothesized that this gene provided "protective properties against alcohol."

8. Edwin M. Lemert, "Alcoholism: Theory, Problem and Challenge. Part III, Alcoholism and the Sociocultural Situation," *Quarterly Journal of Studies on Alcohol* 17 (1956): p. 310.

9. *Hadassah Magazine,* Dec. 1986.

10. American Psychiatric Association, *Diagnostic and Statistical Manual,* p. 617.

11. Darren Garnick and Yigal Schleifer, "The Jewish Vice," *The Jerusalem Report* (Aug. 16, 1999): pp. 26–33.

12. Aliyah Baruchin, "Why Jewish Girls Starve Themselves," *Lilith* (spring 1998): p. 5.

13. Catherine Steiner-Adair, "Bagel Politics: Jewish Women, American Culture and Jewish Culture." Keynote address, "Food, Body Image and Judaism": Conference on Ethnicity and Eating: Cultural Influences, Disorders and Resources for Change. Philadelphia, May 1998 (Kolot and the Renfrew Center, conveners).

14. Adapted from Joseph A. Pursch, "Is there a common basis for all addictions?" *Medicine and Behavior* (June 1998): pp. 33–34.

15. D. Donovan and G. Marlatt, *Assessment of Addictive Behaviors* (New York: Guilford, 1988), pp. 5–6.

16. American Psychiatric Association, *Diagnostic and Statistical Manual,* p. 181.

17. Ibid., pp. 182–83.

18. Ibid., pp. 609–21.

19. National Institute on Alcohol Abuse and Alcoholism, Project MATCH Monographs Series (Rockville, Maryland: National Institute on Alcohol Abuse and Alcoholism, 1995).

20. M. L. Selzer, "The Michigan Alcoholism Screening Test: The Quest for a New Diagnostic Instrument," *American Journal of Psychiatry* 127 (1971): pp. 1653–58, H. A. Skinner and J. L. Warren, "Alcohol Dependence Scale" (Toronto: Addiction Research Foundation, 1984); "What Are the Signs of Alcoholism?" (New York: National Council on Alcoholism, 1987); W. R. Miller, J. S. Tonigan,

and R. Longabaugh, "The Drinker Inventory of Consequences (DrInC): An Instrument for Assessing Adverse Consequences of Alcohol Abuse, Test Manual," National Institute on Alcohol Abuse and Alcoholism, vol. 4 of Project MATCH Monographs Series (Rockville, Md.: National Institute on Alcohol Abuse and Alcoholism, 1995). DrInC is in the public domain and is available at no charge from The National Institute on Alcohol Abuse and Alcoholism. For a more comprehensive treatment of addiction assessments see Donovan and Marlatt, *Addictive Behaviors*.

21. Yaacov J. Kravitz, *Pathways to Recovery: Sources and Spiritual Tools for a Jewish 12 Step Program* (Melrose Park, Pa.: Yaacov Kravitz Publisher, 1997), pp. 7–10.

22. Hyman Goldin, trans., *Ethics of the Fathers* (New York: Hebrew Publishing Company, 1962), 4:2, p. 22.

23. Kravitz, *Pathways;* Kerry M. Olitzky and Aaron Z., *Renewed Each Day: Daily Twelve Step Recovery Meditations Based on the Bible* (Woodstock, Vt.: Jewish Lights Publishing, 1992); Kerry M. Olitzky and Stuart A. Copans, *Twelve Jewish Steps to Recovery: A Personal Guide to Turning from Alcoholism and Other Addictions* (Woodstock, Vt.: Jewish Lights Publishing, 1991); Abraham J. Twerski, *Self-Improvement? I'm Jewish!: Overcoming Self-Defeating Behavior* (Brooklyn, N.Y.: Shaar Press, 1995).

24. Kravitz, *Pathways*, pp. 9–10; Goldin, *Ethics*, 1:2, p. 9.

25. See Maimonides, Mishneh Torah, Laws of Repentance, for a complete discussion of *teshuvah*.

26. Many people made suggestions and recommendations for this chapter. We thank Rabbi Michael Signer, Rabbi Paul Kipnes, Rabbi Sheila Weinberg, Dennis Brown, Barbara Teller, and Betty Batenburg.

Bibliography

Alcoholics Anonymous: The Story of How Many Thousands of Men and Women Have Recovered from Alcoholism (The Big Book of A.A.). New York: Alcoholics Anonymous World Service, 1950.

Glass, Carol. "Addiction and Recovery Through Jewish Eyes." *Addiction and Spirituality: A Multidisciplinary Approach,* edited by Oliver J. Morgan and Merle Jordan. St. Louis, Mo.: Chalice Press, 1999.

Kravitz, Yaacov J. *Pathways to Recovery: Sources and Spiritual Tools for a Jewish 12 Step Program.* Cheltenham, Pa.: Y. J. Kravitz, 1997. (Available from the author at 215-635-3011 or from www.spiritualintelligence.com.)

Levy, Stephen, and Sheila Blume, eds. *Addictions in the Jewish Community.* New York: Federation of Jewish Philanthropies, 1986.

Olitzky, Kerry M., and Stuart A. Copans. *Twelve Jewish Steps to Recovery: A Personal Guide to Turning from Alcoholism and Other Addictions.* Woodstock, Vt.: Jewish Lights Publishing, 1991.

Pita, Dianne Doyle. *Addictions Counseling: A Practical Guide to Counseling People with Chemical and Other Addictions.* New York: Crossroad Publishing, 1994.

Spiegel, Marcia Cohn. *The Heritage of Noah: Alcoholism in the Jewish Community Today.* Ann Arbor, Mich.: University Microfilms, 1979.

Twerski, Abraham J. *Addictive Thinking: Understanding Self-Deception.* Center City, Minn.: Hazelden Foundation, 1989.

White, Robert Kenneth, and Deborah George Wright, eds. *Addiction Intervention: Strategies to Motivate Treatment-Seeking Behavior.* Binghamton, N.Y.: Haworth Press, 1998.

Other Resources

Alcohol/Drug Action Program of Jewish Family Service of Los Angeles and *L'Chaim*: A 12-Step Workshop for Jews and Their Families in Recovery, 5700 Wilshire Blvd., Los Angeles, CA 90048; 323-651-5688. Sponsors educational programs, meetings, retreats, and holiday events.

Alcoholics Anonymous (AA), General Service Office, 475 Riverside Dr., New York, NY 10115; 212-870-3400; www.aa.org.

JACS (Jewish Alcoholics, Chemically Dependent Persons, and Their Significant Others), Jewish Board of Family and Children's Services, 426 West 58th Street, New York, NY 10019; 212-397-4197; fax: 212-489-6229; E-mail: jacs@jacsweb.org; Web site: www.jacsweb.org. Sponsors educational and training programs, informational videos, meetings, retreats, holiday events. Their Web site includes extensive information and articles on addiction, recovery, twelve steps, lists of recovery programs and meetings throughout the United States.

National Council on Alcoholism and Drug Dependence (NCADD), 12 West 21st St., New York, NY 10010; 212-206-6770; 1010 Vermont Ave., NW, Suite 710, Washington, D.C. 20005; 202-737-8122; www.ncadd.org.

SMART Recovery (Self Management and Recovery Training), 7537 Mentor Ave., Suite #306, Mentor, OH 44060; 440-951-5357; www.smartrecovery.org.

Rabbi Yaacov Kravitz, Ed.D., is a licensed psychologist and a Fellow of the American Association of Pastoral Counselors. He is author of *Pathways to Recovery: Sources and Spiritual Tools for a Jewish 12 Step Program,* and maintains a private practice in Jenkintown, Pennsylvania.

Marcia Cohn Spiegel, M.A.J.C.S., Jewish Communal Service, Hebrew Union College–Jewish Institute of Religion, was one of the first people to describe the problem of alcoholism in the Jewish community. She is the founder of the Alcohol/Drug Action Program of Jewish Family Service, Los Angeles, and of *L'Chaim:* Twelve Steps to Recovery. She has served on the Los Angeles County Commission on Alcoholism and worked with special populations.

Letting Their Faces Shine: Accompanying Aging People and Their Families

Rabbi Dayle A. Friedman

In this chapter, Rabbi Dayle A. Friedman investigates the spiritual challenges of growing older. She articulates the *Mitzvah* model, which is based on traditional perspectives on aging, and demonstrates how it can be used to help older adults and their families to address aging's spiritual challenges. Rabbi Friedman explores four key aspects of the pastoral caregiver's role with older people: fostering a life of meaning, facilitating a life of celebration, enabling a life of connection, and accompanying them on their journeys. She gives special attention to the task of working with people with dementia, and with family caregivers of frail elders.

You shall rise before an elder and allow the beauty, glory and majesty of their faces to emerge.

—LEVITICUS 19:32, TRANSLATION BY DANNY SIEGEL

The small room in the old-age home quickly filled as old people arrived on canes and walkers—some talkative, some quiet and withdrawn. I had been invited by a fellow college student to this Shabbat service and was not at all sure that I was happy to be there. As the other students and I took our seats, I looked nervously around and wondered how long a morning lay ahead. One of the students started to sing, and the service continued with old and young people taking turns leading the prayers. To my surprise, the service flew by and it turned out to be the most inspiring worship experience I had had in years. The elders seemed to come alive during the service—singing, clapping, and praying with great enthusiasm. The warmth in the room was palpable.

At the Kiddush after the service, conversation flowed long after the cake and wine had been consumed. The elders begged us to come back and, in essence, I've been coming back ever since. In that brief moment decades ago, I witnessed the promise of Jewish pastoral care. I saw that in reaching out to older people, in connecting them with the blessings of tradition and community, their faces could shine, their beauty emerge.

The graying of the North American Jewish population is dramatic and undeniable. According to the 1990 National Jewish Population Study, at least 18 percent of North American Jews, or 1.1 million individuals, are sixty-five years of age or older, compared with 12 percent of Americans in general. The fastest-growing segment of the Jewish community is those seventy-five and older.[1] People are living ever longer, thus many of us can look forward to two or three decades of being old. Many families have two generations of elderly people— "grandparents" in their sixties or seventies, and "great-grandparents" in their eighties or nineties. This "age wave" has profound implications for the Jewish community.[2]

Issues of aging touch every Jewish pastoral caregiver in one way or another. Acute care chaplains report that the majority of those whom they serve are elderly. Significant proportions of synagogue members are older, and issues of aging may well dominate congregational clergy members' pastoral counseling work. Even if the caregiver does not work directly with older persons, he or she may encounter aging issues in the struggles of the so-called sandwich generation, those who are simultaneously caring for aging parents and young children.

This chapter offers guidance for the pastoral caregiver working with older persons or their families. My experience as a chaplain in long-term care and other work with elders over the past two decades have shaped the perspectives I share here. During my twelve years as Director of Chaplaincy Services at Philadelphia Geriatric Center, I witnessed enormous challenges to dignity and well-being; I also observed amazing resiliency in the remarkable older adults I served. I have been inspired by the wisdom and the courage of my congregants, and by the power of Jewish tradition and community to transform aging from a wilderness to blessing. The stories of the radiant *neshomes* (souls) I have been privileged to meet in pastoral care with older adults are at the center of this text. I am grateful for all of them.

In the discussion that follows, I begin by addressing the special spiritual challenges posed by the aging process. Next, I offer a Jewish perspective that can address those challenges. Drawing on resources in Jewish tradition, I describe the *Mitzvah* model, a Jewish vision for aging, and apply that model to the pastoral caregiver's work with aging Jews and their families. In the *Mitzvah* model, there are three core aspects of the pastoral caregiver's role with aging persons: fostering a life of meaning, facilitating a life of celebration, and enabling a life of connection. I highlight some of the special aspects of working with elders with dementia and also outline key aspects of supporting family members caring for frail elders. Lastly, I identify some of the unique rewards of working as pastoral caregivers with aging persons.

Spiritual Challenges of Aging

Aging is a time of opportunity and also of great spiritual challenge. Despite the heterogeneous nature of the elderly, it is possible to outline three basic challenges that the aging person is likely to encounter on his or her journey from midlife to life's end: finding meaning, confronting empty, burdensome time, and counteracting disconnection and disjunction.

Finding Meaning

"What good am I anymore? All my life, I gave to my *shul*, to my husband, to my nieces and nephews." Esther, aged eighty-six and a widow, has lived in the nursing home for four years. Arthritis pains her daily and has deprived her of the ability to walk. She depends on staff to help her to get dressed, go to the bathroom, and get to meals. "Now, I can't do anything for anyone; why doesn't God just take me?"

The aging process challenges a person's sense of who she is, who she has been, and who she will yet be. The accumulation of losses, of the "little deaths" of the aging process, moves us to redefine ourselves. As people grow older, they are almost inevitably stripped of roles, relationships, and capacities. What are our lives about if the people with whom we share a history are no longer alive? Who are we, outside of our roles as workers, as children to our parents, as partners to our spouses? In a society that takes an instrumental view of persons—judging them by what they can do, or give—it is easy to feel worthless when one no longer has clear roles.

The frailty that often accompanies the later phases of aging is particularly provocative, as it forces us to confront dependency.[3] How can we understand our place in the world when we are no longer creating or giving but rather needing the support of others? In a society that trivializes older people, it is a challenge for elders to find a way to continue to make a contribution, to reach beyond themselves, to share the wisdom accumulated over many years.

As people age, they are drawn to look back on their lives, to take stock of their accomplishments and failures.[4] This process of life review can be affirming if the picture we see is of a full, satisfying life. On the other hand, life review can also make us aware of our failings, of relationships that have broken down, of dreams unfulfilled. Like *cheshbon hanefesh,* the self-examination and appraisal that precedes the High Holy Days, this life review process can potentially spark repentance. Growing older can provide us with an opportunity to turn our lives around, to mend damaged relationships, to take on new life missions, and to make peace with our limits. For many older people, this promise is sadly unfulfilled because they are paralyzed by fear, grief, or resentment, wishing somehow that things could just be the way they used to be.

Time

When older people leave behind their well-established routines, time can weigh heavily. A man who has worked since the age of twenty-one may find he does not know how to fill his days once he retires. A woman who has invested her energy in caring for her children and her spouse may be daunted by the empty time ahead when her spouse has died and her children have established homes and families a great distance away. Cut off from her moorings, she may "kill time" through habitual television watching or compulsive shopping. Without external or long-established structures, old age can feel like a desert in time.[5]

Time can be particularly burdensome for frail elders who reside in nursing homes or other institutional settings. Time in institutions is marked by routinized rhythms of care tasks that are done *to* the older person. There is a time for everything—a time to eat, a time to go to the bathroom, a time to go to sleep. Unfortunately, this schedule is often based on staff and administrative convenience and efficiency rather than on the personal rhythm or preferences of the resident. In the absence of meaningful tasks and activities, much of a resident's time is spent *waiting*—for meals, care, or the recreational activities that break up the routine.[6]

Disconnection and Disjunction

Old age often brings on isolation or disconnection. As friends and partners die or become incapacitated, an individual may find herself or himself cut off from social contact. Physical incapacity can also limit connection because one may no longer be able to seek out social settings. Macular degeneration may not only deprive an older man of his ability to drive; it may also mean that he can no longer attend synagogue because he has no transportation.

In addition, older persons may find themselves cut off from past and future. If dear ones who shared precious past memories are gone, the past itself may feel out of reach. If his or her present home or activities are not linked to roles or physical setting, an older person may feel bereft. Similarly, hopelessness may cut off the older person from the future. What lies ahead includes disability and death; thus older people may be unable to look forward to the future if no one is willing to acknowledge this reality or explore the profound feelings with them.

The Mitzvah *Model: Judaism's Vision for Aging*

Jewish tradition offers aging persons a unique perspective on their lives, one which addresses the spiritual challenges of meaning, time, and connection. This perspective, the *Mitzvah* model, provides spiritual resources that can empower the Jewish person to meet the key challenges of aging. The *Mitzvah* model certainly does not eliminate the painful aspects of aging, but it can foster resiliency in response to them.

Every Jewish person is born not only into their loving family, but also into the *brit* (covenant) between God and the Jewish people. The covenant, established at Sinai, binds each Jew to the *mitzvot*. The existential state of a Jewish person is *metzuveh*, obligated to fulfill the covenant through performance of the *mitzvot*, the ritual and ethical commandments given in the Torah and interpreted and applied by Jews through the generations. Traditional belief suggests that one's fate beyond this world hinges on one's record of observing the *mitzvot*. In addition, the redemption of the Jewish people rests on the collective fulfillment of the covenant through *mitzvot*.[7]

In this classical Jewish worldview, each Jewish person's actions have cosmic significance. On the more mundane plane, one's performance of *mitzvot* affects one's social and religious status. Exemplary performance of *mitzvot*, such as remaining faithful to the *mitzvot* in difficult or dangerous circumstances, earns a person *kavod* (honor). Imbuing one's observance with particular fervor and *kavvanah* (intentionality) merits admiration. Enabling others to fulfill their obligations gains the highest distinction, hence it is a coveted honor to lead others in the recitation of prayers, and to be counted in the *minyan* (the quorum for prayer) or *birkat hamazon* (grace after meals).

Traditionally, the state of being *metzuveh* conveys a message of the individual's infinite worth. We know that obligation has a very definite point of onset: bar or bat mitzvah, when a child is twelve or thirteen. Do obligations have an end-point? In fact, there is neither retirement from *mitzvot* nor any "senior citizen discount." The tradition demands that we continue to engage in a life of *mitzvot* until we die. The older person thus is seen as one who counts, who has a role to play in the community and the cosmos.

This message of a person's importance is not obliterated by the incapacities that all of us will face if we live long enough. The obligation to *mitzvot* is on a sliding scale. One is obligated to do as much as one *can*; one's obligation is adapted to one's capacity. For example, a Jew's obligations in daily prayer are considerably altered if he or she is physically or mentally incapable of performing them in their entirety.[8] A person who is frail and unable to stand may recite the *amidah*, the standing prayers, while sitting down.[9] If he or she does not have the endurance to recite the whole prayer, an abridged version is available.[10] And if the individual cannot speak to recite the prayer, he or she may mentally recite or meditate on the words.[11] Even the *Shema* can be abridged to include only the first line if a person is limited in strength or concentration.[12]

Two aspects of the *mitzvah* sliding scale are key for us as pastoral caregivers. First, the *mitzvah* is tailored to the capacities of the individual. Second, when one fulfills a *mitzvah* to the fullest extent of his or her ability, the person is considered to have fully discharged his or her obligations. Incapacity thus need not perforce stand in the way of dignity and spiritual satisfaction.

The *Mitzvah* model offers a view of the aging person that follows the teaching of Abraham Joshua Heschel.

> What a person lives by is not only a sense of belonging but a sense of indebtedness. The need to be needed corresponds to a fact: something is asked of a [person], of every [person]. Advancing in years must not be taken to mean a process of suspending the requirements and commitments under which a person lives. To be is to obey. A person must not cease to be.[13]

The obligations of the older Jew can be categorized according to the pillars on which the world stands: Torah, *Avodah* (worship/service of the Divine), and *gemilut chasadim* (deeds of loving-kindness [Pirke Avot 1:2]). Put differently, the *mitzvot* enable an older person to participate in a life of meaning, a life of celebration, and a life of connection. The central role of the pastoral caregiver is thus to enable aging people to participate in these three aspects of a life of "significant being."[14]

The Role of the Pastoral Caregiver

Fostering a Life of Meaning

The pastoral caregiver can make a tremendous difference in the lives of older persons by facilitating opportunities for them to take part in a life of meaning. Fundamentally, the caregiver's task is to create opportunities for older adults to perform adaptive *mitzvot,* doing sacred acts to the fullest extent of their capacities. This approach is relevant to pastoral relationships with individual older adults and to work with communities and groups that include elders.

> Rose was a sprightly woman who at ninety-two had lived in the nursing home since a stroke six months before had paralyzed one side of her body. Rose had been active in her traditional

synagogue and had greatly enjoyed participating in Shabbat services at the home. At a Shabbat morning service, Rose had her first-ever opportunity to come to the *bimah*. She was called for the honor of *gelilah* (wrapping the *sefer Torah*). A volunteer pushing her wheelchair helped Rose to approach the reading table, which was not on the raised *bimah*, but on the same level as the pews. The rabbi wrapped the cloth binder around the Torah, until the two ends of the fabric were facing one another. Rose used her "good" hand to press the two ends together, and helped the rabbi to pull down the mantle. Beaming, she said, "This is the biggest honor of my life."

Although on the surface the action that Rose took was a tiny one, its import for her was enormous. In spite of her frail body, she was able to experience herself as a person worthy of honor and as a person contributing to the community's worship experience. The facilitating action of the volunteer and the rabbi made this possible.

Access

In facilitating full participation in the life of *mitzvot*, the pastoral caregiver needs to address issues of access on many fronts. Making Jewish life accessible can be costly in terms of money and human resources, thus it is essential that the pastoral caregiver be a leader in this effort. Access begins with transportation. Elders cannot join in religious activities if they can't get to them. Transportation becomes a critical issue, both for elders living in the community and for individuals in long-term care facilities who are not able independently to get to programs and services. If getting the person to the activity is not possible, it might be possible to "bring" it to him or her, using the telephone or even a radio broadcast.[15] The physical accessibility of the space in which activities are held is also vitally important. Not only must people in wheelchairs be able to get in the door, they need to be able to sit in a space which is part of any group and, of course, to have accessible bathrooms as well.

The perceptual challenges of older persons require another aspect of access. Prayer books or printed materials need to be in large type and lightweight to be usable by those with impaired vision.[16] Of course, a microphone should be used in speaking with groups that include older people, but it is also essential that the sound system have as little distortion as possible.[17]

In enabling full participation of older persons, timing is of the essence. Daytime events may be preferable for those who do not drive or go out at night. Many frail elders are strongest and most lucid in the earlier part of the day. If a nighttime event is planned, even more attention needs to be given to transportation. Program length is another aspect of accessibility because some older adults will find it difficult to participate in events that are very long.

Helping Aging Persons to Continue to Learn and to Grow

Everyone is required to study Torah. Whether rich or poor, of sound body or suffering from infirmities, young or very old and weak....[18]

The big day had arrived. Twenty students had studied hard in preparation for this Confirmation ceremony. Garbed in white robes, they came to the front of the sanctuary. The procession took quite awhile, as the confirmands, aged seventy-five to ninety-five, approached the *bimah* using walkers, canes, and wheelchairs. These confirmands were residents of a nursing home. During the months their class had met, Sylvia, age ninety, had been diagnosed with pancreatic cancer. She was at the end stage of her disease, and was not with her classmates as the service began because she had been taken to the hospital that morning. Amazingly, Sylvia got back in time to join the service in process. Wearing her robe, lying on a geri-chair (a kind of chair-bed) and incredibly weak, Sylvia came to the front of the room where 250 friends and family had gathered. She chanted *aleynu*, her part in the service, and received a certificate of confirmation. Sylvia received congratulations from the friends and family who had traveled to witness this event. Sylvia died less than a week later, gratified that at the very end of her life she had reached for and accomplished this.

Aging can present wonderful opportunities to study Torah and to grow in knowledge. The wisdom gained from experience makes the encounter with sacred text a rich dialogue. The pastoral caregiver can help to bring this wealth to aging persons by teaching in a way that begins with what is familiar and extends toward the unknown. This approach, called andragogy, is deeply respectful of the older person.[19] It does not require either that we focus on topics or texts directly connected to the aging experience or that we offer older adults study opportunities only in age-segregated settings. Rather, teaching andra-gogically is the best way to teach *any* adult.

For some aging persons, later-life learning is simply a natural ex-tension of lifelong study. For most, this part of the life cycle may pre-sent a new chance to engage seriously in *talmud torah*, mining our tradition and history for meaning. The pastoral caregiver can nurture the thirst for knowledge and wisdom and provide sustenance both through direct teaching and through helping people to learn by themselves.

In addition to learning more about Judaism, old age can be a time to grow spiritually. The very old often lose much of their body fat, literally being reduced to a life closer to the bone, the *etzem,* the essence of life. There is a way in which life is taken down to its essence in old age. As roles and relationships fall away, as one's equilibrium is challenged by the ever-present specter of death, grappling with exis-tential questions becomes more urgent. The pastoral caregiver can help to nurture spiritual growth, fostering connection to meditative and reflective ritual techniques, as well as engaging older people in di-alogue about their spiritual lives.

Empower Elders to Make a Contribution

The *Mitzvah* model suggests that aging individuals have much to con-tribute to their community and their world. Fostering a life of mean-ing empowers older people to make that contribution. Giving help to others helps to transform difficulty and suffering. The Jungian psycho-analyst Polly Young-Eisendrath teaches that compassion is an antidote to suffering and counteracts alienation: "In learning the freedom and wisdom of suffering-with . . . [sufferers] discover a new, bigger context in which their lives make sense."[20] Becoming aware of the suffering of others and reaching out to help them can actually salve the wounds of one who suffers. One natural forum for this contribution is sharing the wisdom of elders with young people through intergenerational ties.

> At seventy years of age, Frances, a retired executive secretary, was one of the youngest residents of the nursing home. Some of the others, in fact, were old enough to be her mother! But Frances had

a progressive neurological disease, which confined her to a wheelchair and had destroyed the use of her hands. Frances was the first person that Adam met when he came to visit the nursing home with his synagogue youth group. Adam was fourteen, and more than a little bit shy. He sat down at Shabbat dinner with Frances and worried that they would have nothing to talk about.

Before he knew it, Frances had drawn him out about his two great passions: baseball and guitar. The two discovered they were both Yankees fans, and Frances had played piano, so they had music in common, as well. As they shared Shabbat dinner once a month, Frances asked Adam many questions about Jewish observance because she had come from a socialist family and had only become interested in the religious aspect of her tradition recently. Adam, who attended day school, patiently answered all of her questions. He felt proud that he could actually teach Frances something. Adam continued to visit Frances throughout his high school years, and even wrote her occasional cards when he went to college.

Frances and Adam's connection illustrates some key features of successful intergenerational connections. Older persons have much to give. Children who live far away from grandparents revel in the loving attention of caring elders. Elders' long view on life can help to put the dilemmas of adolescence in perspective. Adam was not there to serve Frances; their sharing was mutual. Reciprocal relationships between elders and adolescents can build self-esteem for both sides.

Programs that bring children simply to perform for elders or for one-shot visits often fail to tap this precious resource. Children need to be well prepared for encountering older people, to learn how to communicate with people whose vision or hearing is impaired, or who are confused. They need an opportunity to express fears about the upcoming encounter and to be equipped with strategies for coping. They also need opportunities to "debrief" their experiences, articulating strengths they found in themselves, sharing struggles, and remembering lessons learned from the elders.

In addition to intergenerational relationships, older people can be helped to make a contribution through volunteering. Using skills gained from long years of work, family life, and community service, older people can help to fill the vacuum in Jewish life left by two-career families and the over-busy schedules of today's families.

Supporting older people to give of themselves requires assessing their particular gifts and interests and matching them with programs, organizations, and individuals who can benefit. Here, too, adapting opportunities in order to facilitate maximal opportunity is key. A homebound older woman might be just the person to edit a congregational bulletin. A frail older man might not be able to come to services, but he might indeed be able to call ill members of the congregation to offer support. Even residents of a nursing home can make a difference.

> Thirty residents of the nursing home gathered to hear a speaker about Ethiopian Jewry. Many had never heard of this ancient African Jewish community, and were surprised to learn there were black Jews. The speaker invited the residents to "adopt" Yonah, aged twenty-six, an Ethiopian Jew airlifted to Israel during Operation Moses. Yonah's mother and siblings were still in Ethiopia. He was barely subsisting on government stipends and trying to find work in his new land. The residents decided to adopt him. They wrote letters (with the help of volunteers, who took dictation from them). They sent photos and expressed sentiments such as, "Hang in there, you'll soon be with your family," and "I remember when I left my family in Russia when I came to America as a young man. I wish you strength," and, "God should watch over you and your family." They raised money to help Yonah's family, contributing dimes and quarters from their meager allowances of spending money and asking family members to donate as well. Yonah wrote back, "When you write, I feel like I have brothers who care about me. Everything you wrote, it has come to be. You wrote that God would bring my family to me. At Pesach, my mother and brother came to Israel."

The nursing home residents had transcended their roles as recipients of care. They had become *redeemers*. Yonah's letter told them that they had participated in the sacred *mitzvah* of *pidyon shevuyim*, redeeming the captive. These frail elders made this difference with their prayers, their caring, and their money. This real contribution was made possible by conscious facilitation on the part of the volunteers, staff, and rabbi.

Maggie Kuhn, the founder of the advocacy group the Gray Panthers, wrote, "What can we do, those of us who have survived to this advanced age? We can think and speak. We can remember. We can give advice and make judgments. We can dial the phone, write letters, and read. We may not be able to butter our bread, but we can still change the world."[21] With the help of the pastoral caregiver, older persons can find their own way to change the world. These efforts do not just offer the elderly a life of meaning; the elders genuinely help to repair our broken world.

Facilitating a Life of Celebration

The pastoral caregiver can facilitate a life of celebration for older persons by enabling them to live "in Jewish time." As Heschel has eloquently pointed out, time is the sanctuary in which we meet God.[22] In contrast to the empty time that can stretch out endlessly before an aging person, in Jewish life time is filled with moments of celebration. We live in cycles of significant moments: the cycles of the week, the month, and the year. We are always living in relationship to holy moments. Today is not just Wednesday, which looks just like Tuesday, it is the 5th of Iyar, Yom ha-Atzmaut (Israel's Independence Day), the 20th day of the Omer, the period between Passover and Shavuot, and three days before Shabbat. This moment, and every moment, has a "location" in time. There is always something to look forward to, always something to savor. Participating in Jewish time offers older people what Heschel calls, "the marvel . . . discovered in celebration."[23]

Jewish time also connects an older person to past and future. When Reba, an assisted living resident who is eighty-one years old, is invited to bless the Shabbat candles, she remarks, "I remember my mother doing this." In this act, Reba experiences a thread of connection to her previous life, to beloved experiences and people. The loneliness and frustration of her current life are, for a moment, softened.

> Max is quite depressed. He recently lost his wife, Sophie, and his visual impairment and advanced heart disease make him unable to live alone. He's come to the nursing home at age seventy-six. Often, he confides in his rabbi, "I know I shouldn't say this, but

to tell you the truth, every night I pray that God should take me." This night, however, Max has something different to say. He is just leaving the synagogue of the nursing home at the end of the Shabbat. As he greets his rabbi, Max says, "We should live and be well and do the same thing next year."

Max is still bereaved and frail after the *Shabbat* service, but participating in that moment of holiness and community has made him hope for a future of more such moments. Jewish time connects older people to the future in another way. Aging persons living in Jewish time know that these cycles of holy moments went on long before them and will continue long after them. This awareness offers a foothold in a future they will not personally witness, an awareness that something precious to them will endure beyond their lives.

> The nursing home congregation has just observed Tisha B'Av. Minnie comments as she leaves the service, "That was wonderful!" What was wonderful? They have sung songs of lament, read from the Book of Lamentations, and recounted moments of loss and destruction in our Jewish past! What was wonderful for Minnie was that the community's worship touched the brokenness and sadness in her own life. As she sat and cried in the service, Minnie's feelings were acknowledged, validated, even sanctified.

The life of celebration available through Jewish time does not refer simply to moments of lightness and joy. The holy days that punctuate the Jewish year reflect the entire spectrum of human emotion. From the outrageous levity of Purim to the solemnity of Yom Kippur, the pure joy of Sukkot to the abject sorrow of Tisha B'Av, every feeling a human being experiences finds reflection in Jewish religious life. This spectrum of emotional opportunity is a tremendous resource for older people.

The pastoral caregiver's role is to link older people with this life of celebration. First, we are called to make sure that older persons in our care have opportunities to participate in the holy moments of Shabbat and the holidays. For example, consider Shabbat. What are the ways in which individuals with different levels of capacity can participate in Oneg Shabbat (Shabbat joy)? For older people living in their own apartments, transportation to services might be what is needed; for those living in the community who are too frail to attend services, a volunteer might deliver chalah or the congregation arrange a telephone connection so that they could listen to services. A rabbi, cantor, or team of volunteers could hold a service for elders in nursing homes and other long-term care facilities. For many older adults, living the life of celebration requires such enabling action on the part of the pastoral caregiver.

The life of celebration need not be limited to rituals and ceremonies that are familiar from an older person's past experience. For instance, Rosh Chodesh can be a beautiful chance to mark time for older people, either on their own or with younger people. Stopping to note and to hallow the beginning of each month can add a dimension of holiness to life. Offering prayers for the coming month for oneself, one's family, the community, and the world connects one to hope and to one's power as a source of blessing.

Lastly, the pastoral caregiver can facilitate a life of celebration by helping older persons mark the transitions of late life with ritual. We know the power of ritual to aid in transitions early in life. Wedding ceremonies contain the tremendous anxieties and fears about entering marriage and give expression to the elation felt by bride, groom, family, and community. Funerals and all of the traditional mourning rites help to hold us together in times of loss.

The many transitions of aging also call for such acknowledgment and celebration. Retirement is an enormously challenging passage from past engagement and accomplishment toward an often-uncharted future territory: Leaving a home of long standing can be a loss of great significance; becoming a grandparent may represent a precious new beginning; giving up driving can signal an end to independence; entering a nursing home or care facility may be frightening and sad. All of these moments, joyous and sad, can and should be marked ritually.[24] The pastoral caregiver can both respond to requests for such rituals, and actively encourage their creation.[25]

Enabling a Life of Connection

The third pillar of the pastoral caregiver's work with aging persons is to facilitate a life of connection. The connection we enable is multidimensional. We have already explored a kind of vertical connection, the link through time to past and future. Another vital aspect of connection is the horizontal link, the connection to community. As mentioned earlier, building intergenerational ties is one means of linking elders to community. Making it possible for elders to participate in the religious life of a congregation is another. Caring relationships, such as those created through *bikur cholim,* are still another way of touching older people and of ensuring that they are not cut off or left behind. This last dimension of connection cannot be characterized by a physical direction, for it is the connection to God, to the soul. The way in which we forge this connection is through accompanying aging persons on their journey.

Accompanying Aging People on Their Journeys: *Hitlavut Ruchanit*

As noted in the introduction to this volume, Rabbi Margaret Holub speaks of the rabbinic task as an *accompanying.*[26] More than fixing or changing people, our job, she says, is to walk along with people through the sorrows, joys, and everyday moments of their lives. The pastoral caregiver is a witness, companion, and tangible manifestation of God's caring. Here, *hitlavut ruchanit* is often the most powerful thing we can offer.[27]

To accompany older adults on their journeys through change, loss, frailty, and limits, we may have to notice and seize opportunities to reach out to them. They will probably not ask for our care and support because they are not aware of their needs, they are embarrassed to call attention to themselves, or they hesitate to burden us. We need to be present to them, sometimes grasping opportunities for pastoral intervention at unlikely moments, whether it is in conversation at the synagogue Oneg Shabbat, or while making rounds at tables in the nursing home dining room. I call this approach "guerilla counseling." We make ourselves available in settings and situations that are normative and not stigmatized. We listen deeply and faithfully to a person's expressions of need, pain, or joy, and we carefully decide how and when to respond. With information gleaned in a casual encounter, we might decide to follow up in greater depth in a more private setting. Our response always begins with making ourselves available.

Two qualities essential in *hitlavut ruchanit* with older adults are humility and respect. Working with people who have seen the world for seven or eight decades, or even a century, we have to assume that they know better than we do what they need and what is right for them. We should also assume that we have much to learn from elders with whom we work. Furthermore, we must approach elders with awe and respect, careful in every interaction to accord them the dignity mandated by our tradition: "Rise before the gray-haired, and grant glory to the face of the elder" (Leviticus 19:32). We need to watch our tone of voice, choice of salutation, and physical situation, for example, to make sure that we do not treat elders like what Maggie Kuhn called "wrinkled babies."[28] We need always to take them and their struggles seriously. We can serve as faithful companions on older persons' journeys only to the extent that we do so with love and honor.

Telling Their Stories: Life Review

When we are present and available, one important service we can perform is to enable elders to tell their stories as they engage in life review. Through telling their stories, older people have an opportunity to savor successes and pleasures and to acknowledge their strengths. Viktor Frankl points to memory as a powerful source of meaning. Older people can draw upon "the full granaries of the past into which they have brought the harvest of their lives: the deeds done, the loves loved and last, but not least, the sufferings they've gone through with courage and dignity." Although the elderly may not have further opportunities for creating meaning in their future, they can draw upon the assets of their past accomplishments, "the potentialities they have actualized, the meanings they have fulfilled, the values they have realized—and nothing and nobody can ever remove these assets from the past."[29]

Our pastoral task is to listen attentively, and to reflect the triumphs, losses, and conflicts that are of primary concern for the person at this stage of his or her journey.

Life review also enables older people to work through unfinished business. Long-ago hurts compounded by years of resentment may come into stark relief as one looks back on one's life. Coming on these experiences anew can impel an elder to work toward forgiveness, toward letting go of anger and healing old wounds.

> Harry is ninety-one years old. Over the past few years, he has become completely blind. He has a loving daughter and grandchildren

and has made a positive adjustment to living in the nursing home despite his difficulties in getting around. In a conversation with the chaplain, Harry says, "I know why I became blind. God struck me blind because I didn't go to my sister's funeral." After exploring Harry's feelings of guilt and remorse, the chaplain suggests that Harry ask for forgiveness from his sister. She invites him to write a letter to his sister, sharing his shame and regret and requesting forgiveness. She invites Harry to perform an act of *tzedakah* as part of his *teshuvah* (repentance), and he makes a gift to a local charity. Lastly, the chaplain and Harry pray together, "Forgive us, God, for we have sinned; have mercy upon us, for we have . . ."

Rabbi Zalman Schacter-Shalomi's work, Spiritual Eldering, has developed very useful techniques to support older people's work of forgiveness and spiritual healing.[30] Conveying the message that *teshuvah* and transformation are possible until the very moment of death, the pastoral caregiver can foster courage and hope.

In the course of telling their stories, older people may also identify losses for which they have never truly grieved, providing an opening for pastoral care intervention.

Hannah lost a two-week-old baby forty years ago. With the birth of her first grandchild, a daughter, she finds herself recalling long-forgotten details of that experience, which was never mentioned in her family. Hannah is very emotional, crying frequently, and constantly anxious about the health and safety of her granddaughter. Hannah speaks to her rabbi about this. He suggests that she visit the cemetery where her infant daughter is buried. Hannah reports that she went to the cemetery with her son (which she had never done before), and together they said *Kaddish* for the child whom they never got to know.

The pastoral caregiver accompanies older people reliving unfinished grief, and may choose to create rituals to mark and contain the feelings of loss.

Sharing the Spiritual Search

"God forgot about me." "God is with me every moment." Older people often search for God with greater intensity than younger people.

They may profoundly feel God's presence amidst their joys and suffering. On the other hand, in coping with frailty, loss, and mortality, the faith of a person can be shaken fundamentally.

Accompanying aging people involves sharing their search for God. The pastoral caregiver will find that many older adults welcome the opportunity to talk about faith, religious experience, doubt, and evil. These questions are not filed away in some remote recess of the mind, but are right at the surface, gnawing, challenging, and urging the older person toward exploration and growth. Sharing the questions is, of course, far more important than attempting to provide answers, although sometimes careful attention to the person's experiences and relationship to God will foster clarity or comfort.

Praying with older people can be a concrete way of sharing the spiritual search. Using traditional psalms and blessings may be sustaining. In addition, empowering the older person to articulate and to utter his or her own prayer or blessing, including his or her very personal hopes, fears, doubts, and dreams, may touch the person profoundly. Sometimes we as pastoral caregivers have to get over our own shyness, embarrassment, or fear of rejection in order to allow the elders whom we serve the gift of prayer.

Looking to Death and Beyond

For all aging persons, death looms large. However long this third age of the life cycle may be, what will inevitably follow it is death. Death is the neighbor next door who might drop by for a visit at any moment. Perhaps that visit will be for the older person herself or himself, or perhaps for a dear friend or family member.

> Edith, an eighty-year-old woman, is sharp and always has a humorous word to say. She stops the cantor visiting the assisted living facility and says, "Where do you think we go when we die? What happens to us? Do we just rot, or do we go someplace? My husband, he's been gone twenty years. Not a letter, not a phone call! Whatever that place is, *nobody's come back to tell us about it!*"

The pastoral caregiver can accompany the older person as she or he prepares for the journey away from this life. Although Edith's remarks were humorous on the surface, in reality, she was deeply curious and troubled by her lack of knowledge about what lay ahead for her. She welcomed an opportunity to talk about her beliefs, and also to hear about Jewish teachings about the afterlife.[31]

Most of us do not take a major trip without rather careful preparation. We pack the things we'll need, we put in order the home we are leaving behind, and we may read and learn about the place we're going. There is no greater journey than the one to the unknown after this life. It behooves us as pastoral caregivers to support older people with whom we work in preparing for death. It may be that, like Edith, a person will wish to speculate on life after death. However, someone else may be moved to put his or her affairs in order, attending to passing on material goods in an orderly fashion. That same individual may also choose to create a spiritual legacy by writing an ethical will, a document spelling out the values one wishes to pass on to loved ones who will survive him or her, and one's hopes and dreams for them.[32]

Bioethical Dilemmas

Elders may need practical help to prepare for dying. In this context, pastoral caregivers can be particularly helpful. We can assist older adults to execute advance directives, living wills, and healthcare proxies to ensure that their wishes regarding their medical treatment will be carried out should they be unable to express them at the time. As part of this process, we can help people to clarify their own values and goals. We can also teach about the Jewish tradition's perspectives on care at the end of life, balancing reverence for the sanctity of life with a realistic acceptance that there is "a time to die."[33]

In the wrenching dilemmas that can emerge in end-of-life medical care, the pastoral caregiver is a resource for older people and their families. With constantly intensifying medical technology, it is possible to extend life far beyond what most elders could have imagined would be the case. Medical technology has outstripped our capacity to discern its appropriateness. Moreover, many deaths have become "deaths by decision." Aside from withdrawing life-sustaining treatment, many other issues of forgoing treatments may present themselves to patients or family members. For example, the family might have to decide whether to use antibiotics for pneumonia for a woman who is ninety-nine years old and has recently been rendered unconscious by a stroke; or whether to consent to the amputation of a foot for a diabetic man who is eighty-five years old and in the end stages of congestive heart failure; or whether to agree to insert a feeding tube for a woman who is seventy-nine years old and in the final stages of Alzheimer's disease and hasn't spoken for years.

The pastoral caregiver can be a resource in analyzing the choices facing a patient or family. He or she can help them look at the bigger picture, including the individuals' most fundamental values and goals, hopes, and fears. The pastoral caregiver may assist decision makers to weigh the potential benefits and burdens of a proposed treatment. The pastoral caregiver can provide a forum for patients and family members to hear one another out, which is difficult in the heat of emotional disputes. He or she can share teachings from Jewish tradition that illuminate and clarify the choices at hand. And he or she can accompany those who must ultimately make choices in the face of uncertainty, offering them support and compassion.

Pastoral Care with People with Dementia

Preserving the *Tzelem Elohim* (Image of God)

Dementia is the nightmare people pray to avoid. Not only are individuals with advanced dementia robbed of memories, cognition, and control over bodily functions, they also are frequently stripped of their dignity. The pastoral caregiver has the sacred responsibility of responding to each person, perhaps especially those suffering from Alzheimer's and other dementing illnesses, as beings created *b'tzelem Elohim* (in the Divine image). We are called to offer the respect and honor due them, to take them seriously, to see past "the wrinkles and the tears"[34] to the soul within that is aching for contact, for love, and for dignity. When we treat those with dementia in this manner, we serve as witnesses, signaling to paid caregivers burdened by numbing and ill-compensated work that they are entrusted with a sacred task. We may need to go beyond witnessing to actively advocate for the dignity and needs of demented individuals for whom we care.

Connecting to the Part That Is Still Whole

Tillie had not spoken for months. She usually sat quietly, sometimes humming to herself, but not responding to attempts to engage her in conversation or activity. One Friday, Tillie was brought to a Shabbat service in her nursing home. As the rabbi chanted *Shalom Aleichem,* Tillie clapped her hands. When the rabbi sang *Shema,* Tillie sang along. When the rabbi wished her "*Shabbat shalom*" after the service, Tillie said, "*Gut shabbos!* It's so nice to be here."

Amidst the broken synapses, thoughts, and memories of persons with dementia, a part that is whole persists. Ritual and music can help a pastoral caregiver touch the part that is whole, to enable the person to find joy, meaning, and relationship. The keys in making these connections are to craft experiences that include as much of familiar rituals and melodies as possible, and to shape observances which are brief, dignified, and joyous.

One-to-One Relationship

The pastoral caregiver should never assume that a person is too confused to connect, although it is tremendously challenging to notice a connection to an individual who seems unresponsive or completely disoriented. We may need to measure our accomplishment in millimeters rather than inches. Despite the sometimes formidable challenge of communicating with persons with dementia, there are approaches that can help.

It is helpful to use touch and position to establish connection and to introduce ourselves at the beginning of an encounter, even if we have met the person before. We need to remember that beneath confusion and unreality are emotional truths. As we listen and respond, we can focus on those.

Sarah, a ninety-year-old woman who has lived in the nursing home for three years, is wandering up and down the hallway with great agitation. She stops the chaplain and says, "I have to go home now. My mother is waiting for me and she'll be worried." The chaplain responds, "It sounds like your mother was very concerned about you. She must have really loved you." Sarah answers, "Oh, yes, she's the best mother, and I don't want her to be scared." The chaplain says, "I can see you really love your mother, and you're trying to take care of her, too." Sarah is visibly less agitated, and allows the chaplain to escort her to dinner.

By acknowledging and validating the emotions reflected in the apparently "unreal" content, we can reach and honor the confused older person. When persons are aphasic, or otherwise unable to express themselves, we can sometimes help "give voice" to them by articulating what we observe them to be experiencing or expressing nonverbally, such as, "I notice that you are crying, Sam. You seem very sad today. I know that you can't use words to tell me more."

As we work with older persons with dementia, we need not only to brace ourselves for loss and sadness but also to be alert for magic moments, for nuggets of insight and wisdom. When we least expect it, a very confused person may suddenly speak the deepest truth.

> Anna had lived in the nursing home for many years. She was a feisty, fun-loving person, who had formed many close friendships with other residents. Only when she passed age 100 did she begin to be confused, and a hip fracture, at age 103, caused her great pain. One day, Anna was lying in her geri-chair in the day room, saying over and over, "Oy, mama, oy, mama." The chaplain sat down next to Anna and took her hand. "You're thinking a lot about your mother, aren't you, Anna?" Anna turned to the chaplain and said, "It's always Mom in the end."

Anna could not have said what day of the week it was, nor did she necessarily remember the chaplain sitting next to her. But Anna knew what really counted: She realized that she was near the end of life. She was aware that she longed for the comfort of her mother, and she believed she would soon be joining her.

Pastoral Support for Family Caregivers

Pastoral caregivers have an important role to play with family members caring for aging relatives. Their task is formidable and they need spiritual support and succor.

The Myth of Abandonment

Many people believe that adult children today fail to care for their parents in the way that previous generations did. The perception that there has been widespread abandonment of the elderly by their families is simply not accurate.

> Ira, a resident who is ninety-seven and requires personal care, has just fallen. He is taken to the emergency room and needs stitches for a gash in his head. The resident and attending physician has called his family, but no one has come to be with him. Knowing that he has a daughter-in-law, Ricki, who is usually quite involved, the personal care facility staff are surprised. They comment that perhaps Ricki isn't as interested in Pop as she once was. When Ricki comes in the next day, she explains that she couldn't come sooner because on the very same day on which Ira was injured, her brother died and her husband was rushed to the hospital with chest pains. Ricki literally didn't know what to do first: Should she stay at the hospital with her husband during his catheterization, make funeral arrangements for her brother, or go to be with Pop, who must be very frightened and upset at being taken to the emergency room alone?

Like Ricki, many family caregivers of frail elders are performing Herculean tasks with few supports. Many caregivers are pulled between multiple concurrent responsibilities for dependent elders, not to mention jobs and caring for young children. Often, the caregivers' efforts are neither seen nor acknowledged and their pain is faced alone.

This reality runs counter to the commonly held perception that today's elders have been abandoned by their children and that previous generations were more devoted and more constant in their care. As the gerontologist Elaine Brody eloquently argues, this "myth of abandonment" is rooted in our guilt at the limits of what we can give our aging parents.[35] The myth also stems from a failure to apprehend the unique challenges posed by today's caregiving task. Increased longevity, mobility, and decreased birthrates means that more and more elders are cared for over increasingly long periods of dependency by fewer and fewer caregivers. Despite the tremendously demanding nature of the caregiving task, family members provide the majority of all care for dependent elders, and adult daughters or daughters-in-law most often provide this care.

Challenges Facing Family Caregivers

Guilt

No matter how much they are doing, family caregivers feel that they never do enough. As Brody points out, in part, this is because we can never repay our parents in kind for the care they provided us when we were totally dependent children.[36] In addition, all caregivers have competing claims on their time and resources. In an important way, the caregiving task itself is impossible, as frail elders typically do not get better, but rather, become more frail and more dependent over time. In this way, there is actually no such thing as "success" in caregiving.

Conflict Among Family Members

The caregiving task almost inevitably elicits conflict within families. Perhaps the daughter who is dutifully caring for Mom is offended when her brother, who lives 3,000 miles away, comes to visit and proceeds to tell her what she needs to do about Mom's care. Perhaps a son believes his mother needs to move from her home to an assisted living facility, and she angrily rejects this notion. The stresses of caregiving bring long-dormant family conflicts to the fore and may provoke new rifts along those fault lines. Sadly, only rarely do these challenging situations bring previously distant family members together.

Hard Choices

Caring for a dependent elder inevitably presents agonizing dilemmas. Often, the wish of the family caregiver to protect the elder conflicts with the elder's desire for autonomy. Family caregivers wishing to be respectful wonder how to decide how much to do for an older person, and how much to let him or her do, even if doing so might pose some financial, social, or physical risk. When—if ever—does a caregiver need to take over an impaired parent's finances? Should an elder suffering from dementia be allowed to continue to drive? When is it time for a frail elder to move into a nursing home or other long-term care facility? Most wrenching is a decision of when it is *et lamut* (time to die)? When does medical treatment cease serving to preserve life and instead serve to prolong the dying process? Caregivers struggle mightily with these hard choices, and often feel they have nowhere to turn in their search for answers.

What Can Pastoral Caregivers Do?

Normative Support

Pastoral caregivers can help caregivers by offering normative support. Rather than perpetuating the myth of abandonment, pastoral caregivers can acknowledge family members' heroic efforts and painful challenges. From the *bimah* and at the bedside, the pastoral caregiver can note the efforts of family caregivers. The pastoral caregiver can also support the caregiver in accepting his or her limits in the face of seemingly infinite tasks.

Offer Guidance

Rabbis and cantors can support family caregivers facing puzzling dilemmas. When asked, they can offer guidance based on the values embedded in Jewish tradition. This guidance must be offered thoughtfully, of course, responding to the needs and concerns of the family caregiver and without imposing a solution or course of action. One insight from tradition that may be particularly helpful is the recognition that obligations to parents have always been understood to be qualified by competing claims, such as obligations to spouses, or to children.[37]

Presence

Harold, seventy-five years old and a retired housepainter, visited his mother, Becky, ninety-seven years old, nearly every day during the years she was in the nursing home. Although Becky was confused about time and place, she still recognized him. Both Harold and Becky enjoyed the times he pushed her wheelchair out to the garden, and he loved it when she would sing her endless repertoire of Yiddish songs. As Becky's Alzheimer's disease progressed, she gradually became less alert, until she could no longer recognize Harold, and then she stopped talking altogether. Harold's visits became more sporadic, and he often looked on the verge of tears as he sat silently holding his mother's hand. The chaplain made a point of catching Harold in the corridor one day when he was visiting at the home. She said, "You look so sad as you sit there with your mom." Harold's tears flowed, and he talked of his love for his mother, his grief at losing her by inches, watching her fade away before his eyes. Harold shared stories about his mother from his youth. The chaplain asked Harold if he would like to say a prayer. He said, "I just pray that Mom knows I love her."

Harold's pain and loneliness were apparent. He had actually lost the mother he'd known, but had had no chance to say goodbye or to grieve that loss. Joining with Harold, enabling him to give voice to his sadness, pierced his loneliness. Praying allowed him to connect to his own spiritual resources. This connection can be enormously helpful for burdened, depleted caregivers. Whether those resources are faith, spiritual practices, or communal ties, research has shown that having access to resources can ease the stresses of caregiving and help in coping.[38] Often, caregivers need to be reminded that they are deserving of care, including attending to their own spiritual lives.

Connecting to Other Resources

It is vitally important that the pastoral caregiver be aware of resources in the community that can support family caregivers, such as counseling services, support groups, and respite services, as well as resources available to frail elders, such as adult day care, in-home services, and long-term care facilities. Professionals who work with caregivers have noted that family members can be resistant to accepting help. Therefore, referral in these situations may require extra support and encouragement. Pastoral caregivers in a congregational context may want to specially reach out to congregants who are intensively caring for frail relatives, and inquire about their needs and what can be done to enable the caregiver to continue to participate in the life of the community.

The Gifts of Working with Older People

Those who do not work with the elderly often believe that their pastoral care is a dreary, draining affair. On the contrary, serving older adults is work that offers rich rewards. In my experience as a pastoral caregiver, not a day has gone by without my receiving beautiful gifts from my elderly congregants; I have been immeasurably enriched by their love, their humor, their perspective, and their wisdom.

Although we are called to make one hundred blessings a day, I have often felt that working with the elderly allows me to *receive* one hundred blessings a day. In almost every encounter, I note that those I am supposed to be helping are reaching out to offer me precious hopes and prayers. It is the currency with which they transform a relationship of professional caregiving into a mutual exchange. "May you live to be my age, but well!" "May you have many children." "When you were born, God made a *bashert* (destined partner) for you. You will find him in a *vinkl* (corner)." "I wish you everything you wish yourself."

I pray that pastoral caregivers who choose to work with the aging—and those who have it thrust upon them—will take in the blessings showered upon them, and that these blessings will sustain them amid pain, loss, and limits, both in working with older people and in aging themselves.

Notes

1. Allen Glicksman and Tania Koropeckyj-Cox, "Jewish Aged in the United States: Sociodemographic and Socioeconomic Characteristics," in *Jewish Aged: Ethnicity, Diversity and Services,* eds. Ze'ev Harel, David Biegel, and David Guttman, (New York: Springer Press, 1994).

2. Ken Dychtwald and Joe Flower, *Age Wave: The Challenges and Opportunities of an Aging America* (New York: Bantam, 1990).

3. See Wendy Lustbader, *Counting on Kindness: An Exploration of Dependency* (New York: Free Press. 1991), for a fascinating examination of the meaning of dependency in a society that prizes independence above almost all else.

4. Robert N. Butler, "The Life Review: An Interpretation of Reminiscence in the Aged," *Psychiatry* 26 (1963): pp. 65–76.

5. Florida Scott Maxwell, *The Measure of My Days* (New York: Penguin, 1979).

6. For a fuller treatment of this topic, see Dayle A. Friedman, "Spiritual Challenges of Nursing Home Life," in *Aging, Spirituality and Religion: A Handbook*, eds. Melvin Kimble, et al. (Minneapolis: Fortress Press. 1995), pp. 362–73.

7. The concept of *mitzvah* may be interpreted differently in liberal and traditional communities. Traditional Jews hold that one learns of one's precise obligation through Halacha; posthalachic Jews maintain that one "hears" the commandment in community, or through one's own autonomous relationship with God. Regardless of which view one holds, participating in the *mitzvot*, what Mordechai Kaplan called "sancta," grants one a connection to holiness and meaning.

8. Orthodox tradition continues to view women as exempt from time-bound *mitzvot;* Reform and Reconstructionists hold that they are obligated equally, and

Conservatives hold that a woman may voluntarily take on time-bound commandments.

9. Shulchan Aruch Orach Chayim 94:6.

10. Ibid., 110:1

11. Ibid., 94:6.

12. Mishnah Berurah Orach Chayim 100:21.

13. Abraham Joshua Heschel, "To Grow in Wisdom," in *The Insecurity of Freedom* (Philadelphia: Jewish Publication Society, 1966), p. 78.

14. Ibid., p. 77.

15. For example, homebound elders can participate in a synagogue service via a telephone hook-up to the public address system. See Amy L. Sales and Shira Kandel, *Synagogue Hope: Help, Opportunities and Programs for Jewish Elders* (Waltham, Mass.: Brandeis University, 1998). In addition, some congregations broadcast Shabbat, High Holy Day services, or both over the radio to those who are too ill or frail to attend services. Finally, ill or homebound people can join in study with each other and a teacher using conference-call technology.

16. For information about appropriate print size and format for individuals with low vision, contact the Jewish Braille Institute, 110 E. 30th St., New York, NY 10016, 212-889-2525.

17. A sound system that includes infrared amplification with headsets for individuals who are hearing impaired is an option to consider.

18. Maimonides, Hilchot Talmud Torah 1:6, translated by Danny Siegel.

19. For an explication of the theory of andragogy, see Malcolm Knowles, *The Modern Practice of Adult Education: From Pedagogy to Andragogy* (Cambridge, Mass.: Cambridge Book Company, 1988).

20. Polly Young-Eisendrath, *Gifts of Suffering* (Reading, Mass.: Addison-Wesley, 1996), p. 59.

21. Maggie Kuhn, et al., *No Stone Unturned: The Life and Times of Maggie Kuhn* (New York: Ballantine Books, 1991).

22. Abraham Joshua Heschel, *The Sabbath: Its Meaning for Modern Man* (New York: Farrar, Straus & Giroux, 1951).

23. Heschel, *The Sabbath* (1966), p. 82.

24. For examples of rituals of this sort, see Cary Kozberg, "Let Your Heart Take Courage: A Ceremony for Entering a Nursing Home," pp. 289–97; Paul Citrin, "A Testament to Growing Older: The Av/Em Eitza Program," pp. 267–69; Marcia Cohn Spiegel, "Havdalah: A Time to Acknowledge Growing Old," pp. 275–78, in *A Heart of Wisdom: Making the Jewish Journey from Midlife through the Elder Years*, ed. Susan Berrin (Woodstock, Vt.: Jewish Lights Publishing, 1997).

25. For extremely practical and helpful guidance on creating rituals of transition, see "How to Create a Ritual," ed. Debra Orenstein, in *Lifecycles, Vol. 1: Jewish Women on Life Passages and Personal Milestones* (Woodstock, Vt.: Jewish Lights Publishing, 1994), pp. 359–76.

26. Rabbi Margaret Holub, personal communication.

27. See my introduction to this volume for an explanation of this new Hebrew term for pastoral care.

28. See also BT Baba Kama 92b: "Now that we're old, we're treated like infants."

29. Viktor Frankl, *Man's Search for Meaning: An Introduction to Logotherapy* (New York: Touchstone Books, 1984), p. 151.

30. See, for example, the exercises in "Healing a Painful Memory," "Giving Yourself the Gift of Forgiveness," and "A Testimonial Dinner for the Severe Teachers," Zalman Schacter-Shalomi, *From Age-ing to Sage-ing* (New York: Warner Books, 1995), pp. 276–80.

31. See chapter 16 in this book, "Grief and Bereavement," p. 342.

32. *So That Your Values Live On: Ethical Wills and How to Prepare Them,* eds. Jack Riemer and Nathaniel Stampfer (Woodstock, Vt.: Jewish Lights Publishing, 1991).

33. Rabbi Richard Address has compiled an excellent manual for older adults to use in preparing for death and dying. *A Time to Prepare: A Practical Guide for Individuals and Families in Determining One's Wishes for Extraordinary Medical Treatment and Financial Arrangements* (New York: Union of American Hebrew Congregations, 1992) contains advance directive forms, background on Jewish values, a format for a person to indicate wishes about his or her funeral, and an ethical will format.

34. Kathy Levine, founder of "Magic Me," a national intergenerational program. Personal communication.

35. See Elaine M. Brody, "Parent Care as a Normative Family Stress," *The Gerontologist* 25, no. 1 (1985): 19–29.

36. Ibid.

37. See, for example, Maimonides, Mishneh Torah, Ishut 13:14 on obligations to one's spouse that may take precedence over obligations to parents. Mamrim 6:10 suggests that when a parent is mentally impaired and caring for him or her becomes "unbearable" for the adult child, the child is to leave and arrange for someone else to provide the direct care for the parent.

38. See, for example, P. V. Rabins, et al., "Emotional Adaptation Over Time in Caregivers for Chronically Ill Elderly People," *Age and Aging* 19 (1990): pp. 185–90.

Bibliography

Berrin, Susan, ed. *A Heart of Wisdom: Making the Jewish Journey from Midlife Through the Elder Years.* Woodstock, Vt.: Jewish Lights Publishing, 1997.

Journal of Religious Gerontology. The Haworth Press, Inc., 10 Alice St., Binghamton, NY 13904-1580. E-mail: getinfo@haworthpressinc.com; Web site: www. haworthpressinc.com

Kimble, Melvin, et al., eds. *Aging, Spirituality and Religion: A Handbook.* Minneapolis: Fortress Press, 1995.

Koenig, Harold G., and Andrew J. Weaver. *Counseling Troubled Older Adults: A*

Handbook for Pastors and Religious Caregivers. Nashville: Abingdon Press, 1997.

Knudson, Lois. *Understanding the Senior Adult: A Tool for Holistic Ministry.* Washington, D.C.: Alban Institute, 2000.

Mace, Nancy, and Peter Rabins. *The 36-Hour Day: A Family Guide to Caring for Persons with Alzheimer's Disease, Related Dementing Illnesses and Memory Loss in Later Life.* Baltimore: Johns Hopkins University Press, 1981, 1991.

Sales, Amy L., and Shira Kandel. *Synagogue Hope: Help, Opportunities and Programs for Jewish Elders.* Waltham, Mass.: Brandeis University, 1998.

Schacter-Shalomi, Zalman, and Ronald S. Miller. *From Age-ing to Sage-ing.* New York: Warner Books, 1995.

Other Resources

The Center for Aging, Religion and Spirituality (CARS), Luther Seminary, 2481 Como Ave., St. Paul, MN 55108-1496; phone: 651-641-3581; fax 651-641-3425; E-mail: CARS@luthersem.edu; Web site: www.luthersem.edu/cars. Publishes newsletter on aging and spirituality and holds an annual summer gerontology training program for clergy.

Committee on Older Adults, Department of Jewish Family Concerns, Union of American Hebrew Congregations, 633 Third Ave., New York, NY 10017-6778; phone: 212-650-4193; Web site: www.uahc.org. Publishes materials for congregations and lay people on issues of aging and spirituality, caregiving, healthy aging, and congregational programming for older adults.

Forum on Religion, Spirituality, and Aging, American Society on Aging, 83 Market St., Suite 516, San Francisco, CA 94103-1824; phone 415-974-9600; fax 415-974-0300; Web site: www.asaging.org. Holds annual conference and publishes quarterly newsletter, *Aging and Spirituality.*

Rabbi Dayle A. Friedman, M.A.J.C.S., M.S.W., is the director of the Geriatric Chaplaincy program at the Reconstructionist Rabbinical College, where she also serves as a spiritual director. She has served for many years as a nursing home chaplain, and as a clinical supervisor to rabbinic and cantorial students in geriatric internship programs.

Walking in the Valley of the Shadow: Caring for the Dying and Their Loved Ones

Rabbi Amy Eilberg

Rabbi Amy Eilberg guides Jewish pastoral caregivers in working with the dying. She presents an analysis of Jewish attitudes toward death and investigates the central needs of the dying and of their loved ones. Rabbi Eilberg explores Jewish principles of care for the dying and applies them to the pastoral relationship, making a passionate case for Jewish chaplains to be advocates for hospice care. In closing, she examines the meaning of encounters with the dying to the pastoral caregiver.[1]

I still remember one of my first experiences with death, which occurred very early in my work as a chaplain. I was on call at the hospital when I was asked to be with a family whose loved one was dying in the intensive care unit (ICU). Life support had been disconnected; there was nothing to do but wait for death. Family members gathered around the death bed, the eerie sounds of the ICU in the background, as they held vigil for the woman who was wife, mother, and grandmother. The vigil, as it turned out, went on for some hours. I spent time with the family and then went to visit with other hospital patients, checking back from time to time. I remember little about what was said during that time. What I remember most is the silence, the hush, the sensation of our watching the monitors together. Finally, the line on the heart monitor went flat. There were tears and prayers, and a bit of relief. Most of all, I remember the sense of awe, the awareness that we had all stood in a holy place.

Even after many years of experience, standing in the presence of death still inspires awe in me. How could it be otherwise? Caring for the dying, we find ourselves at the mysterious nexus of life and death. No matter how familiar these encounters become, they still cause us to reflect on our own lives, our own fears, our own mortality. These moments touch our own personal grief and remind us of our own vulnerability. They can bring us to painful confrontation with the raw face of injustice when a death is untimely or, in our judgment, preventable. They make us acutely aware of our own powerlessness. However, we still strive to offer comfort and wisdom, and most of all, to bring ourselves fully to the side of the person in pain.

Each encounter with another human being is unique; each person's life story is a world of its own. To each encounter we bring ourselves, our own wisdom, our own experiences, and our own needs. Each encounter calls on a different part of us and has different things to teach us. Therefore, there can never be a map of the territory of dying: The territory is too complex for charting. However, it is possible to sketch some of what we find when we work in the presence of death; more aware of the nature of the territory, we can be clearer about how the chaplain can be of help.

Jewish Attitudes Toward Death

People live their lives with very different attitudes toward the nature of life and death. These attitudes, a combination of temperament, learning, and experience, have a significant impact on how a person copes when confronted with life-threatening illness.

I have discerned at least three distinct views of death, which are present to a greater or lesser degree in Jewish tradition, and are common among the Jews with whom I have worked. Of course, one person may hold several different attitudes simultaneously and different views at different phases of their illness. I explore these attitudes in this chapter because they so frequently underlie the journey of the dying through terminal illness. Recognizing these often-subconscious assumptions may help the chaplain hear the dying more fully and possibly help them consider views that may serve them better.

Death as the Enemy

For many Jews in America, death is an adversary to be defeated at all costs. In this view, to be Jewish is to fight valiantly to the end, regardless of circumstances. Death, when it finally comes, is viewed as a kind of defeat, a capitulation to an enemy.

Of course, there is significant basis for this view of death in Halacha (Jewish law), and certainly in Jewish history. The halachic view that all but three *mitzvot* are to be abrogated in the service of *pikuach nefesh* (life-saving activity) has clearly contributed to the notion that we are to value life above all.[2] Beyond the teachings of Jewish law, our path through history has taught us to fight, to survive, and to thrive as a people.

Throughout much of our lives, even in the face of life-threatening illness, fighting for life is surely the appropriate response. I think of the eighty-year-old father of a friend, lying in the ICU after a massive, sudden heart attack, silently struggling to live, eloquently laboring to communicate with his family, to let them know he was not ready to let go. I think of a young woman with breast cancer, struggling with all her might to win a little more time to live with her young child. I think of a mother searching for anything or anyone that could help her desperately sick child. There is a time to fight.

For many Jews, particularly in America where the culture reinforces denial of death in so many ways, this view has seemed to be the only one possible. Many Jews have forgotten that, although there is a time to fight, there is also a time to let go. When death is clearly approaching, the fighting attitude can deprive the person and loved ones of using the time remaining in the richest possible way. For some, to accept the reality of death even seems like a betrayal of our people, of our view of ourselves as survivors. Convinced that being Jewish is synonymous with defying the odds and vanquishing death, many have considered the term *Jewish hospice* an oxymoron, an impossibility. But of course, this is not the only Jewish view of death. If read carefully, our rich tradition offers us other ways to understand the place of death in life.

Death as a Part of Life

One can open almost any classical Jewish book and find evidence of a very different Jewish attitude toward death. The view of death that is best represented in classical Jewish sources is that death is a part of life, a part of God's creation.

Jewish tradition is rich with texts that cultivate our awareness of mortality as a part of the divine plan for humankind. Death is a part of life; it is as predictable a part of living as being born and growing, a necessary end to a life well lived. Jewish sources that cultivate this perspective emphasize God's role as Creator, the immensity of God and the universe in contrast to the short span of human life. Yet, there is some comfort in its brevity: This is the way life is supposed to be, full and rich and finite.

For example, consider the following classic statement from Psalm 90:

> Your sleep, [O God] engulfs all mortals.
> They flourish for a day, like grass.
> In the morning it sprouts afresh;
> by nightfall it fades and withers. . . .
> Three score and ten our years may number,
> four score years if granted the vigor.
> Laden with trouble and travail,
> life quickly passes and flies away. . . .
> Teach us to use all of our days,
> that we may attain a heart of wisdom.[3]

Or consider the midrash from Kohelet Rabbah (7:4). The midrash reflects on the puzzling verse from Ecclesiastes, "A good name is better than fine oil; the day of death is better than the day of birth" (7:1) The day of death is better than the day of birth? How could this be? Birth is a time of joy, of promise, of awareness of miracles. Death is a time of grief, confusion, and bitterness. Yet, this midrashic author reverses our usual understanding, using the metaphor of a ship's journey. He says that most people celebrate when a boat sets off to sea, and offer no acknowledgment when the boat returns safely home: "When a ship sets out from harbor," says the midrashist, "one never knows what storms it may encounter, what obstacles may impede its journey. It is when the ship returns safely and successfully at the end of the journey that one does well to celebrate. So, too, it is at the end of life's journey, when one knows that life has been well lived, that is the time for satisfaction, for peace, even for celebration."

In its wisdom, our tradition understands profoundly how much pain the journey toward death can bring. Yet, this midrash also embodies a truth worth pondering: The essence of life can be known most fully at its end rather than at its start; in fact, life's finiteness is a part of its beauty.

I remember David, a man who was forty-five when I first met him, only months before the end of his life, as it turned out. David was a physically beautiful man who had known much professional success, traveled around the world, had a large circle of loving friends and family, and had deep connections in two religious communities. He had lost a life partner and many, many friends to acquired immune deficiency syndrome (AIDS), and now he was dying of the disease. "I have done everything I wanted to do," he told me, extraordinarily, having moved past a time of anger at the disease. He was not afraid of death; he had seen death's face so many times. He trusted that his profound spiritual life would help him to face his own. "I am afraid of the dying part," he said. For David, the hardest part would be the unpredictable, uncontrollable ups and downs of the disease process.

There were, in fact, many twists and turns, times of horror and times of beauty, as his body grew weaker and as his loved ones wrapped David in love. Even during hard times, he loved the fact that he could stay in his own home, in his own room; for moments at a time, he could savor the fire crackling in his fireplace, listen to the sound of the rain, treasure the stillness of this place that was his home.

One day, shortly before he died, David was moving in and out of consciousness as we visited. He opened his eyes for a moment, got very clear, and said, "You know, people have been doing this for a long time." Even as he came close to death, he was able for a moment to see himself as part of the whole circle of humanity.

It is not our role as chaplains to persuade people to adopt a different attitude toward death. People have developed these views over a lifetime, often for very good reasons. Pastoral care is enhanced by our awareness that people can become trapped in a view of death that is too small, or one that has outgrown its usefulness by the end of an excruciating illness.

Death as a Teacher

It seems that there are lessons that we learn best when we are in close contact with the reality of death. When we have no choice but to recognize that life is finite, that we and everyone we will ever love will die, we are often catapulted into an intense experience of the preciousness of life.

Death can be a teacher about the fragility of life and its beauty, about the deep importance of loved ones and of treasured values, about the ways in which life gives us extraordinary gifts, that even loss sometimes brings blessing in its wake. Death is a teacher about God's presence in the world, about human goodness, compassion, and love. Death teaches courage and hope and faith, about believing in what we cannot see, about moving through the valley of the shadow until light is visible again.

In fact, one finds embedded in Jewish liturgy references to death that can be understood as death-awareness practices, as rituals that specifically direct our attention to our own mortality. These prayers, recited daily over a lifetime, offer the chance to cultivate the capacity to tolerate the reality of death and to embrace its teachings throughout our lifetime until, perhaps, our own final moments.

Consider the *keri'at Shema al hamita*, the recitation of the *Shema* every night before going to sleep. It is surely no coincidence that the *Shema* is also to be recited just before death. In instituting these practices, the Rabbis almost certainly intended to have us treat the process of going to bed each night as a daily rehearsal for the final moments of life. Each night, we relinquish our conscious control over our lives. We descend into darkness, into a state in which we have little control over our bodies or our thoughts, a state that the Rabbis called a one-sixtieth part of death.[4] Each night, we place our lives in the hands of God, just as we will when we close our eyes for the last time. Each night, we are to practice trusting that somehow, without our knowledge or control, everything will be okay.

On awakening in the morning, we recite: "*Modeh ani/modah ani lefanech*" (I thank You, Ever-living God, that You have returned my soul to me in love. Your faithfulness is very great). We are to begin each morning with the awareness that the soul that we had placed in God's care the previous night has been returned to us once more this morning as a loving gift. It seems clear that the rabbis hoped that if one actively cultivated awareness of the precious gift of life, one would live differently, and perhaps, die just a little differently when the time came.

As chaplains, there are moments of grace when we witness a person's recognition of death's teaching in their life. There is nothing one needs to do in such a moment, except perhaps to whisper, "Amen." Such encounters enrich our sense of what is possible, and we bring this awareness into our encounters with others.

The Needs of the Dying and Their Loved Ones

Every stage of life has its own challenges and opportunities. Babies learn to live in the world, to receive nourishment, to trust, and to love. Toddlers, when unimpeded by illness or deprivation, naturally learn to walk and to talk. Adolescents instinctively turn to explore their own unique identities. People who know that death is near also have characteristic feelings and needs and a particular set of developmental challenges to face. There are areas of pain that need soothing, and sometimes, the challenges seem to present possibilities for learning, growth, and healing, even at the end of life.

Care for the dying requires enormous respect and humility, and I do not mean to suggest that the following are necessarily the right feelings to have or appropriate tasks to face. These tasks are also not to be seen as the chaplain's agenda of things to work on in relationship with a dying person. One must be alert to the tendency of so-called experts who seem to think they know the "right" way to approach dying. What a *chutzpah*! I suggest the following rather as a partial sketch of what dying people tend to experience and long for. Knowing as much as we can about the territory we may encounter, we enter each room and listen.

Fear

People who face death often live with fear. Some are most afraid of death itself, of the prospect of facing the end of life, the end of relationships, the end of their individuality and conscious being. For others, the reality of death is tolerable, but the prospect of dying alone is a source of terror. For still others, what is most frightening is the potential for pain, or the unpredictability of the dying process ("the dying part") that is most distressing.

I do not believe that it is necessarily the chaplain's job to make a person less afraid of death: Would that this were always possible! Sometimes, the fear is too powerful to be soothed. We should rather concentrate on being as present as we can be in the hope that our love may offer comfort.

> I remember Renée, a woman in her fifties whom I had the blessing to know shortly before her death. She was a person with a rich array of loving relationships. This was no accident; she had a great gift for loving, thus many friends and family members stood by her, tending to her needs with exquisite care. I had been surprised when I encountered Renée just prior to a Rosh Hashanah service, which we both assumed, correctly, would be her last. She fell into my arms in tears, crying, "Promise me that I won't be alone when I die." I took the chance and made a promise I was not sure I could keep. Yet somehow, I felt certain that this woman would not be alone. (Thank God, this turned out to be true.) Even though surrounded by a circle of loving people, dying alone was her greatest fear.

Life Review

One desire that seems to come naturally when death is approaching, whether at the end of a long lifetime or during an illness that is sure to bring premature death, is to look back over the life one has lived. People are moved to review the story of their lives, to savor and to celebrate the gratifying pieces, and to acknowledge, to grieve, and perhaps to make peace with the painful places. Seen from this perspective, the propensity of older people to tell stories is just as basic a developmental need as the toddler's desire to practice walking and talking. When death is near, this work becomes particularly important because the person needs to sum up and affirm his or her time on this earth, to savor the harvest of contributions he or she has made, and to identify areas still in need of repair while there is still time. For chaplains, their work is as basic as good listening with respect and reverence for the tapestry of another person's life.

Grief

Most people facing death find themselves grieving. Grief can encompass a wide range of emotional issues—sadness about leaving loved ones behind, pain about coming to the end of this life, regrets about the life one has lived, fear about what death may bring. It may also include anger about the illness, resentments of caregivers, guilt, and relief, to name a few.

In this emotional territory, the chaplain needs to do nothing more than listen fully. We can be grateful for those graced occasions when talking through grief can bring relief. Sometimes, the sadness cannot find relief, and we must remember that our compassionate presence nonetheless makes a difference.

Finishing Business

In reflecting on their lives when death is near, many people find that there is "business" to finish, in relation to the self (making peace with perceived failures, disappointments, resentments, self-criticism), in relation to others, and in relation to God. This is not to suggest that people must neatly tie up all of the threads of a long life to die "a good death." Rather, it is useful for caregivers to be aware of the many ways in which people can be helped to make peace with some of the painful baggage they carry as they reflect on their lives. A person can sometimes make peace with a painful episode simply by telling the story to a compassionate listener: telling and hearing the story in this awesome time is sometimes enough to reframe it as forgivable.

When the painful issue is in relationship to another person, the path to healing may lie in a conversation with this person. This takes great courage, and sometimes the chaplain can be the one to encourage or even facilitate such a meeting. Such encounters can transform the person's sense of her life, and the legacy she or he leaves behind. When a live encounter with the other person is impossible (because the estranged person is dead or unwilling to communicate), it is still possible to write a letter, even if the letter is never sent. Even encouraging the person to imagine what they might like to say to their estranged loved one can sometimes bring a sense of release.

Many people who are dying but still have strength find that they have unresolved issues with God or with their community. The chaplain in this case can serve, either explicitly or subconsciously, as the representative of God and Jewish community. This may mean listening to a lifetime of anger. The chaplain's ability to embody a loving image of God and Jewish community in relationship with the dying person can sometimes help the person to transform old resentments. To help someone to die a little more at peace with God and with Judaism is very holy work.

Reconciliation/Forgiveness

I rarely meet a person who has no regrets at the end of a life. Imperfect creatures that we are, we invariably have memories of personal failures and regret, hurt, and estrangement. For some people, the burdens are too great to address and are carried painfully to the grave. Some lucky people, who have had the good fortune to recognize the reality of death while they still have strength, can actively seek forgiveness from within, from another, or from God for mistakes made, for wounds inflicted, for things left undone. Those who are able to seek forgiveness may find that the path toward death becomes a little more bearable. In my experience, the *Viddui*, especially if recited while the dying person can still participate, can serve as a powerful vehicle for acknowledging and releasing areas of regret.

> I remember Sam, aged twenty-seven, who lived with cystic fibrosis. He called me, the hospital's rabbi, to his bedside in the middle of the night to recite the *Viddui*, the final confessional prayer. The staff people were confused; medically speaking, there was no reason to believe that death was imminent. But Sam insisted on saying the *Viddui*. With remarkable clarity and courage, he then picked up the phone and called several estranged loved ones around the country to say good-bye. His doctors didn't understand until it became clear that death, in fact, was coming. The doctors wanted to try one more procedure. Sam calmly explained that he was dying, but he agreed to give the doctors three days to try their treatment. After that, he insisted that they promise to let him go. He told them he was ready, that it was okay.

Leaving Legacy

In addition to material preparations (distributing personal property, ensuring care for children, making financial arrangements, and so forth), people long to know that their legacy will continue after their death. For some people, writing an ethical will or a letter to children (or friends or community members), making a videotape, and so forth satisfies a profound need to bequeath their commitments, beliefs, and memories to loved ones in tangible form.[5] The process of creating such a document is always an enormous aid to the dying person in summing up the essence of his or her life. It is frequently a wonderful trigger for loving conversations about values and relationships, and it remains as a treasured gift in the lives of the survivors after death has taken their loved one.

Plans

Many people have a strong need to participate in their own funeral plans; others do not want to have anything to do with planning their own funeral. For those who wish to and are able to move beyond the initial awkwardness, the process can become a way to exert control while they still can. It can also relieve those left behind of the full burden of decision making when death comes. The funerals I have attended that were planned by the dying person have had an extraordinary richness, a palpable sense of the presence of the one who has died with the mourners, which can be a remarkable gift to all. The dying person sometimes chooses the chaplain as the guardian of his desires for the funeral. This is a great privilege.

Saying Good-bye

I am always surprised when I work with people who feel there is nothing left to say as death approaches: "I said 'I love you' every day," or "I've said everything I need to say." These people and their families are lucky.

Many of us, not so lucky, often leave important things, especially loving things, unsaid until endings are near. The ability to say words of love and appreciation at the end of life can bring comfort and blessing to both the dying person and the loved ones. It is an opportunity to acknowledge the strength of relationship, to share tears and love together as death approaches. The final days of life are enriched, and the precious words exchanged at this time become a part of the legacy of love that the survivors will carry with them through their lifetime.

People sometimes feel that saying good-bye will hasten the moment of death. In my experience, this is almost never the case. If more time remains after good-byes have been said, that time is likely to be more filled with a sense of connection and richness. Time lived in this way, even as we anticipate death, can be a great blessing.

> As a younger chaplain, I was rather dogmatic on this point, certain that saying good-bye could not hasten the moment of death. I once worked with a woman with advanced metastatic cancer who would not discuss her illness, and she often talked with me about elaborate plans for travel in her future. The woman had a psychiatric history, and I confess that I heard some of these musings as denial, even as "craziness." One day, the woman began to talk about her cancer; it was a wonderful session. When I said good-bye, the woman said to me, "So I won't see you again, right?" At that time, there was absolutely no medical reason to believe that death was imminent; I thought it was only her pathology talking. As one might reassure a child I told her that, although life and death were in God's hands, I would see her again on my regular visit, two weeks later. The woman knew something that I didn't know. She died two days after this visit.

Did she die, after all, because she finally spoke the dreaded word, cancer? Or was she able, at last, to speak of her illness because on some level she knew that death was near? Did saying good-bye to me somehow hasten her death? This experience humbled me. Perhaps some people know that they dare not speak the word, cancer, or say good-bye, because doing so will rob them of their ability to fight for life. Yet, I believe these are the exceptions that prove the rule: Encouraging people to say good-bye usually brings more richness, blessing, and love to the final days of life.

Cultivating Moments of Acceptance

Dying is rarely beautiful. Most people struggle against death's approach, and find this time awesomely painful. Although miraculous moments of transformation do occasionally unfold, people usually die the way they lived. It is unrealistic, and profoundly disrespectful, to expect people to face the challenges of death in the way that we judge the most healthy, enlightened, or wise.

However, there are occasionally moments of awesome beauty, times when it seems that everything will be okay. The dying person may seem to feel cared for, that life is just as it should be, that loved ones are precious. It takes a person unafraid of death to share such moments with a dying person, to listen quietly and reverently as a person speaks the truth of their experience at this awesome time. If we remember that such fleeting moments are possible, even in the midst of many hours and days of intense suffering, we may occasionally be blessed to see such a glimmer of light cross the otherwise bleak landscape of dying. We can be the one to say "yes" to the dying person or the loved one, who needs a witness to this moment of blessing.

Jewish Principles of Care for the Dying

Given what we know about what dying people need, how can the chaplain best be of help? What can we bring that addresses the pain, needs, and longings of a dying person? We carry many things with us when we enter the room or the home of a dying person. We bring our own presence and our capacity for love and compassion. We carry our own years of experience caring for others at the end of life, the memories of their pain, and the teachings they have given us. We carry our own life experiences that have taught us—not just in the head, but deep in the *kishkas*—what this time of life is about. We carry our own knowledge of the riches of Jewish wisdom about death and about life.

As chaplains attending to the dying, we are not primarily teachers. It is not our primary goal to educate, inform, or even to persuade the person to "do things right" according to Jewish tradition; but we embody much Jewish wisdom about dying and about living. Even if we never speak these words, our presence conveys our convictions about what is possible and helpful in facing the end of life.

I offer the following principles of care for the dying in this spirit—certainly not as an agenda for conversation with the dying person and their loved ones. It is not a time for lecturing or sermonizing, but as we enter a relationship with the person, these are some of the valuable things we bring with us.

Affirmation of *Tzelem Elohim* (Image of God)

Entering the room of a dying person, we see someone who, like us, was created in the image of the Divine. This reality is true no matter how long one has to live, no matter how righteous or full of regret one's life has been. No matter how the body is working, no matter how much time remains until the moment of death, this person embodies the spark of the Divine. Our primary task is to see beyond the illness, the prognosis, the tubes and machines, the desperation or denial. If we can perceive and affirm the *tzelem Elohim* in this person even now, we have done a great deal.

Refuat Hanefesh (Healing of Spirit)

In relationship with a dying person, we always remember that healing of spirit—healing of the person, healing of the person's life—is possible until the very last breath. Not infrequently, the final stage of life offers the possibility of the healing of relationships, of guilt and regret, of isolation, of lifelong emotional or spiritual pain. This healing is available even when healing of the body is no longer possible. We need not try to convince the person to engage in this work; it is enough to know what is possible, to remember healings of spirit we have witnessed at the end of life. Embodying this sense of possibility is enough.

Perhaps this is, in part, why we continue to offer the *Mishebe-rach,* the prayer for healing, even when it appears that a healing of body is not possible. So many kinds of healing can still unfold. We pray for God to bring the most perfect healing to this person. After all, how do we know what kind of healing God may envision, even as death approaches?

Refa'ela was fifty-three years old when we met, as ovarian cancer ravaged her body. She told me that she had been a classic "type A" before cancer came into her life, a high-powered lawyer with little time for her family and friends, much less her spiritual life. It was hard to imagine this exquisite, gentle, open-hearted woman that way, but it was clear that during her valiant battle with a terrible cancer she had developed an extraordinary gift for gratitude. She found herself taking pleasure in the small blessings of her life: She loved the sunshine; she loved the rain; she loved working in her garden; she savored the taste and smell of food, knowing that someday her bowel would be blocked and she would be unable to eat. Later, when she was only able to take nutrition through her intravenous line, she asked me for a *beracha* she could recite over this strange and terrible new food that nonetheless, she knew, sustained her life.

In her last two years of life, after many years of anger and distance, Refa'ela set out to heal her relationship with Judaism. Shortly before her death, she celebrated an adult bat mitzvah, along with her twenty-year-old daughter. It was an extraordinary Shabbat morning, full of love and joy and pain.

Teshuva: Repentance/Turning/Atonement

Rabbi Eliezer taught, "Do *teshuvah* (repentance) the day before you die."[6] This Talmudic teaching, of course, is directed to those of us who believe that we have years to live, encouraging all of us to live our lives in such a way that we will be ready when death comes. So, too, this teaching is a poignant promise to those for whom death is imminent. The stories of a lifetime cannot be rewritten; not all mistakes can be remedied. But the heartfelt intention to repent can cast a person's past wrongdoings in a different light; brief words of apology from the heart can transform memories.

As chaplains, we cannot do another person's *teshuvah*, as much as we would like to. But when we encounter places of pain, we can encourage people to use the time they have to apologize, to turn, to seek forgiveness. We may offer classical understandings of the *teshuvah* process; we may encourage people to pick up the phone; occasionally, we may even tell stories of reconciliation that we have witnessed at the end of life. It is sometimes enough for us simply to hold the conviction that extraordinary moments of transformation can and do happen right up to the end.

Hopefulness

I do not believe in the cheer-up theory of pastoral care. It is not necessarily my goal to make a patient smile, for I cannot assume that a patient will feel better after my visit. I am very careful not to encourage unrealistic expectations on the level of physical healing, lest the patient and loved ones feel shattered when this hope proves unjustified. Certainly, false reassurance (e.g., "Everything will be okay") is never helpful.

But I have learned that an attitude of hopefulness is possible even in dark times, and this may mean a prayer for an unexpected shift in the course of the disease. Even when death is fast approaching, we can still sometimes find a moment to remind ourselves and others that we just don't know, that perhaps there may be some relief. Much of our pastoral visit may be spent in simply sharing moments of suffering, yet we may find the time to offer a prayer or a hope for a day freer of pain, for a beautiful visit with a loved one, for a moment of peace. Although we witness and receive the pain that people feel, we may also convey in our pastoral conversation the conviction that as long as there is life, there is hope.

> Tommy was twelve years old when we met, but he seemed more like nine. Many years of cancer treatment and hospitalization had affected his growth, and he seemed like a sweet little boy, although he brought remarkable maturity and grace to his dying process. Tommy's mother had always wanted nothing more than a loving family with lots of children. She had lost two other children, and her marriage had ended in a terrible way. The pain of watching Tommy's decline was unbearable, and yet she often knew just what to do.
>
> When Chanukah approached, Tommy asked for a new bike. Tommy's mother knew that it was unlikely that Tommy would live to see the spring when he could use that new bike, but she bought that bike for her little boy, supporting him in living with hope, just as kids are entitled to do. Later, the Make-a-Wish Foundation made it possible for Tommy and his mother to travel to Disneyland. And when death was near, she gave a big party for her son. Faced with the possibility that she would see all her loved ones together only at her son's funeral, she decided instead to have a big party—a huge, joyous celebration of Tommy's life, while there was still time.

Community

Inevitably, we die alone, in our own body, on our own solitary journey, yet, as with every phase of our life as Jews, we journey with others—with those who have gone before, those who stand with us now, those who know the same sorrow and fear. We are part of a large community (a Jewish community and a human community) that has known death, and will continue to live after our bodies are gone. As Jews, we are part of a large circle—*she'ar chole Yisrael* (All the ill of the Jewish people [as in the *Misheberach* for healing]), and *she'ar avele Zion Viyerushalayim* (All the mourners of Zion and Jerusalem [as in the greeting to mourners]).

Our very presence as Jewish chaplains at the bedside of the dying shows that they are not alone in their suffering. We are there as representatives of a community that cares about their pain and their fear. Our visits mean that this person is part of the Jewish people around the world and throughout history. Our presence serves as a reminder that this person is part of something that is stronger than death.

Appreciation of Everyday Miracles

Quite often, the reality of the nearness of death naturally awakens a powerful appreciation of the wondrousness of being alive: It seems that we most value what we know we will soon lose. Perhaps this is why dying people and their loved ones frequently grow in awareness of the "miracles that are with us, morning, noon, and night."[7]

As pastoral caregivers, we must not turn away from people's pain by encouraging them to "look at the bright side." Yet, when a person's awareness naturally turns toward gratitude, we can acknowledge the wonder. We can mirror and marvel at a person's perception of the beauty of life, even then. Serving as a witness, we help the person to feel and to claim her or his gratitude more fully. In effect, we say "Amen" to another's prayer of gratitude, and we thank God for the blessing conveyed on us when we witness such holy moments.

I remember a woman named Michelle who suffered from several degenerative chronic illnesses, including a serious lung disease that had repeatedly threatened to take her life. Michelle told me that she had lived most of her life primarily concerned with externals—beauty, wealth, and social status. With her illness, new awareness had been birthed in her. She would awaken each morning grateful to find herself alive and breathing, for the warmth of the sunshine coming through her window, for a day when she had the strength to shower. Knowing that she could die any night in her sleep, she began to live each day as if it were her last, seeking to resolve any conflicts with loved ones on the day they occurred, lest this be the last opportunity. Michelle began to notice that she was no longer alone. People wanted to be near her, blessed by the grateful awareness that now filled her life.

Afterlife

It is remarkable how many of our people have lost contact with our tradition's rich teachings on life after death. Perhaps just as remarkably, in our generation there is great hunger for this wisdom, particularly among those facing death. It is my experience that people with a strong afterlife belief usually have an easier time making their way toward the time of death. It is a very great *mitzvah* to respond to people's questions about the afterlife, or even to ask whether this is a part of a person's belief.

I find it most powerful to begin by asking the person what he or she believes about what happens to us after we die, or whether he or she has ever had an experience of contact with someone who had died. There are so many versions of Jewish afterlife belief that almost any image that a person believes in can be located in Jewish teaching. We can then tell the person that their tentatively held belief ("Is this a little crazy?") has ancient roots in Jewish thought. Learning that Judaism teaches that life continues after the grave can be a great source of comfort.[8]

The Chaplain as Advocate for Hospice Care

One of the most potent ways in which the chaplain can help the dying person and his or her family is to encourage the family to engage hospice care, preferably sooner rather than later. In a sense, much of what the chaplain offers is the spiritual component of hospice care, regardless of who is coordinating the patient's medical care. But when the chaplain can help the family overcome their resistance to hospice care, new possibilities of healing and comfort become available to the dying person and the entire family.

In many ways, hospice care epitomizes what all medical care should be, and it exemplifies the Jewish vision of healing, addressing both *refuat hanefesh* and *refuat haguf*, healing of the body and healing of the spirit. Hospice care—whether provided in a residential center or in the patient's home—addresses the possibilities of healing when the time to fight for cure has passed. With hospice care, the focus shifts from the frantic search for one more treatment to the process of reducing suffering and giving the dying person his or her best chance to live the time remaining in the richest possible way.

Hospice is care of the whole person—care of the person's body and emotions and spiritual life, care for the whole family and the person's circle of caregivers, care for the context in which the person will live the last chapter of life. Hospice care is offered by a team of care providers who talk to one another, who understand that the parts of the person are interconnected and that the best care is care that recognizes and honors those connections. Hospice is care that is loving, fierce in its determination to alleviate pain, free of ill-timed concerns about addiction or conventional doses of medication. Hospice, at its best, is care that is unafraid of death and pain, aware of the limitations of medical technology, mindful of the power of compassion, and reverent of the mysteries of life and death.

Hospice workers are frequently frustrated by the all-too-common late referral—the family that waited so long that hospice had only days to offer care to their dying loving one. Why does it take so long for families to choose hospice? And why do so many families not avail themselves of hospice care at all? Clearly, denial of death is still deeply imbedded in the American psyche; but in my experience, hospice care providers around the country acknowledge that Jewish use of hospice is even lower than the national average. What keeps Jews, in particular, from choosing hospice?

Resistance to Hospice Care: Questions of *Halacha*

Some families are concerned about halachic teachings on care for the terminally ill. Some traditional families need to turn to their own rabbi for a *pesak* (legal ruling) on the permissibility of hospice care, but frequently this question is addressed to the chaplain at the bedside. The chaplain can provide an invaluable service by helping such families to recognize that a broad consensus exists among religious authorities of all movements about the permissibility, even the desirability, of hospice care.

Without entering into complex halachic explanations, some families might respond to the evocative imagery of the following source from the twelfth-century work of ethics and theology, the *Sefer Hasidim*: "'There is a time to be born and a time to die' (Ecclesiastes 3:2). Why did *Kohelet* say this? With respect to one who is dying, a *goses*, we do not cry out on his behalf [in the hope] that his soul will return; he can at best live only a few days, and in those days he will suffer greatly. Thus it says, 'a time to die.'"[9]

Rabbi Solomon Freehof uses this source as warrant even for passive euthanasia.[10] For Freehof and other authorities, it is the sacred duty of a life-affirming tradition to recognize and to honor the moment when the time has come to die. In their view, even clearer is the case of hospice, which is not a choice to terminate treatment at all, but a choice to shift the focus of medical care from the pursuit of cure to the management of pain and the offer of comfort.

Rabbi Elliot Dorff has demonstrated that Jewish tradition grants the patient a significant degree of autonomy in choosing among several medically justifiable courses of treatment. His close reading of halachic texts finds that the patient is entitled to reject even potentially effective treatments whose risks or side effects are unbearable to a patient. In the view of the *Tosafot*, a patient may reject treatments that are not *letovato* (not to his or her benefit) as this person experiences it.[11] In the Talmud's lyrical formulation, "The heart knows its own bitterness," which cites Proverbs to assert eloquently that only the patient knows which treatments he or she can tolerate.[12]

Therefore, although the sick person may choose to undergo painful and risky treatments in the continuing hope for cure, he or she may also choose to reject such treatments as excessively painful and essentially hopeless. For Rabbi Dorff and many halachic authorities across the spectrum of Jewish life, by this reasoning "hospice care becomes not only a permissible option, but, at least in most cases, the Jewishly preferable one," because it directly addresses the unique needs of the person facing death.[13]

Resistance to Hospice: The Jewish Psyche

In my own hospice work, it has been remarkable to see how many nontraditional Jewish families, not particularly observant or literate in classical Jewish text, are convinced that Jewish law teaches that one must never give up on life. For such families, although they are correct in sensing that Jewish law is profoundly concerned with protecting life, another dynamic is at work. Why do families otherwise disconnected from the dictates of Jewish law feel so concerned about following Halacha in this matter?

Like everyone else, Jews struggle with denial, fear, grief, and uncertainty in the face of death. Yet for us, these personal feelings are also interwoven with national feelings, a passion for life that lies deep within the Jewish psyche, in our collective consciousness, shaped and reinforced throughout Jewish history.

As I indicated earlier, for many Jews, death is an enemy to be vanquished at all costs. The determination to defeat death feels like the ultimate *mitzvah*, the essence of Jewish identity. Through the history we have studied, the stories we have learned, and the spirit we have inherited, we carry within us the collective determination to survive. Perhaps Jewish law would have taught that life is the ultimate value even if our people had undergone a different journey through history. But that piece of classical teaching took on visceral meaning for our people. I think that this is why so many Jews—long since removed from Jewish ritual practice or traditional learning—feel in their core that fighting for life is quintessentially Jewish, and that to give up is a betrayal, a defeat.

Unfortunately, this collective story of survival, so essential to Jewish continuity and pride, translates imperfectly into the life of the individual Jew. Chaplains regularly see people suffering unnecessarily, unable to put their last days and weeks to good use because they feel they had no choice but to fight to the very end. I have seen people miss the chance to say good-bye, to say "I'm sorry," to say "I love you," because they did not have the help they needed to learn—not just in theory but for themselves—that just as there is a time to be born, so too, there is a time to die.

The Jewish chaplain can fulfill a pivotal role in addressing resistances to hospice care when the time has clearly come. The decision must ultimately reside with the dying person and his or her family, and we must respect the decisions that people make for themselves, but the Jewish chaplain is often the person who stands with the dying at the time when hospice care can be made available. The chaplain's ability to communicate the gifts of hospice care, to simply and clearly convey that the choice of hospice is a profoundly Jewish choice, can perform a great *mitzvah*.

What Can We Do in the Face of Death?

Paradoxically, it can be important to remind ourselves of the limits of our ability to help in the presence of death. We so wish we could reverse the person's illness, keep them alive, defeat death's power. We long to alter the terrible injustice of what is happening to this person, but we cannot. We yearn to take away a person's sadness, guilt, regret, or fear; even these we can rarely do. We cannot, after all, change the person's life story, transform their relationships, or change their characteristic way of being in the world. Even with the best of our skills and wisdom, we cannot make death beautiful, easy, or devoid of pain.

Miracles of transformation do sometimes happen at the end of life: Occasionally, a person is able to choose a fundamentally different way of being when death is near, but such miracles are rare and mysterious. We cannot and should not assume that it is in our hands to bring them about.

How, then, can we help in the face of death? What we can do? As in all pastoral care, we can bring ourselves. We can bring our own love and care, showing the dying person by our presence that their pain matters to us, that their life has made a difference. We can listen quietly, reverently, and joyfully to the stories of the person's life, the achievements and regrets, the joys and shame. We can listen to a person's thoughts and feelings about living and about dying without letting our own judgments, fears, and grief interfere. We can tolerate listening to all kinds of powerful and contradictory feelings. We can hear unspeakably painful things without wavering. We can listen to talk about death without running away or shutting down. We can help a person feel less alone. We can represent the caring of community, and of God. These are great gifts.

Our wisdom may sometimes bring a degree of comfort or

enlightenment: We may be able to facilitate encounters that lead to reconciliation, or help a person to bequeath their values to loved ones in tangible form. Occasionally, we can help a person with a piece of *teshuvah*, or help them recognize a moment of blessing along the way.

Of course, we can be the voice of Jewish tradition, conveying the sense that our people have been doing this for a long time, and that our tradition has much to offer in guiding and embracing the person, even now. For those who so desire, we can provide information about Jewish ritual. For those who have the strength and longing to know, we can share the riches of Jewish afterlife beliefs to help the person know that she or he is not heading into the void. When death is very near, we can be present for the sacred moments of the *Viddui*, a time of closure, farewell, forgiveness, and surrender into God's hands.

The Chaplain's Encounters with Death

We are so often asked, "How can you do this work? It must be so hard!" In a way, this is true. We walk amid a great deal of sadness, grief, and fear. We regularly encounter the face of injustice, and we frequently find ourselves in the midst of trauma and conflict. It is, indeed, a heavy burden to carry.

This demands a great deal of us. It calls on the best of our capacity for compassion. It requires us to be courageous and wise, generous and unwavering. It requires a complex dance of giving and limit-setting, of opening the heart and of clear boundaries. We regularly come face-to-face with our own mortality, when we find ourselves at the deathbed and the graveside.

Nevertheless, this work also gives us great gifts: We witness much holiness and beauty. We have the privilege of being invited into the most sacred and intimate moments of another's life. We encounter extraordinary acts of love and devotion, of trust and courage. Our days contain many moments of awe.

Encounters with death teach us things that could not be learned in any other way. Death can be a lesson about how fragile and precious life is, about how important it is to make the most that we can of every day. In the presence of death, we have a front-row seat on life's wonders and blessings, as well as its awesome pain. Sitting in the presence of death, we may paradoxically find beauty in the process of living and dying, discovering some measure of trust and acceptance in the way in which life unfolds.

> A close friend of mine once had the terrifying experience of facing a terminal diagnosis. During a long period of time when multiple tests were being conducted and interpreted, she sat with the possibility that her life would be cut short; then miraculously, the dire diagnosis was ruled out. She still had many health challenges ahead of her, but she knew that she would live. She told me that she had been given the double blessing of receiving the clarity and wisdom that encounters with death often provide, and the time to weave these lessons into her life.

As pastoral caregivers, we have the extraordinary privilege of stepping into the territory of dying with our own health still intact. We can learn what death has to teach and take these lessons forward, God willing, into many years of healthy living. If we are able to maintain healthy boundaries and humility, we can continue to serve others in times of great need, and to weave the blessings of awe and wisdom that death bequeaths into our own lives.

May we always be inspired to serve the Divine and God's creatures. May life nourish our capacity for compassion and for joy. May we always have what we need to continue to make ourselves a blessing to others; and may the holiness of our work be an ongoing source of blessing in our own lives.

Notes

1. A version of this chapter will appear in the forthcoming work, *The Jewish Book of Healing* (Jewish Publication Society), by Rabbi Nancy Flam and Rabbi Amy Eilberg.
2. *Ketubot* 19a.
3. Rabbi Jules Harlow, trans., *Siddur Sim Shalom* (New York: The Rabbinical Assembly, 1985).
4. *Berachot* 57b.
5. For more information on ethical wills, see Bibliography.
6. *Shabbat* 153a.
7. From the *Amidah* prayer.
8. See p. 342 in this book "Grief and Bereavement."
9. Cited in Louis Newman, *Past Imperatives* (Albany: State University of New York Press, 1998), p. 164.

10. Ibid.
11. *Tosafot* to *Avodah Zarah* 27b, cited in *Conservative Judaism* (spring 1991): p. 16.
12. Proverbs 14:10, quoted in *Yoma* 83a.
13. *Conservative Judaism* 43, no. 3 (spring 1991): p. 26.

Bibliography

Brener, Anne. *Mourning & Mitzvah: A Guided Journal for Walking the Mourner's Path Through Grief to Healing.* Woodstock, Vt.: Jewish Lights Publishing, 1993.

Gillman, Neil. *The Death of Death: Resurrection and Immortality in Jewish Thought.* Woodstock, Vt.: Jewish Lights Publishing, 1997.

Isaacs, Ron H., and Kerry M. Olitzky. *A Jewish Mourner's Handbook.* Hoboken, N.J.: KTAV, 1991.

Lamm, Maurice. *The Jewish Way in Death and Mourning.* New York: Jonathan David, 1969.

Riemer, Jack. *Jewish Reflections on Death.* New York: Schocken Books, 1974.

_____, and Nathaniel Stampfer. *So That Your Values Live On: Ethical Wills and How to Prepare Them.* Woodstock, Vt.: Jewish Lights Publishing, 1991.

_____. *Wrestling with the Angel: Jewish Insights on Death and Mourning.* New York: Schocken, 1995.

Shapiro, Rami M. *Open Hands: A Jewish Guide on Dying, Death and Bereavement.* Miami: Temple Beth Or, 1986.

_____. *Willow Baskets, Colored Glasses: A Friend's Guide to Comforting Mourners.* Miami: Temple Beth Or, 1988.

_____. *Last Breaths: A Guide to Easing Another's Dying.* Miami: Temple Beth Or, 1993.

Syme, Daniel, and Rifat Sonsino. *What Happens After I Die?: Jewish Views of Life After Death.* New York: UAHC Press, 1990.

Wolfson, Ron. *A Time to Mourn, a Time to Comfort: A Guide to Jewish Bereavement and Comfort.* New York: Federation of Jewish Men's Clubs, 1993.

Rabbi Amy Eilberg, M.S.W., was the first woman ordained by the Jewish Theological Seminary. Since ordination she has worked as a hospital and hospice chaplain, and a national leader in the Jewish Healing movement. She currently serves as a pastoral counselor in Palo Alto, California, where she also teaches and writes on Jewish spirituality and healing.

Grief and Bereavement

Simcha Paull Raphael

Dr. Simcha Paull Raphael provides unique tools and perspectives for caring for the bereaved. He synthesizes theoretical frameworks by offering a four-stage model of the grief process that links the emotional and the spiritual experience of the mourners to the rituals of Jewish mourning at the various stages of bereavement. He guides the pastoral caregiver in using the frameworks of mourning rituals in responding. Dr. Raphael also retrieves and summarizes Jewish teachings on the afterlife, demonstrating how they can be helpful spiritual resources at each stage of the grief process.

Centuries ago, whenever the great Rabbi Israel Baal Shem Tov sought divine guidance, it was his custom to go to a certain spot in the forest to meditate. He would light a fire, say a special prayer, and the wisdom he needed would be granted to him. Later, when his disciple, the celebrated Magid of Mezritch, needed to seek divine wisdom, he would go the forest and say, "Master of the Universe, listen! I do not know how to light the fire, but I am still able to say the prayer," and again the wisdom needed would be granted to him. Still later, Rabbi Moshe-Leib of Sasov, in times of dire need, would go the forest and say, "I do not know how to light the fire, I do not know the prayer, but I know the place, and this must be sufficient." It was sufficient, and his request for divine guidance was granted. The time came when Rabbi Israel of Rizhyn needed divine guidance. Sitting in his armchair, head in his hands, he spoke to God, "I am unable to light the fire, and I do not know the prayer; I cannot even find the place in the forest. All I can do is tell the story, and this must be sufficient." And it was sufficient.[1]

Since the advent of modernity, many Jewish spiritual practices have been lost through acculturation and assimilation. The efficacious secrets that Jews once used to attain wisdom and to live a spiritually inspired lifestyle have been watered down or forgotten, or have simply disappeared. This is particularly the case with regard to Jewish teachings about death and grief, which can be a precious resource both for grieving Jews and for pastoral caregivers working with them.

Less than 200 years ago in the *cheder* of Eastern Europe, young children were taught *Hilchot Avelut*, the laws of mourning, as part of the standard curriculum of study. At the same time, ideas about life after death were accepted as part and parcel of Jewish learning and liturgy. The community as a whole had an understanding of how death rituals functioned during times of loss, as well as of a spiritual framework that provided meaning when they were confronted with death and loss. As a result, there was little need for social workers, psychologists, pastoral counselors, and chaplains to help individuals and families deal with grief and with the existential and spiritual crises precipitated by death.

By contrast, in the contemporary Jewish community, adults and children frequently have little knowledge of Jewish rituals of dying, death, and mourning. They know to bring food to a *shiva* house, to stand when saying the words of the mourner's *Kaddish,* to light a *yahrzeit* candle on the anniversary of a death, and to go to synagogue, perhaps only on Yom Kippur, for a *yizkor* service. However, as a result of secularization and assimilation, all too often absent from the Jewish knowledge of most Jews are the specifics of Jewish death rituals, the deeper psychological and spiritual wisdom inherent in mourning observances, and Jewish teachings about life after death. As a consequence, the spiritual malaise commonly engendered by the death of a loved one sends mourners scrambling to find meaning in other traditions, or to psychologically oriented grief workshops. If the fire has been extinguished and the words of the prayers forgotten, it is little wonder that faced with an encounter with death and grief, many Jews walk around lost, looking for a place outside of Jewish communal life to do their grief work and spiritual seeking.

Nonetheless, wise and profound Jewish resources for dealing with death and grief do exist. It is the role of the pastoral caregiver to help connect Jews in mourning with the legacy of available Jewish resources.

The classical Jewish phases of the mourning process—*aninut,* funeral, *shiva, sheloshim, Kaddish, yahrzeit,* and *yizkor*[2]—and the ritual practices associated with these phases constitute a complete psychosocial system for dealing with bereavement. Long before Sigmund Freud, Judaism created a community-based approach for the healing of grief. These practices were first developed during the rabbinic era and reached classical form during the medieval period when Jews were confronted with the traumatic deaths of the Crusades and the Black Plague.[3] These seven phases are designed to take mourners through the stages of grief—from the initial, shocking encounter with death through the difficult phases of deep sorrow and mourning to the healing and renewal of a grief resolved.

In spite of the often-presumed point of view that Judaism believes in "life and the living, the here and not the hereafter," Judaism has an extensive belief in the survival of the soul after death.[4] Normative and mystical Jewish teachings about the journey of the soul after death can provide spiritual comfort and meaning to mourners wrestling with loss.

However, to heal grief, it is not enough to expound what traditional Jewish sources have to say about mourning and the afterlife. Such teachings were created in a time and a cultural context different than ours, thus classical knowledge alone may be a helpful but insufficient resource for mourners. To make the wellspring of Jewish teachings available to individuals and families in grief, the pastoral caregiver must reframe them in a context appropriate for Jewish life in the twenty-first century.

Prompted by the pioneering work of Elisabeth Kübler-Ross, profound changes have taken place in cultural attitudes toward the dying and bereaved.[5] Since the late 1960s, many scholarly studies and self-help manuals on death and bereavement have been published, resulting in a much broader popular understanding of death and grief, and an impressive array of resources, tools, and methodologies that can be used for grief care. The Jewish approach to pastoral care for the bereaved draws on current developments in this burgeoning field and uses emerging perspectives on death and mourning to translate the rich legacy of the Jewish past into a viable pastoral psychology of grief.

The late Rav Kook taught that "the old will be made new, and the new will be made holy."[6] In that spirit, this chapter presents a contemporary pastoral model of the stages of the grief journey. This model integrates an understanding of the psychospiritual function of Jewish death rituals with Jewish concepts about the afterlife survival of the soul. Drawing from professional case work, this chapter also presents guidelines for pastoral care professionals and paraprofessionals who walk with others the ever-changing and mysterious grief journey, the slow and arduous trek from the valley of the shadow of death to the mountaintop of healing, renewal, and community reintegration.

The Grief Journey: A Fourfold Model

Psychological and pastoral models have been developed to describe the grief experience, and to explain how grief changes over time.[7] Knowledge of the specific phases of grief is helpful to understand the psychodynamics of this process and to determine the kind of pastoral support needed at each stage of the journey. The four-stage model that follows, adapted from the works of William Worden,[8] Michelle Goodman,[9] and Howard Clinebell,[10] is useful as both a descriptive and a prescriptive framework for understanding the dynamics of the grief process.

In the encounter with grief, individuals frequently experience the following stages,[11] which correspond approximately to the cycle of Jewish mourning rituals:

Phase One: The Initial Shock and Denial

- *Aninut*
- Funeral
- *Shiva*
- *Sheloshim*

Phase Two: Facing the Painful Truth

- *Shiva*
- *Sheloshim*
- *Kaddish*

Phase Three: Putting the Pieces Together

- *Kaddish*
- *Yahrzeit*

Phase Four: Affirming Life and Legacy

- *Yahrzeit*
- *Yizkor*

Phase One: The Initial Shock and Denial

Psychological Dimensions

During the first phase of the grief journey, which occurs immediately after receiving the news of a death, mourners are often numb, in a seemingly unreal, foglike state of shock. It is as if the psyche allows people to adjust gradually to the reality of the loss. Many mourners have described enduring the whole ordeal of preparing for a funeral, dealing with all the minute details, and even making it through a week of *shiva* before the full impact of death sets in. One father described it as follows:

> I was called in the middle of the night with the news that my son had been killed in a car accident. I just moved into gear: the police, the morgue, the funeral, and making arrangements for our daughter to return home from Israel. I remember feeling in control of everything, in shock, numb. Only weeks after the *shiva* did I begin to realize the full impact of what I had just been through.

This first stage of the grief journey corresponds, in part, with the phase of *aninut*—the short period of time between the first news of a death and the funeral. It is a time of hyperacute grief, when the bereaved are still in shock and must first and foremost deal with preparing for the funeral. For the pastoral caregiver, it is important to realize that regardless of whether the bereaved exhibit numbing shock or overt catharsis of grief, in this early phase they are often in coping mode and not yet able to fully enter into deeper emotional experiences of mourning, which will come later.

In this phase of the grief journey, the central task for the bereaved is to accept the reality of death. The main function of pastoral care and ritual practices at this stage is to make death real in their lives with honest, gentle, and compassionate caring. It is common to hear them speak of the deceased in present tense: "He is such a wonderful father"; or to speak of oneself as a "we": "We were so happy together." This is a clear indication that the full impact of death has not yet hit. This is a normal response, so much so that Jewish tradition prohibits one from attempting to console a person in *aninut*,[12] as if to say, "How can one attempt to take away such pain, when their beloved one is lying dead before their eyes?"

One of the first rituals performed by mourners is *keriah*, the rending of a garment of clothing. Today, this often done just before the funeral, and the modern Jewish funeral custom has transformed the practice of literally ripping one's clothing into a more "proper" symbolic act of wearing a black ribbon.

> A young woman reported that at her father's funeral, the funeral director pinned a black button and ribbon on her dress collar and had her recite a blessing by rote. But the meaning of the ritual and the prayer were never explained to her, thus she was unable to take advantage of the psychoemotional function of this ritual act.

Wearing a symbolic *keriah* ribbon is an option today—but this is not at all how *keriah* was traditionally designed to function as a mourning practice. From a psychological vantage point, it is vital to help mourners understand that this ritual is not just a symbolic act but a visceral one. There is a gut level reality to death when a mourner literally rips clothing they are wearing on their body, as if to say, "I am torn apart by this death, and I express my grief and pain in this act of ripping my clothing!" *Keriah* is an embodied ritual act that functions to help make death real, both to the mourners and to those around them.

The Jewish funeral is another ritual that takes place during this early phase of the grief journey. The pinnacle of the Jewish funeral, the act of shoveling earth on a coffin, is likewise a ritual act designed to declare with no reservations the finality of death. Death has a bodily essential quality to it when one hears the sound of earth striking a coffin. As one mourner noted:

> When my father died I recall being in a stupor for days; but then at the cemetery, at the first sound of the earth hitting the box, I was jolted into an undeniable sense of reality that he was dead. I had a vision of seeing every clump of earth that had ever hit the coffin of a Jewish man being buried. At that moment, I felt myself an orphaned son, aligned with every other Jewish child who had ever buried his father. As I look back, I see that the fog began to lift and that was the moment at which I knew that my father had died.

Given the potency of this ritual, it is good pastoral care to encourage all primary mourners to participate in the act of shoveling earth on a grave. For the sake of convenience, cemetery workers sometimes like for everyone to leave the graveside quickly so that the grave can be covered back up using a backhoe, but burial of the dead is a communal ritual, and it is important to notify cemetery and funeral home staff that mourners and their friends and family will be invited to participate in the act of covering the casket with earth. Filling the grave can be cathartic and healing.

In a similar way, the act of sitting *shiva* is also designed to help the bereaved accept the reality of death. During the first days of *shiva*, particularly when there is a sudden tragic death, mourners are still in a state of shock. Even though death and burial have taken place, the full emotional impact has not yet set in. However, when visitors come day in and day out to honor a person who has died, and when mourners' prayers are recited in a *shiva* home, the irrevocable nature of death begins to dawn. Slowly but surely, mourners begin to sense that they are no longer going to see their loved one again in physical form.

To help mourners move toward a fuller acceptance of death, it is important for pastoral caregivers to be aware of language used in conversations with the bereaved during *shiva*. Our culture as a whole tends to use polite euphemisms that soften death. People don't die: They expire, depart, pass away, pass on; one loses someone. Visitors in a *shiva* house may respond to their own discomfort by steering the conversation toward mundane topics and away from the death, and yet, a gentle but realistic, questioning approach can help the bereaved talk openly about the impact of death. It is helpful and healing to say: "Tell me about your mother." "What were the circumstances of your father's death?" "Was this death a surprise to you?" "What was it like as your mother spent her last days fighting cancer?" Doing so will communicate openness toward death and a willingness to listen to what mourners have to say. Listen! Mourners do have a great deal to say.

Mourners need to speak about the illness, accident, or tragedy that ended the life of their loved one. They also have a deep desire to reminisce and to talk about the person who has died. A pastoral caregiver can actively encourage those sitting *shiva* to have photographs on display, to tell family stories about distant relatives and ancestors, and to talk about and to invite others to share remembrances of the life of the person who has died. This kind of conscious remembering allows mourners to achieve the tasks of the earliest phase of the grief journey, to allow the reality of death to sink in, so that the mourning can proceed.

By example and by teaching, the pastoral caregiver can help community members stay focused on the tasks of *shiva*—to honor the memory of the person who died and to offer consolation for the bereaved. Above all, it is important to help both mourners and community members understand that *shiva* is more than just a catered party with a lot of food. Both the Jewish funeral and the experience of sitting *shiva*, which take place during the first phase of the grief journey, have great psychological efficacy in the healing of grief.

Spiritual Dimensions

In the early phase of the grief journey, an understanding of Jewish teachings on life after death can help inform the approach of pastoral caregivers. According to Jewish tradition, immediately after a death it is said that the soul of the deceased may be potentially confused, unaware whether it is still alive or departed from the world. This phase of the postmortem journey is called *chibbut hakever*, "the pangs of the grave," and is described in Jewish sources as a process of three to seven days of the gradual separation of the soul from the body.[13] During this phase, the disembodied being undergoes a process of purification that enables it to give up attachments to the physical realm. For those beings who are attached to physical existence and materiality, the process of separation can be painful. The disembodied soul, according to the Zohar, "wanders about the world and beholds the body [that] was once its home devoured by worms and suffering the judgment of the grave [*chibbut hakever*]."[14] On the other hand, for those beings who have cultivated a sense of spiritual awareness in their lives, leaving behind the body and material existence may be effortless, less painful, "like drawing a hair out of milk."[15]

Mourners in the state of *aninut* before a funeral are often confused, uncertain of how to contain or to focus their own grief. In some cases, especially if caregivers have an inclination to reflect on ideas about the survival of the soul after death, letting mourners know what Judaism has to say about afterlife can be therapeutic.

One rabbi reported having the following conversation with a grieving congregant the night before a funeral:

Michelle had been inconsolably distressed as she and her brother were making arrangements for her father's funeral. She had been out of town when her father died and had not had an opportunity to say her last good-byes to him. After her brother left, I sat with her a while longer and said to her, "Our tradition suggests that immediately after a death, a soul may be in close connection with loved ones in this world. I imagine that in your heart and mind is an incomplete conversation with your dad. After you leave here, I suggest you go home, light a candle, and sit quietly, imagining tuning into your father's soul, wherever he may be now. Have a conversation with him, let him know how you are feeling, continue the unfinished symphony of the love you shared together as father and daughter." Michelle reported later that taking time the night before the funeral to be with her father's soul had been an important experience. She felt that she was able to reach a new level of healing in their relationship that had not been possible while he was alive.

Immediately before or right after a person's death, a sense of contact with the deceased being is not at all uncommon. Many people have reported having had a dream or an apparition near the time of a person's death, and that they have often experienced it as a sense of closure or completion. We find one such anecdote in the folk literature of Chasidism:

> Rabbi Jacob Samson of Spitkova, who resided in the Holy Land, had a very powerful dream vision. He saw the *Shechina*, God's Divine Presence, in the form of a woman in lamentation. He sensed that her lamentation was for a friend of her youth who had died. He immediately awoke, and cried out with grief: "Reb Pinchas of Koretz has died." And so it was at that moment, on the continent of Europe, Reb Pinchas of Koretz had breathed his last.[16]

This kind of phenomenon happens not only to great rebbes but is widely reported, as the following anecdote shows:

> Eddie was a young adult who had been drawn to countercultural activities quite foreign to his father, a Holocaust survivor. Eddie had not seen his father in many months and was at a gathering at a wilderness site, completely cut off from the outside world. One

evening while sitting in a sweat lodge singing and chanting, he suddenly began singing the *niggunim* (wordless melodies) that he had learned from his father on Shabbat afternoons as a young child. He was possessed by these chants and for hours could not stop singing them. He felt his father's presence with him and experienced a deep exchange of love between them. Almost a week later, when he returned and contacted his family, he was told that his father had died and it had been exactly at the time he had been chanting *niggunim* in the sweat lodge. He had missed his father's funeral and almost the entire week of *shiva,* but the feelings of deep connection with his father had a profound impact on his grief and allowed him to accept his father's death with a sense of spiritual equanimity.

It is important for pastoral caregivers to help mourners talk openly about such experiences, particularly because contemporary society denies the reality of postmortem contact, causing them to be exceptionally reluctant to talk about such occurrences. A simple question such as: "Have you ever had a sense of connection with your father [mother/husband/wife] since they died?" can open the door for people to talk deeply about their grief and their relationship with the deceased, which includes a sense of contact with the person's spirit. A mourner may tell a pastoral caregiver: "I saw or felt my brother's presence standing by my bed at night. Am I going crazy?" The best response is: "Our tradition suggests that these kinds of experiences do occur. I'm interested in how you make sense of your experience." Although that phenomenon does occur, it need not be the central element to focus on in offering pastoral care. In counseling the bereaved, it is helpful to explore how an experience of postmortem contact affects a mourner's spiritual beliefs and ongoing process of grief.

Another context in which afterlife beliefs come into play is at the funeral. From a psychological and communal point of view, the goal of the Jewish funeral is to honor and to remember the life of the deceased and to provide mourners with communal support and an opportunity to grieve. But afterlife teachings about *chibbut hakever* suggest another dimension to the Jewish funeral. It is a time of helping the soul leave behind the physical world. In this way, a funeral might be thought of as a "soul-guiding" ritual.[17] Such a perspective can transform how mourners experience the time of burial, as illustrated by the following recollections of this young man of his grandmother:

> At Bubbe Jenny's funeral, I knew in my heart that she was watching us. She always loved people and would have delighted in seeing so many of us gathered together. In my eulogy, I spoke about her long life and her impact on the people who had known her. I then said to those gathered, "We all have memories of Bubbe Jenny, a picture in our mind of her speaking, laughing, telling a story: Take a moment and let a memory or an image of her come to mind." I paused, then continued, "Our Jewish tradition suggests that right now she may be somewhere in an afterlife, a realm we do not know very much about; but let us hold that picture or memory of her in our minds, and let us all send her love as she commences her journey in the afterlife." I then stopped speaking and we spent a moment in silence—it was very powerful. I had the sense we were giving Bubbe Jenny a grand send-off to the other world.

Silence is a powerful tool that can allow for a sense of connection between the world of the living and the world beyond. It needs to be used more frequently at Jewish funerals, and especially during the *shiva*.

Shiva is another time when ideas about the afterlife can help mourners in the grief journey. A simple and useful liturgical intervention is to include a few moments of silence at the beginning or end of any *minyan* during *shiva*. It is important for the silent time to be framed as an opportunity for mourners and all present to commune in their heart and mind with the deceased person. Many people may be suspicious about ideas of life after death, thus one can introduce a moment or two of silence in a subtle way, by saying, for example: "Here is a chance for each of us present to engage in a silent conversation of heart and mind with [the name of the person who has died] and to imagine their incomplete conversation with us." Again, the intention is neither to force a belief in afterlife on mourners nor to assume that in a silent moment a spirit will appear to everyone present. The aim instead is to communicate the concepts that human consciousness survives bodily death and that communion between the world of the living and the world of the dead is possible. Allowing for silence and for connection with the soul of the deceased helps mourners accept the reality of death and move on with their grief journey.

Phase Two: Facing the Painful Truth

Psychological Dimensions

In the second phase the numbness of shock wears off and the process of mourning enters a more intense period. Forced to live life without a beloved family member or friend, mourners begin to feel anguish, despair, intense sadness, or all of these. As the reality of death becomes increasingly apparent, mourners are often burdened with confusing and conflicting emotional and physical reactions. Tears, depression, physical exhaustion, insomnia, anger, and guilt are all very common reactions to grief. The central task of this stage is to experience fully the pain of grief, as difficult as it may be. The bereaved do not need advice at this time; they need someone who can listen to what they are experiencing, without judgment or denial of the pain.

This phase might begin during the first week of *shiva*, but it intensifies over the coming weeks and months. During the *shiva*, it is important to allow mourners to experience their emotions, no matter how intense they are. When a family member begins to cry, others may feel uncomfortable. The following anecdote suggests how a caregiver can intervene in a positive way with a family when there is a discomfort with overt expression of grief:

> A young woman whose mother had died was weeping uncontrollably one afternoon during *shiva*. Trying to be helpful, her aunt said, "Don't cry, Judy, your mother would want you to be strong!" The rabbi overheard this comment and intervened, saying, "I didn't know your mother very well, Judy, but I sense that your tears are tears of sadness and of love. In a *shiva* house, both laughter and tears can be healing." Turning to the aunt, he said, "Tell me a story of how you remember Judy's mother." The woman was silent for a moment but then her eyes began filling up with tears as she told the story of the first time she met the woman who was to become her sister-in-law and friend for many years. In this way, both daughter and aunt were given ways to express their grief.

In the weeks after *shiva*, the support that the bereaved receive from friends and family begins to dissipate, and after the intensity of *shiva*, there is a slow return to the ongoing demands of life. Children go back to school, neighbors and friends become absorbed in their own lives, and the bereaved begin to feel increasingly alone, and often bewildered, not sure what steps are needed to cope with this loss. The painful truth that must be faced during this time is that one's love will not return. Life has been forever transformed.

In Jewish tradition, the thirty-day period, *sheloshim*, is a time of gradual readjustment. It is helpful to recognize *sheloshim* as a time of transition marking the shift from "initial shock and denial" (Phase One) to "facing the painful truth" (Phase Two).

As the first month passes, shock dissipates, and the emotional intensity of grief is heightened. Frequently, mourners have a much more difficult time emotionally during the six to eight weeks after a death than during the first week or two immediately after *shiva*. This point is essential for pastoral caregivers to remember. To be helpful, continue to be present for mourners after *shiva* and *sheloshim*. Do not say, "Call me if you need me!" because people usually will not respond to such an offer. This phase of the grief journey is at times so painful and overwhelming that people do not have the energy or self-esteem to reach out for help. Mourners need a caregiver who cares enough to reach out to them, who can stay with them in their pain and grief without trying to make the pain go away. They need gentle acceptance, a compassionate heart, and a good listening ear.

During the long stretch of time during the middle of the first year after a death, grief is often most intense. This period corresponds with the phase of the Jewish ritual cycle of saying *Kaddish*. However, in today's Jewish community many are uninvolved in synagogue life and do not recite *Kaddish,* especially as a three-times-a-day practice. Nonetheless, the grief journey does intensify, and it is common for mourners to experience a time of increased emotional pain, anguish, and grief. It is not unrealistic to assume that individuals and families may have the most difficult time between four to eight months after a death.

The type and the intensity of grief reaction varies from person to person and often depends on the circumstances of the death. It is essential for caregivers to help mourners understand that what they are experiencing is natural. In fact, even the standard reference book of modern psychiatry, The American Psychiatric Association's *Diagnostic and Statistical Manual of Mental Disorders*, fourth edition (DSM-IV), has created a mental health classification called Bereavement Reaction[18] (understood to refer to normal bereavement), which suggests that, given the emotional challenges of grief, the seemingly abnormal reactions one experiences in bereavement are quite normal. During the first year of mourning, it is natural to experience sadness, anger, depression, lack of energy, or physical ailments. The bereaved also often have great difficulty simply coping with the demands of daily life. These are all predictable responses to the loss of a loved one. It is critical for caregivers to encourage an acceptance of the emotions and to help mourners understand that bereavement is a process that intensifies as healing proceeds, eventually subsiding during the journey toward acceptance and resolution. Caregivers can say to someone in grief: "What you are experiencing is a normal part of the grief journey. You are not crazy! This pain is an essential dimension of the healing process."

Pastoral caregivers need to be aware of the differences between normal and pathological grief responses. If intense and unrelenting grief continues for longer than two years after a death, or if a person is chronically numb and the mourning process is delayed or inhibited, it is likely that the response is pathological. The concept of grief as a process is central here. Is the mourner going through a process that is changing, or is he or she fixated in one place? Mourning is problematic when any of the following symptoms persist after a considerable period of time: a lack of acceptance of the death, an avoidance of experiencing the pain of grief, a resistance to continuing on with daily living, an unwillingness to be comforted by others, a lack of desire to form new relationships, and a continued sense of spiritual despair and anger at God. In such cases, referral to a professional psychologist or grief counselor is in order.

The task of this second stage is to fully experience the pain of grief, thus there are certain counseling techniques that enable mourners to move toward resolution. First, it is essential to allow the bereaved to tell their stories—over and over again, if necessary. Mourners often have a desperate need to talk about the person who has died, particularly a few months after the death when others around them seem to have forgotten their grief. Pastoral caregivers should encourage them to talk about the person they are mourning, to tell tales of her or his life, and to talk about the circumstances of death. Mourners may be experiencing conflicting emotions, and it is important to give them permission to speak whatever is on their heart and mind. As long as a person needs to talk, encourage them to do so. The morning *minyan*, often followed by conversation over coffee and bagels, is a successful ritual event in Jewish life because it enables mourners to exchange stories about the person who has died and their process of coping with grief and loss. This principle can be applied directly to pastoral counseling of the bereaved with this simple question: "What do you want to tell me today about your wife [father/mother/brother]?" There is always more to be told. This is how grief moves toward resolution.

In the months (and sometimes years) after a death, it is common for mourners to find themselves having subtle but ongoing conversations in their hearts and minds with a loved one who has died: This is how the psyche works toward completion and closure in a relationship ended by physical death. Frequently, whether alone or with others, mourners may be thinking about and conversing with their loved one. How can a pastoral caregiver help mourners externalize conversations of the heart in ways that facilitate the healing of grief?

One useful technique used in counseling the bereaved is the "chair dialogue." Adapted from Gestalt psychology, this technique consists of the bereaved person imagining a parent, spouse, or sibling who has died sitting in a chair opposite her or him, with the caregiver facilitating a conversation between the bereaved and the deceased.

> After her husband's sudden and violent death, Ellen wrestled for many months with the intensity of her feelings. Using the chair dialogue, she screamed and railed at her husband because he had left without saying good-bye, but she continued to be very depressed about her life, unable to move on from the grief.
>
> One day, after expressing a great deal of pent-up rage, her counselor asked, "Can you tell your husband about the hurt behind the anger?" Suddenly, she began to sob uncontrollably, contacting a deep sadness and longing underneath all the rage. Using the chair dialogue, she was able to speak about how much she missed the shared communication with her husband, how lonely

she was without him, and how afraid she was going forward and rebuilding her life. Having these conversations helped Ellen reach a place of deep love in her heart for her husband and an increasing ability to forgive him for leaving without warning.

A pastoral caregiver might say to a widow, "If your husband were here today, what would you want to say to him?" To enhance this imagined encounter, the pastoral caregiver might also ask, "If I were to be in the presence of your spouse sitting in that chair, what would I see? What would he look like—his posture, his physical features?" In this way, a mourner can use the imagination to visualize a deceased loved one before their eyes. Emotions and imagination are closely linked, thus developing an imagined sense of the person in doing this exercise allows the mourner to release the many of the feelings that are bottled up inside.

What is apparent at this stage of the grief journey is that people typically have conflicting emotions toward the person who has died. Love and hate, ambivalence and guilt are key to the grieving experience. The conversation between mourner and deceased loved one might be something like: "I love you, but I hate you because you abandoned me (or you were a smoker and would have lived longer if you had taken care of your health)." Or, "I want to mourn your death but I am numb because I keep blaming myself for not getting you to a doctor on time."

It is important for pastoral caregivers to help mourners identify and sort out the conflicted emotions by saying, for example: "Speak to your mother as the daughter who loved her." After allowing that conversation to come to a conclusion ("Is there any more you need to say right now as the loving daughter?"), invite her to speak to her mother as the angry, rebellious daughter. It is possible to move back and forth, to hear both sides of the conflict. Another example is to say: "Speak to your father and share with him your guilty feelings, then tell him about the feelings of loss and longing you have had buried away inside." These kinds of conversations can go on for months, reflecting the changing nature of grief.

Spiritual Dimensions

During this second phase of mourning, ideas about life after death can enhance a caregiver's work with the bereaved. This period of the bereavement journey, characterized by a deep intensification of emotions, corresponds with saying *Kaddish* and with the second stage of the afterlife journey, when the soul of the deceased is said to be in a state of purgation known as *Gehenna*, or *Gehinnom*.[19]

Traditionally, within the rabbinic worldview, *Gehenna* is an abode of punishment for those who have not lived in accordance with the ways of God and Torah.[20] Although many horrific torments await the wicked in *Gehenna*, rabbinic literature teaches that it is a realm of purification, in most cases lasting a maximum of twelve months.[21] According to the kabbalists, *Gehenna* is understood not only in moral and ethical terms, but also in more of a psychological and psychospiritual sense. *Gehenna* is regarded as a process in which any incomplete or unresolved emotional dimensions of life experience are cleansed and transformed.[22]

Like the Rabbis, the kabbalists affirmed that punishment in *Gehenna* was to be endured for a maximum of twelve months, which, interestingly, corresponds with the time of saying *Kaddish*.[23] Traditionally, Judaism has taught that the act of saying *Kaddish* enables the soul of the deceased to be redeemed from the purgations of *Gehenna*. This point is expressed in the following Midrash:

> Rabbi Akiva once saw in a vision the shadowy figure of a man carrying a load of wood upon his shoulders. "What ails you?" asked the rabbi. "I am one of those forlorn souls condemned for his sins to the agony of hellfire," replied the shadow. "And there is no hope for you?" inquired the rabbi further in great compassion. "If my little son, who was a mere infant when I died, could be taught to recite the *Kaddish*, then and only then would I be absolved." The rabbi took the boy under his care and taught him to recite the *Kaddish*. He was then assured that the father had been released from *Gehenna*.[24]

What does it mean for us today to think about how a mourner can redeem a soul from the purgations of *Gehenna*? Our post-Enlightenment mentality tends to reject any notion of postmortem torment, as well as the belief that prayers can affect the fate of the soul in the hereafter.

It is essential to understand this story beyond its narrow, literal sense. What we glean from this tale is the idea that after death *there continues to be a spiritual connection between the mourner and the soul of the person who has died,* between the living and the dead. During the often gut-wrenching process of grief, the mourner and the soul of a beloved parent, sibling, spouse, or friend are in an interactive relationship working to transform unresolved feelings of anger, rage, resentment, guilt, sadness, and longing into a deeper sense of love, peace, and forgiveness. One of the primary goals of pastoral bereavement counseling is to help facilitate this process for the mourner.

There are a number of methods that can help the mourner in this process. The act of saying *Kaddish* can be a powerful way of deepening one's internal conversation with the soul of a deceased loved one. On a psychological level, saying *Kaddish* is a way to remember the deceased with respect and reverence, and it facilitates a gradual acceptance of death and loss. On a spiritual level, saying *Kaddish* mediates the ongoing relationship between the bereaved and the soul of the person who has died. It is a way of continuing the healing and "finishing old business"[25] between the living and the dead.

Therefore, a pastoral counselor might explore with mourners what happens in their heart and mind while reciting *Kaddish* in a *minyan*. One of the psychospiritual functions of *Kaddish* is to help mourners experience the fullness of their grief; thus one can suggest that mourners use the time before and after saying *Kaddish* to focus on their relationship with the deceased and to imagine their ongoing dialogue with each other. This act of focusing will enable mourners to continue the process of resolution with the person who has died.

In addition, the chair dialogue method can be used to evoke the continuing conversation between a mourner and a deceased loved one, as in the following case:

Marian was an only child whose father had died when she was quite young. She and her mother had an exceptionally close, although conflicted, relationship. When her mother died after three years in a nursing home, Marian was wracked with guilt and remorse. She felt she had been cruel to her mother because she had been angry at how much of her life she had had to give up to care for her. At the same time, she missed her mother a great deal. One day while talking about her mother, Marian suddenly had a sense of her mother's presence in the room. Using the chair dialogue, she was able to imagine asking her mother for forgiveness for the way she had been impatient with her. In response, she felt that her mother was saying to her, "Sure, I forgive you, *Maideleh*" (the term of endearment her mother had used for her as a child). This conversation and sense of soul contact were very helpful for moving Marian along in her grief.

One additional technique for counseling the bereaved is to use a photograph of the deceased person to enable the ongoing conversation to unfold. Looking at the photograph will elicit deep memories and feelings in a mourner and may also be a catalyst for evoking the ongoing relationship between this world and the world of the dead.

A bereaved person might ask, "Do you think my father really hears what I have to say?" A pastoral caregiver might answer by saying, "According to Jewish tradition there is certainly a sense that even after death the interconnection between the living and the dead continues." This reply allows a mourner to continue the process of wrestling with the relationship with the person who has died and with their evolving sense of spiritual views of life after death.

At this stage of the journey, the main task for the caregiver is to help the grieving express the various dimensions of their bereavement reactions, as difficult as they may be. Doing so makes it possible for mourners to move on with life and to be increasingly unencumbered by grief.

Phase Three: Putting the Pieces Together
Psychological Dimensions

In the third phase of the grief journey, the bereaved continue to sort through their feelings and thoughts, and slowly adapt to life without the deceased. Although the pain of loss and the memories of a loved one persist, the mourner is increasingly able to find ways to affirm that life goes on. The goal for the mourner during this phase of bereavement is to learn to adjust to an environment in which the deceased is missing. It is a time for restructuring one's life, both functionally and emotionally.

If the previous phase of the bereavement process was marked by an intensification of emotional pain, this third phase is characterized by intermittent periods of grief. The emotional anguish of loss does not dissipate suddenly; rather, it cycles in and out. The pain of yearning may leave momentarily, perhaps even for days at a time. Periods of intense sadness, loneliness, and anger are punctuated by intervals of rest, but predictably, grief returns with greater intensity. "Putting the pieces together" is a slow and arduous process that requires wisdom and patience on the part of caregiver and bereaved alike.

This third phase of the grief journey frequently corresponds to the second half of the period of saying of *Kaddish* and is often marked by an unveiling or, sometimes, the first *yahrzeit*. Although everyone's experience of grief is unique, one of the main issues that mourners deal with at this time is learning to function without the deceased and that life will never return to the way it once was. A new life of "normal functioning" must be established, without the deceased. The bereaved learn to reorganize their daily routine and to acquire new skills, both social and functional: A young widow learns to raise children alone, a family adjusts to not having a cherished elderly grandmother to connect grown children and their families, and children cope with living without a parent. All of this can be difficult, but with the passing of time the necessary adaptive skills are learned.

From a pastoral point of view, it is especially important to help the bereaved prepare in new ways for the celebration of Jewish holy days, or even a secular day of celebration like Thanksgiving. If the deceased person was central in bringing together family members for a Seder, or a Yom Tov meal, mourners may feel that a tradition has been broken by death and be reluctant to have such a gathering without their loved one. To help families observe these traditions without the person who has died, it is important to encourage them to plan ahead and to find ways of acknowledging the absence of the deceased loved one as they celebrate.

One family found it comforting to leave an empty chair at the Seder table in honor of a deceased grandfather, and they invited everyone present to share their beloved memories of him. Another family set up a table with Yom Tov and *yahrzeit* candles surrounded by photos and mementos of a deceased mother to acknowledge the important role she continued to play in her family's thoughts and emotions.

Similarly, birthdays, anniversaries, and dates of personal significance that mourners shared with a deceased loved one can be exceptionally difficult during the first year after a death. It is helpful to warn mourners to anticipate that these occasions might be times of intensified sadness. Reaching out to friends or family members, planning to spend part of a day with others, as well as part of it alone to acknowledge their mourning, are ways in which mourners can allow the process of grief to unfold in a healthy way.

Another challenge during the grief journey is for mourners to integrate what they have learned from the person who has died, claiming those skills, resources, and gifts that are worthwhile, and letting go of those attributes and characteristics that may be less than wholesome and healthy. Children learn both good and bad habits from parents, and after a parent dies, they sometimes feel a sense of freedom and an unbinding of psychic patterns. A pastoral caregiver can help mourners wrestle with the legacy that a deceased loved one left behind.

A helpful way of thinking about this part of the grief journey is through Rabbi Zalman Schachter-Shalomi's concept of "*Kaddish* College." Reb Zalman describes *Kaddish* as a psychospiritual process during which one works toward deep resolution with a parent or another who has died. He tells about a conversation that he had with his deceased father:

> After my father died, I was driving from Boulder back to Winnipeg, where I was living at the time. In those years I drove a truck, and as I was getting on the highway someone cut me off. I rolled down the window and let out a string of curses–Polish, Yiddish—every obscenity in my vocabulary. As I did that I could hear the echoing of my father's voice. It was exactly as he would curse and swear while driving at the wheel. Shaken up, I stopped the truck, and said aloud, "Papa, this is one of yours! This one you can have back." I realized that I was just beginning to sort out my *yerishah*, my inheritance from Papa. In saying that to him it dawned on me that I could now claim as my own what his legacy was to me, keep all the good stuff I had been given, and reject what was his, not mine, and no longer useful in my life.[26]

Pastoral caregivers can help mourners extract from the mourning experience the gifts they have been given from the person who has died. Doing so helps them move forward in the grief process.

Spiritual Dimensions

As mourners work through this third stage of the bereavement journey, there is a subtle but observable shift of perspective. Issues of existential and spiritual meaning move increasingly into the foreground. The pain of grief does not necessarily disappear, but it can recede into the background of awareness. Frequently, this third phase of the mourning cycle can be characterized as a time of contemplation, a season of life in which mourners look closely at the things that are important to them. Questions about the meaning of life, death, suffering, and their understanding of God begin to emerge.

Timing is of utmost importance in pastoral interventions involving exploration of theological questions. In the early phases of bereavement, when mourners are still in shock dealing with the chaotic ever-changing emotions of grief, they do not have the psychic energy available to wrestle with questions of spirituality and meaning. Bringing up theological conversations about God, religion, and the hereafter when they are trying to arrange carpools and settling legal matters of estates and wills is inappropriate, at best, and "bad theology" at worst. The following tale from Zen tradition makes this point quite clearly:

> A famous Zen master had died. One of his students, a young monk, was grief-stricken, crying inconsolably. His friend, another young monk, came up to him and said, "Why are you crying? We have learned so much about impermanence, about death not being finite. Why are you crying?" With clarity, the other monk looked at him and replied, "I am crying because I am sad, you fool!"[27]

Pastoral grief work sometimes requires simply knowing when to share the bereaved one's sadness, holding a mourner's hand and allowing her or him to be in touch with the longing of a hurting heart. However, as the emotional intensity recedes, the mind of the mourner yearns to understand about God, spirits, life after death, and other matters of ultimate concern. Pastoral caregivers can speak about what Jewish spirituality has to say about these topics, and invite mourners to share their own reflections and concerns. Given many contemporary Jews' lack of awareness of Jewish spiritual resources, pastoral caregivers may actively need to point a questing mourner toward Jewish approaches to meditation, mysticism, and other spiritual practices. A spiritual perspective helps mourners transform the experience of bereavement from mourning to meaning, from longing to legacy.

In the third phase, as well as earlier in the grief journey, another useful spiritual resource to work with is dreams. Psychologically, dreams can help mourners access deep, unconscious feelings about a person who has died. It is also common for the bereaved to have dreams in which there is a strong sense of connection with the one who has died. Sources such as Rabbi Yehuda HaChasid's medieval ethical manual, *Sefer Chasidim,* suggest that it is possible for the dead to communicate with the living in dreams.[28] Toward the end of a year of grief, the bereaved are often reluctant to give up their mourning because they feel as if they will lose their last thread of contact with the one who has died. However, at this time (as well as earlier in the year of mourning) mourners can sometimes have a powerful sense of connection with the deceased through the dream world.

It is important to give mourners an opportunity to share their dreams about the one who has died and to help them make sense of the meaning in the dream. If a bereaved person reports having a dream and asks if it is a real contact with the person who has died, it might be helpful to say, "We cannot be certain that it was the spirit of your loved one that appeared to you in that dream, but it is certainly a possibility, and Jewish tradition affirms that these kinds of connections between the world of the living and the world of the dead do happen." This response allows mourners to be open to their own sense of connection with the one who has died, as shown in the following anecdote:

> As Beth's wedding day approached, her mother was dying of cancer. Her mother was not well enough to leave the hospital, thus on the afternoon before the wedding the rabbi performed a "mock" marriage ceremony at the hospital. Beth and her new husband left for their honeymoon after the actual wedding, but were called back five days later for her mother's funeral. Starting married life was exceptionally problematic for this young woman. On one hand, she could not fully be with her husband because she was mourning her mother; on the other hand, she was furious with her mother for dying when she did. In grief counseling Beth slowly sorted through and resolved her conflicted feelings. Almost nine

months after her mother's death she had a dream in which her mother stood near her, healthy and vital, wearing a blue dress that Beth described as having a luminous radiance. Her mother smiled lovingly and said, "Go be with your husband, Bobby; I am fine where I am now!" Waking up from the dream, Beth had a sense of having had contact with her mother's spirit presence. She felt this dream allowed her to let go of her grief. Her mourning shifted radically in the weeks after this dream experience, and she was able to move on with her life.

Jewish afterlife teachings speak of a third stage of the postmortem journey called *Gan Eden*, the heavenly Garden of Eden, described in rabbinic literature as a realm of divine bliss[29] and in kabbalistic tradition as a state of consciousness of supernal repose of the soul.[30]

Was this a dream in which Beth's mother is letting her know she has entered the heavenly Garden of Eden? Obviously, there is no way to know, but Beth was profoundly affected by the luminous quality of the blue dress her mother was wearing. Interestingly, this image echoes the mystical writings of Zohar, which teach that "when the soul mounts on high through that portal of the firmament [to *Gan Eden*], other precious garments are provided for it of a more exalted order."[31]

The work of healing in the face of grief is challenging for both mourners and caregivers, but there is no doubt that helping mourners cultivate a spiritual perspective in the face of loss strengthens their ability to deal with loss.

Phase Four: Affirming Life and Legacy

Psychological Dimensions

In the final phase of the bereavement journey, as the more intense waves of grief wind down, mourners begin to claim a new life and to reinvest energy in new relationships and activities. The task of this phase is to say yes! to life, to affirm its fullness, given the reality of mortality and the finite nature of human relationships. As the first *yahrzeit* of a death approaches, even though grief may continue in subdued ways, mourners discover that they can talk about a deceased loved one without feeling the same intensity of pain and heartache as in the past.

It is common during this phase of the grief journey for the bereaved to rearrange personal priorities and to reenter life with newfound meaning and purpose. Mourners may discover a newly developed sense of spiritual renewal, recommit to Jewish community life, or become involved in a new creative endeavor. Some mourners find meaning in working on a particular charitable project, such as cancer research; others may create in memory of a loved one, or perhaps name a child after one who has died.

However, given the durative and cyclical nature of bereavement, even in this phase it is important to remember that grief can suddenly reappear with painful intensity. Even though mourners have adjusted to new routines of everyday life, special occasions such as a wedding, bar/bat mitzvah, holy day, birthday, or anniversary can often be quite difficult and bittersweet, reawakening feelings of longing and grief. The task of this phase is continually finding ways to affirm that life goes on, without denying the pain of loss. It is important for pastoral caregivers to help mourners honor their grief—even when they are celebrating joyous occasions—by remembering and not forgetting, by treasuring precious memories of those who have died. Consider the following example:

> Allan was preparing for his wedding fifteen months after his father had died. Although he had finished saying *Kaddish* and was technically no longer a mourner, his grief persisted, particularly when he thought of walking to the *chupah* without his father, who had been a very strong presence in the family. It was clear that everyone at the wedding would feel his absence. After conversations with Allan, the rabbi encouraged him to visit his father's grave before the wedding—a traditional Jewish act—and also to write a letter to his father, sharing his feelings about his wedding and about his father's absence in his life. Further, Allan and his mother asked the rabbi to chant the *el maleh rachamim* (memorial prayer) under the *chupah* to invite his father's presence to be part of the wedding ceremony. At first, the rabbi was hesitant to do so, suggesting instead that the prayer be chanted in private with the family before the wedding ceremony, but Allan insisted and the rabbi honored his request. The prayer turned out to be a powerful and moving part of the ceremony. Had his father's memory been

ignored, Allan and his family's feelings would still have been there, but without having a ritual context for their expression. By including the *el maleh rachamim* in the ceremony, Allan and his family found a way to affirm life as well as to honor the memory and legacy of his father.

If mourners have completed the previous tasks of mourning, as the bereavement process comes to completion they move from mourning to memorialization, from grieving a loss to honoring the memory and the legacy of the one who has died. As throughout the process of bereavement, Jewish death rituals at this stage—*yahrzeit* and *yizkor*, in particular—help mourners make the transition though the next stages of grief.

In a psychological sense, the *yahrzeit*, the commemoration of the anniversary of a death, has a simple but important function: it provides mourners with the opportunity to remember the dead person and the legacy that she or he has left behind. Observing the *yahrzeit* allows mourners to remain in touch with the memory of the deceased one as the cycle of life moves on.

As the first year of mourning comes to an end, the *yahrzeit* can be an especially moving event because it brings home to mourners the reality that they have made it through an entire cycle of the year—birthdays, anniversaries, holidays, and changes of seasons—without the physical presence of their loved one. The *yahrzeit* can be a time of intense sadness as they recall the time of death, the funeral, and the bereavement journey. Although grieving often continues long after the first anniversary of a death, particularly when the relationship has been especially close or conflicted, the first *yahrzeit* marks a transition in the bereavement experience. A pastoral caregiver can help mourners prepare for the first *yahrzeit* by using the passing of time as a yardstick to evaluate how they have grown and what lessons have been learned during the year of mourning and healing.

It is also important to provide mourners with guidelines to ritualize formally the passing of a *yahrzeit*. All too often, in the reality of North American Jewish life, *yahrzeit* has been reduced to lighting a candle or screwing in the light bulb on the synagogue wall. The psychospiritual task of *yahrzeit* is memorialization. Families need to be encouraged to find a way to gather together, to share a meal, to remember and reminisce. A widowed mother sometimes spends the anniversary of a death alone, not wanting to disturb her children with the reemergence of her grief. Similarly, adult children might avoid talking to their mother about their father, thinking that not mentioning him makes it easier. However, memorialization, remembering, and reminiscing are the very activities that help the grieving continue healing, through feeling an ongoing connection with the deceased loved one.

Like *yahrzeit*, *yizkor* (traditionally recited four times a year, on Yom Kippur and on the three pilgrimage festivals) provides a sacred time to remember and to honor those who have died. During the regular, ongoing cycle of life, it is easy to be preoccupied with the demands of daily living, and it is often difficult to take the time to remember the people who once were part of our life. But Judaism recognizes that death is part of life, and it is the duty of the living to remember the dead. *Yizkor,* the time for the remembrance of souls, is also a psychologically sound ritual practice: It provides an opportunity to connect with the memories of the person who has died. By remembering those who have lived and died throughout the seasons and from year to year, their lives and legacies live on.

Spiritual Dimensions

From a spiritual point of view, there is yet another way to consider *yahrzeit* and *yizkor*. There is a mystical belief that reciting the *Kaddish* at the time of a *yahrzeit* "elevates the soul every year to a higher sphere in [Gan Eden]."[32] Like the funeral, *yahrzeit* can be seen as a "soul-guiding" ritual, a process that acknowledges that the living and the dead are in an ongoing process of interconnection. Observing the anniversary of a death with ritual intentionality, with *kavannah* of heart and mind, strengthens the spiritual bond between the world of the living and the soul of the departed. This spiritual bond allows the living to live fully in the present, connected through mystical kinship to those ancestors whom they have known and loved.

In a similar way, *yizkor* is also a soul-guiding ritual that acknowledges that there is a window, not a wall, between the world of the living and the world of the dead. Judaism has a great tradition of petitionary prayers offered at *yizkor*, asking the deceased to intervene in a benevolent way in the mourner's life. Historically, it was common for young women struggling with issues of infertility to pray to a deceased mother or grandmother, requesting that they intervene on their behalf in the heavenly spheres.[33] Therefore, *yizkor* is another ritual form that allows mourners dealing with grief and loss to continue the relationship with a deceased long after the deceased have departed this world.

This *kavannah*, or meditation, for *yizkor* suggests the ongoing, soul-guiding connection between the living and the dead. It could be used in the context of a *yizkor* service:

> As you recite *Yizkor* prayers let your senses and imagination serve as the vehicle of interconnection. For whom are you saying *Yizkor* today? Can you imagine that person's face before your eyes? See their smile, visualize how they might be carrying their body standing next to you. Do you recall the sound of their voice? Hear their words as you stand in prayer. Feel their presence right in this moment. In your mind, in your heart, allow a conversation between the two of you to unfold. What needs to be communicated this year? What's the message you need to hear today? What are the silent prayers of the heart? What remains unspoken? Speak. Listen. Take your time. There is no reason to hurry. This is a timeless moment. Let all the radiance of their love be with you right now.[34]

Final Thoughts

There is much to learn about providing a spiritual presence with those who are walking on the journey through the valley of the shadow of death. Jewish tradition has much to teach, but ultimately, what caregivers offer is their own depth of heart and spirit. This difficult journey can take a mourner from the depths of agony to renewed heights of spiritual union. The following teaching, attributed to Professor Abraham Joshua Heschel, perhaps sums up the grief journey:

> There are three ways to mourn: to weep, to be silent, and to sing.
>
> *The first way to mourn is to weep:* even if our tears are for ourselves, for our ache of loneliness, for our pain of loss, they are still sacred, for they are the tears of love. But we may weep only if we do not weep too long, only if the spark of our own spirit is not

quenched by a grief too drawn out, only if we do not indulge ourselves in the luxury of grief until it deprives us of courage and
even the wish for recovery.

The second way to mourn is to be silent: to behold the mystery of love, to recall a shared moment, to remember a word or a
glance, or simply at some unexpected moment, to miss someone
very much and wish that he or she could be here. The twinge lasts
but a moment, and passes in perfect silence.

The third way to mourn is to sing: to sing a hymn to life, a
life that still abounds in sights and sounds and vivid colors; to sing
the song our beloved no longer has the chance to sing. We sing the
songs of our beloved; we aspire to their qualities of spirit; and we
trust in our heart that there is a God who hears the bittersweet
melody of our song.[35]

Notes

1. Adapted by the author from Elie Wiesel, *The Gates of the Forest* (New York:
   Avon Books, 1974).
2. These terms are familiar to the Jewish pastoral caregiver; however, for the sake of
   those who may be unfamiliar with the tradition of Jewish grief rituals, they can
   be explicated briefly as follows:
   Aninut is the period from the announcement of death until the funeral. It is a
   time of hyperacute grief when the bereaved must first and foremost deal with the
   practical functional realities of preparing for a funeral.
   Shiva is a seven-day period of ritualized mourning in community.
   Sheloshim is a thirty-day period of intensive mourning from the time of burial, including and continuing beyond the period of *shiva*. It is a transitional period between the initial impact of death and burial, and the gradual reestablishment of
   the daily rhythms of life.
   Kaddish, in the context of mourning, refers to a prayer recited in memory of the
   deceased. When a parent dies, *Kaddish* is recited for eleven months; for other
   family members, for thirty days. In a psychological sense, *Kaddish* may be seen as
   a durative eleven-month process when the mourner is engaged in the deep, transformative experiences of grieving a loss.
   Yahrzeit means literally *year's time,* the anniversary of a death. It is a time on an
   annual basis to remember and to honor the one who has died through recitation
   of *Kaddish*, and by making a memorial donation to *tzedakah*, charity. In a psychological sense, *yahrzeit* is a time for remembering the ongoing connection between the living and the dead.
   Yizkor is a memorial prayer recited four times a year: at Yom Kippur, Sukkot,

Passover, and Shavuot. Like *yahrzeit, yizkor* is a time for the remembrance of souls. It provides mourners with opportunity to connect with memories of one who has died, and to reflect on their life and their legacy.

3. Solomon B. Freehof, "*Hazkarath Neshamoth,*" *HUCA* 36 (1965), pp. 179–85; Sylvie Goldberg, *Crossing the Jabbok—Illness and Death in Ashkenazi Judaism in Sixteenth- Through Nineteenth-Century Prague,* trans. Carol Cosman (Berkeley: University of California Press, 1996).

4. This quote appeared in 1981 in a newspaper article about a rabbi who had given a lecture on the Jewish approach to biomedical ethics. When asked by a young nurse, "Does Judaism believe in an afterlife?" he responded as quoted here. Jean Herschaft, "Patient Should Not Be Told of Terminal Illness, Rabbi," *The Jewish Post and Opinion* (New York), March 13, 1981, p. 12.

5. Elisabeth Kübler-Ross, *On Death and Dying* (New York: Macmillan, 1970). This was Kübler-Ross's pioneering study of care for the dying. In the three decades since the book was published, there has been an extensive proliferation of resources and programs designed to care for the dying and bereaved. See also Kübler-Ross, *The Wheel of Life—A Memoir of Living and Dying* (New York: Scribner, 1997).

6. Igrot HaRaya [Letters], 164.

7. Through the work of Elisabeth Kübler-Ross, the stages of dying—shock, anger, depression, bargaining, and acceptance—have become well known. However, strictly speaking, Kübler-Ross's model refers to the experiences a dying person goes through in preparation for physical demise. They are not stages of the mourning process per se. See Kübler-Ross, *On Death and Dying.*

8. J. William Worden, *Grief Counseling and Grief Therapy: A Handbook for the Mental Health Practitioner,* 2nd ed. (New York: Springer, 1991), pp. 10–18.

9. Michelle B. Goodman, *Nichum Avelim: Comforting the Mourners* (Toronto: Benjamin Family Foundation, 1987), pamphlet 27.

10. Howard Clinebell, *Basic Types of Pastoral Care and Counseling: Resources for the Ministry of Healing and Growth* (Nashville: Abington Press, 1984), pp. 218–42.

11. For the pastoral caregiver, it is essential to remember that grief is always personal, and that no two people go through the experience in identical ways. The model presented here may be useful to assess an individual's encounter with grief, but must not be imposed upon a person's experience.

12. Binyamin Ze'ev, No. 427. This is a Talmudic directive and is based on the following Midrash:

> When the children of Israel were exiled to Babylonia, God mourned for them, as it is written: "On that day the Lord God of Hosts, called to weeping and lamentations . . ." (Isaiah 22:12). The angels sought to console Him but He said: "Do not hasten to comfort Me. Your condolences are blasphemy in My eyes." He refused to accept consolation until He

had imposed the children of Israel the full measurement for their sins. Only then, when He saw that no one dared to console Him, did He say, "Comfort, comfort, My people . . . (Isaiah 40:1)."

Cited by Chaim Press, *Concerns for the Living* (New York: Feldheim, 1990), pp. 39–40.

13. BT Sanhedrin 47b; Lev. R. 18:1; Gen. R. 100:7; PRE 34. See also Simcha Paull Raphael, *Jewish Views of the Afterlife* (Northvale, N.J.: Jason Aronson, 1994).

14. Zohar II, 141b–142a.

15. Ber. 8a.

16. Louis Newman, ed. and trans., *The Hasidic Anthology—Tales and Teachings of the Hasidim* (New York: Schocken Books, 1975), p. 71.

17. For further discussion on "soul-guiding" see Simcha Steven Paull [Simcha Raphael], "Judaism's Contribution to the Psychology of Death and Dying," Ph.D. dissertation, California Institute of Integral Studies, 1986; and Lewis Solomon, *Jewish Book of Living and Dying* (Northvale, N.J.: Jason Aronson, 1999).

18. American Psychiatric Association, *The Diagnostic and Statistical Manual of Mental Disorders,* 4th ed., rev. (Washington, D.C.: American Psychiatric Association, 1994), classification number V62.82.

19. This term is derived from *Gei-Hinnom,* the Valley of Hinnom (Joshua 15:8, Jeremiah 7:30–34, a location south of Jerusalem where idolatrous child sacrifices had been offered to the god Moloch. Repeatedly condemned by the prophets and many Judean kings as a total abomination to the loyalty-demanding YHVH, these ritual sacrifices were eventually wiped out in the seventh century B.C.E. However, *Gei Hinnom* came to be associated with depravity and evil and, eventually, became the term used to describe the underworld of punishment and torment. See R. H. Charles, *Eschatology: The Doctrine of a Future Life in Israel, Judaism and Christianity* (New York: Schocken Books, 1963), pp. 161–62.

20. See, for example, Ex. R., 2:2.

21. According to Shabbat 33b, "The punishment of the wicked in *Gehenna* is twelve months."

22. Zohar II, 129b. Gershon Winkler, in *The Soul of the Matter* (New York: The Judaica Press, 1982), p. 20, describes this process as follows:

How much a person invests in the cultivation of his soul while yet alive, will determine the reaction of the soul when it confronts the ultimate of purity and perfection (G-d) after "death." The less one permits himself to draw from the absolute focal point of reality, G-d, the less prepared he will be, and the more intense will be the contrast when he is faced with that reality after death. For having been preoccupied with the excessive material indulgence while alive, the soul, after death, maintains these same spiritual yearnings but now without the benefit of the physical outlets and faculties to facilitate their satisfaction. The "purification" is then the painful process of "cold turkey" withdrawal of the disembodied consciousness from its heretofore exclusive relationship with the material, enabling it subsequently to bask in the eternal bliss of the purely spiritual *Gan Eden.*

23. When the year of *Gehenna* ends, according to Zohar, the soul is prepared to enter the next phase of the afterlife journey: "The body is punished in the grave and the soul in the fire of *Gehinnom* for the appointed period. When this is completed she rises from *Gehinnom* purified of her guilt like iron purified in the fire, and she is carried up to the *Gan Eden*" (Zohar III, 53a.)

24. Sanhedrin 104a. One of most complete versions of this Midrash is found in Isaac B. Moses of Vienna (1180–1250), *Or Zarua, Hilkhoth Shabbat,* 50. See also Tzvi Rabinowicz, *A Guide to Life—Jewish Laws and Customs of Mourning* (Northvale, N.J.: Jason Aronson, 1989), p. 73; Rabbi Simcha ben Samuel of Vitry, *Mahzor Vitry,* ed. Simon Hurwitz (Berlin: M'kize Nirdamim, 1893), pp. 151, 117; Solomon B. Freehof, "Ceremonial Creativity Among the Ashkenazim," *The Seventh-Fifth Anniversary Volume of the Jewish Quarterly Review,* ed. Abraham A. Neuman and Solomon Zeitlin (Philadelphia: JQR, 1967), pp. 212–13; Solomon Ganzfried, ed., *Kitzur Shulchan Aruch,* I, 26, p. 83; Michael Edward Panitz, "Modernity and Mortality: The Transformation of Central European Jewish Responses to Death, 1750–1850," Ph.D. dissertation, Jewish Theological Seminary, 1989, pp. 34–36.

25. Elisabeth Kübler-Ross, *To Live Until We Say Goodbye,* photographs by Mal Warshaw (Englewood Cliffs, N.J.: Prentice-Hall, 1978), p. 55.

26. Zalman Schachter-Shalomi, "On the Afterlife," unpublished audiocassette tape in the archive of ALEPH, distributed by B'nai Or Religious Fellowship (Philadelphia, 1980).

27. Stephen Levine, "Conscious Living, Conscious Dying," audiotape (Chamisal, N.M., n.d., Warm Rock Tapes, P.O. Box 108, Chamisal, NM 87521).

28. Avraham Yaakov Finkel, ed., *Sefer Chasidim—The Book of the Pious by Rabbi Yehudah HeChasid* (Northvale, N.J.: Jason Aronson, 1997), p. 341; see also Joshua Trachtenberg, *Jewish Magic and Superstition—A Study in Folk Religion* (New York: Athenum, 1974), pp. 223, 234.

29. Yalkut Shimoni, Bereshit 20.

30. Zohar I, 129b.

31. Zohar II, 210b.

32. Attributed to Isaac Luria; quoted in Rabinowicz, *Guide to Life,* p. 105.

33. G. Selkovitsch, ed. and trans., *Maaneh Lashon—Memorial Prayers and Meditations* (New York: Hebrew Publishing Co., 1910).

34. Simcha Paull Raphael, "A Meditation for Yizkor," in *Kol Haneshamah Prayerbook for the Days of Awe* (Wyncote, Pa.: Jewish Reconstructionist Fellowship, 1999), p. 1005.

35. Quoted by Rabbi Jack Stern, "How We Should Mourn" (source unknown).

Bibliography

Raphael, Simcha Paull. *Jewish Views of the Afterlife*. Northvale, N.J.: Jason Aronson, 1994.

Solomon, Lewis. *Jewish Book of Living and Dying*. Northvale, N.J.: Jason Aronson, 1999.

Worden, J. William. *Grief Counseling and Grief Therapy: A Handbook for the Mental Health Practitioner*, 2nd ed. New York: Springer, 1991.

Simcha Paull Raphael, Ph.D., completed his doctorate in psychology at the California Institute of Integral Studies, and received ordination from Rabbi Zalman Schachter-Shalomi as a Rabbinic Pastor. He is a psychotherapist in private practice, affiliated with Mt. Airy Counseling Center in Philadelphia. He teaches in the Department of Religion of La Salle University in Philadelphia and serves as a Spiritual Director at Reconstructionist Rabbinical College. For the past two decades, Dr. Raphael has worked as a death awareness educator, teaching and leading workshops on various aspects of death and the afterlife in Judaism. He has also worked as a hospice counselor, and as resident psychologist in a Jewish funeral home. He is the author of *Jewish Views of the Afterlife*.

Trauma: A Jewish Pastoral Response

Rabbi Nancy Fuchs-Kreimer
Paula Goldstein

Rabbi Nancy Fuchs-Kreimer and Paula Goldstein help the pastoral caregiver prepare for the unexpected. They draw from the field of trauma studies to define trauma and its impact on individuals and communities. Using the model of critical incident work, they propose a role for the pastoral caregiver in caring for people affected by trauma. Fuchs-Kreimer and Goldstein show how Judaism can provide a framework of meaning in trauma's wake. They caution pastoral caregivers about the costs of this work and the importance of getting appropriate support.

Who shall die by fire, and who by drowning . . .
Who by an earthquake, who by a plague,
Who shall be strangled and who shall be stoned,
Who shall dwell in peace, and who be uprooted. . . .

—HIGH HOLIDAY LITURGY

It was a beautiful June afternoon, and Rabbi Cohen was just finishing the filing of the last materials from the Hebrew School year. She was looking forward to a quiet month. Today, the youth group was out together on a trip to a lake about an hour from the synagogue. A phone call interrupted her work. The youth group leader was calling from her cell phone. The bus was almost back at the synagogue and she wanted to warn the rabbi that the day had not been a happy one. The students had witnessed a freak accident: A seven-year-old stranger had drowned in front of their eyes. They had been present for all the resulting tumult and terror, including the child's parents' arrival at the scene. The teenagers from the synagogue were exhibiting symptoms of shock and fear. Some were crying, some were numb. Rabbi Cohen glanced at her bookcase, wondering if buried among all those texts was some wisdom to help her. Uttering a quick, silent prayer, she went off to greet the bus.

Trauma and Critical Incidents

God created the world out of nothingness
But the nothingness shines through
—PAUL VALÉRY

The need to endure harrowing, often violent, events is part of the human condition. According to the first eleven chapters of Genesis, the early history of humanity was filled with trauma: exile (The Garden of Eden), murder (Cain and Abel), natural disaster (The Flood), and technological catastrophe (The Tower of Babel). However, it is interesting that only in the last twenty-five years has research formalized the discussion of the psychological suffering that can ensue from violent events. Not until 1980 was the diagnosis of posttraumatic stress disorder (PTSD) legitimized by the American Psychiatric Association in its *Diagnostic and Statistical Manual,* third edition (DSM–III). The combination of the women's movement's recognition of the suffering of sexual abuse victims and of Vietnam veterans' articulation of the psychic fallout of their combat experiences led to a surge of interest in this field.[1]

What constitutes a trauma? A traumatic event, referred to as a "critical incident" when it affects a group, is an extremely stressful life occurrence that happens "outside the range of usual human experience." Although a couple might report to a rabbi that they have been "traumatized" by the news of their daughter's impending intermarriage, the word *trauma* refers in this chapter to highly stressful and overwhelming events, which almost always involve a threat to perceived or actual safety. This chapter focuses on critical incidents likely to be encountered by Jewish pastoral caregivers: premature or violent death, assault or rape of a member of a group, traffic accidents, and plane crashes or natural disasters, such as earthquakes or hurricanes. As in our opening story, a group will sometimes experience the incident together; other times, a trauma experienced by an individual will have repercussions for the group of which the individual is a part. Obviously, the definition of a critical incident is culturally relative. In our communities, unlike many in the past, a young mother's dying in childbirth would probably constitute a critical incident, because it would upset people's basic assumptions about a relatively normal life event.

Most individuals use expectations of predictability to guide them through the day. Traumatologist Ronnie Janoff-Bulman refers to these as "over-generalizations [that] are extremely adaptive."[2] In traumatic events, these expectations are shattered. Although those closest to the event are obviously at the greatest risk of developing long-term, dysfunctional responses to the experience, everyone in a community, to a greater or lesser degree, should be considered when responding pastorally to a critical incident. When Janie, a thirteen-year-old, died suddenly of a virus, it was a traumatic experience for her entire school community, students and teachers alike. Viruses are supposed to be curable; thirteen-year-olds are not supposed to die suddenly. In a critical incident, we need to bring all of the resources available to us as representatives of the culture and community in response to the disruption of our normal way of seeing.

Clearly, some reactions to trauma are similar to those in any case of sorrow and suffering. Some aspects of the response to trauma are shared more generally with the response to death. However, trauma also has unique features, including specific physiological components. This chapter focuses on the features of traumatic stress that distinguish it from ordinary bereavement. We need to recall that the qualitatively different features of trauma coexist with features that are similar to those of all loss. The family of a murder victim is likely to be suffering from both grief and trauma; it is often helpful for the pastoral caregiver to notice and to name both of these dimensions of their suffering.

The study of trauma raises fascinating theological issues. It is not coincidental that those traumas with no human perpetrator are commonly referred to as "acts of God." In earthquakes and floods, we confront the flip side of the creation that we usually evoke as proof of God's goodness. Even more devastating are the traumas created by human agency: murders, assaults, nuclear waste accidents, etc. In these events, we confront human nature at its worst.

On the other hand, when working with groups confronted by trauma, we are often privileged to witness astounding examples of human buoyancy, cooperation, and generosity. One of the findings of this field is that, although many victims of trauma bear the consequences in psychic suffering, a startling number actually carry on with a resilience that mystifies researchers. In some cases, trauma can precipitate a move toward emotional growth. We are able to see first-hand how the human ability to create religions, cultures, and communities helps us flourish despite the most overwhelming events.

How the Mind and the Body Respond to Trauma

> After great pain,
> A formal feeling comes.
> This is the hour of lead.
> —EMILY DICKINSON

Those involved in a critical incident, or even confronted with the news of it, are at risk of developing certain physiological and psychological symptoms in the immediate aftermath of the event. In many cases, these predictable responses (a normal response to an abnormal situation) will be short-term and mild, and those involved will then move on with their lives. In others, depending on the severity of the stress, prior exposure to trauma, and the unique psychic makeup of the individual, more serious outcomes such as acute stress disorder (ASD) or, later, PTSD, can occur. Researchers understand increasingly more about the changes in the brain after a traumatic event. The damage is not done by the trauma itself, but by the way in which the individual's mind and body react to the trauma.

We are all aware that our memory is selective; extraordinary moments are seared into our memories in a way that ordinary ones are not. Most people old enough to remember know exactly what they were doing on November 22, 1963, when they heard that President John F. Kennedy had been shot, although they may have no specific recollection of November 21. Recent research has indicated that truly catastrophic stress, such as being the victim of a life-threatening crime, can actually change the chemistry of the brain. Victims may be altered biologically by such events. It appears that the brain takes a snapshot of highly fraught events and preserves their memory acutely, sometimes at the cost of appropriate functioning later in life.[3]

All of this can occur at greater and lesser degrees of severity. One need not be a direct witness to a traumatic event to have some of the symptoms, albeit usually less intense, of PTSD. For example, Fran was an American-born daughter of Holocaust survivors. Over the years, she heard many frightening stories. As an adult, she took a tour through Europe. In Germany, she found herself responding with physiological arousal and a completely inappropriate affect to benign situations, such as being asked for her train ticket by a German-speaking, uniformed conductor.

A greater understanding of PTSD has led to a commitment on the part of mental health professionals to reach people quickly after critical incidents occur and to intervene in a way that can help reduce the more serious and long-term consequences of trauma. Increasingly, pastoral care professionals may have access to social workers or psychologists trained in critical incident response work. It is important to understand the benefits and the limits of the role of these professionals because it may often be wise for the pastoral caregiver to arrange for such services to complement his or her own skills.

There are two ways in which critical incident response teams are called in. The first is immediately after a critical incident occurs, which is referred to as crisis work. The goal during the first day or two is to help those involved restore a sense of safety, maintain basic functions, and cope with the daily tasks of living. The most important intervention is to reunite individuals as speedily as possible with their families and loved ones. Children, in particular, appear to be phenomenally resilient as long as trusted caregivers are close at hand; they are correspondingly devastated by trauma when these caregivers are absent, or worse, are the cause of the violence or fright. During the first hours and days after a critical incident, mental health professionals may be stationed at the school or synagogue and be available to help in this restorative process on a one-to-one basis, as needed.

The second phase is critical incident stress debriefing (CISD). This activity, usually facilitated in small groups by one therapist—or, preferably, several—formalizes the kind of talking-through of a traumatic event that occurs organically in all cultures through such institutions as *shiva* or a wake. Intuitively, it makes sense that people would benefit from talking about an upsetting event that has evoked strong emotions. Research into the nature of PTSD bears out that intuition. People suffering from PTSD are unable to find words for the horror, and consequently, they relive it over and over with the same strong emotions that occurred during the original incident. When words can be used, the retelling can often lessen the intensity of the emotions.

In CISD, therapists encourage people to retell the story of what they witnessed (or the story of how they first heard about the crisis), to share feelings stirred up by the event, and to support each other in the process. In addition, these groups offer education to individuals about common and expected stress reactions. Ideally, these sessions are timed after people have recovered from the initial shock of the crisis. CISD should take place while people are still in the acute phase of reaction to the trauma, preferably several days after the event. If the debriefing takes place too late, it can have the undesired effect of disrupting people's hard-won coping and defense mechanisms. When a beloved Hebrew School teacher died over the summer, social workers were called to the synagogue's school that fall to help the children process the event. However, during the debriefing sessions they encountered resistance from the students, who were not eager to revisit their intensive grief feelings. Timing is critical.

There is much value in involving trained therapists in this work. These professionals can, with authority, educate people about the expected course of reactions. When symptoms are understood in the context of the traumatic event, the symptoms are normalized. Professionals can also alert people to long-term problems and inform them about to where and how to seek more extensive help, if needed. Those who have been affected by trauma should be warned that an initial, healthy adjustment does not guarantee that problems will not develop at a later stage, and they should be made aware of the possible trigger points and danger signs.[4] In addition, the professionals responding to critical incidents are in a position to observe the affected individuals in a group setting and to make note of those who may need special attention.

Lastly, the organization making use of these services has an opportunity to demonstrate its concern for its constituents. For example, in our opening story, the rabbi involved could call on the local Jewish Family Service for social work assistance, thereby assuring the parents of the teens that she is conscientiously addressing the risk to their emotional well-being. This kind of intervention has the added benefit of reducing the inevitable stress of the parents involved.

Even strong advocates for professional psychological intervention often agree that the single most important response is to reconnect an individual to his or her regular systems of support. The pastoral caregiver's role goes well beyond that of the critical incident intervention team. The remainder of this chapter explores the special contributions of the pastoral caregiver in (1) connecting traumatized individuals to community and reconnecting traumatized communities; (2) sustaining individuals during crises of faith, particularly through the use of ritual; and (3) situating individuals in a framework of meaning, a source of hope.

Critical Incidents as Community Challenges

The first job of a pastoral caregiver is to connect people, if possible, to their communities and to encourage them to exploit the resources available to them by turning outward. This is almost literally a case of the famous Talmudic dictum, *o chevruta, o mituta*, translated loosely as "Give me companionship or give me death" (BT Ta'anit, 22a). When a major earthquake devastated the Los Angeles community, rabbis quickly arranged for opportunities for their congregants to gather and to reflect as a community.

Rabbis in congregations instinctively know that the community seeks opportunities to be together in times of shock. A prayer community is a setting in which people are already accustomed to opening their hearts; it is thus, in many ways, an ideal place to turn after trauma. For example, when Yitzhak Rabin was assassinated, many rabbis scheduled and led emergency services in the days immediately following his death rather than wait a full week until the next regularly scheduled Shabbat service. It is enormously powerful for people simply to be together at times of shock. What is said at services such as these is far less important than the fact of people gathering in the same place to comfort one another.

Sometimes a pastoral caregiver needs to go out and find those in need of connecting to community.

Rabbi White learned that a carload of teenagers, several of whom attended the high school that most of his teenaged congregants also attended, had crashed, killing all the youths. The high school was using the services of a team of crisis intervention specialists. Rabbi White called the school principal and asked if he might be of service. The principal was happy to welcome him into the school and accompany him through the various classrooms as psychological support groups were in session. The simple presence of a rabbi, *yarmulke* on head, seemed important to a number of students, some of whom later called the rabbi at his office, attended services that Friday night, or both.

Working with a community over time when some of its members have experienced a trauma is a tremendous challenge: The pastoral caregiver becomes aware that everyone in the community is, to some degree, a victim; thus, the group will need attention. The primary victims, of course, will need a great deal of support, and one might expect that this support would be forthcoming from the rest of the community, but it does not always work that way. For example, a teenager is murdered, and the rabbi, in good Jewish fashion, reaches out to the family and assures them, with the best of intentions, that the entire community is there for them. However, she discovers to her surprise that the community is actually not as present for the family as she had hoped.

What is happening? If we think of trauma as the shattering of our assumptions about an orderly and reliable world, it is clear that most people, given a choice, would like to distance themselves from such disruptive information. Most of us cherish the belief that we and our families are safe, and we like to think that our safety is within our control. People find themselves thinking things like: "That girl hung around with a wild crowd." If they can find some blame to assess, they will not have to confront the randomness of life; the world can still make sense. In a cruel turn of fate, community members, despite their goodwill, want less to do with the victimized family.

This phenomenon has been observed so often after rapes, murders, and traumas of all kinds that it even has a name. The victim's family, already suffering terribly, now receive from their own communities the so-called second injury. Rather than feeling enveloped in love, the family begins to feel like they are freaks. Some people simply are not able to reach out to victims because of their own vulnerabilities. On the other hand, with enough support from a pastoral caregiver, others may be alerted to their own distancing process, and some of the worst consequences of the human need for denial may be mitigated.

In some disasters, such as a terrorist attack, there are multiple victims. In those cases, although the families of the victims are less likely to be shunned and isolated, a different problem may occur. The whole community is so swept up in the tragedy that family members sometimes feel that the specificity of their own grief or the memory of their own beloved is being obscured in the general confusion, which can be experienced as yet another loss. Again, the sensitive pastoral care professional, in the midst of attending to so many individuals in trauma, will be scrupulous about giving each individual who died or lost someone close to them their chance to be named and recognized.

Trauma and Faith Development

Critical incidents bring people beyond the everyday distractions of life and force them to confront the limits of their faith and worldview, which can be seen as an entirely negative occurrence or be reframed as Laurie Ann Pearlman does by calling it a "disruption."[5] Assuming that one can avoid the long-term pathology discussed earlier, this kind of event can hold the potential for growth and development in the realm of faith and spirit. Given a choice, most of us would not choose trauma and suffering, even when apprised of its putatively pedagogic value. However, we are not given a choice, so it is worthwhile to consider what groups and individuals might gain from such experiences in the extended aftermath of traumatic events.

The Swiss psychologist Jean Piaget showed the world that as we grow, we learn not only more facts but also new and more sophisticated ways of processing facts. We actually think differently at different stages of development; movement through these stages can be predicted and, in some cases, even hastened.[6] Lawrence Kohlberg, building on Piaget's work, focused his own study of cognitive development on one particular area, moral reasoning. He found he could chart how people developed more complex, more adequate ways of thinking about moral issues as they moved through predictable stages.[7] Lastly, James Fowler, a theologian whose interest turned to cognitive developmental psychology, documented that one can also chart the way people think about faith, noting stages that build upon each other in ever more sophisticated ways.[8]

According to all three theorists, movement through stages is not inevitable. The precipitating factor for growth in all three theories is crisis, defined as the failure of the current stage to explain and process new information adequately. In other words, we outgrow our old ways of understanding when they no longer work for us. We are then pushed to reformulate our thinking at a higher stage. Another way of looking at shattered assumptions is growth opportunities, or in popular parlance: "If your stomach is churning, you are learning."

Of course, this sounds entirely too upbeat. No one denies that, in fact, this process is often painful for the individual and for those around him or her. Nevertheless, the study of faith development—especially those difficult times of transition between stages—has yielded some insights that are useful in responding to people after the acute phase of the trauma has passed. First, it helps to think about a crisis of faith in terms of a movement through stages, rather than simply the collapse of a worldview. Transitions are difficult, but when understood as the inevitable passage from one stage to another, they can be endured with more grace. Robert Kegan, a developmental psychologist, has suggested that when one is between stages one feels, quite literally, "beside oneself." Bible scholar Aviva Zornberg describes Sarah's state after learning of the binding of Isaac as "spiritual vertigo."[9] It helps to be told that this set of feelings is to be expected; it is also helpful to be "held" during that time by family and community members who knew you before and will know you in the future. This ideal "holding environment," as Kegan call it, assures the person in passage that despite her or his own sense of loss of identity, he or she is actually recognized and cherished. The holding environment asks little of the individual during this time of trial but gives much. At its best, ritual can be seen as a kind of holding environment pending the reconstruction of one's worldview and the reordering of life.

The Role of Ritual in
Responding to Trauma

As students of human behavior have long noted, rituals help individuals control their emotions, order their behavior, link the sufferers more intimately to the social group, and serve as symbols of continuity.

—MARTIN DEVRIES, "TRAUMA IN CULTURAL PERSPECTIVE,"
IN *TRAUMATIC STRESS*

Ritual is a particularly powerful tool because it can continue to provide nurture even when beliefs are under siege. Scholars of contemporary Judaism have noted that ritual observance in our era is not necessarily correlated with belief. Jews are drawn to the Passover Seder in record numbers, even as they are increasingly doubtful of the core beliefs of the ceremony. Arnold Eisen has suggested that ritual may be attractive to Jews in our day precisely because "it continues even in the absence of God's felt presence and compensates for that absence. . . . God inhabits the ritual and the stories, regardless of an individual's level of belief."[10] In other words, people who have been traumatized should be assured that there is nothing unusual in allowing their ritual behavior to move out ahead of their beliefs.

In a time of crisis, of "ontological chill," engaging in so-called mindless ritual can often be a powerful tonic, precisely because of its mindless quality. A notable example of this phenomenon is the mourner's *Kaddish*, which evokes strong emotional resonances for many Jews despite the fact that it is recited in Aramaic and most could not say what the words mean. The response is to the prayer's sounds, cadence, and nonverbal messages. The prayer speaks to Jews of mystery, of order, of continuity; indeed, that its literal meaning is not understood is a plus. It works at times when clear statements about God might be at best confusing, and at worst offensive. The world may have been shattered, but the *Kaddish* sounds the same as it always has.

Similarly, in the aftermath of a critical incident, one is struck by the power and the wisdom of the custom of *shiva* (seven days of mourning conducted within the home of the bereaved). At a time when people are shocked and frightened, wandering in emotionally unfamiliar terrain, they are told to remain in the most safe and recognizable environment—their own home. Those who come to call on them participate in services and pay their respects in the home, a place that is comforting by its familiarity and informality. The message of the setting—the normalcy of a home—is a powerful antidote to the confusion, strangeness, and unreality of the event itself.

Jewish tradition has a ritual already built into its structure that explicitly addresses critical incidents. There is a blessing called *gomel* (literally, the One who bestows) that is recited by a person on living through or witnessing a life-threatening event. The blessing is said in the presence of a *minyan* (ten adult Jews). The individual who has experienced the event stands in front of the group and says, "Blessed are You, our God, Sovereign of all the worlds, who bestows good things on one in debt to you, and who has granted me all good." The group responds, "May the One who has bestowed upon you good, continue to bestow upon you good. Let it be so!"

Notice that the theology underlying this blessing is quite problematic, especially at a time such as this. If God chose to save this individual from death, why did God cause the near-death experience in the first place? If others involved were not as lucky, what does that say about those who suffered a different fate? However, the ritual does not ask one to probe that question so much as it invites the person to take several very positive steps: First, it requires the person to leave his or her home and connect with community; second, it allows her or him to let the community know about an experience that is out of the ordinary, which allows the community's support to be mobilized; and third, it locates the sense of fear and terror around the event within the more comfortable context of the Hebrew prayer service. Much of life is mysterious: Critical incidents are encounters with the terrifying side of that mystery. The traditional Jewish liturgy addresses that mystery in its more positive dimensions. The prayer also turns the individual's thoughts away from the past and toward the future.

In recent years, some Jews have begun exploring the use of the *mikveh* (ritual bath) as the occasion for a ritual of transformation. *Mikveh* was originally concerned with ritual purity and impurity, a category primarily relevant to the Temple in Jerusalem. After the destruction of the Temple, total immersion in the living waters of the *mikveh* was reserved primarily for two functions: a conversion to

Judaism and the purification of women during their monthly menstrual cycle. However, the contemporary reclamation of the waters of the *mikveh* for use in a ritual after a trauma uses the metaphoric associations of rebirth and spiritual cleansing to effect psychological transformation.

Rabbi Elyse Goldstein uses the *mikveh* as spiritual therapy, a tool in pastoral encounters after trauma. She notes that it offers "no quick fix but acts as one part of the healing process." She tells the story of a congregant who was raped by a handyman she had hired to work in her home. After months of therapy, she still felt dirty. Rabbi Goldstein suggested using the *mikveh* as a ritual experience that might help "cleanse both her body and her soul. As it turned out, the experience was profoundly moving and healing."[11]

However, given what we know about trauma, it is important not to place on rituals any unrealistic expectations of closure. As Deborah Spungen teaches about traumatic experiences, "There is no such thing as closure. There is only the new normal."[12]

When we think of ritual, we often think first of a funeral, a synagogue, or a special event like going to a *mikveh*. But ritual can be as simple and as ordinary as a bedtime routine or a family mealtime at which certain dishes are usually served. Families in times of stress should be encouraged to hold on to all the traditions and rituals in their repertoire and to create new routines to foster safety and acceptance. When Susan, a teenager, learned of the sudden death of a close friend and classmate, she experienced a "free fall" from all sense of meaning and reliability in the world. After a few days of the expected symptoms of acute stress, she found herself recalling her bedtime ritual from childhood in which her mother would envelop her with a billowing sheet while singing the words to the Hebrew prayer, "Spread over us your *sukkah* (tent) of peace." She then experienced on a visceral level—far from her challenged theology—that there was indeed a *sukkah* of peace under which she dwelt. Perhaps this ritual offered Susan a symbolic holding environment.

Judaism as a Framework of Meaning

According to Ernest Becker, like any culture, Judaism is an effort to deny that we are born to die. As Becker puts it: "Our symbolic world is an attempt to deny our biological fate." Critical incidents confront us, abruptly and often in a terrifying manner, with our own mortality. What role does the symbolic world have in such a situation? In some important ways, it is our symbolic world, our culture, that can help to sustain us in times of crisis.

What is culture? Culture may "be viewed as the protective and supportive system of values, lifestyles and knowledge. . . . Culture thereby buffers its members from the profound impact of stressful experiences by furnishing social support, providing identities in terms of norms and values, and supplying a shared vision of the future."[13] The relevance for the representative of Jewish culture should be clear. Notice that no mention is made here of providing meanings or answers. Although Judaism, like other cultures, offers many responses to the problem of suffering and injustice, it is not these answers that are central, but rather, the simple fact of being part of something larger than oneself.

The Jewish people existed before the crisis and will exist after it; indeed, in its long history, the Jewish people have known much crisis. It is not a coincidence that the Book of Genesis opens with the exile of Adam and Eve from the garden: The community that first canonized the book was dealing with its own exile. Every critical incident is like the exile from the garden, from being cast out of the paradise of a world that makes sense into a world where all bets are off. When the Jewish people lost the Temple and its cult, they faced a crisis of staggering proportions: They literally had to reinvent themselves and their faith.

This is the heart of the cognitive work of trauma recovery. Simply locating oneself in the master story of Jewish history can provide grounding. The story is one of almost indefatigable ability to recover from loss and disruption. The individual's story is set within a context. Cultural stories highlight communal trauma and thus "allow individuals to reorganize their often catastrophic reactions to losses. Culture . . . locates experiences in historical context and forces continuity on discontinuous events."[14] The yearly cycle of the Jewish calendar exposes one to the triumphs and tragedies of our communal past. "Trauma can lead to extremes of retention and forgetting"[15]; thus one aspect of trauma recovery is restoring the delicate balance between forgetting and remembering. Our religious tradition has worked out its own methodology of remembering and forgetting, of grieving and celebrating. Exposure to this complex way of coping with history and prevailing may be a source of inspiration for the individual.

In the Jewish yearly cycle, there is an ongoing engagement with the most powerful issues of life and death, loss and vulnerability. Healing from traumatic incidents is a long process, and a Jewish pastoral caregiver is sometimes in a position to help people revisit the trauma at various points along the healing journey. By setting the story within the larger story of the Jewish year, one is able to counteract the sense of horror and disconnection, allowing people to integrate the experience into their ongoing worldview.

> When two first-graders were killed in a schoolyard accident, Rabbi Israel offered emergency pastoral care to the many families in his congregation with children in that school, including the family of one of the girls who were killed. Although the funeral and *shiva* provided the structure for the initial grieving and trauma response, the rabbi realized that the event was hardly over weeks or even months later. The accident had occurred during the spring. That Tisha B'Av, Rabbi Israel invited a therapist in the congregation to speak about recovery from trauma with special reference to the event that had rocked the congregation a few months before. Noting that Tisha B'Av was a time for the Jewish people as a whole to revisit a traumatic event in its history, the rabbi understood that it was important to acknowledge the ongoing nature of the task of assimilating the tragedy.
>
> That fall, during High Holy Days, the rabbi again chose to address the traumatic loss his community had undergone. He knew there were concepts people could hear then that could not have been heard six months before. The Jewish people's annual confrontation with the fragility of life provided an opportunity to look at the terrifying event through yet another lens. Each spring, when the anniversary of the young girl's death occurs, her name is read aloud on the *yahrzeit* list along with the names of other congregants who died over the years. In this way, an event that was so shocking as to seem virtually impossible to assimilate became

normalized as it was taken up into memory as one piece of a larger story, a larger framework of meaning.

The sacred story that the Jewish people preserves is one that widens the lens, setting our own national history in a larger tale that begins with the creation and ends with redemption. Once again, the issue in the end is simply that of hope. For people to move beyond trauma they need to find a way to focus positively on the future. Judaism suggests that redemption is a real possibility and that human beings need to contribute actively to the struggle. Volunteering, *tzedakah*, and *tikkun olam* can all be integral parts of a healing path for people after critical incidents. Organizations like Mothers Against Drunk Driving (MADD) help people move beyond trauma to response. In the cultural symbol system of Judaism, the presumption that—despite current evidence to the contrary—the world is moving toward the time of the Messiah suggests that there is an imperative to act, as well as reason to hope.

Caring for the Caregivers

Traumatologists know that this kind of work changes people. There are many covictims in any trauma, and a good caring professional will be on the lookout for the victims of secondary traumatic stress (STS) or vicarious traumatization. Most obviously, these include the witnesses to a horrific event, their family and friends, and a host of professionals who may experience residual effects from the "emotional contagion." These include police and firefighters, doctors, nurses, social workers, lawyers, and even journalists. Hearing about a traumatic event can put the listener at risk, especially when the listener exhibits a high degree of empathy.

Pastoral caregivers must be alert to two tasks, the second more difficult than the first. First, they ought to help the entire system recover after a trauma and be constantly vigilant for the forgotten victims, including support staff and children. For example, in a teen suicide, all the professionals involved will be aware that the immediate family is at serious risk and indeed are covictims. However, the rabbi might be the one to recall that not only the student's immediate peers, but all the children in the school or synagogue are going to be affected by this news. Furthermore, depending on their personal history with teenage suicide, some adults in the community may have strong reactions.

Second, pastoral caregivers must recall that they, too, are at risk. Pastoral care workers need to take special responsibility to protect themselves from what has come to be known as "compassion fatigue."[16] Compassion fatigue, or compassion stress, is widely recognized as a risk for therapists involved in trauma work.[17] The literature distinguishes STS from generic burnout, although some symptoms may be shared. STS is a very specific version of burnout, one whose onset can be quite sudden rather than gradual and cumulative. The literature stresses that the person suffering from STS can exhibit any and all of the symptoms of PTSD. The pastoral caregiver must beware. In fact, some trauma specialists contend that it is actually "unethical for therapists to work with traumatized clients if the therapist does not have a professional support system."[18]

It is particularly challenging to serve a traumatized community of which one is a part. In such cases, recourse to mental health professionals trained in critical incident intervention work may be indicated.

> Rabbi Levy was the chaplain in a large urban hospital when one of the beloved women doctors on staff was murdered on the premises. Rabbi Levy devotedly ministered to the staff in a variety of ways, including counseling numerous individuals and conducting a memorial service. What Rabbi Levy failed to appreciate at the time was how deeply burdened he was by grief, shock, and genuine fear. Given that the rabbi shared the struggles of the rest of the staff, outside professional trauma response specialists would have been a desirable additional support.

In some ways, pastoral caregivers may be at greater risk than therapists when it comes to STS. Therapists often work in settings where they have some control over their caseload. The pastoral caregiver, on the other hand, often does not have that luxury. For example, in the story we used at the beginning of this chapter, Rabbi Cohen was not able to say, "Sorry, I have some personal history with the death of a young child and I think I'll sit this one out."

Second, and perhaps more important, many therapists work in settings with a group of professionals whom they regularly consult about cases and, especially for trauma work, with whom they routinely debrief. Debriefing involves a review of the critical incident and the particular stresses the individual experienced as a result of the work. Many pastoral caregivers do not enjoy that level of collegiality on a daily basis. Although many pastoral care professionals share their concerns with colleagues, close family members, and therapists, it is usually on a more ad hoc basis. A discussion with a group of rabbis on this topic yielded such comments as: "If I am not too exhausted at night, I tell my wife," or, "I try to talk things over with a colleague by the end of the week," or, "If I have a therapy appointment and something has been difficult personally, I bring it up." According to standards of self-care established in the therapeutic community, this is simply not enough.

On the other hand, the structure of the job for the pastoral caregiver in some ways works to their advantage. One of the findings of those who study compassion fatigue in therapists is that therapists who specialize in trauma are at heightened risk; a frequent suggestion is that therapists diversify their caseload. For a rabbi in a congregation, such diversity of caseload is the norm. Although Rabbi Cohen may have to deal with the children after their witnessing a critical incident, by the very nature of her job, she may also be officiating at a baby naming the next day. This is all to the good, for it allows the pastoral caregiver to remind herself of the range of human experiences and emotions. If diversification is not built into the job, it should be.

Some of the findings concerning self-care for therapists at risk for STS are of interest to the Jewish pastoral care professional. One suggestion is to make sure that one's life is balanced between work and relaxation. Observing Shabbat can help to provide just such balance. It is also strongly recommended that therapists be members of supportive communities. Although it is likely that a pastoral caregiver has such a community, he or she ought to cherish and nurture those ties. Finally, in anticipation of working with trauma, pastoral care professionals should be aware of the traumas in their own lives so that they can do the personal work necessary to be able to deal with others in crisis. It may sound obvious that pastoral caregivers ought to be self-aware, but it is actually a more specific warning. The nature of adaptation to trauma is such that many people have dealt with traumatic events so efficiently that they do not come up, even in therapy. Given the trigger of this kind of work, however, caregivers may find themselves confronting long-forgotten material.

Self-awareness is essential in understanding our own comfort level and ability to help others during their times of great vulnerability. Needless to say, the more comfortable one is with one's own belief system and the more one has thought about the theological questions, the easier it will be to be a nonanxious presence in the midst of stress. A pastoral caregiver may sometimes simply need to bring another person to the scene to deal with an individual, family, or community when he or she is not able to handle the distress the particular incident may trigger. As Hillel wrote, "If I am not for myself, who shall be for me?"

Responding to a critical incident pushes one to reexamine one's own assumptions and to experience the limits of one's self-sufficiency. This is a costly enterprise for the individual. At the same time, it can be incredibly fruitful. Having discussed the stresses of this kind of work for the rabbi or cantor, we must also recognize how much strength and inspiration can be derived from this work. In fact, human beings are amazingly resilient and creative when forced to cope with unbelievable life events. Through crisis work, we can often witness the human spirit at its most courageous. Professionals who become involved in this work often find themselves moved by the way members of communities rally to support one another. In one case, a rabbi, along with a social worker he had invited, conducted a debriefing session with the teens in his community after the suicide of their peer. In addition to the fear and the trauma surrounding the event, the teens shared fond, sometimes humorous memories of their friend. They were uncommonly tender and compassionate with one another. The rabbi felt he had been privileged to know these teenagers in a different way than he had before. Many of the teens continued to check in with the rabbi after the incident, and he continued to be moved by their sweetness, loyalty, and strength.

Providing pastoral care in response to critical incidents is a profound opportunity to be with people at the very edges of what human beings can bear. It is an opportunity to catch a glimpse of the ultimate "holding environment," which Paul Tillich called "the Ground of Being." We see that which permits all of us to survive despite terror, and, in some cases, to quote Faulkner, not only to survive, but to prevail.

Notes

1. Judith Herman, *Trauma and Recovery* (New York: Basic Books, 1992).
2. Ronnie Janoff-Bulman, *Shattered Assumptions: Toward a New Psychology of Trauma* (New York: Free Press, 1992), pp. 4–12.
3. Daniel Goleman, "New Kind of Memory Found to Preserve Moments of Emotion," *The New York Times*, Oct. 25, 1994.
4. Trigger points refer to situations that *bring the person back* to the trauma and will probably occur for anyone who has experienced a traumatic event. Danger signs are symptoms of emotional distress that suggest that the individual may not have resolved the trauma sufficiently. Danger signs include chronic depressive symptoms, preoccupation with health, increased anxiety, dependence on drugs or alcohol, and low impulse control.
5. Laurie Ann Pearlman, "Self-Care for Trauma Therapists: Ameliorating Vicarious Traumatization," in *Secondary Traumatic Stress*, ed. B. Hudnell Stamm (Lutherville, Md.: Sidran Press, 1995), p. 51.
6. Jean Piaget, *The Child and Reality* (New York: Penguin, 1976).
7. Lawrence Kohlberg, *The Philosophy of Moral Development* (San Francisco: Harper & Row, 1981).
8. James W. Fowler, *Stages of Faith: The Psychology of Human Development and the Quest for Meaning* (San Francisco: Harper and Row), 1981; Robert Kegan, "There the Dance Is: Religious Dimensions of a Developmental Framework, Toward Moral and Religious Maturity," in *The First International Conference on Moral and Religious Development* (Morristown, N.J.: Silver Burdett Company).
9. Aviva Gottlieb Zornberg, *The Beginnings of Desire: Reflections on Genesis* (New York: Doubleday, 1995), p. 127
10. *Rethinking Modern Judaism: Ritual, Commandment and Community* (Chicago: University of Chicago, 1998), p. 256.
11. Elyse Goldstein, *ReVisions: Seeing Torah Through a Feminist Lens* (Woodstock, Vt.: Jewish Lights Publishing, 1998), p. 129.
12. Deborah Spungen, lecture for the Jewish Family and Children's Service of Greater Philadelphia, May 1999.
13. DeVries, "Trauma," p. 400–01.
14. Ibid.
15. Bessel van der Kolk, "Trauma and Memory," in *Traumatic Stress*, eds. Bessel van der Kolk, Alexander C. McFarlane, and Lars Weisaeth (New York: Guilford, 1996), p. 282.
16. The phrase was first used by C. Johnson in "Coping with Compassion Fatigue," *Nursing* 22, no. 4 (1992): pp. 116–22.
17. Charles R. Figley, "Compassion Fatigue: Towards a New Understanding of the Costs of Caring," in *Secondary Traumatic Stress: Self-Care Issues for Clinicians, Researchers and Educators,* ed. B. Hudnall Stamm (Lutherville, Md.: Sidran Press, 1995), p. 11. Figley suggests that the terms *compassion fatigue* or

compassion stress are good substitutes for the more widely used "secondary victimization."

18. J. F. Munroe, "Compassion Fatigue: Secondary Traumatic Stress from Treating the Traumatized," Symposium at the 10th Annual Meeting of the International Society for Traumatic Stress Studies, Chicago, 1994.

Bibliography

Figley, C. *Trauma and Its Wake,* Volume II, *Traumatic Stress Theory, Research, and Practice.* New York: Brunner/Mazel, 1986.

Horowitz, M. D. *Stress Response Syndromes,* 2d ed. Northvale, N.J.: Jason Aronson, 1986.

Janoff-Bulman, Ronnie. *Shattered Assumptions: Towards a New Psychology of Trauma.* New York: Free Press, 1992.

Herman, Judith. *Trauma and Recovery.* New York: Basic Books, 1992.

Stamm, B. Hudnall. *Secondary Traumatic Stress: Self-Care Issues for Clinicians, Researchers, and Educators.* Lutherville, Md.: Sidran Press, 1995.

Van der Kolk, Bessel, Alexander C. McFarlane, and Lars Weisaeth, eds. *Traumatic Stress.* New York: Guilford, 1996.

Rabbi Nancy Fuchs-Kreimer, Ph.D., is the Director of the Jewish Identity Program at the Jewish Family and Children's Service of Greater Philadelphia. She has taught at the Reconstructionist Rabbinical College for twelve years. She is the author of *Parenting As a Spiritual Journey: Deepening Ordinary & Extraordinary Events into Sacred Occasions* (Jewish Lights Publishing).

Paula Goldstein, L.S.W., is the Codirector of the Lieberman Jewish Family Life Education Department of the Jewish Family and Children's Service of Greater Philadelphia.

Para-Chaplaincy: A Communal Response to the Ill and Suffering

Rabbi David J. Zucker

Rabbi David J. Zucker analyzes the need for para-chaplains, and explores traditional sources that mandate the involvement of lay Jews in the work of caring for ill and suffering people. He explores three key aspects of the para-chaplain's role: one-to-one relationship, advocacy, and Jewish programming. He provides direction in establishing a para-chaplaincy program and suggests a structure for training and supervision. Rabbi Zucker's chapter provides support for an adjunct to the professional caregiver and is a valuable resource for communities without adequate professional pastoral care resources.[1]

Miriam, a para-chaplain, reflects in the following on a powerful encounter:

> George Levy was a resident on the specialized Alzheimer's unit of the nursing home. He had not spoken in years; nonetheless, we brought him to the model Seder. We were at a table, with the Seder plate before us. When we began to recite the four questions, George suddenly connected. For a few moments, he was reciting the words alongside me: "*Mah nishtanah halailah hazeh*" (How different this night is!). It was a minor miracle, a brief moment of personal redemption. I will never forget that occasion.[2]

They might be called the invisible Jews—men and women, often elderly, who because of limited financial circumstances or compromised health find themselves isolated from the general Jewish community, living in non-Jewish institutions such as nursing homes. They often have no relatives who visit them regularly or anyone to advocate on their behalf. These institution-bound Jews cannot be adequately served by congregational clergy or by professional chaplaincies. Congregational rabbis and cantors do not have the resources to serve those outside their own membership, and most of these isolated people are not affiliated with any congregation. Although some institutional and community chaplaincies have been established to serve these so-called invisible Jews, the need far outstrips supply.

Some Jewish communities have responded to the spiritual concerns of people who are living in isolated circumstances by training lay members, called para-chaplains, to serve Jews who are homebound or in nursing homes, hospices, mental health centers, or prisons. Para-chaplaincy has been developed in various cities across North America, including Minneapolis, Los Angeles, Chicago, Palm Beach, Philadelphia, and Denver. The oldest of these programs has been in place for approximately twenty years. All of these programs include recruitment, formal training, placement, supervision, and interagency cooperation between organizations such as the Board of Rabbis and Jewish Family Service.[3]

Para-chaplains help isolated Jews by forging one-to-one relationships, by fostering Jewish ritual and programming, and by advocating for the needs of residents within institutions in which they serve. It is important to note that para-chaplains are not trained to provide pastoral care. They are not intended to be a substitute for professional pastoral caregivers. Para-chaplains should not be expected to address spiritual crisis, conflicted family dynamics, acute grief, and other complex situations that require a professional pastoral care response. Ideally, a para-chaplain functions under the supervision of and as an adjunct to a professional pastoral caregiver.

In this chapter, the description of para-chaplaincy concentrates on para-chaplaincy services to residents of nursing homes. Some brief comments are offered about services in other settings such as hospices, psychiatric hospitals, and prisons, which, although fundamentally similar, may differ in important ways. This chapter does not address acute care hospitals, where patients are usually best served by professional pastoral caregivers.

The Mandate for Para-Chaplaincy in Tradition

Although para-chaplaincy in its current form is a recent phenomenon, it has a strong basis within the history of Jewish communal life. Classic rabbinic texts underscore the importance of the *mitzvah* of *bikur cholim* (visiting the ill or suffering). All members of the community are obligated to engage in *bikur cholim* and *gemilut chasadim* (acts of loving-kindness), para-chaplaincy is a natural extension of this tradition because it engages members of the community in helping one another. In fact, *bikur cholim* committees of lay Jews have a long and exalted history as a communal institution.[4]

Two talmudic stories highlight the Rabbis' concerns with visiting those who are ill:

> One of Rabbi Akiva's students was ailing. For some reason—and we do not know if it was fear of contagion or neglect—no one came to visit this person. Finally Rabbi Akiva himself went to the ill student's bedside and began to sweep and make some order. The student subsequently recovered and credited his recovery to Rabbi Akiva's visit.[5]

There are several lessons to be learned from the narrative of this encounter. Those who are ill need to be visited. When we are sick—or infirm—we often feel cut off from the world, and social isolation can be devastating to morale. Rabbi Akiva understood that he needed to be personally involved in the healing process. Furthermore, Rabbi Akiva assessed what was needed and offered it. In this case, his help was of a practical nature. In being with someone who is ill, words are sometimes of help. At other moments one's presence brings comfort, and at still other times the situation calls for concrete measures, such as making a person feel comfortable (by getting water or adjusting pillows, for example.)

> Once, Rabbi Yohanan's colleague, Rabbi Hiya bar Abba, fell ill. Rabbi Yohanan visited Rabbi Hiya, took his hand, and cured him. Later, Rabbi Yohanan fell ill. A third colleague, Rabbi Hanina, visited him in turn. Rabbi Hanina took Rabbi Yohanan's hand, and Rabbi Hanina cured him.[6]

Of course, we might wonder: If Rabbi Yohanan had the power to cure others, why could he not heal himself? The text provides this answer: Just as prisoners who are incarcerated cannot free themselves, so prisoners of wounded bodies, ailing spirits, and devastated souls cannot heal themselves. Even this illustrious rabbi needed another person—or perhaps another person's touch—to facilitate his healing.

These tales remind us of our "power to bring wholeness, *refuat hanefesh* (healing of body) through our presence and our caring."[7]

The caring, presence, and concrete assistance of a caring person can help heal another. The para-chaplain, a caring representative of the Jewish community, can be that person.

The Role of the Para-Chaplain

One-to-One Relationship

Howard, a para-chaplain, recalls his relationship with Manny, a nursing home resident who was eighty-four years old:

> When we first met through para-chaplaincy, Manny became my teacher because of his intellect; in time, he became my friend. His deteriorating physical condition led him to become angry and bitter, which was difficult for me, but I understood that one must "meet people where they are," and that was where he was. It was sometimes hard to visit him, but I always felt better after going; Manny has no one else visiting him except those from Jewish Family Service. Now he is dying and does not have much time left. After five years of friendship, I will miss him. I have bonded to Manny and I have loved him. This has been an incredible experience—a real learning, rewarding experience.

Para-chaplains forge relationships with individuals on a one-to-one basis, providing a living Jewish presence for the person before them. In their roles as para-chaplains they may offer a sympathetic listening ear, enabling the person to share memories, fears, and joys as well as concrete, current concerns. The para-chaplain may also respond to the resident's spiritual needs by offering or sharing prayer.

Para-chaplains' very presence in a nursing home provides a tangible connection to the organized Jewish community. In addition to offering personal presence, para-chaplains can also bring other forms of connection, such as flyers or newsletters from local synagogues or communal organizations. If the resident wishes, para-chaplains can also provide links to a rabbi, cantor, or home congregation and request a visit or notifying them of a person's needs.

Advocacy

Helen, a para-chaplain, notes the impact of her presence on a nursing home resident's well-being:

Joan, a woman in her eighties, had been living at Sunrise Manor for three or four years. She was a fairly quiet person. She had been widowed for years. Joan's children lived out of town, and although she was reasonably friendly with the other Jewish resident at the nursing home, they were not close. After I began regular, weekly visits with Joan as part of the para-chaplaincy program, I noticed that the staff seemed to pay more attention to her. On a couple of occasions, I mentioned to staff that Joan seemed to be wearing the same dress, or that her hair needed some attention. Afterwards, she seemed to be better groomed. Suddenly, Joan was more than just "another resident" to the staff. She was someone who had outside connections. There was someone who was looking out for her.

The para-chaplain can serve as the advocate for an individual. Volunteer para-chaplains usually visit a person weekly or twice a month. In a broad sense, they are part of a professional team that interacts with residents, although they serve in an adjunct role. The residents' daily needs are met by nurses, nursing assistants, doctors, social workers, and support staff. These regular team members have ongoing relationships with residents. Most of residents' care is provided by nursing assistants. These direct-care staff perform challenging and stressful work, often with poor compensation and minimal training. Abuse and neglect are, unfortunately, part of the reality in a minority of staff–resident relationships.

Often, residents do not have regular visitors from *outside* the institution. A visit by a para-chaplain may have the added benefit of raising the profile of the resident, demonstrating to staff members that someone from outside the institution cares about this individual. Furthermore, the resident may share needs and concerns with a para-chaplain that he or she might not express to staff members, or which have not been responded to by staff. By making these needs known, the para-chaplain can be a liaison between the resident and the staff.

A delicate aspect of interacting with the institutional staff members is the difficulty of assessing the accuracy of a resident's complaints or allegations of neglect or abuse. A resident's statement that she was not given breakfast that morning, that a staff member took a long time to answer the call button, or that clothes and money are missing may or may not be true. The resident may or may not be a chronic complainer, or she may be demented. On the other hand, the resident's complaint may be accurate. Para-chaplains should find out if residents would like concerns to be shared with facility staff or the para-chaplaincy coordinator. If residents are unable to grant permission, the para-chaplains may consider reporting the problem based on their observations.

Jewish Programming

Michael, a para-chaplain, was thrilled to share a moment of celebration with isolated Jewish nursing home residents:

> At Cornerstone Nursing Home, there were three long-time Jewish residents, and they were isolated from the 100 or so non-Jewish residents. At Chanukah, I came equipped with a small *chanukiyah* for each of the Jewish residents; I brought candles and *dreidels* and even *latkes* and applesauce. They were touched that someone would care enough to fry the *latkes* and get the *dreidels*. At this season, they felt particularly alienated by the Christmas festivities. Although the staff wanted to include the Jewish residents, Christmas parties could not meet their emotional and spiritual needs. I could see that our Chanukah get-together made a difference to them.

When there are few Jewish residents in a facility, there will likely be limited Jewish programs, if there are any at all. Most staff are not Jewish, and understandably have a limited knowledge of Judaism. The Jewish resident may feel alienated when surrounded by extensive programs and worship marking Christian holidays; thus, the para-chaplain may be the resident's only link to Judaism. The para-chaplain can make a difference by conducting a brief Shabbat or holiday service on the actual day or a few days in advance. A number of community para-chaplaincy programs have developed abridged Shabbat and festival services appropriate for frail and elderly nursing home residents.[8]

The para-chaplain can also bring other aspects of Jewish culture to the isolated resident. These might include literature, photographs, pamphlets, and recordings of Jewish music or videos of Jewish interest. Materials pertaining to the State of Israel may be of particular interest to some residents.

In many situations, all that is required of the para-chaplain is simply to being present as a caring emissary of the Jewish community; this is a goal in itself. Although many nursing home residents want the para-chaplain to bring *Yiddishkeit* (Jewishness) into their lives, other residents simply need the companionship of another Jewish person. The presence of a representative of the Jewish community is valuable not only to nursing home residents but also to those individuals who are more socially isolated, such as those in a hospital or hospice or who are homebound or in prison.

Organizing a Para-Chaplaincy Program

A Home for the Program

There is no automatic home base for the para-chaplaincy program. One natural setting is a Jewish Family Service agency. Other possibilities are the Jewish Federation or a community chaplaincy program. The Jewish Family Service agency may be the most natural fit if it has a nursing home coordinator or a unit serving older persons. The nursing home coordinator and the para-chaplains can share important information with each other.

Staffing: The Para-Chaplaincy Coordinator

Since a para-chaplaincy program requires recruitment, screening, coordination, and the ongoing supervision of para-chaplains, it is essential to have a professional para-chaplaincy coordinator. The para-chaplaincy coordinator should have social work, chaplaincy, or other related clinical training. Necessary skills for the coordinator include organizational ability, willingness to be a team player, and active listening acumen, both for screening potential para-chaplains and for the ongoing support that she or he will offer them as well. A sense of humor is always a valuable asset.

Budget

The budget for the para-chaplaincy program should include funds for the para-chaplaincy coordinator (salary and benefits); design, printing, and mailing of para-chaplaincy brochures; advertisements in the local Anglo-Jewish press; food for training sessions; and honoraria for speakers. It should also allow for production of a para-chaplaincy calling card (leaving a space for the para-chaplain to fill in his or her name) as well as identification badges for para-chaplains to wear when they are visiting. The para-chaplaincy program should also allot funds for Judaica materials that para-chaplains may leave with the residents: prayer/blessing cards, cassette tapes, holiday foods, and ritual items.

Bring the Local Rabbis and Cantors on Board

Para-chaplains can embody the vital message to a Jewish person in an institution that the community has not forgotten him or her, and their visits can serve as a complement to the invaluable visits of rabbis and cantors. When clergy are unable to visit, para-chaplains' presence is especially beneficial. Rabbis and cantors should thus be natural allies and strong supporters of the para-chaplaincy program. It is important for those creating a para-chaplaincy program to communicate with local rabbis and cantors, to explain the nature of the program, to allay any concerns, and to obtain their help in recruiting volunteers.

Some synagogues have *bikur cholim* committees that visit ill members of their own congregation, and sometimes other Jews in nearby hospitals or nursing homes. In principle, para-chaplaincy could coordinate with such groups. Although *bikur cholim* volunteers provide a caring presence on an occasional basis, para-chaplains provide more in-depth service to individuals and establish *ongoing* relationships. These two missions can complement one another. The para-chaplaincy coordinator can contact local congregations to find out what efforts are already in place. For some congregations, joint training might be desirable.

Recruitment

Potential para-chaplains may be found among volunteers in local synagogues, communal organizations, or the Jewish Federation. Area rabbis and cantors, Jewish communal professionals, and volunteers can be good referral sources both for current volunteers and for those without a history of volunteering.

Recruitment is often a one-on-one effort. It takes time to explain properly this unique volunteer opportunity and the responsibilities that it carries. It is advisable to recruit more para-chaplains than are actually needed because there is inevitably attrition over the course of training and preparation. Although there are great joys in this work, it also contains many moments of stress and sadness. Para-chaplaincy encourages people to encounter fragility and mortality, and some who volunteer will realize that it is too uncomfortable for them.

Screening

Candidates for para-chaplaincy must be carefully screened. Para-chaplains should be outgoing, friendly, and communicate easily; they must be able to listen and to be silent. A basic knowledge of Judaism is also important. Not everyone who comes forward to volunteer is suited for this kind of work. Applications should require a detailed reference from a local rabbi or communal professional, and all candidates should be interviewed. It is important to be cautious in considering candidates who have recently suffered a bereavement or serious illness of their own because they may not be ready to confront the emotional challenges of para-chaplaincy. In addition, people who cannot commit enough time to this program and those who have failed to follow through on past volunteer commitments should not be accepted: Consistency is important.

After a training period, para-chaplains are asked to commit to visiting their clients for a six-month period; less than six months is an insufficient return on the amount of time taken to train the para-chaplain. It also would be disruptive for the clients who are visited. Para-chaplains should commit to visiting their clients a certain number of times per month, usually every week or two. For administrative purposes, a minimal number of clients may be suggested. Alternatively, the para-chaplain might be assigned to a particular facility and to be available to any Jewish resident within that facility who would welcome a visit.

Training

There is no one way to train para-chaplains; likewise, there is no special order to the content of the training. The subjects and concepts in the outline below represent a suggested core curriculum. The length of each session may vary, but the first session will probably require a minimum of three hours. This initial training session ideally will include a shared meal, which helps participants establish rapport and begin to build relationships with each other and the professional staff. It is valuable to offer refreshments at each subsequent session and to schedule break times.

Six sessions are a reasonable time frame for covering the material necessary to prepare para-chaplains. Various pedagogic modalities might be used, including didactic presentations, small group discussions, experiential exercises, role-playing, and visits to a nursing home.

Para-Chaplaincy Training Program: A Suggested Curriculum

Session 1: Introduction to Para-chaplaincy

- A description of the program
- The need for para-chaplaincy
- The distinction between the roles of para-chaplain, chaplain, and congregational rabbi or cantor
- The traditional mandate for para-chaplaincy: textual study on *bikur cholim*
- The perspective of previously trained para-chaplains

Session 2: Older Adults and the Aging Process

- Characteristics of the elderly and the aging process
- Spiritual challenges and needs of aging persons
- An understanding of dementia
- Ethical issues in dealing with the aging

Session 3: Jewish Views of Dying and Death

- Core Jewish values on caring for the dying person
- Traditional and liberal Jewish perspectives on end-of-life medical decisions
- Jewish views on the afterlife
- Explanation how residents cope with other residents' deaths
- Exploration of para-chaplains' feelings about death and their own mortality

Session 4: Listening Skills and Being Present

- Listening with a discerning ear
- Responding to anger, grief, and other emotions
- Talking to a resident who has a different approach to Jewish tradition
- Meeting the resident where he or she is
- Using "validation" as a technique for working with those with dementia[9]

Session 5: Bringing Judaism to the Nursing Home

- Fostering Jewish life in a non-Jewish nursing home
- Using prayer in encounters (spontaneous or liturgical)
- Leading worship services, celebrations
- Sharing Jewish resources with residents

Session 6: Becoming an Effective Para-Chaplain

- The relationship of the para-chaplain to the care team: collaboration and advocacy
- Respect for confidentiality
- Infection control
- Knowing one's own limits/reaching out for support

Identifying Individuals to Serve

Referrals of people to visit may come to the para-chaplaincy program from a number of sources. The nursing home coordinator at Jewish Family Service or other communal agencies may have a list of names of Jewish nursing home residents. Referrals may come from a relative, a friend or acquaintance, or a staff member at the facility. Ideally, nursing home residents should give permission before being visited by a para-chaplain, perhaps through a rabbi, community chaplain, or a social worker from the facility or a communal agency. However, it is not always possible to secure consent, thus the para-chaplain may simply ask the person if he or she would like a visit.

In all cases, confidentiality is required. Visiting at a hospice, a psychiatric hospital, a prison, or in a private home may require the person's advance consent. The Jewish person to be visited may be embarrassed about being in any of these settings, or may simply wish to maintain his or her privacy. Concerns such as these demonstrate the care and planning required in bringing para-chaplaincy to these contexts.

Supervision

The para-chaplaincy program should develop standards and procedures for monitoring the work of the para-chaplains. Under some circumstances, a para-chaplain may need to be dismissed or given a leave of absence. Reasons might include refusal to accept supervision; inappropriate behavior with a resident; showing disrespect for a resident's religious beliefs; failure to visit regularly; or other concerns raised by the institution's personnel.

The para-chaplaincy coordinator will probably serve as the supervisor. The supervisor should maintain regular contact with the institutions served, to communicate about potential problems or successful programming. It is also desirable to develop a process to evaluate para-chaplains on a regular basis. This process might include the para-chaplain's self-evaluation and input from facility staff and the supervisor.

The supervisor should maintain both telephone and face-to-face contact with para-chaplains themselves. In regular supervisory conversations, the supervisor can draw out strengths and weaknesses and check to ensure that para-chaplains are honoring their time commitment. The supervisor can support para-chaplains and provide concrete suggestions and techniques for problem solving. When a para-chaplain is new, bimonthly, in-person supervision sessions are particularly beneficial. Although documentation of para-chaplains' work can be helpful, it is time-consuming and may discourage volunteers. On the other hand, documentation allows for heightened accountability of the program. It also facilitates demonstration of the impact of the program by providing statistics on numbers of people served and of time spent with them.

Group Support for Para-Chaplains

Para-chaplains should meet as a group on a monthly basis to share their experiences and to debrief, at least for the first few months after their training. It is empowering and meaningful for para-chaplains to learn from each other's experiences. They may find comfort and inspiration in sharing the often complex emotions evoked by their para-chaplaincy work. Developing a supportive peer group is essential.

Conclusion

A para-chaplaincy program can provide enormous gifts to the community. Para-chaplains are living links to the Jewish community who perform the *mitzvah* of *bikur cholim*. They extend caring to isolated people who are very much in need of regular and personal visits. Para-chaplains can serve as the community's eyes and ears, as helping hands, as people who are present. Para-chaplaincy is an honorable and honored position in which to serve: Their very presence is a manifestation of God's presence.

Notes

1. I am very grateful to Sandie Eichberg, former Director of Volunteer Services at Jewish Family Service in Denver and founding Para-chaplaincy coordinator; Rabbi Deborah Pipe-Mazo, who was the creator of the Para-Chaplaincy program in Philadelphia; Rabbi Alan Sherman, Community Chaplain, Jewish Federation of Palm Beach County, Florida, who has been involved in the Chaplain Aides program for many years in Florida; Rabbi E. Robert Kraus who was involved with Para-Chaplaincy for the Southern California Board of Rabbis; and Chaplain Sheila Segal of the Board of Rabbis of Greater Philadelphia. All read this chapter in draft form and offered valuable suggestions.

2. This and other case vignettes in this chapter are told in the words of the para-chaplains who reported them.

3. For example, see Marilyn Silverstein, "Chaplain Brings God into a House of Pain," *Jewish Exponent,* Philadelphia (Jan. 27, 1995), p. 6; Ron Hayes, "Volunteer a Rabbi in Spirit," *The Palm Beach Post,* Palm Beach, Fl. (July 6, 1998), p. 1B; "Para-Chaplains Offer Comfort," *Family Matters,* a publication of Jewish Family Service, Denver (May 1998), p. 1.

4. For a historical account of the development of such committees, see Joseph S. Ozarowski, "*Bikur cholim* Committees," in *To Walk in God's Ways: Jewish Pastoral Perspectives on Illness and Bereavement* (Northvale, N.J.: Jason Aronson, 1995), pp. 64–66.

5. BT Nedarim 40a.

6. BT Berachot 5b.

7. Adapted from Bonita E. Taylor and David J. Zucker, "Everything I Wish My Non-Jewish Supervisors Had Known about Me as a Jewish Supervisee." Tentative title, article forthcoming.

8. Large-print, abridged Shabbat prayer books are available from Rabbi Cary

Kozberg, Chaplain, Wexner Heritage Village, 1151 College Avenue, Columbus, OH 43209-2827. Packets with Shabbat and holiday programs designed for Jewish nursing home residents are available from Sacred Seasons, Reconstructionist Rabbinical College, Church Road and Greenwood Avenue, Wyncote, PA 19095, 215-576-0800.

9. See Naomi Feils, *The Validation Breakthrough: Simple Techniques for Communicating with People with "Alzheimer's-Type" Dementia* (Baltimore: Health Professions Press, 1993).

Bibliography

Ellis, Susan J. *The Volunteer Recruitment Book.* Philadelphia: Energize, Inc. (5450 Wissahickon Avenue, Philadelphia, PA 19144).

Feils, Naomi. *The Validation Breakthrough: Simple Techniques for Communicating with People with "Alzheimer's-Type" Dementia.* Baltimore: Health Professions Press, 1993.

McCurley, Steve, and Rick Lynch. *Volunteer Management: Mobilizing All of the Resources of the Community.* Heritage Arts Publishing (1807 Prairie Avenue, Downers Grove, IL 60515).

Hill, Patrick. *The Challenges of Aging: Retrieving Spiritual Traditions* (Park Ridge Center, 211 E. Ontario, Suite 800, Chicago, IL 60611, 1999). Training program with leader guide and videotapes for congregational volunteers serving nursing home residents.

Ozarowski, Joseph S. *To Walk in God's Ways: Jewish Pastoral Perspectives on Illness and Bereavement.* Northvale, N.J.: Jason Aronson, 1995. See in particular, *"Bikur cholim* Committees," pp. 64–66.

Schirn, A. "In Praise of Para-Rabbinics," *Reform Judaism* 16 (fall 1987).

Rabbi David J. Zucker, Ph.D., is the Director of Pastoral Care and Recreation at Shalom Park in Aurora, Colorado. A former congregational rabbi and Jewish Community Chaplain, he serves on the national board of the National Association of Jewish Chaplains, and he chaired their 1999, 2000, and 2001 national conferences.

Glossary

Aggadah (aggadic): legends, tales included in rabbinic literature.

Adonai: my Lord; one of the names for God.

Amidah (literally, standing): prayer—19 benedictions recited in daily worship services.

Aliyah: the honor of being called to the Torah.

Avel: a mourner.

Bar (Bat) mitzvah: ceremony at which a Jewish thirteen-year-old (some girls do this at twelve) is called to the Torah to mark their entry to the community as an adult.

Bet Din: rabbinic court.

Ben gil: a peer.

Bikur cholim: visiting the sick.

Bimah: pulpit from which services are led and where the *Aron Kodesh* (holy ark that holds the Torah scrolls) is found.

Birkat hamazon: grace after meals.

Brit mila: circumcision.

Chalah: braided egg bread eaten on Shabbat.

Cheder: school for teaching Torah to young children.

Chanukah: holiday commemorating rededication of the Temple in Jerusalem after it was defiled; a celebration of freedom and light.

Choleh: ill person.

Chesed: loving-kindness.

Chupah: marriage canopy; marriage ceremony.

Davven: pray.

Dreidel: top used for Chanukah game.

Gemilut chasadim: deeds of loving-kindness.

Get: Jewish divorce.

Gomel: blessing recited after surviving a life-threatening situation.

Gut Shabbes: greeting to wish someone a good Sabbath (Yiddish).

Haggadah: liturgical text for the Passover Seder; tells the story of the Exodus from Egypt.

Halacha (halachic): Jewish law/legal interpretation.

Hamakom: the Place, a name for God.

Hamotzi: blessing over bread.

Hitlavut ruchanit: spiritual accompanying. A term for Jewish pastoral care.

Kaddish: memorial prayer for the dead, recited by close relatives of the deceased for eleven months after the death, and thereafter on the anniversary of the death.

Kashrut: Jewish dietary laws.

Kavannah: sacred intention.

Kedushah: holiness; one of the central prayers in the daily worship service.

Keriah: rending of one's garments upon hearing of the death of a loved one.

Kiddush: blessing over wine expressing sanctity of Shabbat and each festival; also, reception after festival or Shabbat morning services.

Kishkas: "guts."

Latkes: potato pancake eaten on Chanukah.

Machzor: High Holy Day prayer book.

Maror: bitter herbs eaten at the Passover Seder to symbolize the bitterness of slavery in Egypt.

Matzah: unleavened bread eaten on Passover.

Menorah: nine-branched candelabrum lit on Chanukah; also *chanukiyah*.

Misheberach: blessing for healing.

Midrash: rabbinic explication or expansion of Bible story.

Minyan: quorum of ten adult Jews necessary for reciting certain prayers.

Mitlaveh/mitlavah ruchanit: pastoral caregiver (spiritual accompanier).

Mitzvah (plural, *mitzvot*): commandment or religious obligation; colloquial: good deed.

Nefesh: soul.

Neshamah (Yiddish, *neshomeh*): soul

Niggun: wordless melody.

Oneg Shabbat: Shabbat joy; also, reception after Friday evening services.

Refuah shelemah: a full healing.

Refuat haguf: physical healing.

Refuat hanefesh: spiritual healing.

Rosh Chodesh: the new moon; beginning of month on the Hebrew calendar.

Seder: ritual meal on Passover, at which the story of the Exodus from Egypt is told.

Sefer Torah: Torah scroll.

Shabbat: Jewish Sabbath, Friday sundown to Saturday night after sundown. A day of rest and holiness.

Shabbat Shalom: greeting wishing someone Sabbath peace.

Shaliach: emissary, messenger.

Shalom aleichem: peace unto you, a greeting; also a song for the eve of Shabbat.

Shechina: the Divine Presence.

Shechita: [kosher] slaughter.

Shema: central Jewish prayer affirming God's unity.

Shofar: ram's horn blown on Rosh Hashanah, the Jewish New Year.

Shiva: week of mourning after a funeral, when the bereaved stay at home and are visited by friends and members of the community.

Shul: synagogue (Yiddish).

Siddur: prayer book.

Sukkah: temporary shelter/hut built for the holiday of Sukkot/Tabernacles; represents temporary homes of the Israelites during the wandering in the wilderness; symbol of human fragility and God's protection.

Talmud Torah: Torah study.

Tallit: prayer shawl, worn at morning services.

Tefilah: prayer.

Tefillin: phylacteries, traditionally worn during morning worship.

Teshuvah: repentance.

Tzedakah: righteous action, such as giving charity.

Viddui: final confessional prayer, recited on one's deathbed.

Yizkor: special memorial prayers recited for the deceased on Yom Kippur and on the festivals of Shemini Atzeret, Passover, and Shavuot.

Yom Tov: festival.

Yohrtzeit (or *yahrzeit*): the anniversary of a death, marked by lighting a memorial candle and reciting of the *Kaddish* prayer (Yiddish).

Index of
Terms and Concepts

Index of Classical Sources Cited (Biblical and Rabbinic)

Torah

Notes

Notes

Notes

Notes

About JEWISH LIGHTS Publishing

People of all faiths and backgrounds yearn for books that attract, engage, educate and spiritually inspire.

Our principal goal is to stimulate thought and help all people learn about who the Jewish People are, where they come from, and what the future can be made to hold. While people of our diverse Jewish heritage are the primary audience, our books speak to people in the Christian world as well and will broaden their understanding of Judaism and the roots of their own faith.

We bring to you authors who are at the forefront of spiritual thought and experience. While each has something different to say, they all say it in a voice that you can hear.

Our books are designed to welcome you and then to engage, stimulate and inspire. We judge our success not only by whether or not our books are beautiful and commercially successful, but by whether or not they make a difference in your life.

We at Jewish Lights take great care to produce beautiful books that present meaningful spiritual content in a form that reflects the art of making high quality books. Therefore, we want to acknowledge those who contributed to the production of this book.

Stuart M. Matlins, Publisher

PRODUCTION
Marian B. Wallace & Bridgett Taylor

EDITORIAL
Sandra Korinchak, Emily Wichland,
Martha McKinney & Amanda Dupuis

JACKET DESIGN
Bridgett Taylor

TEXT DESIGN & TYPESETTING
Sans Serif, Inc., Saline, Michigan

JACKET / TEXT PRINTING & BINDING
Lake Book, Melrose Park, Illinois

Spirituality

Does the Soul Survive?
A Jewish Journey to Belief in Afterlife, Past Lives & Living with Purpose
by *Rabbi Elie Kaplan Spitz;* Foreword by *Brian L. Weiss, M.D.*

Do we have a soul that survives our earthly existence? To know the answer is to find greater understanding, comfort and purpose in our lives. Here, Spitz relates his own experiences and those shared with him by people he has worked with as a rabbi, and shows us that belief in afterlife and past lives, so often approached with reluctance, is in fact true to Jewish tradition. 6 x 9, 288 pp, HC, ISBN 1-58023-094-6 **$21.95**

The Women's Torah Commentary: *New Insights from Women Rabbis*
on the 54 Weekly Torah Portions Ed. by *Rabbi Elyse Goldstein*

For the first time, women rabbis provide a commentary on the entire Torah. More than 25 years after the first woman was ordained a rabbi in America, these inspiring teachers bring their rich perspectives to bear on the biblical text. In a week-by-week format; a perfect gift for others, or for yourself. 6 x 9, 496 pp, HC, ISBN 1-58023-076-8 **$34.95**

Bringing the Psalms to Life
How to Understand and Use the Book of Psalms by *Rabbi Daniel F. Polish*

Here, the most beloved—and least understood—of the books in the Bible comes alive. This simultaneously insightful and practical guide shows how the psalms address a myriad of spiritual issues in our lives: feeling abandoned, overcoming illness, dealing with anger, and more. 6 x 9, 208 pp, HC, ISBN 1-58023-077-6 **$21.95**

Stepping Stones to Jewish Spiritual Living: *Walking the Path Morning, Noon, and Night*
by Rabbi James L. Mirel & Karen Bonnell Werth
6 x 9, 240 pp, Quality PB, ISBN 1-58023-074-1 **$16.95**

The Business Bible
10 New Commandments for Bringing Spirituality & Ethical Values into the Workplace
by Rabbi Wayne Dosick 5½ x 8½, 208 pp, Quality PB, ISBN 1-58023-101-2 **$14.95**

Moses—The Prince, the Prophet: *His Life, Legend & Message for Our Lives*
by Rabbi Levi Meier, Ph.D. 6 x 9, 224 pp, Quality PB, ISBN 1-58023-069-5 **$16.95**

Ancient Secrets: *Using the Stories of the Bible to Improve Our Everyday Lives*
by Rabbi Levi Meier, Ph.D. 5½ x 8½, 288 pp, Quality PB, ISBN 1-58023-064-4 **$16.95**

Or phone, fax, mail or e-mail to: **JEWISH LIGHTS Publishing**
Sunset Farm Offices, Route 4 • P.O. Box 237 • Woodstock, Vermont 05091
Tel: (802) 457-4000 • Fax: (802) 457-4004 • www.jewishlights.com
Credit card orders: **(800) 962-4544** (9AM–5PM ET Monday–Friday)
Generous discounts on quantity orders. SATISFACTION GUARANTEED. Prices subject to change.

Spirituality & More

The Jewish Lights Spirituality Handbook
A Guide to Understanding, Exploring & Living a Spiritual Life
Ed. by *Stuart M. Matlins, Editor-in-Chief, Jewish Lights Publishing*
Rich, creative material from over 50 spiritual leaders on every aspect of Jewish spirituality today: prayer, meditation, mysticism, study, rituals, special days, the everyday, and more.
6 x 9, 304 pp, Quality PB, ISBN 1-58023-093-8 **$16.95**; HC, ISBN 1-58023-100-4 **$24.95**

Six Jewish Spiritual Paths: *A Rationalist Looks at Spirituality*
by *Rabbi Rifat Sonsino*
The quest for spirituality is universal, but which path to spirituality is right *for you*? A straightforward, objective discussion of the many ways—each valid and authentic—for seekers to gain a richer spiritual life within Judaism. 6 x 9, 208 pp, HC, ISBN 1-58023-095-4 **$21.95**

Restful Reflections: *Nighttime Inspiration to Calm the Soul,*
Based on Jewish Wisdom by *Rabbi Kerry M. Olitzky* and *Rabbi Lori Forman*
Wisdom to "sleep on." For each night of the year, an inspiring quote from a Jewish source and a personal reflection on it from an insightful spiritual leader helps you to focus on your spiritual life and the lessons your day has offered. The companion to *Sacred Intentions: Daily Inspiration to Strengthen the Spirit, Based on Jewish Wisdom* (see below).
4½ x 6½, 448 pp, Quality PB, ISBN 1-58023-091-1 **$15.95**

Sacred Intentions: *Daily Inspiration to Strengthen the Spirit, Based on Jewish Wisdom*
by Rabbi Kerry M. Olitzky and Rabbi Lori Forman
4½ x 6½, 448 pp, Quality PB, ISBN 1-58023-061-X **$15.95**

The Enneagram and Kabbalah: *Reading Your Soul*
by Rabbi Howard A. Addison 6 x 9, 176 pp, Quality PB, ISBN 1-58023-001-6 **$15.95**

Embracing the Covenant: *Converts to Judaism Talk About Why & How*
Ed. and with Intros. by Rabbi Allan L. Berkowitz and Patti Moskovitz
6 x 9, 192 pp, Quality PB, ISBN 1-879045-50-8 **$15.95**

Shared Dreams: *Martin Luther King, Jr. and the Jewish Community*
by Rabbi Marc Schneier; Preface by Martin Luther King III
6 x 9, 240 pp, HC, ISBN 1-58023-062-8 **$24.95**

Mystery Midrash: *An Anthology of Jewish Mystery & Detective Fiction*
Ed. by Lawrence W. Raphael; Preface by Joel Siegel, ABC's *Good Morning America*
6 x 9, 304 pp, Quality PB, ISBN 1-58023-055-5 **$16.95**

Wandering Stars: *An Anthology of Jewish Fantasy & Science Fiction* Ed. by Jack Dann; Intro. by Isaac Asimov 6 x 9, 272 pp, Quality PB, ISBN 1-58023-005-9 **$16.95**

More Wandering Stars
An Anthology of Outstanding Stories of Jewish Fantasy and Science Fiction
Ed. by Jack Dann; Intro. by Isaac Asimov 6 x 9, 192 pp, Quality PB, ISBN 1-58023-063-6 **$16.95**

Spirituality—The Kushner Series
Books by Lawrence Kushner

The Way Into Jewish Mystical Tradition

Explains the principles of Jewish mystical thinking, their religious and spiritual significance, and how they relate to our lives. A book that allows us to experience and understand the Jewish mystical approach to our place in the world.   6 x 9, 176 pp, HC, ISBN 1-58023-029-6 **$21.95**

Eyes Remade for Wonder
The Way of Jewish Mysticism and Sacred Living
A Lawrence Kushner Reader Intro. by *Thomas Moore*

Whether you are new to Kushner or a devoted fan, you'll find inspiration here. With samplings from each of Kushner's works, and a generous amount of new material, this book is to be read and reread, each time discovering deeper layers of meaning in our lives.
6 x 9, 240 pp, Quality PB, ISBN 1-58023-042-3 **$16.95**; HC, ISBN 1-58023-014-8 **$23.95**

Because Nothing Looks Like God

by *Lawrence and Karen Kushner*; Full-color illus. by *Dawn W. Majewski*

What is God like? The first collaborative work by husband-and-wife team Lawrence and Karen Kushner introduces children to the possibilities of spiritual life with three poetic spiritual stories. Real-life examples of happiness and sadness—from goodnight stories, to the hope and fear felt the first time at bat, to the closing moments of life—invite us to explore, together with our children, the questions we all have about God, no matter what our age.
11 x 8½, 32 pp, HC, Full-color illus., ISBN 1-58023-092-X **$16.95**

    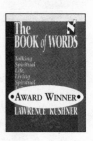

Invisible Lines of Connection: *Sacred Stories of the Ordinary* AWARD WINNER!
6 x 9, 160 pp, Quality PB, ISBN 1-879045-98-2 **$15.95**; HC, ISBN 1-879045-52-4 **$21.95**

Honey from the Rock SPECIAL ANNIVERSARY EDITION
An Introduction to Jewish Mysticism 6 x 9, 176 pp, Quality PB, ISBN 1-58023-073-3 **$15.95**

The Book of Letters: *A Mystical Hebrew Alphabet* AWARD WINNER!
Popular HC Edition, 6 x 9, 80 pp, 2-color text, ISBN 1-879045-00-1 **$24.95**; *Deluxe Gift Edition,* 9 x 12, 80 pp, HC, 2-color text, ornamentation, slipcase, ISBN 1-879045-01-X **$79.95**; *Collector's Limited Edition,* 9 x 12, 80 pp, HC, gold-embossed pages, hand-assembled slipcase. With silkscreened print. Limited to 500 signed and numbered copies, ISBN 1-879045-04-4 **$349.00**

The Book of Words: *Talking Spiritual Life, Living Spiritual Talk* AWARD WINNER!
6 x 9, 160 pp, Quality PB, 2-color text, ISBN 1-58023-020-2 **$16.95**;
152 pp, HC, ISBN 1-879045-35-4 **$21.95**

God Was in This Place & I, i Did Not Know
Finding Self, Spirituality and Ultimate Meaning
6 x 9, 192 pp, Quality PB, ISBN 1-879045-33-8 **$16.95**

The River of Light: *Jewish Mystical Awareness* SPECIAL ANNIVERSARY EDITION
6 x 9, 192 pp, Quality PB, ISBN 1-58023-096-2 **$16.95**

Life Cycle & Holidays

How to Be a Perfect Stranger, In 2 Volumes
A Guide to Etiquette in Other People's Religious Ceremonies
Ed. by *Stuart M. Matlins* & *Arthur J. Magida* AWARD WINNER!

What will happen? What do I do? What do I wear? What do I say? What are their basic beliefs? Should I bring a gift? In question-and-answer format, explains the rituals and celebrations of America's major religions/denominations, helping an interested guest to feel comfortable, participate to the fullest extent possible, and avoid violating anyone's religious principles. Not presented from the perspective of any particular faith.

Vol. 1: *America's Largest Faiths*, 6 x 9, 432 pp, HC, ISBN 1-879045-39-7 **$24.95**
Vol. 2: *Other Faiths in America*, 6 x 9, 416 pp, HC, ISBN 1-879045-63-X **$24.95**

Putting God on the Guest List, 2nd Ed.
How to Reclaim the Spiritual Meaning of Your Child's Bar or Bat Mitzvah
by *Rabbi Jeffrey K. Salkin* AWARD WINNER!

The most influential book about finding core spiritual values in American Jewry's most misunderstood ceremony. 6 x 9, 224 pp, Quality PB, ISBN 1-879045-59-1 **$16.95**

For Kids—Putting God on Your Guest List
How to Claim the Spiritual Meaning of Your Bar or Bat Mitzvah
by Rabbi Jeffrey K. Salkin 6 x 9, 144 pp, Quality PB, ISBN 1-58023-015-6 **$14.95**

Bar/Bat Mitzvah Basics: *A Practical Family Guide to Coming of Age Together*
Ed. by Cantor Helen Leneman 6 x 9, 240 pp, Quality PB, ISBN 1-879045-54-0 **$16.95**;
HC, ISBN 1-879045-51-6 **$24.95**

The New Jewish Baby Book AWARD WINNER!
Names, Ceremonies, & Customs—A Guide for Today's Families
by Anita Diamant 6 x 9, 336 pp, Quality PB, ISBN 1-879045-28-1 **$16.95**

Hanukkah: The Art of Jewish Living
by Dr. Ron Wolfson 7 x 9, 192 pp, Quality PB, Illus., ISBN 1-879045-97-4 **$16.95**

The Shabbat Seder: The Art of Jewish Living
by Dr. Ron Wolfson 7 x 9, 272 pp, Quality PB, Illus., ISBN 1-879045-90-7 **$16.95**
Also available are these helpful companions to *The Shabbat Seder:* Booklet of the Blessings and Songs, ISBN 1-879045-91-5 **$5.00**; Audiocassette of the Blessings, DN03 **$6.00**; Teacher's Guide, ISBN 1-879045-92-3 **$4.95**

The Passover Seder: The Art of Jewish Living
by Dr. Ron Wolfson 7 x 9, 352 pp, Quality PB, Illus., ISBN 1-879045-93-1 **$16.95**
Also available are these helpful companions to *The Passover Seder:* Passover Workbook, ISBN 1-879045-94-X **$6.95**; Audiocassette of the Blessings, DN04 **$6.00**; Teacher's Guide, ISBN 1-879045-95-8 **$6.95**

The Jewish Gardening Cookbook: *Growing Plants & Cooking for Holidays & Festivals*
by Michael Brown 6 x 9, 224 pp, Illus., Quality PB, ISBN 1-58023-116-0 **$16.95**;
HC, ISBN 1-58023-004-0 **$21.95**

Theology/Philosophy

A Heart of Many Rooms: *Celebrating the Many Voices within Judaism*
by *Dr. David Hartman* AWARD WINNER!
Addresses the spiritual and theological questions that face all Jews and all people today. From the perspective of traditional Judaism, Hartman shows that commitment to both Jewish tradition and to pluralism can create understanding between people of different religious convictions. 6 x 9, 352 pp, HC, ISBN 1-58023-048-2 **$24.95**

A Living Covenant: *The Innovative Spirit in Traditional Judaism*
by *Dr. David Hartman* AWARD WINNER!
Winner, National Jewish Book Award. Hartman reveals a Judaism grounded in covenant—a relational framework—informed by the metaphor of marital love rather than that of parent-child dependency. 6 x 9, 368 pp, Quality PB, ISBN 1-58023-011-3 **$18.95**

 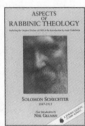  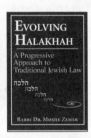 

These Are the Words: *A Vocabulary of Jewish Spiritual Life*
by Arthur Green 6 x 9, 304 pp, Quality PB, ISBN 1-58023-107-1 **$18.95**

Evolving Halakhah: *A Progressive Approach to Traditional Jewish Law*
by Rabbi Dr. Moshe Zemer 6 x 9, 480 pp, HC, ISBN 1-58023-002-4 **$40.00**

The Death of Death: *Resurrection and Immortality in Jewish Thought* AWARD WINNER!
by Dr. Neil Gillman 6 x 9, 336 pp, Quality PB, ISBN 1-58023-081-4 **$18.95**;
HC, ISBN 1-879045-61-3 **$23.95**

Aspects of Rabbinic Theology by Solomon Schechter; New Intro. by Dr. Neil Gillman
6 x 9, 448 pp, Quality PB, ISBN 1-879045-24-9 **$19.95**

The Last Trial: *On the Legends and Lore of the Command to Abraham to Offer Isaac as a Sacrifice* by Shalom Spiegel; New Intro. by Judah Goldin
6 x 9, 208 pp, Quality PB, ISBN 1-879045-29-X **$17.95**

Judaism and Modern Man: *An Interpretation of Jewish Religion* by Will Herberg;
New Intro. by Dr. Neil Gillman 5½ x 8½, 336 pp, Quality PB, ISBN 1-879045-87-7 **$18.95**

Seeking the Path to Life AWARD WINNER!
Theological Meditations on God and the Nature of People, Love, Life and Death
by Rabbi Ira F. Stone
6 x 9, 160 pp, Quality PB, ISBN 1-879045-47-8 **$14.95**; HC, ISBN 1-879045-17-6 **$19.95**

The Spirit of Renewal: *Finding Faith after the Holocaust* AWARD WINNER!
by Rabbi Edward Feld
6 x 9, 224 pp, Quality PB, ISBN 1-879045-40-0 **$16.95**

Tormented Master: *The Life and Spiritual Quest of Rabbi Nahman of Bratslav*
by Dr. Arthur Green
6 x 9, 416 pp, Quality PB, ISBN 1-879045-11-7 **$18.95**

Ecology/Spirituality

Torah of the Earth: *Exploring 4,000 Years of Ecology in Jewish Thought*
In 2 Volumes Ed. by *Rabbi Arthur Waskow*

Major new resource offering us an invaluable key to understanding the intersection of ecology and Judaism. Leading scholars provide us with a guided tour of ecological thought from four major Jewish viewpoints.

Vol. 1: *Biblical Israel & Rabbinic Judaism,* 6 x 9, 272 pp, Quality PB, ISBN 1-58023-086-5 **$19.95**
Vol. 2: *Zionism & Eco-Judaism,* 6 x 9, 336 pp, Quality PB, ISBN 1-58023-087-3 **$19.95**

Broken Tablets: *Restoring the Ten Commandments and Ourselves*
Ed. by *Rabbi Rachel S. Mikva*; Intro. by *Rabbi Lawrence Kushner*;
Afterword by *Rabbi Arnold Jacob Wolf* **AWARD WINNER!**

Twelve outstanding spiritual leaders each share profound and personal thoughts about these biblical commands and why they have such a special hold on us.
6 x 9, 192 pp, HC, ISBN 1-58023-066-0 **$21.95**

Ecology & the Jewish Spirit: *Where Nature & the Sacred Meet* Ed. and with Intros.
by Ellen Bernstein 6 x 9, 288 pp, Quality PB, ISBN 1-58023-082-2 **$16.95**;
HC, ISBN 1-879045-88-5 **$23.95**

God & the Big Bang
Discovering Harmony Between Science & Spirituality **AWARD WINNER!**
by Daniel C. Matt
6 x 9, 216 pp, Quality PB, ISBN 1-879045-89-3 **$16.95**

Israel—A Spiritual Travel Guide AWARD WINNER!
A Companion for the Modern Jewish Pilgrim
by Rabbi Lawrence A. Hoffman 4¾ x 10, 256 pp, Quality PB, ISBN 1-879045-56-7 **$18.95**

Godwrestling—Round 2: *Ancient Wisdom, Future Paths* **AWARD WINNER!**
by Rabbi Arthur Waskow
6 x 9, 352 pp, Quality PB, ISBN 1-879045-72-9 **$18.95**; HC, ISBN 1-879045-45-1 **$23.95**

The Year Mom Got Religion: *One Woman's Midlife Journey into Judaism*
by Lee Meyerhoff Hendler 6 x 9, 208 pp, Quality PB, ISBN 1-58023-070-9 **$15.95**

Israel: *An Echo of Eternity* by Abraham Joshua Heschel; New Intro. by
Dr. Susannah Heschel 5½ x 8, 272 pp, Quality PB, ISBN 1-879045-70-2 **$18.95**

The Earth Is the Lord's: *The Inner World of the Jew in Eastern Europe*
by Abraham Joshua Heschel 5½ x 8, 112 pp, Quality PB, ISBN 1-879045-42-7 **$13.95**

A Passion for Truth: *Despair and Hope in Hasidism* by Abraham Joshua Heschel
5½ x 8, 352 pp, Quality PB, ISBN 1-879045-41-9 **$18.95**

Your Word Is Fire: *The Hasidic Masters on Contemplative Prayer*
Ed. and Trans. with a New Introduction by Dr. Arthur Green and Dr. Barry W. Holtz
6 x 9, 160 pp, Quality PB, ISBN 1-879045-25-7 **$14.95**

Children's Spirituality

ENDORSED BY CATHOLIC, PROTESTANT, AND JEWISH RELIGIOUS LEADERS

Because Nothing Looks Like God
by *Lawrence and Karen Kushner*
Full-color illus. by *Dawn W. Majewski*

For ages 4 & up

MULTICULTURAL, NONDENOMINATIONAL, NONSECTARIAN

What is God like? The first collaborative work by husband-and-wife team Lawrence and Karen Kushner introduces children to the possibilities of spiritual life. Real-life examples of happiness and sadness—from goodnight stories, to the hope and fear felt the first time at bat, to the closing moments of life—invite us to explore, together with our children, the questions we all have about God, no matter what our age.

11 x 8½, 32 pp, HC, Full-color illus., ISBN 1-58023-092-X **$16.95**

Where Is God? (A Board Book)
by *Lawrence and Karen Kushner;* Full-color illus. by *Dawn W. Majewski*

For ages 0–4

Gently invites children to become aware of God's presence all around them. Abridged from *Because Nothing Looks Like God* by Lawrence and Karen Kushner.
5 x 5, 24 pp, Board, Full-color illus., ISBN 1-893361-17-9 **$7.95**

Sharing Blessings
Children's Stories for Exploring the Spirit of the Jewish Holidays
by *Rahel Musleah* and *Rabbi Michael Klayman*
Full-color illus. by *Mary O'Keefe Young*

For ages 6 & up

What is the spiritual message of each of the Jewish holidays? How do we teach it to our children? Many books tell children about the historical significance and customs of the holidays. Now, through engaging, creative stories about one family's preparation, *Sharing Blessings* explores ways to get into the *spirit* of 13 different holidays.
8½ x 11, 64 pp, HC, Full-color illus., ISBN 1-879045-71-0 **$18.95**

The Book of Miracles
A Young Person's Guide to Jewish Spiritual Awareness
by *Lawrence Kushner*

For ages 9 & up

Introduces kids to a way of everyday spiritual thinking to last a lifetime. Kushner, whose award-winning books have brought spirituality to life for countless adults, now shows young people how to use Judaism as a foundation on which to build their lives.
6 x 9, 96 pp, HC, 2-color illus., ISBN 1-879045-78-8 **$16.95**

Children's Spirituality

In Our Image
God's First Creatures
by *Nancy Sohn Swartz*
Full-color illus. by *Melanie Hall*

For ages 4 & up

A playful new twist on the Creation story—from the perspective of the animals. Celebrates the interconnectedness of nature and the harmony of all living things. "The vibrantly colored illustrations nearly leap off the page in this delightful interpretation." —*School Library Journal*

9 x 12, 32 pp, HC, Full-color illus., ISBN 1-879045-99-0 **$16.95**

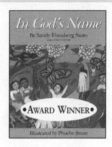

God's Paintbrush

For ages 4 & up

by *Sandy Eisenberg Sasso*; Full-color illus. by *Annette Compton*

Invites children of all faiths and backgrounds to encounter God openly in their own lives. Wonderfully interactive; provides questions adult and child can explore together at the end of each episode.

11 x 8½, 32 pp, HC, Full-color illus., ISBN 1-879045-22-2 **$16.95**

*Also available: **A Teacher's Guide: A Guide for Jewish & Christian Educators and Parents***
8½ x 11, 32 pp, PB, ISBN 1-879045-57-5 **$6.95**

God's Paintbrush Celebration Kit 9½ x 12, HC, Includes 5 sessions/40 full-color Activity Sheets and Teacher Folder with complete instructions, ISBN 1-58023-050-4 **$21.95**

In God's Name

For ages 4 & up

by *Sandy Eisenberg Sasso*; Full-color illus. by *Phoebe Stone*

Like an ancient myth in its poetic text and vibrant illustrations, this award-winning modern fable about the search for God's name celebrates the diversity and, at the same time, the unity of all the people of the world.

9 x 12, 32 pp, HC, Full-color illus., ISBN 1-879045-26-5 **$16.95**

What Is God's Name? (A Board Book)

For ages 0–4

An abridged board book version of the award-winning *In God's Name*.

5 x 5, 24 pp, Board, Full-color illus., ISBN 1-893361-10-1 **$7.95**

The 11th Commandment: Wisdom from Our Children

For all ages

by *The Children of America*

"If there were an Eleventh Commandment, what would it be?" Children of many religious denominations across America answer this question—in their own drawings and words. "A rare book of spiritual celebration for all people, of all ages, for all time."—*Bookviews*

8 x 10, 48 pp, HC, Full-color illus., ISBN 1-879045-46-X **$16.95**

Children's Spirituality

God Said Amen

by *Sandy Eisenberg Sasso*
Full-color illus. by *Avi Katz*

For ages 4 & up

A warm and inspiring tale of two kingdoms: one overflowing with water but without oil to light its lamps; the other blessed with oil but no water to grow its gardens. The kingdoms' rulers ask God for help but are too stubborn to ask each other. It takes a minstrel, a pair of royal riding-birds and their young keepers, and a simple act of kindness to show that they need only reach out to each other to find God's answer to their prayers.

9 x 12, 32 pp, HC, Full-color illus., ISBN 1-58023-080-6 **$16.95**

For Heaven's Sake

by *Sandy Eisenberg Sasso*; Full-color illus. by *Kathryn Kunz Finney*

For ages 4 & up

Everyone talked about heaven: "Thank heavens." "Heaven forbid." "For heaven's sake, Isaiah." But no one would say what heaven was or how to find it. So Isaiah decides to find out, by seeking answers from many different people.
9 x 12, 32 pp, HC, Full-color illus., ISBN 1-58023-054-7 **$16.95**

But God Remembered

Stories of Women from Creation to the Promised Land

by *Sandy Eisenberg Sasso*; Full-color illus. by *Bethanne Andersen*

For ages 8 & up

A fascinating collection of four different stories of women only briefly mentioned in biblical tradition and religious texts. Vibrantly brings to life courageous and strong women from ancient tradition; all teach important values through their actions and faith.
9 x 12, 32 pp, HC, Full-color illus., ISBN 1-879045-43-5 **$16.95**

God in Between

by *Sandy Eisenberg Sasso*; Full-color illus. by *Sally Sweetland*

For ages 4 & up

If you wanted to find God, where would you look? A magical, mythical tale that teaches that God can be found where we are: within all of us and the relationships between us.
9 x 12, 32 pp, HC, Full-color illus., ISBN 1-879045-86-9 **$16.95**

A Prayer for the Earth: The Story of Naamah, Noah's Wife   AWARD WINNER!

by *Sandy Eisenberg Sasso*; Full-color illus. by *Bethanne Andersen*

This new story, based on an ancient text, opens readers' religious imaginations to new ideas about the well-known story of the Flood. When God tells Noah to bring the animals of the world onto the ark, God also calls on Naamah, Noah's wife, to save each plant on Earth.
9 x 12, 32 pp, HC, Full-color illus., ISBN 1-879045-60-5 **$16.95**

Spirituality

My People's Prayer Book: *Traditional Prayers, Modern Commentaries*
Ed. by *Dr. Lawrence A. Hoffman*

Provides a diverse and exciting commentary to the traditional liturgy, helping modern men and women find new wisdom in Jewish prayer, and bring liturgy into their lives. Each book includes Hebrew text, modern translation, and commentaries *from all perspectives* of the Jewish world.
Vol. 1—*The Sh'ma and Its Blessings*, 7 x 10, 168 pp, HC, ISBN 1-879045-79-6 **$23.95**
Vol. 2—*The Amidah*, 7 x 10, 240 pp, HC, ISBN 1-879045-80-X **$23.95**
Vol. 3—*P'sukei D'zimrah* (Morning Psalms), 7 x 10, 240 pp, HC, ISBN 1-879045-81-8 **$23.95**
Vol. 4—*Seder K'riat Hatorah* (The Torah Service), 7 x 10, 264 pp, ISBN 1-879045-82-6 **$23.95**

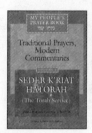   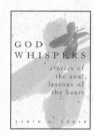 

Becoming a Congregation of Learners
Learning as a Key to Revitalizing Congregational Life by Isa Aron, Ph.D.;
Foreword by Rabbi Lawrence A. Hoffman, Co-Developer, Synagogue 2000
6 x 9, 304 pp, Quality PB, ISBN 1-58023-089-X **$19.95**

Self, Struggle & Change
Family Conflict Stories in Genesis and Their Healing Insights for Our Lives
by Dr. Norman J. Cohen 6 x 9, 224 pp, Quality PB, ISBN 1-879045-66-4 **$16.95**;
HC, ISBN 1-879045-19-2 **$21.95**

Voices from Genesis: *Guiding Us through the Stages of Life*
by Dr. Norman J. Cohen 6 x 9, 192 pp, Quality PB, ISBN 1-58023-118-7 **$16.95**;
HC, ISBN 1-879045-75-3 **$21.95**

God Whispers: *Stories of the Soul, Lessons of the Heart*
by Rabbi Karyn D. Kedar 6 x 9, 176 pp, Quality PB, ISBN 1-58023-088-1 **$15.95**

Being God's Partner: *How to Find the Hidden Link Between Spirituality and Your Work*
by Rabbi Jeffrey K. Salkin; Intro. by Norman Lear **AWARD WINNER!**
6 x 9, 192 pp, Quality PB, ISBN 1-879045-65-6 **$16.95**; HC, ISBN 1-879045-37-0 **$19.95**

ReVisions: *Seeing Torah through a Feminist Lens* **AWARD WINNER!**
by Rabbi Elyse Goldstein 5½ x 8½, 224 pp. Quality PB, ISBN 1-58023-117-9 **$16.95**;
208 pp, HC, ISBN 1-58023-047-4 **$19.95**

Soul Judaism: *Dancing with God into a New Era*
by Rabbi Wayne Dosick 5½ x 8½, 304 pp, Quality PB, ISBN 1-58023-053-9 **$16.95**

Finding Joy: *A Practical Spiritual Guide to Happiness* **AWARD WINNER!**
by Rabbi Dannel I. Schwartz with Mark Hass
6 x 9, 192 pp, Quality PB, ISBN 1-58023-009-1 **$14.95**; HC, ISBN 1-879045-53-2 **$19.95**

"Who Is a Jew?" *Conversations, Not Conclusions* by Meryl Hyman
6 x 9, 272 pp, Quality PB, ISBN 1-58023-052-0 **$16.95**; HC, ISBN 1-879045-76-1 **$23.95**

Life Cycle/Grief

Moonbeams
A Hadassah Rosh Hodesh Guide
Ed. by *Carol Diament, Ph.D.*

This hands-on "idea book" focuses on *Rosh Hodesh*, the festival of the new moon, as a source of spiritual growth for Jewish women. A complete sourcebook that will initiate or rejuvenate women's study groups, it is also perfect for women preparing for *bat mitzvah*, or for anyone interested in learning more about *Rosh Hodesh* observance and what it has to offer. 8½ x 11, 240 pp, Quality PB, ISBN 1-58023-099-7 **$20.00**

Mourning & Mitzvah: *A Guided Journal for Walking the Mourner's Path through Grief to Healing, 2nd Ed.* with *Over 60 Guided Exercises*
by *Anne Brener, L.C.S.W.*; Foreword by *Rabbi Jack Riemer*; Intro. by *Rabbi William Cutter*

For those who mourn a death, for those who would help them, for those who face a loss of any kind, Brener teaches us the power and strength available to us in the fully experienced mourning process. 7½ x 9, 304 pp, Quality PB, ISBN 1-58023-113-6 **$19.95**

 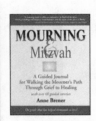   

Tears of Sorrow, Seeds of Hope
A Jewish Spiritual Companion for Infertility and Pregnancy Loss
by Rabbi Nina Beth Cardin   6 x 9, 192 pp, HC, ISBN 1-58023-017-2 **$19.95**

Lifecycles
V. 1: *Jewish Women on Life Passages & Personal Milestones* AWARD WINNER!
Ed. and with Intros. by Rabbi Debra Orenstein
V. 2: *Jewish Women on Biblical Themes in Contemporary Life* AWARD WINNER!
Ed. and with Intros. by Rabbi Debra Orenstein and Rabbi Jane Rachel Litman
V. 1: 6 x 9, 480 pp, Quality PB, ISBN 1-58023-018-0 **$19.95**; HC, ISBN 1-879045-14-1 **$24.95**
V. 2: 6 x 9, 464 pp, Quality PB, ISBN 1-58023-019-9 **$19.95**; HC, ISBN 1-879045-15-X **$24.95**

A Heart of Wisdom: *Making the Jewish Journey from Midlife through the Elder Years*
Ed. by Susan Berrin; Foreword by Harold Kushner
6 x 9, 384 pp, Quality PB, ISBN 1-58023-051-2 **$18.95**; HC, ISBN 1-879045-73-7 **$24.95**

Grief in Our Seasons: *A Mourner's Kaddish Companion*
by Rabbi Kerry M. Olitzky 4½ x 6½, 448 pp, Quality PB, ISBN 1-879045-55-9 **$15.95**

Parenting As a Spiritual Journey
Deepening Ordinary & Extraordinary Events into Sacred Occasions
by Rabbi Nancy Fuchs-Kreimer 6 x 9, 224 pp, Quality PB, ISBN 1-58023-016-4 **$16.95**

A Time to Mourn, A Time to Comfort: *A Guide to Jewish Bereavement and Comfort*
by Dr. Ron Wolfson 7 x 9, 336 pp, Quality PB, ISBN 1-879045-96-6 **$16.95**

When a Grandparent Dies
A Kid's Own Remembering Workbook for Dealing with Shiva and the Year Beyond
by Nechama Liss-Levinson, Ph.D.
8 x 10, 48 pp, HC, Illus., 2-color text, ISBN 1-879045-44-3 **$15.95**

So That Your Values Live On: *Ethical Wills & How to Prepare Them*
Ed. by Rabbi Jack Riemer & Professor Nathaniel Stampfer
6 x 9, 272 pp, Quality PB, ISBN 1-879045-34-6 **$17.95**

Spirituality/Jewish Meditation

Discovering Jewish Meditation
Instruction & Guidance for Learning an Ancient Spiritual Practice
by *Nan Fink Gefen*

Gives readers of any level of understanding the tools to learn the practice of Jewish meditation on your own, starting you on the path to a deep spiritual and personal connection to God and to greater insight about your life. 6 x 9, 208 pp, Quality PB, ISBN 1-58023-067-9 **$16.95**

Entering the Temple of Dreams: *Jewish Prayers, Movements, and Meditations for the End of the Day* by *Tamar Frankiel* and *Judy Greenfeld*

Nighttime spirituality is much more than bedtime prayers! Here, you'll uncover deeper meaning to familiar nighttime prayers—and learn to combine the prayers with movements and meditations to enhance your physical and psychological well-being.
7 x 10, 192 pp, Illus., Quality PB, ISBN 1-58023-079-2 **$16.95**

The Handbook of Jewish Meditation Practices
A Guide for Enriching the Sabbath and Other Days of Your Life
by *Rabbi David A. Cooper*

Gives us ancient and modern Jewish tools—Jewish practices and traditions, easy-to-use meditation exercises, and contemplative study of Jewish sacred texts—to help us quiet our minds and refresh our souls. 6 x 9, 208 pp, Quality PB, ISBN 1-58023-102-0 **$16.95**

   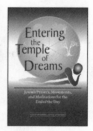 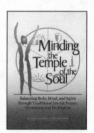

Meditation from the Heart of Judaism
Today's Teachers Share Their Practices, Techniques, and Faith
Ed. by Avram Davis 6 x 9, 256 pp, Quality PB, ISBN 1-58023-049-0 **$16.95**;
HC, ISBN 1-879045-77-X **$21.95**

The Way of Flame: *A Guide to the Forgotten Mystical Tradition of Jewish Meditation*
by Avram Davis 4½ x 8, 176 pp, Quality PB, ISBN 1-58023-060-1 **$15.95**

Minding the Temple of the Soul: *Balancing Body, Mind, and Spirit through Traditional Jewish Prayer, Movement, and Meditation*
by Tamar Frankiel and Judy Greenfeld 7 x 10, 184 pp, Quality PB, Illus.,
ISBN 1-879045-64-8 **$16.95**; Audiotape of the Blessings and Meditations (60-min. cassette),
JN01 **$9.95**; Videotape of the Movements and Meditations (46-min.), S507 **$20.00**

The Empty Chair: *Finding Hope and Joy—*
Timeless Wisdom from a Hasidic Master, Rebbe Nachman of Breslov AWARD WINNER!
4 x 6, 128 pp, Deluxe PB, 2-color text, ISBN 1-879045-67-2 **$9.95**

The Gentle Weapon: *Prayers for Everyday and Not-So-Everyday Moments*
Adapted from the Wisdom of Rebbe Nachman of Breslov
4 x 6, 144 pp, Deluxe PB, 2-color text, ISBN 1-58023-022-9 **$9.95**

Healing/Wellness/Recovery

Jewish Pastoral Care
A Practical Handbook from Traditional and Contemporary Sources
Ed. by *Rabbi Dayle A. Friedman*

Gives today's Jewish pastoral counselors practical guidelines based in the Jewish tradition.
6 x 9, 464 pp, HC, ISBN 1-58023-078-4 **$35.00**

Healing of Soul, Healing of Body
Spiritual Leaders Unfold the Strength & Solace in Psalms
Ed. by *Rabbi Simkha Y. Weintraub, CSW,* for The National Center for Jewish Healing

A source of solace for those who are facing illness, as well as those who care for them. Provides a wellspring of strength with inspiring introductions and commentaries by eminent spiritual leaders reflecting all Jewish movements.
6 x 9, 128 pp, Quality PB, Illus., 2-color text, ISBN 1-879045-31-1 **$14.95**

Jewish Paths toward Healing and Wholeness
A Personal Guide to Dealing with Suffering
by *Rabbi Kerry M. Olitzky*; Foreword by *Debbie Friedman*

Why me? Why do we suffer? How can we heal? Grounded in personal experience with illness and Jewish spiritual traditions, this book provides healing rituals, psalms and prayers that help readers initiate a dialogue with God, to guide them along the complicated path of healing and wholeness.
6 x 9, 192 pp, Quality PB, ISBN 1-58023-068-7 **$15.95**

Twelve Jewish Steps to Recovery: *A Personal Guide to Turning from Alcoholism & Other Addictions . . . Drugs, Food, Gambling, Sex . . .* by Rabbi Kerry M. Olitzky & Stuart A. Copans, M.D. Preface by Abraham J. Twerski, M.D.; Intro. by Rabbi Sheldon Zimmerman; "Getting Help" by JACS Foundation 6 x 9, 144 pp, Quality PB, ISBN 1-879045-09-5 **$13.95**

One Hundred Blessings Every Day: *Daily Twelve Step Recovery Affirmations, Exercises for Personal Growth & Renewal Reflecting Seasons of the Jewish Year* by Rabbi Kerry M. Olitzky 4½ x 6½, 432 pp, Quality PB, ISBN 1-879045-30-3 **$14.95**

Recovery from Codependence: *A Jewish Twelve Steps Guide to Healing Your Soul* by Rabbi Kerry M. Olitzky 6 x 9, 160 pp, Quality PB, ISBN 1-879045-32-X **$13.95**; HC, ISBN 1-879045-27-3 **$21.95**

Renewed Each Day: *Daily Twelve Step Recovery Meditations Based on the Bible* by Rabbi Kerry M. Olitzky & Aaron Z. *Vol. I: Genesis & Exodus; Vol. II: Leviticus, Numbers and Deuteronomy*
Vol. I: 6 x 9, 224 pp, Quality PB, ISBN 1-879045-12-5 **$14.95**
Vol. II: 6 x 9, 280 pp, Quality PB, ISBN 1-879045-13-3 **$14.95**

The Way Into... Series

A major 14-volume series to be completed over the next several years, *The Way Into...* provides an accessible and usable "guided tour" of the Jewish faith, its people, its history and beliefs—in total, an introduction to Judaism for adults that will enable them to understand and interact with sacred texts. Each volume is written by a major modern scholar and teacher, and is organized around an important concept of Judaism.

The Way Into... will enable all readers to achieve a real sense of Jewish cultural literacy through guided study. Forthcoming volumes include:

   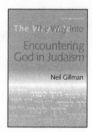

The Way Into Torah
by *Dr. Norman J. Cohen*

What is "Torah"? What are the different approaches to studying Torah? What are the different levels of understanding Torah? For whom is the study intended? Explores the origins and development of Torah, why it should be studied and how to do it.
6 x 9, 176 pp, HC, ISBN 1-58023-028-8 **$21.95**

The Way Into Jewish Prayer
by *Dr. Lawrence A. Hoffman*

Opens the door to 3,000 years of the Jewish way to God by making available all you need to feel at home in Jewish worship. Provides basic definitions of the terms you need to know as well as thoughtful analysis of the depth that lies beneath Jewish prayer.
6 x 9, 224 pp, HC, ISBN 1-58023-027-X **$21.95**

The Way Into Jewish Mystical Tradition
by *Rabbi Lawrence Kushner*

Explains the principles of Jewish mystical thinking, their religious and spiritual significance, and how they relate to our lives. A book that allows us to experience and understand the Jewish mystical approach to our place in the world.
6 x 9, 176 pp, HC, ISBN 1-58023-029-6 **$21.95**

The Way Into Encountering God in Judaism
by *Dr. Neil Gillman*

Explains how Jews have encountered God throughout history—and today—by exploring the many metaphors for God in Jewish tradition. Explores the Jewish tradition's passionate but also conflicting ways of relating to God as Creator, relational partner, and a force in history and nature.
6 x 9, 240 pp, HC, ISBN 1-58023-025-3 **$21.95**